T0235362

Lecture Notes in Computer Science 9469

Commenced Publication in 1973
Founding and Former Series Editors:
Gerhard Goos, Juris Hartmanis, and Jan van Leeuwen

More information about this series at http://www.springer.com/series/7409

Robert B. Allen · Jane Hunter
Marcia L. Zeng (Eds.)

Digital Libraries: Providing Quality Information

17th International Conference on Asia-Pacific
Digital Libraries, ICADL 2015
Seoul, Korea, December 9–12, 2015
Proceedings

 Springer

Editors
Robert B. Allen
Yonsei University
Seoul
Korea (Republic of)

Jane Hunter
School of ITEE
University of Queensland
St. Lucia, QLD
Australia

Marcia L. Zeng
School of Library and Information Science
Kent State University
Kent, OH
USA

ISSN 0302-9743   ISSN 1611-3349   (electronic)
Lecture Notes in Computer Science
ISBN 978-3-319-27973-2   ISBN 978-3-319-27974-9   (eBook)
DOI 10.1007/978-3-319-27974-9

Library of Congress Control Number: 2015957784

LNCS Sublibrary: SL3 – Information Systems and Applications, incl. Internet/Web, and HCI

This Springer imprint is published by SpringerNature
The registered company is Springer International Publishing AG Switzerland

Preface

This volume contains the papers presented at ICADL 2015, the 2105 Asian Digital Library Conference, held during December 9–12, 2015, in Seoul, Korea. This was the 16th event in the ICADL conference series. Since its beginnings in Hong Kong in 1998, ICADL has become one of the premier international research meetings about digital libraries. The conference series explores digital libraries as a broad foundation for interaction with information and information management in a digital world. The papers for this 2015 conference cover topics such as digital preservation, gamification, text mining, citizen science, data citation, linked data, and cloud computing. Overall, there were 31 full and short papers along with 18 poster papers. In addition, these proceedings include short descriptions of the presentations from the two panel sessions: one about digital humanities and the other about eScience. The proceedings also include brief papers from students participating in the doctoral consortium.

The Conference Committee consisted of Profs. Sung Been Moon, Min Song, and Giyeong Kim in addition to Prof. Robert B. Allen all of Yonsei University. As co-chairs of the Technical Program Committee, we would especially like to thank all of the Program Committee members for their effort. We also thank Prof. Soohyun Joo of the University of Kentucky and the review committee he assembled for their exceptional effort in reviewing the posters.

We are grateful to Prof. Kiduk Yang of Kyungpook National University who organized the doctoral consortium with the support of a strong panel of faculty mentors. We further thank Prof. Kyong Eun Oh of Simmons College for her help with publicity.

Two exceptional workshops were co-located with ICADL 2015. The NKOS (Networked Knowledge Organization Systems) workshop was held on December 9. This was organized by Profs. Xia Lin, Jian Qin, and Marcia Zeng and was the first workshop in that series to be held in Asia. The CiSAP (Consortium of Information Schools Asia-Pacific) was held on December 12 with Profs. Emi Ishita and Chern Li Liew as chairs.

We gratefully acknowledge the Yonsei University Graduate School for its financial support. We would also like to thank the Yonsei Department of Library and Information Science and its students for their assistance.

November 2015

Robert B. Allen
Jane Hunter
Marcia L. Zeng

Organization

Technical Program Committee

Palakorn Achananuparp	Singapore Management University, Singapore
Robert Allen	Yonsei University, South Korea
Mauricio Almeida	Universidade Federal de Minas Gerais, Brazil
Kanwal Ameen	University of the Punjab, Pakistan
Lu An	Wuhan University, China
Tobias Blanke	University of Glasgow, UK
Shu-Jiun Chen	Academia Sinica, Taiwan
Youngok Choi	Catholic University of America, USA
Sayeed Choudhury	Johns Hopkins University, USA
Gobinda Chowdhury	Northumbria University, UK
Sally Jo Cunningham	Waikato University, New Zealand
Giorgio Maria Di Nunzio	University of Padua, Italy
Ismail Fahmi	University of Groningen, The Netherlands
Myung-Ja Han	University of Illinois at Urbana-Champaign, USA
Bernhard Haslhofer	Austrian Institute of Technology, Austria
Jieh Hsiang	National Taiwan University, Taiwan
Xiao Hu	University of Hong Kong, SAR China
Jane Hunter	University of Queensland, Australia
Emi Ishita	Kyushu University, Japan
Adam Jatowt	Kyoto University, Japan
Kiran K.	University of Malaya, Malaysia
Min-Yen Kan	National University of Singapore, Singapore
Emad Khazraee	University of Pennsylvania, USA
Christopher Khoo	Nanyang Technological University, Singapore
Kyung-Sun Kim	University of Wisconsin-Madison, USA
Claus-Peter Klas	Leibniz Institute for Social Sciences, Germany
Chernli Liew	Victoria University of Wellington, New Zealand
Xia Lin	Drexel University, USA
Keven Liu	Shanghai Library, China
Devika Madalli	Indian Statistical Institute, India
Elli Mylonas	Brown University, USA
Michael Nelson	Old Dominion University, USA
Jungran Park	Drexel University, USA
Helen Partridge	Queensland University of Technology, Australia
Hsiao-Tieh Pu	National Taiwan Normal University, Taiwan
Jian Qin	Syracuse University, USA
Edie Rasmussen	University of British Columbia, Canada

Soo Young Rieh	University of Michigan, USA
Laurent Romary	Inria and HUB-ISDL, France
Seamus Ross	University of Toronto, Canada
Shigeo Sugimoto	University of Tsukuba, Japan
Tamara Sumner	University of Colorado at Boulder, USA
Kulthida Tuamsuk	Khon Kaen University, Thailand
Pertti Vakkari	University of Tampere, Finland
Karin Verspoor	University of Melbourne, Australia
Yejun Wu	Louisiana State University, USA
Long Xiao	Beijing University Library, China
Marcia Zeng	Kent State University, USA

Posters Committee

Namjoo Choi	University of Kentucky, USA
Soohyung Joo, Chair	University of Kentucky, USA
Youngseek Kim	University of Kentucky, USA
Kun Lu	University of Oklahoma, USA
Jin Mao	University of Arizona, USA
Adam Worrall	University of Alberta, Canada
Shuheng Wu	Queens College, City University of New York, USA
Seungwon Yang	Louisiana State University, USA
Yan Zhang	University of Texas at Austin, USA

Contents

Posters

Visual Topical Analysis of Museum Collections

Lu An[1], Liqin Zhou[1], Xia Lin[2], and Chuanming Yu[3(✉)]

[1] School of Information Management, Wuhan University, No. 299 Bayi Road,
Wuchang District, Wuhan 430072, Hubei Province, China
[2] College of Computing and Informatics, Drexel University,
3141 Chestnut Street, Philadelphia, PA 19104, USA
[3] School of Information and Safety Engineering, Zhongnan University
of Economics and Law, No. 182 Nanhu Ave,
East Lake High-Tech Development Zone, Wuhan 430073, Hubei Province, China
yuchuanming2003@126.com

Abstract. Museums are highly specialized cultural institutions. Obstacles exist between the knowledge and terminology of the museum professionals and that of the general public. Topical analysis of museum collections can reveal topical similarities and differences among museums and facilitate museum tours with recommended professional guides. In this study, 7177 French artworks collected by 90 art museums worldwide were investigated. The Self-Organizing Map (SOM) technique, an unsupervised artificial neural network method, was applied to visually analyze similarities and differences among the museums. The Treemap technique was also employed on a large dataset to reveal the distribution of the specific themes among the investigated museums. Finally, a comprehensive museum tour recommendation mechanism is established for tourists.

Keywords: Museum collections · Topical analysis · Information visualization · Self-Organizing Map · Treemap

1   Introduction

Museums are cultural institutions which collect, preserve and display objects with scientific, artistic or historical significance in the long or short term. With the development of human civilization and accumulation of knowledge, museum collections become richer and more varied. As museum collections are highly specialized, obstacles exist between professional museum collections and the knowledge structure of the non-professional general public. With limited knowledge of artworks and art museums, the general public usually tends to tour some very well-known art museums (such as the Metropolitan Museum of Art in New York) or artworks (such as those by Pablo Picasso) and ignore the rest. Due to limited time and energy, it is not realistic for tourists to visit all the museums. How is it possible to facilitate tourists choosing the most interesting museums in the most economical way within limited time? To satisfy the topical preferences of tourists, how can they find nearby museums with

© Springer International Publishing Switzerland 2015
R.B. Allen et al. (Eds.): ICADL 2015, LNCS 9469, pp. 1–11, 2015.
DOI: 10.1007/978-3-319-27974-9_1

collections of similar subjects to a specific museum? How can they find nearby museums with collections of quite different subjects from a specific museum? Which museums are worth touring given subject preferences of tourists? Answers to these questions will not only help ordinary tourists select suitable museums, but also facilitate understanding of the collection status of one museum compared with other museums and promote cooperation or communication among museums. The purpose of this study is 1) to reveal topical similarities and differences among the investigated museums, and 2) to establish a reasonable museum tour recommendation mechanism based on themes of artworks. The findings of the study can provide operational methods and data support to build a museum recommendation system which can be used by the public to find a suitable museum with desirable collections.

2   Related Research

2.1   Topical Analysis of Museum Collections

Many researchers studied contents and displays of museum collections [1,2] and advocated separating a museum into several thematic areas [3]. Some researchers proposed the strategy of determining exhibition themes and displaying selected cultural relics [4]. However, these types of research simply classified and organized museum collections by topics or themes. Deep analyses and mining of collection themes were seldom conducted.

Some scholars also realized the importance of thematic analysis of museum collections. For example, Hu [5] believed that understanding of the rich information within collections can promote display quality. However, little was addressed regarding detailed and operational procedures of topical analysis of collections. In addition, Gao and Wu [6] and Zhang [7] made in-depth analyses of museum collections of specific categories, such as baby clothing, horse paintings and potteries. Such analyses heavily depend on domain knowledge and are hard to transfer to other types of collections.

In this study, we will reveal the thematic structure of museum collections and discover similarities and differences among art museums to provide appropriate museum tour recommendations for tourists.

2.2   Self-Organizing Map

The Self-Organizing Map (SOM) technique is an unsupervised learning algorithm which visualizes the high-dimensional input data in a low-dimensional space and preserves the topology of the input data through competitive machine learning [8]. The SOM display is composed of a two-dimensional orderly grid of nodes. Each SOM node corresponds to an n dimensional weight vector, where n equals the number of attributes of the input data. The input data with similar properties are projected onto the same node or adjacent nodes.

Ultsch and Siemon [9] proposed a novel SOM display named U-matrix map to explore the clustering structure of input data, which can effectively reveal differences between weight vectors associated with SOM nodes. The value of each element in the

U-matrix equals the sum of distances from a node to all its immediate neighbors normalized by the largest occurring value in the SOM grid. The higher element value in the U-matrix means greater differences between the weight vectors associated with the corresponding SOM node and adjacent nodes and vice versa. High U-matrix values represent borders between clusters, while low U-matrix values represent clusters themselves. Values in the U-matrix are then converted to specific colors to reveal differences. Users can observe similarities and differences of input data from positions of input data in the SOM display and background colors defined by the U-matrix.

Compared with other clustering techniques, e.g. k-means and hierarchical clustering, the SOM technique can visualize similarities and dissimilarities among input data even in the same cluster. It can process higher dimensional data more efficiently than other visual clustering techniques, e.g. Multi-Dimensional Scaling (MDS). Existing information visualization tools usually target on literature analysis or are based on citations and co-citations, e.g. CiteSpace and SCI. The SOM technique has been widely used in many fields and disciplines. Recent examples of data exploration include abstract clustering [10], topical analysis of journals [11], subject directory analysis [12] and analysis of technical competitive intelligence [13]. In this study, we investigate topical similarities and differences among art museums with the SOM technique and build a museum tour recommendation mechanism upon the analysis results.

2.3 Treemap

Treemap is a visualization method widely used in various disciplines to display a large number of hierarchical data sets [14]. Examples in the field of library and information science include exploratory visualization of decision trees in the process of knowledge discovery in databases [15] and interfaces of personal digital libraries [16]. The Treemap algorithms include binary tree, square [17], Voronoi [18], etc. The square algorithm is the most frequently used since it is easy to observe and provides sufficient insights into the investigated data. In this study, the Treemap technique and the square algorithm are employed to reveal distribution of themes among museum collections.

3 Data and Method

3.1 Data Source and Collection

The data source in this study comes from the database of French artists by Getty Research Institute.[1] The database contains 7177 records of French artworks collected by 90 art museums in the United States, United Kingdom and Ireland. Each record has the attributes of serial number, title of the artwork, museum name, museum location, subjects of the artwork, etc. Each artwork in the database was assigned with several subjects. After removing stop words, such as "with", "of", etc. from subjects of artworks and word stemming, we obtained 3538 subject terms in total.

---

[1] http://www.getty.edu/research

3.2   Definition of the SOM Input Matrix

In this study, an SOM input matrix M with k rows and l columns was constructed. See Eq. (1), where the rows (k) of the matrix represent the objects (namely museums, ranking from 1 to k) to be visualized in the SOM display, and the columns (l) of the matrix define the attributes of the objects (namely subjects, ranking from 1 to l). In Eq.(1), d_{ij} (i=1, 2, ...,k; j=1, 2, ..., l) is defined as the number of the artworks with the jth subject collected by the ith museum. If the ith museum collected no artwork with the jth subject, then d_{ij} is equal to 0.

$$M = \begin{pmatrix} d_{11} & d_{12} & \cdots & d_{1l} \\ d_{21} & d_{22} & \cdots & d_{2l} \\ & & \cdots & \\ d_{k1} & d_{k2} & \cdots & d_{kl} \end{pmatrix} \tag{1}$$

4   Results Analysis and Discussion

This section presents results that can be used to provide museum tour recommendations for tourists based on their topical preference. Here, topical preferences of tourists are divided into three types. The tourists with the first type of topical preferences tend to visit the museums with similar subjects to the museum that they toured. On the contrary, the tourists with the second type of topical preferences tend to visit the museums with different subjects to the museum that they toured. The tourists with the third topical preferences tend to visit museums which collect artworks of specific subjects, e.g. landscape or flower.

Due to travel costs, the target museum to be recommended to the tourists will need to be as close as possible to the starting museum, ideally in the same state (or nation). For example, a tourist just visited the Chicago Museum. Even if a museum located in Ireland collect artworks with highly similar or different subjects to the Chicago Museum, the tourist is unlikely to travel a long distance from USA to Europe. It is worth noting that adopting states to determine nearby museums has some disadvantage. As areas of different states vary, two museums in a large state can be further away from each other than those in two adjacent small states. Although physical distances are more accurate than states, the former data are difficult to obtain. Thus, in this study, we adopted states to determine nearby museums.

4.1   Museum Tour Recommendations Based on Topical Similarities

For the first two topical preferences, the input matrix M was constructed, which consisted of 90 rows (museums) and 3538 columns (subjects). Although locations of museums are important for tourists to decide whether to visit them, the attribute of location was not considered in the input matrix M. Since the matrix has too many attributes of subjects, if locations were considered as an attribute, it would not really play a role in the SOM training process. If the attribute of location were to be weighted, it would be difficult to select suitable weights to balance subjects and locations. Notice that different subjects may have different occurring frequencies in the investigated museums. For example, the frequency of *landscape* varied from 0 to 141 while the frequency of *angel* varied from 0 to 7. Thus, different attributes or columns in the input matrix M may have different value ranges. In order to avoid attributes with large value ranges dominating the SOM display, the input matrix M was first normalized with the "Var" method [19], in which variances of attributes are linearly normalized to 1. In this case, attributes with different value ranges were equally treated in the SOM training process. The toroid space was employed in the SOM display to reduce the "border effect" [8]. The SOM display in the toroid space is dough-nut-shaped, in which the upper edge of the SOM display is connected to the bottom edge and the left edge is connected to the right edge [20]. The normalized input matrix was then trained by liner initiation and batch learning since related studies by [11] showed that this combination obtained the smallest final quantization error compared with other combinations of random/linear initiation and sequential/batch learning. Values of the U-matrix were calculated and applied to the background color for the SOM display. See Fig.1.

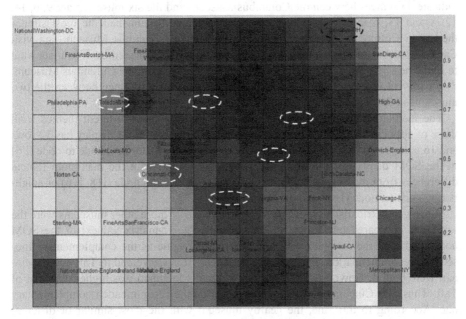

Fig. 1. The SOM display labeled with museum abbreviations and locations

Color bars on the right indicate U-matrix values for each color. Labels (namely abbreviations of museums) in Fig. 1 represent different museums and their locations (states or nations). The SOM display contained 12 rows and 16 columns. The SOM node located at the ith row and j^{th} column was denoted as node (i, j). According to the principle of the SOM technique presented by Kohonen [8], the input data which are projected onto the same or adjacent SOM nodes have highly similar attributes. Those which are projected onto the SOM nodes in far distance have very different attributes. The geometric distance between two SOM nodes reflects similarity of attributes of the input data which are projected onto the two SOM nodes, respectively. To discriminate the distance between two SOM nodes, the geometric distance between a node and its immediate neighbors is defined as 1 and the distance to its diagonal neighbors is defined as 2 and so on. Note that the toroid space was used in the SOM display. Thus, the distance from node $(12, j)$ to $(1, j)$ was 1 and the same was true with the distance from node $(i, 16)$ to $(i, 1)$.

Tourists may take two strategies to select museums to visit. The first one is to find a nearby museum with the most similar collection themes to the museum that they visited. The second one is to find a nearby museum with the most different collection themes from the museum that they visited. If museum A has the most different collection themes from museum B among all the museums, museum A is the complementary museum for museum B. For example, a tourist visited the Columbus Museum in Ohio (abbreviated as Columbus-OH), which is located at node $(1,14)$ as the black circle indicates in Fig. 1. Notice that six other museums in OH are located at nodes $(4, 8)$, $(5, 12)$, $(7, 6)$, $(8, 9)$, $(6, 11)$ and $(4, 4)$ in the SOM display as the white circles indicate. Distances between the Columbus Museum and the six museums are 9, 6, 14, 12, 8 and 13, respectively. This means that Canton Museum had the most similar themes to Columbus Museum. Tourists who visited Columbus Museum can visit Canton Museum to find more collections with highly similar themes. If tourists want to find a nearby museum with the most different themes from the Columbus Museum, they can visit the Cincinnati Museum since the geometric distance between the two museums in the SOM display is the longest.

The method for finding a nearby museum with the most different themes from those of a specific museum is relatively complex. Since the SOM display has 12 rows and 16 columns, it can be proved that node $(i+8, j+6)$ is the farthest node to node (i, j) in the SOM display of toroid space. Thus the museum with the maximum topical differences from the museum at node (i, j) was mapped onto node $(i+8, j+6)$ or neighboring node (if node $(i+8, j+6)$ was empty).

When geometric distances from a museum to two or more other museums were the same, we compared background colors (namely the U-matrix values) of the SOM nodes and took the museum with higher U-matrix value as the complementary museum of recommendation. For example, distances from Cleveland to Taft and Cincinnati were both 4. However, the U-matrix value of Cincinnati was higher than that of Taft. Thus, the Cincinnati Museum was taken as the recommended complementary one. According to this rule, the nearby museum with the most similar or different themes for each museum and geometric distances between them were summarized in Table 1. The top three similar or different subjects of collections by similar or complementary museums were also provided.

To explore specific similarities and differences among museums in Table 1, take the group of Ireland, Wallace and Dulwich for example. A scrutiny of subjects and their counts in collections by the three museums revealed that Ireland and Wallace collected similar counts of collections regarding "horse", "woman", "man", "life", "still", "child", etc. However, these subjects were nearly invisible in collections of Dulwich. Instead, the latter collected artworks of "harbor", "baptiste", "israel", etc. Results in Table 1 can provide data support for the museum recommendation system.

Table 1. The nearby museums with the most similar or different themes

Starting Museum	Node	Similar Museum	Geo. Dist.	Similar Subjects	Complementary Museum	Geo. Dist.	Different Subjects
Allen-OH	(4,8)	Toledo	4	landscape France water	Columbus	9	forest boy church
Ashmolean-England	(8,9)	Walker	0	landscape life still	NationalLondon	9	storm angel festivities
Bowdoin-ME*	(12,11)	Hood	3	landscape woman person	Hood	3	art differentia-tion formal
Canton-OH	(5,12)	Taft	2	landscape France forest	Cincinnati	8	woman life still
Chicago-IL	(8,16)	Krannert	7	landscape woman cattle	Contemporary	12	cup figure human
Cincinnati-OH	(7,6)	Allen	5	landscape France woman	Columbus	14	artist boy church
Cleveland-OH	(8,9)	Taft	4	landscape child man	Columbus	12	forest France river
Columbia-SC	(3,10)	Bob	6	king	Bob	6	child christ angel
Columbus-OH	(1,14)	Canton	6	landscape France boy	Cincinnati	14	symbol country evening
Ireland-Ireland*	(11,5)	Wallace	1	woman girl scene	Dulwich	10	him baptiste Israel

Note: In some states (such as ME, CO, MI, etc, with * mark) or nations (e. g. Ireland), there is only one museum or two museums were mapped onto the same SOM node. Then it is necessary to find a museum with the most similar or different themes in neighboring states or nations.

Users can select or input a museum that they already toured and the system will show nearby museums with collections with the most similar or most different subjects.

4.2   Museum Tour Recommendations Based on Specific Thematic Preferences

Some tourists have special preferences for particular themes, such as landscape, figures or flowers. To recommend museums to tourists in accordance with their preferences, we imported the museum data to the Treemap tool and grouped them successively by collection subject, museum location and museum name. The background, size and color of labels were determined by frequencies of the subjects involved in museum collections.

In order to show the distribution of significant subjects clearly, the top 15 subjects were selected to generate the Treemap display. See Fig. 2 for results, in which we can zoom in and out, drill down and roll up to observe more details.

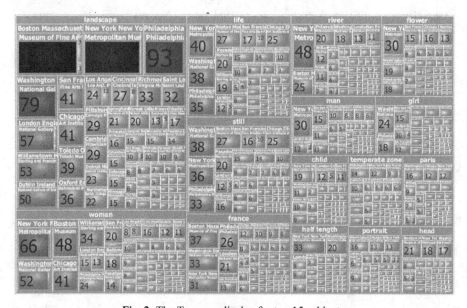

Fig. 2. The Treemap display for top 15 subjects

The distributions of top 15 significant subjects were summarized in Table 2.

It shows that the salient topics among the investigated museum collections were "landscape", "woman", "life", "still", "France", "river", "flower", "man", "girl", "child", "temperate zone", "Paris", "half length", "portrait" and "head". It is easy to understand that salient topics included "France" and "Paris" since the dataset in this study comes from the database of French artists by the Getty Research Institute. It means that French artists tend to create artworks of topics related to their own country. It is also found that artworks related to "woman" attracted more attention than those related to "man". A sub-category of "girl" even existed separately. The Treemap display and Table 2 can provide data support for the museum recommendation system. Users can select or input a subject of their interests, e.g. landscape, and the system will show museums with the most collections on this subject. Then tourists can choose a museum at their convenience to visit according to their specific topical preferences.

Table 2. Distributions of top 15 subjects among museum collections

Subjects	Museums	Locations	Frequencies
Landscape	Museum of Fine Arts	Boston, Massachusetts	141
	Metropolitan Museum of Art	New York, New York	131
	Philadelphia Museum of Art	Philadelphia, Pennsylvania	93
Woman	Metropolitan Museum of Art	New York, New York	66
	National Gallery of Art	Washington District of Columbia	52
	Museum of Fine Arts	Boston, Massachusetts	48
Life	Metropolitan Museum of Art	New York, New York	40
	National Gallery of Art	Washington District of Columbia	38
	Philadelphia Museum of Art	Philadelphia, Pennsylvania	35
Still	National Gallery of Art	Washington District of Columbia	38
	Metropolitan Museum of Art	New York, New York	36
	Philadelphia Museum of Art	Philadelphia, Pennsylvania	33
France	Museum of Fine Arts	Boston, Massachusetts	37
	National Gallery of Art	Washington District of Columbia	33
	Metropolitan Museum of Art	New York, New York	31
River	Metropolitan Museum of Art	New York, New York	48
	Museum of Fine Arts	Boston, Massachusetts	25
	Philadelphia Museum of Art	Philadelphia, Pennsylvania	20
Flower	Metropolitan Museum of Art	New York, New York	30
	National Gallery of Art	Washington District of Columbia	19
	Philadelphia Museum of Art	Philadelphia, Pennsylvania	18
Man	Metropolitan Museum of Art	New York, New York	30
	Museum of Fine Arts	Boston, Massachusetts	15
	National Gallery	London, England	12
Girl	National Gallery of Art	Washington District of Columbia	24
	Philadelphia Museum of Art	Philadelphia, Pennsylvania	18
	Museum of Fine Arts	Boston, Massachusetts	15
Child	Metropolitan Museum of Art	New York, New York	19
	National Gallery	London, England	12
	Fine Arts Museums of San Francisco	San Francisco, California	11
Half length	Metropolitan Museum of Art	New York, New York	33
	National Gallery of Art	Washington District of Columbia	20
	National Gallery	London, England	9
Temperate zone	Philadelphia Museum of Art	Philadelphia, Pennsylvania	14
	Metropolitan Museum of Art	New York, New York	12
	National Gallery of Ireland	Dublin, Ireland	10
Paris	National Gallery of Art	Washington District of Columbia	16
	Art Institute of Chicago	Chicago, Illinois	12
	Metropolitan Museum of Art	New York, New York	12
Portrait	National Gallery of Art	Washington District of Columbia	16
	Art Institute of Chicago	Chicago, Illinois	13
	Metropolitan Museum of Art	New York, New York	13
Head	Museum of Fine Art	Boston, Massachusetts	21
	Metropolitan Museum of Art	New York, New York	18
	National Gallery of Art	Washington District of Columbia	17

5   Conclusion

Visual topical analysis of museum collections can facilitate understanding thematic characteristics of museum collections, reveal topical similarities and complementarities among museums, and establish a reasonable museum tour recommendation mechanism for tourists.

In this study, we divided topical preferences of tourists into three types: 1) the preference for visiting another museum with similar themes to the museum that they toured, 2) the preference for visiting another museum with different themes to the museum that they toured, and 3) the preference for visiting a museum with specific themes. A number of 7,177 French artworks and 3,538 subjects from the database of French artists by the Getty Research Institute were investigated.

For the first two preferences, an effective information visualization technique Self-Organization Map (SOM) was employed to visualize the investigated museums in a low-dimensional space. The U-matrix was applied to background colors of the SOM display. According to the geometric distances between the SOM nodes onto which museums were mapped and the U-matrix values of corresponding SOM nodes, we can recommend nearby museums with the most similar or different themes to the museums that tourists toured.

As for the third topical preference, the Treemap technique was used to reveal the distribution of salient themes among museum collections. Using visualization results, tourists can choose suitable museums according to their topical preferences.

Research findings of this study can help tourists understand topical structure of museum collections and plan their visits according to the most interesting nearby museums in the most economical and efficient way. The constructed methods can also be applied to other aspects of museums, such as museum recommendation based on preferences of tourists toward artists, or other types of cultural institutions.

6   Limitations and Future Research

This study has two limitations. The first limitation lies in the analysis of museum tour recommendations based on thematic preferences. The Treemap technique was directly applied to subject terms, which ignored relationships among those terms. In future, we will first cluster subject terms and then apply the Treemap technique to the clustering results, which will better reveal the distribution of art museums among subject clusters. The second limitation lies in using unigrams to analyze subjects of art collections. In future, we will use higher n-grams to analyze phrases in subjects of art collections.

Acknowledgements. We thank the National Social Science Foundation of China (11CTQ025), National Natural Science Foundation of China (71373286) and the China Scholarship Council for financial support. We are also grateful to PhillyCodefest 2015 committee of Drexel University for providing the data of French artworks from Getty Research Institute. Many thanks go to the anonymous reviewers for their invaluable suggestions on the revision of this paper.

References

1. Feng, K.J., Tang, J.G.: Subject Displayed and Expressed of the Museum. J. Yindu Journal **3**, 113–115 (2014)
2. Pang, J.: The Theme Plan of the Phoenix Museum and Show Way. J. Relics and Musicology **4**, 85–90 (2010)
3. Liu, D.Q.: The Pure Geological Museum and Spatial Art Design of the Theme Park-Take the Design of Grand View Garden for Example. J. Literature and Art for the Populace **6**, 85–86 (2014)
4. Lu, Y.M.: Expression of the Displayed Exhibition Theme in Local Comprehensive Museum. J. Literature Life, Next Timothy Publication **12**, 257–258 (2014)
5. Hu, Y.F.: A Brief Discussion on the Research of the Museum Collections and Improvement of Exhibition Quality. J. Chi Zi **10**, 45 (2013)
6. Gao, Q.X., Wu, Z.K.: Appreciation of the WenZhou Infant Played Museum Collections. J. Cultural Relics Appraisal and Appreciation. **6**, 26–29 (2012)
7. Zhang, Z.: The Market Analysis of Chinese Painting and Tri-colored Glazed Pottery of the Tang Dynasty. J. Financial Management **4**, 90–91 (2014)
8. Kohonen, T.: Self-Organizing Maps, 3rd edn. Springer, Berlin (2001)
9. Ultsch, A., Siemon, H.P.: Kohonen's self organizing feature maps for exploratory data analysis. In: Proceedings of International Neural Network Conference, pp. 305–308. Kluwer Press, Dordrecht (1990)
10. Skupin, A.: Discrete and Continuous Conceptualizations of Science: Implications for Knowledge Domain Visualization. J. Informatics **3**(3), 233–245 (2009)
11. An, L., Zhang, J., Yu, C.: The Visual Subject Analysis of Library and Information Science Journals with Self-Organizing Map. J. Knowledge Organization **38**(4), 299–320 (2011)
12. Zhang, J., An, L., Tang, T., Hong, Y.: Visual Health Subject Directory Analysis Based on Users' Traversal Activities. J. the American Society for Information Science and Technology **60**(10), 1977–1994 (2009)
13. An, L., Yu, C.: Self-Organizing Maps for Competitive Technical Intelligence Analysis. J. International Journal of Computer Information Systems and Industrial Management Applications **4**, 83–91 (2012)
14. Asahi, T., Turo, D., Shneiderman, B.: Using Treemaps to Visualize the Analytic Hierarchy Process. J. Information Systems Research **6**(4), 357–375 (1995)
15. Rojas, W.A.C., Villegas, C.J.M.: Graphical representation and exploratory visualization for decision trees in the KDD process. In: Proceedings of the 2nd International Conference on Integrated Information, Budapest, Hungary, pp. 136–144 (2012)
16. Good, L., Popat, A.C., Janssen, W.C., Bier, E.: A fluid interface for personal digital libraries. In: Rauber, A., Christodoulakis, S., Tjoa, A.M. (eds.) Research and Advanced Technology for Digital Libraries. Lecture Notes in Computer Science, vol. 3652, pp. 162–173. Springer, Heidelberg (2005)
17. Bruls, M., Huizing, K., van Wijk, J.J.: Squarified treemaps. In: de Leeuw, W., van Liere, R. (eds.) Data Visualization 2000. Eurographics, Berlin, Heidelberg, pp. 33–42 (2000)
18. Horn, M.S., Tobiasz, M., Shen, C.: Visualizing biodiversity with voronoi treemaps. In: Proceedings of Sixth Annual International Symposium on Voronoi Diagrams in Science and Engineering, pp. 265–270. IEEE press, Copenhagen (2009)
19. SOM Norm Variable. http://www.cis.hut.fi/somtoolbox/package/docs2/somnormvariable.html
20. Ultsch, A.: Maps for the visualization of high-dimensional data spaces. In: Proceedings of Workshop on Self-Organizing Maps (WSOM 2003), Kyushu, Japan (2003)

Experiments on Russian-English Identity Resolution

Zinaida Apanovich[1,2(✉)] and Alexander Marchuk[1,2]

[1] A.P. Ershov Institute of Informatics Systems, Siberian Branch
of the Russian Academy of Sciences, Novosibirsk, Russia
{apanovich,mag}@iis.nsk.su
[2] Novosibirsk State University, Novosibirsk, Russia

Abstract. The focus of this paper is on Russian-English identity resolution when English names of entities have been created by a transliteration or translation of Russian names. A new approach combining attribute-based identity resolution with the text analysis of publications attributed to these entities has been proposed. The dataset of the Open Archive of the Russian Academy of Sciences and digital library SpringerLink are used as test examples.

Keywords: Linked open data · Cross-language identity resolution · Authorship attribution · Self-citation network · Tf-idf · LDA · Jaro-Winkler

1 Introduction

One of the projects carried out at the A.P. Ershov Institute of Informatics Systems of the Siberian Branch of the Russian Academy of Sciences (IIS SB RAS) is aimed at populating the Open Archive of the Siberian Branch of the Russian Academy of Sciences (SB RAS Open Archive, Open Archive)[1] [1] with the data of the Open Linked Data cloud (LOD) [2]. The problem of identity resolution is complicated by the fact that the Open Archive uses names written in Cyrillic, and other data sets use Latin names to identify the same persons. Our recent experiments [3] have shown that this problem has *language specific aspects* because sometimes a name in one language can be obtained by translation or transliteration of the name in another language. Several named entities with distinct English spellings and translations of their names may correspond in reality to the same Russian entity; on the other hand, several distinct entities may be homonyms and share the same name or some forms of this name.

Name ambiguity in the context of bibliographic citation records is a difficult problem that affects the quality of content in digital libraries. The library community has been working on it for a long time [4-6]. In the context of Linked Open Data and increasing data traffic on a global scale, the issues of data quality and confidence have become extremely important. In this environment, errors are promulgated, dispersed, and become difficult to discover and repair. As the number of homonyms and synonyms increases, it becomes crucial to have accurate data identifying various entities.

---

[1] http://duh.iis.nsk.su/turgunda/Home

© Springer International Publishing Switzerland 2015
R.B. Allen et al. (Eds.): ICADL 2015, LNCS 9469, pp. 12–21, 2015.
DOI: 10.1007/978-3-319-27974-9_2

An important aspect of this problem is multilingualism. Multilingual resources such as DBPedia, VIAF, WorldCat, etc., become increasingly common. Our experiments with several multilingual datasets have shown that Russian names admitting several transliterations are often treated as homonyms, and several persons with identical name variations are treated as synonyms.

Experiments with the RKBExplorer datasets[2] have shown that a person of the Open Archive has several matches in the RKBExplorer with different spellings and these matching persons have disjoint lists of their publications. For example, the publications authored or edited by Academician Andrei Petrovich Ershov have been attributed to 18 distinct persons whose names are Andrei P. Ershov, A.P. Yersh'ov, A. Ershov, and A. Yershov in DBLP RKBExplorer. By checking the DBLP Computer Science Bibliography, the counterpart of RKB Explorer DBLP, three distinct persons with publications belonging to Academician Andrei Petrovich Ershov have been identified. Their names are various forms of the Latin transliteration of "Андрей Петрович Ершов".

Experiments with WorldCat.org have shown that this resource, too, is not free from identification errors when Russian authors are considered. For example, the list of WorldCat Identities[3], containing descriptions of particularly prominent personalities, has a record dedicated to Academician Andrei Petrovich Ershov. It contains information about the books and papers authored or edited by Academician A.P. Ershov mixed with the publications authored by another A.P. Ershov (Alexander Petrovich) from Novosibirsk. Articles authored by A.P. Ershov and published between 1989 and 2012 have been described as "publications by Andrei Petrovich Ershov published posthumously" (Academician A.P. Ershov died in 1988). It is possible to find among these "posthumous publications" an article entitled "Capillary Flow of Cationic Polyelectrolyte Solutions". The text of this article indicates the affiliation of its author as the "Institute of Physical Chemistry, Russian Academy of Sciences". Academician A.P Ershov never worked for this organization, which means that this article is authored by another A.P. Ershov (Albert Petrovich).

Another example is VIAF, the Virtual International Authority File. Its web interface is available on http://viaf.org. The source files of VIAF include some of the most carefully curated files of names available. In addition, the bibliographic records using the files are professionally created, often reviewed and corrected by many libraries. In spite of the substantial work put into the creation and maintenance of the files, they still have inaccuracies. For example, VIAF has attributed several papers edited by or written by Academician A.P. Ershov to a person identified as http://viaf.org/viaf/196995053 and named Ershov, Aleksandr Petrovich. On the other hand, among the publications attributed to Academician Andrei Petrovich Ershov there are two books on economics (http://viaf.org/viaf/5347110), which can hardly belong to him.

This paper presents our approach to Russian-English identity resolution using text analysis methods in combination with attribute-based methods. The rest of this paper is organized as follows. Section 2 discusses specific features of our data sets that can

---

[2] www.rkbexplorer.com
[3] www.worldcat.org/wcidentities/lccn-n80162678

be used for identity resolution. Section 3 presents our algorithm along with some experimental results that show its effectiveness. Finally, Section 4 presents our conclusions and outlines future work.

2   Datasets and Evidence Used in the Disambiguation Task

The content of the SB RAS Open Archive provides various documents, mainly photos, reflecting information about people, research organizations and major events that have taken place in the SB RAS since 1957. The Open Archive contains information about the employments, research achievements, state awards, titles, participation in conferences, academic and social events for each person mentioned in the Archive. The Open Archive has 20,505 photo documents and facts about 10,917 persons and 1,519 organizations and events. The data sets of the Open Archive are available as an RDF triple store, as well as a Virtuoso endpoint for the SB RAS Archive. Its RDF triple store comprises about 600,000 RDF triples.

In the SB RAS Open Archive, all persons are specified by means of a normalized name. The format of a normalized name is <LastName, First Name Middle Name>. This attribute has two options: the Russian-language version and the English-language version. The English version is a transliteration of the Russian version. However, several English name variations can correspond to a normalized Russian name. It can be < First Name Middle Name Last Name>, <First Name Last Name>, <First Name First letter of the Middle Name Last Name >, < First letter of the First Name First letter of the Middle Name Last Name >, etc. All this forms should be first generated in Russian and then transliterated in English. Again, every Russian name can be transliterated in many ways. For example, the Russian family name Ершов can be spelt as Ershov, Yershov, Jerszow, and the first name Андрей can be written as Andrei, Andrey, Andrew. Therefore, in order to identify in an English knowledge base all the possible synonyms of a person from the Open Archive, we have to generate the most complete list of English spellings for each Russian name. This procedure is applied in the character by character manner, but some characters need special attention: the vowels such as "я", "ю ", and "e", can be transliterated in many ways. For example, the character "я" can be spelt in English as "ia", "ya", and "ja". The same is true of the consonants such as "й" and "щ". Another source of multiple transliterations is such character pairs as "ья", "ью", etc.

All generated forms of names are used as key words to search for articles in a target database. The authors of the extracted articles can be both homonyms and synonyms. We have to process the list of articles and determine which of their authors are synonyms and which of them are homonyms. In other words, the list of articles should be clustered into subsets S_1, S_2,..., S_n such that each subset of articles is authored by a single person and all his or her name variations are synonyms. Subset S_1 should contain the articles authored by the person from the Open Archive.

A well-known system for attribute-based identity resolution in the context of the Open Linked Data is SILK [7]. The heuristics used by VIAF and DBLP for ambiguity detection are described in [8,9]. However, cross-language entity disambiguation requires taking into account differences in orthography between languages and differences in the way these words in different languages are used to express similar meanings.

Since we need to identify the persons of the Open Archive, we use the Open Archive itself as an additional source of information. It provides the so-called "track records" – a list of affiliations with a related period for every person. For example, the Open Archive contains such facts as "Academician A.P. Ershov was the head of a department at the Institute of Mathematics SB AS USSR from 1959 to 1964 and the head of a department at the Computing Center SB AS USSR from 1964 to 1988".

Another useful kind of information stored in the Open Archive is the list of names for every organization. For example, there is information that the Institute of Computational Mathematics and Mathematical Geophysics SB RAS was called Computing Center SB AS USSR from 1964 to 1991.

The author's affiliations, extracted from SpringerLink, are compared with the information about employment of persons of the Open Archive. Note that the English names of Russian organizations indicated by the authors of articles quite often do not correspond to their standard translations, and can contain unusual abbreviations and nonstandard word order. To tackle this problem, we have developed a cyclic modification of Jaro-Winkler algorithm [10].

Sometimes there is no information about author's affiliation or this information is rather general, such as "Russian Academy of Sciences". To classify this kind of article, we use semantic text analysis methods. Now a large number of publications are digitized, and the most important attribute characterizing each researcher is her or his publications. Nowadays, quite advanced methods of authorship attribution exist, including analysis of character, lexical, syntactic, semantic and application-dependent features [11-13]. The use of these methods is governed by the idea that authors unconsciously tend to use similar lexical, syntactic or semantic patterns. However, when comparing the English texts published by Russian authors, character, lexical, and syntactic methods do not seem to be the most appropriate because different texts of the same author can be translated by different translators who vary in their translation styles. On the other hand, semantic analysis of the texts can reveal, for example, their terminological similarity.

Thus, we suggest a combined use of articles metadata comparison and their text similarity estimation for the cross-language identity resolution.

As a source of detailed meta-data, the digital library SpringerLink has been chosen. SpringerLink is currently one of the largest digital libraries that holds more than 9,000,000 documents in various fields of research: computer science and mathematics, life sciences and materials, philosophy and psychology. Its wide range of fields corresponds well to the multidisciplinary orientation of the SB RAS Archive. SpringerLink contains the full texts of many articles. If the full text of a publication is not available, SpringerLink provides detailed meta-data about the publication, such as ISSN, abstract, the affiliations of its authors (if it is specified in the text of the publication), references etc. Finally, SpringerLink is one of the sources used by a part of the Open Linked Data cloud WorldCat.org (http://worldcat.org).

Basically, our program was used to identify the persons described in the Open Archive. Nevertheless, there is a mode which allows for use of the identity resolution program for persons missing from the Open Archive.

3   Algorithm for Identity Resolution

The general scheme of our algorithm is shown in Fig. 1.

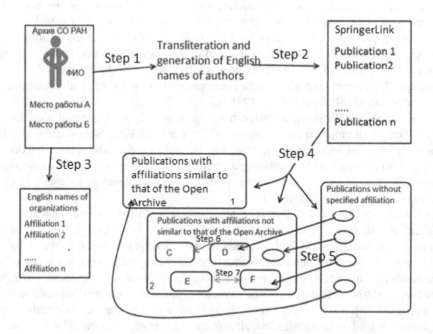

Fig. 1. The general scheme of our algorithm.

1. Our program takes as input a string *R_string,* corresponding to a normalized Russian name, and returns a set of all possible English transliteration and form variations *E_strings* as it is explained in Section 2. Initially, we used Google translate for the *E_strings* generation, but when we noticed some inaccuracies, we developed our own transliteration program. This step should allow the extraction of the most complete set of synonyms for the given person.

2. Each generated string $s \in E\_strings$ is used for key word search in SpringerLink. This search results in a list of documents where the key word can occur in the title of article, in the name of organization, in the reference list, etc. All the articles are filtered, and only publications having one of the key words as the author are retained. Each article is specified by a unique identifier. SpringerLink indexes several kinds of data formats (txt, PDF, PNG). For our experiment, however, we convert non-text formats into text and make use of plain text files. A set of meta-data such as citation_publisher, citation_title, citation_language, citation_pdf_url, citation_author, citation_author_affiliation, etc. are extracted and concatenated to create a text for analysis. The authors of the extracted articles can be both homonyms and synonyms. We have to process the list of articles and determine which of their authors are synonyms and which of them are homonyms. In other words, the list of articles should be clustered into subsets $S_1, S_2, \ldots, S_n$ such that each subset of articles is authored by a single

person and all his or her name variations are synonyms. Subset S_1 should contain the articles authored by the person from the Open Archive.

3. The publication date and authors' affiliations, provided by SpringerLink are compared with the person's list of affiliations specified by the Open Archive. Again, English names of organizations should be compared against their Russian counterpart. At this stage using transliteration is inappropriate, therefore Google translate and viaf.org web services are used for generating the English variants of the Russian names of organizations. For example, "Институт Систем Информатики" is identified in VIAF as VIAF ID: 159616561 (Corporate). Permalink: http://viaf.org/viaf/159616561. Its English name provided by VIAF is "A.P. Ershov Institute of Informatics Systems". However, only 10 percent of the names of organizations occurring in the Open Archive can be found at VIAF.org. If there is no English counterpart for the Russian name of an organization, its Google translation is used.

4. To distinguish persons whose affiliations specified in SpringerLink coincide with these indicated in the Open Archive, we generate a matrix that measures pair wise similarity between stemmed affiliations (names of organizations). Cyclic Jaro-Winkler distance [10] is used as the measurement. That is, a sequence of words that make up the name of the first organization, is cyclicly shifted to find the longest subsequence that matches the name of the second organization. Based on this comparison, the whole list of articles S is subdivided into three subsets P_1, P_2, and P_3, where P_1 is a set of articles whose affiliations are similar to one of the list of affiliations specified for the given person in the Open Archive, P_2 is a set of articles whose affiliations are not similar to any of the list of affiliations specified by the Open Archive for the given person, and P_3 is a set of articles that have no specified affiliation for the considered author. The publications of the subset P_2 are further subdivided into groups of articles $Group_2...Group_K$ such that each group of articles corresponds to exactly one place of work.

5. The program tries to distribute articles without specified affiliations among the groups of publications with specified affiliations. This procedure is based on the text similarity of articles. Two options are available at this stage. One of the most effective methods for the semantic analysis of textual data is Latent Dirichlet Allocation with Cullback-Leibler divergency [14,15]. A simpler and computationally cheaper alternative is to calculate document similarity using the tf-idf weighting with cosine similarity[4]. The results presented in this paper are mainly obtained using the tf-idf weighting with cosine similarity[5]. Before computing the text similarity, the text is cleaned by removing stop words and leaving only plain content-carrying words, then a stemming procedure[6] is applied. If the similarity value for an article A is below threshold for every group of articles $Group_1$, ..., $Group_N$, the program creates a new group $Newgroup_{N+1}$, where $N+1$ is the serial number of the newly created group.

---

[4] http://www.codeproject.com/Articles/12098/Term-frequency-Inverse-document-frequency-implemen

[5] http://www.codeproject.com/Articles/12098/Term-frequency-Inverse-document-frequency-implemen

[6] http://snowball.tartarus.org/

6. Some articles are specified by general affiliation such as "Russian Academy of Sciences". The program tries to distribute articles with more general affiliations among the groups of articles with more specific affiliations. For example, "Siberian Division of the Russian Academy of Sciences" is considered to be more general with respect to "A.P. Ershov Institute of Informatics Systems of the Siberian Division of the Russian Academy of Sciences". More general affiliation is a substring of a more specific one. If the author's affiliation specified in SpringerLink is considered to be a general name of an organization, the program tries to decide which of the more specific names of the organization can be used as author's affiliation. Text similarity of the articles from groups with the exact names of organizations is used at this stage.

7. Text similarity measure is applied again to compare the generated groups of articles and if the similarity value for two groups of articles $Group_i$ and $Group_j$ exceeds the threshold value, the two groups are merged into one.

8. The collection of documents is treated as a graph. Each document is a node identified by its number in the list of documents and every pair of documents is connected by an edge whose weight (W) is given by the similarity between the two documents. A threshold is applied to the similarity matrix to ignore the links between documents with low similarity. The threshold depends on the number of nodes: $k \times N_{nodes}$, where the factor k was chosen experimentally as 0.0015. For example, the threshold is equal to 0.05 for 30 nodes. The obtained graph is drawn by a usual force-directed placement algorithm so that similar documents are placed close to each other. In our case, the force of attraction and the repulsion force both depend on the weight of the edge between vertices.

The result of the program is a set of SpringerLink articles subdivided into several groups. The first group of articles is attributed to the person described in the Open Archive.

4   Results

Experiments have shown that name variations generated by our program were more appropriate than that of Google translate. For example, 408 English variants have been generated by our program for the Russian name "Валерий Александрович Непомнящий," among which only five variations have been discovered in Springer-link: V.A. Nepomnyashchii, Valery Nepomniaschy, V.A. Nepomniaschy, Valery A. Nepomniaschy, V.A. Nepomnyaschy. Google Translate created 160 variants of the same name, but some name variations existing in SpringerLink were absent from Google translate results. For example, the name variation "V.A. Nepomnyaschy" existing in SpringerLink was generated by our program but was not generated by Google Translate at the time of our experiments. A specific point of Google Translate was that along with the transliteration of names, it generated their translations. For example, Google translate generated variants like "Valery oblivious" for the Russian name "Валерий Непомнящий", and "Vadim cats" for the Russian name "Вадим Котов". For the Russian name «Андрей Петрович Ершов» 64 English variants have been generated.

An example of the program, searching for the articles authored by the Russian person "А.П. Ершов" in the digital library SpringerLink is shown in Fig. 2. English variations of a Russian personal name are displayed in the upper left tab. English versions of affiliations for the given person are displayed in the middle left tab. In the center, a graph representing the publications attributed by the algorithm to the person from the Open Archive is shown.

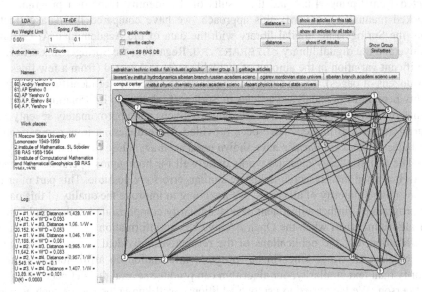

Fig. 2. A placement of several articles attributed to the person named as Андрей Петрович Ершов in the Open Archive. Articles with specified affiliation are shown in a lighter color.

Each node of the graph corresponds to an article of the SpringerLink digital library. 10 white nodes correspond to the articles with a specified affiliation and 7 yellow nodes represent articles without a specified affiliation. This means that for this person 30 percent of publications is correctly attributed due to the text similarity measure. A total of 91 publications have been found for the "А.П. Ершов" query. All these papers were written by several real persons. There were 84 papers belonging to persons named as A.P. Ershov, 5 papers belonging to a person named as Andrei P. Ershov, 1 paper belonging to a person named A.P. Yershov, and 1 paper belonging to Andrei Petrovich Ershov. Academician Andrei Petrovich Ershov (described in the Open Archive) has used all the above variants of his name, and the other persons (Albert Petrovich Ershov, Alexei Petrovich Ershov, Albert Petrovich Ershov...) have always named themselves A.P. Ershov. The program has correctly attributed 17 publications authored by Academician Andrei Petrovich Ershov, as well publications authored by another three A.P. Ershov who are not descibed in the Open Archive. Other groups of articles correspond to homonyms of the person described in the Open Archive.

5   Conclusion

The program has been tested on a test sample of 100 persons employed by the IIS SB RAS at various time periods (about 3,000 publications) and on the articles authored by Academician A.P. Ershov. The names of the IIS SB RAS employees were extracted automatically from the Open Archive, after that their publications were extracted from SpringerLink and the results of the identity resolution program were checked manually. To verify this approach, we have compared the data extracted from the SpringerLink digital library with the data of the Academician A. Ershov's archive and the digital library eLIBRARY.RU. Regarding the SpringerLink articles, a significant variation in the amount of available texts is detected (from a few lines to a few dozens of pages), which significantly affects the accuracy of identification. About eighty percent of the analyzed articles in SpringerLink had no information on the full names of their authors (only short forms were given) and approximately seventy percent of author's affiliations have been provided. Nevertheless, a joint comparison of attributes and text similarities have shown good accuracy, close to 93 percent.

The text similarity measure works quite well for homonyms operating in remote areas, but when their research fields are similar, errors are possible. This part of errors makes up the majority of all errors. We are going to improve the quality of this part of the program by further adjustment of text similarity comparison. Another problem for our algorithm arises when the Open Archive has no information concerning a change in affiliation, but the publications of the respective individual indicate a change in his/her place of work. Since in our program information on affiliations has higher priority than text similarity, our algorithm can produce several distinct persons for one real person. We have tried to use two additional well-known heuristics such as paper venue and information about co-authors for these cases [4]. However, quite often a change of affiliation correlates with a change or research partners and publication venue. In the near future we are going to develop a measure taking into account both text similarity and additional attributes such as paper references.

Acknowledgements. This work has been supported by the RFBR grant 14-07-00386.

References

1. Marchuk, A.G., Marchuk, P.A.: Specific features of digital libraries construction with linked content. In: Proc. of the RCDL 2010 Conf., pp. 19–23 (2010). (in Russian)
2. Schultz, A., et al.: How to integrate LINKED DATA into your application. In: Semantic Technology & Business Conference, San Francisco, June 5, 2012. http://mes-semantics.com/wp-content/uploads/2012/09/Becker-etal-LDIFSemTechSanFrancisco.pdf
3. Apanovich, Z., Marchuk, A.: Experiments on using LOD cloud datasets to enrich the content of a scientific knowledge base. In: Klinov, P., Mouromtsev, D. (eds.) KESW 2013. CCIS, vol. 394, pp. 1–14. Springer, Heidelberg (2013)
4. Ferreira, A.A., Gonçalves, M.A., Laender, A.H.F.: Disambiguating author names. In: Large Bibliographic Repositories Conference: Internat. Conf. on Digital Libraries, New Delhi, India (2013)

5. Song, Y., Huang, J., Councill, I.G., Li, J., Giles, C.L.: Efficient topic-based unsupervised name disambiguation. In: Proc. of the 7th ACM/IEEE-CS Joint Conf. on Digital Libraries, pp. 342–351 (2007)
6. Godby, C.J., Denenberg, R.: Common Ground: Exploring Compatibilities Between the Linked Data Models of the Library of Congress and OCLC. http://www.oclc.org/research/publications/2015/oclcresearch-loc-linked-data-2015.html
7. Isele, R., Jentzsch, A., Bizer, C.: Silk server - adding missing links while consuming linked data. In: 1st Internat. Workshop on Consuming Linked Data (COLD 2010), Shanghai (2010)
8. Ley, M.: DBLP-Some Lessons Learned. PVLDB 2(2), 1493–1500 (2009)
9. Hickey, T.B., Toves, J.A.: Managing Ambiguity In VIAF. D-Lib Magazine 20, July/August, 2014. http://www.dlib.org/dlib/july14/hickey/07hickey.html
10. Cohen, W.W., Ravikumar, P.D., Fienberg, S.E.: A comparison of string distance metrics for name-matching tasks. In: II Web, pp.73–78 (2003)
11. Stamatatos, E.: A survey of modern authorship attribution methods. J. of the American Society for Information Science and Technology 60(3), 538–556 (2009)
12. Rogov, A.A., Sidorov, Y.: Vl. statistical and information-calculating support of the authorship attribution of the literary works. computer data analysis and modeling: robustness and computer intensive methods. In: Aivazian, S., Kharin, Y., Rieder, Y. (eds.) Proc. of the Sixth Internat. Conf. (September 10–14, 2001, Minsk), vol. 2, pp. 187–192. BSU, Minsk (2001)
13. Kukushkina, O., Polikarpov, A., Khmelev, D.: Using literal and grammatical statistics for authorship attribution. Probl. of Info. Trans. 37(2), 172–184 (2001)
14. Blei, D.M., Ng, A., Jordan, M.: Latent Dirichlet allocation. Journal of Machine Learning Research 3, 993–1022 (2003)
15. Steyvers, M., Griffiths, T.: Probabilistic Topic Models Handbook of Latent Semantic Analysis (2007)

Exploring the Kyoto Digital Archives Project: Challenging the Funding Model of Digital Archive Development

Noriko Asato[✉] and Andrew Wertheimer

Library and Information Science Program, University of Hawaii, Honolulu, USA
{asaton,wertheim}@hawaii.edu

Abstract. Within the Japanese world of digital archives, Kyoto plays a key role. The city became a pioneer in digital archive development by partnering with academics, private organizations with cultural treasures, and private industry. They created the Kyoto Digital Archives Project, an organization that developed a profit-sharing model for digitizing materials and overcoming complex issues of intellectual property. This paper examines how it developed, and also looks at its framework for proposing autonomous regional archives over a homogenized national digital archive.

Keywords: Digital archives · E-Japan strategy · Intellectual property · Copyright · Cultural preservation · Funding digital archives · National identity · Regional identity

1 Development of Digital Archives as Part of the National Agenda

In Japan, government policy is usually created from the top-down and national to local. For the most part, digital archive planning is no different. The context for the creation of digital archives in Japan emerged from the government's strategy to establish an environment in which education, culture, and art are all accessible for people living in an advanced and highly networked society. This was executed by a government-led organization, the Japan Digital Archives Association, established in 1996, which laid the foundation for promoting the establishment of local digital archives [1]. In parallel, the government issued a series of IT strategy initiatives incorporating digital archives as an effective medium to carry out these policies. Those initiatives include *e-Japan Strategy II* (2003), in which the Ministry of Internal Affairs and Communications and the Ministry of Cultural Affairs planned to construct a digital archive portal called "Cultural Heritage Online" [2]. Both the *e-Japan Priority Policy Program-2003* and *e-Japan Strategy II Acceleration Package* (2004) emphasized a three-pronged approach of enhancing educational content, dissemination, and utilization [3,4].

More recent national government strategies, *Intellectual Property Promotion Plan 2011* and *2012*, recognize digital archives to be a key "knowledge infrastructure" that

© Springer International Publishing Switzerland 2015
R.B. Allen et al. (Eds.): ICADL 2015, LNCS 9469, pp. 22–32, 2015.
DOI: 10.1007/978-3-319-27974-9_3

guide the creation of new content, intellectual property strategy in Japan, and also increase its competitiveness internationally [5]. The plan's "Cool Japan" strategy promotes cultural content, games, manga, animé, food, and anything that foreigners may find attractive to expand the international marketplace for "Brand Japan."

From the early development of Japanese digital archives in the mid-1990s to the present, we can identify three continuous developmental stages. The first stage is the development of large-scale national digital libraries or ones fostered by the central government. Several studies have explored this period. Koga [6] examined the development of Japanese IT initiatives, and later [7] analyzed the strategic role of electronic services of the National Diet Library (NDL) and National Archives of Japan. Nakayama [8] focused on the NDL's function as a data provider, aggregating data from other digital archives. Shimizu [9] discussed the significance of digital archives in the national strategic plans, such as the "Cultural Heritage Online Project" and "Strategy for the Nation of Tourism."

The main players in the second phase of digital archives development were the digital archives established by prefectural and municipal governments. Literature on this second stage examined themes of sustainability [10]; operations [11] content selection and processing [12,13]; and effects on local communities [14]. Sugimoto [15] discusses the importance of digital archives as memory institutions. Learning from the 2011 Great East Japan Earthquake, Sugimoto argues that digital archives build on a robust information environment, and that metadata and meta-metadata are essential for preserving community memories for the future.

In the third phase, as the effectiveness of digital archives as a medium to disseminate information has become more established, groups of citizens and private organizations launched their own digital archives. Their purpose ranged from merely introducing new IT technologies, revitalization of their organizations to seeking publicity, with objectives shifting over time [16]. Case studies [1] and surveys and reports [17] are typical of research on citizen and community based digital libraries.

On one hand, these three overlapping phases occurred over two decades, with even more digital archives continuously emerging. On the other hand, a significant number have been discontinued or even disappeared from the web. The establishment of digital archives requires various resources and technical and practical skills, which are important, but assuring a digital archive's continued existence requires organizational commitment and vision.

This paper examines one of the rare examples of a very successful municipal project to promote digital archives in Kyoto. We will explore factors that led to the success, especially the philosophical framework that guided their project over several years and helped foster a unique business model that may work for other digital archives holding cultural treasures. A purpose of the Kyoto digital archives project was to create a business model, and develop a pilot project with one digital collection that would generate energy and encourage others to emulate this. It also intended to shift the present paradigm of centralization of culture and media to a local-oriented one. Kyoto is an old capital of Japan, known for its long cultural heritage, yet also thrives as an innovative and entrepreneurial environment. The Kyoto digital archives model, building on the city's countless cultural treasures and international tourist sites, is rather unique and may not be applicable to other local contexts outside Japan or even within the country.

However, its underpinning spirit of creating a new paradigm for digital archives that would meet local needs and conditions is worth examining. The Kyoto digital archives initiative also exemplifies community members' leadership to orchestrate individual efforts to crystalize a distinctive regional style.

2   Local Digital Archives

2.1   Preservation (*tameru*), Dissemination (*tsunagu*), and Utilization (*ikasu*)

As the national government incorporated digital archives measures into national digital strategic plans, many organizations promoting local digital archives in their communities emerged. In 2001, they organized the first convention, the National Council for the Organization of Local Digital Archive Promotion, in Kyoto to exchange information and technologies. Thirteen local organizations participated from all over the nation. Over the following years, national conventions were held in different cities which were spearheading digital archives initiatives. Those organizations shared the view that digital archives are not only to preserve local treasures and historical records, but also that they should have a more "active" function of "disseminating" and focusing on how the information is "utilized." Further, participants agreed that those digitized materials should be aggregated as human knowledge and preserved for future generations. They perceived digital archives as the center of a circular knowledge organism [18].

Digitization of local culture was also seen as a means of local revitalization.   Japanese society is suffering from the graying of society combined with a declining birth rate. An extreme urbanization accelerated depopulation in the countryside and has been greatly diminishing local businesses. Local communities saw digital archives as helping them to brand local culture, food, crafts, and events to attract tourists and rebuild communities. They also hoped that digital projects would encourage the development of IT businesses and human resources and in turn rejuvenate the community. In all, digital archives are perceived to be catalysts to shift the Tokyo-centric media and lifestyle to local oriented ones [1].

2.2   The Kyoto Digital Archives Project

The initiative to create digital archives in Kyoto began with the launch of "Kyoto Digital Archives Plan of 1997." The following August, the Kyoto Digital Archives Promotion Agency was established with the cooperation of Kyoto City, the Chamber of Commerce, and other organizations. In 2000, the project was succeeded by the Kyoto Digital Archives Research Center [18]. The Research Center was a cooperative organization of the Kyoto Municipal Government, a consortium of Universities in Kyoto, and the Chamber of Commerce, as a "membership corporation."[1]

---

[1] Japan Association of Graphic Arts Technology, Degitaru Akaibu: Chuoshuken kara Bunsan e [Digital Archives: From Centralization to Dispersion]. The Kyoto Digital Archives Research Center was closed at the end of 2003. The operation was succeeded by the Advanced Science Technology & Management Research Institute of Kyoto.   Kyoto City Official Website. http://www2.city.kyoto.lg.jp/sogo/seisaku/promop/sub-contents/2_3_3_3%28187%29.htm

The initial objectives of the Kyoto Digital Archives Plan were to 1) digitize the rich history, culture and traditional assets of Kyoto for future generations; 2) create new industries by using these digitized assets; and 3) create an environment that promotes intellectual property rights [19]. The Research Center's main activities included cultivating public awareness, industrial development, and human resources. The Center put the emphasis on building a database for digital archives, development of new products, and producing digital content. Among a number of projects the Research Center produced, we will examine the "National Treasure, Nijo Castle Digital Archives," which created a unique business model for digital archive operations.

2.3   The Nijo Castle Digital Archives

The largest endeavor taken up by the Kyoto Digital Archives Research Center was a digital collection of the National Treasure, Nijo Castle. Nijo Castle is a world cultural heritage site, its Ninomaru Palace is a National Treasure, and 954 out of the 3,411 wall paintings (*fusuma-e*, paintings on Japanese sliding doors) are designated as Important Cultural Properties. In addition, the Kano-Japanese Painting School's *fusuma* paintings and engraved metal objects, and heavy transom, magnificent hallways, and gardens, are all elaborate artworks that capture the essence of Momoyama era culture. Every part of the castle was digitized using the standard of 130 million pixels. However, what makes the castle a "miracle castle" and the digitization project so quintessential is its wall paintings, which present a wide range of vivid colors. The process of digitizing these rare treasures took an extreme level of care and precision so as not to damage these paintings, which are hundreds of years old and susceptible to light damage.

An essential part of the project's purpose was preservation. However, the costs for this scale of preservation project are enormous, so in order to make it possible, they created a venture business using the digitized images to produce unique products. The royalties from the use of the digitized images would be used to finance continued preservation. In other words, the goal of this project was not only preservation of Nijojo artifacts, but also to develop a self-sustaining business model that would motivate others to launch their own efforts to preserve and digitize Kyoto heritage. It would also cultivate human resources and revitalize the city's economy [11].

The Digitization of Nijo Castle received great response: it was a huge success as a business model [18]. The digitized images were used to create wallpapers, floor tiles, subway walls, train bodies, clothes, and everyday goods. The proposal application for the use of Nijo Castle image is now available at the Kyoto Culture Association's homepage.[2]

2.4   Solving Copyright Issues

Besides technical aspects of digitization, one of the biggest challenges encountered related to the digitization of cultural treasures surrounded copyright issues. Negotiation with cultural property owners, such as temples and shrines, and old families, over their intellectual property rights is rarely easy. They worry that their original treasures

---

[2] http://kyo-bunka.or.jp/nijyo.html

would become devalued by the existence of authorized copies, and that unauthorized images would emerge from these. They also were concerned about who would pay for the expenses, how the profit would be divided, and questioned if the digital medium is stable enough to last. In the face of so many difficult-to-answer questions, many cultural property owners simply believed that digitalization was a troublesome process that brought in few rewards, and thus was easy to reject. This situation obviously was a problem for digital archive efforts, especially in Kyoto, where most of the cultural properties were owned by temples or shrines who raise funds by donations or tourists buying tickets or amulets.

The solution was to create a business model for gaining revenue from digitization and to produce success stories. Kazuhiro Shimizu, Deputy Direct of the Kyoto Digital Archives Research Center, argued that the content distribution business consists of two aspects: one is whether the system would work, and the other was whether it could produce sufficient business. More often than not, organizers involved with a digitization project are concerned only with the functionality and security of the system; however, Shimizu explains "that's like putting a carriage before a horse." The first and most important question is to see whether it would produce revenue [11]. Based on this vision, the Research Center focused on the business aspect of digitization and designed the "Kyoto Business Model" for its digital archives projects.

The Kyoto Model is designed based on a profit distribution system. When temples or shrines digitize their cultural properties, they permit companies who are interested in the digitization of a particular object without charging a fee for digitization rights, but costs incurred in the digitization will be at the expense of the company. However, if the digital content is commercialized and produced for profit, a certain percentage of these profits are then shared between the company and the content owner [20].

Figure 1 illustrates the concept of the model. In it, we can see that temples (or shrines or other cultural property owners), would grant "Company A" the right to digitize its images. Company A then self-finances the digitization, but this project could also use subsidies or grants by the government or other organizations. Once digitized, Company A could allow specific usage permission of the digitized image to another business. For example, a hotel might want to use an image as the design for hotel interiors, or even as goods and clothes they would sell. The hotel would then give some portion of the royalties or profit to Company A, which then provides a certain percentage of this royalty with the original property owner.

The fee for using the digitized image would vary depending on the content, quality, purpose of the use and target audience, format of use, and amount produced. The Kyoto Business Model suggests 40% of the product value be paid to the digitization company. For example, if a hotel built an interior wall using the digital image, which has an estimated value of $1 million, Company A would receive $400,000, and half of that, or $200,000 should be paid to the temple.

This system makes digitization of properties possible without the property owner's self-financing and technical skills. It also spares the owners from assessing individual property values and creating different contracts depending on the nature of a project or conditions. It is also a mechanism that allows cultural properties to self-finance their necessary repairs and preservation.

A key factor in the Kyoto Model is that a cultural treasure would not be required to give "Company A" exclusive rights for the digitized images. The property owners would be able to permit other companies under the same conditions. By holding the freedom of sharing the rights of digitization and image use with an unlimited number of users, the property owners can avoid a number of potential problems, such as monopoly, breach of contract, or be stuck with images produced using low quality equipment.

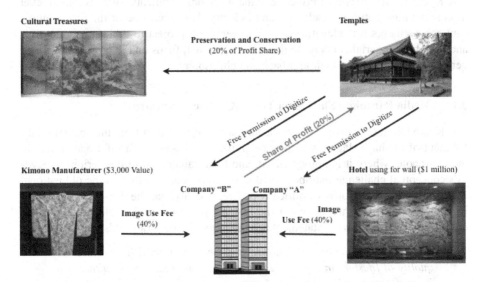

This explanatory graphic is a translation and modification of the one by Shimizu (2006). **Image Credits:**
• Peter Roan Takao in Autumn by Yamamoto Baiitsu (Japanese, 1783–1856)" Creative Commons Flickr.
• Bermi Ferrer, "Kyoto Temples" Creative Commons Flickr.
• Artwork in main lobby (OkiBird, Sep 2013)" at Crowne Plaza Hotel. Tripadvisor.co.uk

Fig. 1. The Kyoto Business Model for Intellectual Property and Preservation

2.5 A Future Model: Decentralized / Clustered Digital Archives

The Research Center staff view the success of the Nijo Castle digitization project as a pivotal point for the development of digital archives in Kyoto. It would shift the present central government led digital projects to the content holders' autonomous movement. They also perceived the initiative as conducive to make the city a treasure of digital archives. The Research Center generated success stories out of the Nijo Castle project to be a model for other digital archives projects. This model encourages temples, shrines, and families with historical records, historic sites, museums, individual artists, and art dealers alike, to become actively involved with establishing their own digital archives. In other words, there would be more independent, decentralized digital archives with unique content that reflect regional cultures. They proposed this bottom-up, more autonomous approach allows the flexibility to highlight unique regional elements and distinctive personality that would otherwise be lost in a highly centralized, top-down model of digital archives, with the usual imposed standards and appearance. Rather, the organizers of the Research Center hoped to see these independent archives increase and be like a regional cluster of digital archives.

3   Discussion

The Kyoto Digital Archives Project had many accomplishments, such as a high level of collaboration between academics and industry. However, one of the most significant achievements was elevating a local government project to a business enterprise and its entrepreneurial concept. In this section, we will focus on the project's business perspectives and analyze their approach and philosophy.

3.1   Media Paradigm Shift from Tokyo-Centric to Localized

The Kyoto Digital Archives Project displays a conceptual shift from the present establishment of media in Japan, which is centralized in Tokyo, with information sent to the metropole, where it is homogenized, and then transmitted to the periphery. Kyoto's conceptual challenge may be rooted in its politics and history as the old national capitol. Kyoto, a traditionally politically progressive city, has the disposition of adopting new ideas and technologies on the outside while preserving old traditions and customs at heart. Shimizu's statement below eloquently illustrates this point.

> When the globalization of culture is promoted, naturally it raises the quality of lifestyle in a global level. At the same time, local culture will be uniformed and eventually disappear. For this, the preservation of any ethnic events, traditional industries, life equipment and tools, documents on ethnic history, which characterize local cultures, is a critical and urgent matter [18].

The e-Japan Priority Policy Program 2002 stated that it aimed to establish an environment where "various cultural property, art, local culture, performing arts, historical documents such as important official documents will be accessible from anywhere without geographical restrictions." Referring to this point, the Ministry of Internal Affairs in its Information Telecommunications report emphasized "digital archives are playing a essential role as a base for integration and dissemination of digital network culture" [21]. This quote shows us the radical example of the Kyoto Digital Archives Project, and how it cleaves to an autonomous emphasis on the local over national identity. It stands for the paradigm of establishing local identities, disseminating local culture, producing new creative local industries, and upgrading a local information infrastructure, which sums up the initiative of establishing independent governance.

3.2   A Business Model for the Management of Intellectual Property Rights

Copyright issues are often seen as one of the leading obstacles for creating digital archives. A 2009 National Diet Library survey on digital archives indicates that reasons that the respondents (cultural and academic institutions) have not created a digital archive include "a lack of budget (79.7%)", "a lack of staff (74.2%)", "a lack of knowledge (59.4%)," and "difficulties with copyright issues (29.9%)" [22].

The Kyoto Digital Archives Project adopted a general business contract without resorting to complex copyright laws. Their "Kyoto Business Model" became a prototype for business using digital content. Creativity and such novelty helped avoid typical problems pertaining to copyright, and managed to launch their project.

3.3   The "Kyoto Business Model" as a Circulatory Model

Kyoto is surrounded by cultural treasures; however, Kyoto Digital Project leaders didn't believe that funding would naturally emerge to finance preservation efforts just because something has special cultural values. Rather, they saw digital images as actual resources that help them gain monetary resources to repair and preserve these treasures. They embodied this concept into a circulatory business model and promoted it for others to follow suit. Shimizu explained that the project adopted three elements; 'preservation', 'dissemination,' and 'utilization,' of the central government's concept of digital archives, but particularly focused on the 'using,' because the first two require substantial funds. This fact itself demanded focus first on making business out of the digitization. He explains that ideally a local government's digitization project should lead to commercial projects; however, it is not easy to overcome barriers such as gaining the understanding of citizens and clearing copyright issues [23]. Many local government digital projects pointed out a large expenditure of digitization limited their work along with a lack of cooperation between industry, academics, and government [1].

3.4   A Digital Archives Project with a Clear Vision

Typical functions of a local government are considered to be the promotion of education, culture, and welfare, but making a profit is seen to belong to the private sector. However, the first and most important goal for the Kyoto Digital Archives Project was to establish a foundation for commercial success, which would stimulate other content holders to follow suit and consequently revitalize the city. It was also to generate funds to preserve and repair cultural treasures.

According to the 2009 National Diet Library's survey on digital archive operations, in which respondents were asked to choose the most important purposes of their digital archives selected: 47.8% of the institutions chose "publicity and promotion of the institution's activities" as the most important purpose, followed by "maintenance and preservation of materials" (23.7%). Among the reasons chosen as second most important were "increase search ability" was most popular, followed by "publicity" [22]. In any case, the questionnaire did not even include "making profit" as a reason although respondents could write their own answer in "other." This again makes a sharp contrast with the Kyoto Digital Archives.

3.5   Frequent Organizational Change in the Promotion Agency

As the Kyoto Digital Archive Initiative developed, it went through many stages. In 1997, the project became the "Kyoto Digital Archive Promotion Agency." Three years later, it was dismantled once it achieved its goals. A new organization, the "Kyoto Digital Archives Research Center" immediately succeeded the mission with new goals, and it was closed in 2004 when the Center fulfilled its promised mandate. The project promotion organization's short period of existence and dissolution was planned, and was not the consequence of an unsuccessful operation.

The missions of the first agent, the "Kyoto Digital Archive Promotion Agency," included the construction of a database for digital archives, the development of new products, and established the foundation for creating a digital content business. The project completion was planned in March 2001, and was successfully achieved, with the agency closed after three years. A new organization, the Kyoto Digital Archives Research Center was formed with the goal of producing a business model in three years, which was met with the production of the Nijo Castle Digital Archives Project and dissolved in 2004. It is said to be the philosophy of Inagaki Kazuo, a leader of the project, who claimed "an essential project to lead the time needs to produce significant results in 1,000 days or three years at longest" [24]. The Project's next step announced for the 21st century archives is aimed to move to dispersion type archives with government subsidies [25].

It is often the case that leaders involved in a public business use the opportunity to advance their own fame or profit; however, their priority was to maintain the organization's energy at the highest level to produce visible success. In order to move on to the next step with new missions, a succeeding agent was to be established, which was to be an opportunity to introduce new generation of staff and technologies. In his survey study of 2011, Kawakami found that digital archives created by local governments tended to have closed down more than those led by private organizations [10]. These results suggest that digital archives need to focus on sustainability. However, the organizers of the Kyoto Model were focusing on a model for sustainability rather than in becoming an agency supporting digital archives or a repository itself.

3.6   The Universality of the Kyoto Digital Archives Project as a Model

Although there are many things we could learn from the Kyoto Digital Archives Project, the Project took place in rather an unusual environment to be seen as a model for a regional digital archival development. Kyoto is an old Japanese capital and holds literally millions of national and regional treasures, which naturally could lead to countless digital projects. In addition, Kyoto had already established its own 'brand' domestically as well as internationally before the digital era as a tourist site and a center of Japanese traditional culture and arts. Therefore, the potential for success was already there.

The Project suggests that participating in a digital archives project led by the central government might not be in the best interest for a regional community since it would lose local autonomy and unique cultures. It rather suggest a future direction to be decentralized, dispersed archives, with individual independent archives forming a cluster type digital archives. In a decentralized archive, digital contents are independently managed within the institutions, and these archives are independent yet connected in a cluster manner instead of being aggregated and mixed in a large national digital entity. This model would again be disadvantageous for a region which does not have as abundant cultural significance that would bring about business opportunities and form an economic foundation.

4   Conclusion

Examining this Kyoto Model from the perspective of archival profession in North America, this is an interesting experiment. The model helps to address two key problems, how to gather materials still in private hands, and also how to gather funds for expensive digitization projects in a time when public funds are in tight supply. On the other hand, it also raises some key questions over such foundational questions of 'what is a digital archive' and the mission of an archive. In North America, the key point would not only be preservation, but also access. Clearly, there is a need for more research from a historical and comparative model. It is essential to develop an understanding of how archives, digital archives, and digital libraries are unique endeavors in each country, and how they develop missions, standards, and sense of national and local identity, reflecting the wider social and political contexts.

References

1. Kanto ICT Promotion NPO Liaison Council.: Degitaru Akaibu Machi Zukuri Jireishu [Case Studies on Digital Archives for Building Communities], pp. 1–47 (2009). http://www.soumu.go.jp/soutsu/kanto/ai/npo/hokokusho/h210603.pdf
2. IT Strategic Headquarters.: e-Japan Strategy II. http://japan.kantei.go.jp/policy/it/0702senryaku_e.pdf
3. IT Strategic Headquarters.: e-Japan Priority Policy Program 2003 (Summary). http://japan.kantei.go.jp/policy/it/0808summary/030808gaiyo_e.pdf
4. IT Strategic Headquarters.: e-Japan Strategy II Acceleration Package. http://japan.kantei.go.jp/policy/it/040318senryaku_e.pdf
5. Intellectual Property Strategy Headquarters.: Chiteki Zaisan Suishin Keikaku [Intellectual Property Promotion Plan 2011], pp. 28–31 (2011). http://www.kantei.go.jp/jp/kakugikettei/2011/__icsFiles/afieldfile/2012/03/12/chizaikeikaku2011.pdf
6. Koga, T.: Access to Government Information in Japan: A long Way toward Electronic Government? Government Information Quarterly 20, 47–62 (2003)
7. Koga, T.: Innovation Beyond Institutions: New Projects and Challenges for Government Information Service Institutions in Japan. IFLA Journal, 1–10, June 9, (2005)
8. Nakayama, M.: Building Digital Archives by the National Diet Library: Toward Knowledge Sharing. Journal of Information Processing and Management 54, 715–724 (2012)
9. Shimizu, H.: Digital Archives as a National Strategy. IEICE Technical Report. Image Engineering 104, 29–34 (2004)
10. Kawakami, K., Okabe, Y., Suzuki, S.: A Study in Communal Image Archive on Web: Focused on Sustainability of Digital Archives. Journal of Japan Society of Information and Knowledge 21, 245–250 (2011)

11. Shimizu, H.: Digital Archives and e-Local Government. Computers and the Humanities **73**, 1–8 (2002)
12. Makishi, E.: Akaibu no Shiryo Shushu Hokan Riyo deno Sozai no Sentei Hyokaho no Kenkyu [Research on the Selection Process for Digital Archives Contents]. Japan Society of Educational Information **29**, 154–157 (2013)
13. Got, M.: The Introduction of Research for Cultural Heritage Using 'Digital Technology': Archive, Repository, Practical Use, and Curation. Computers and the Humanities **73**, 57–64 (2008)
14. Sano, M.: Degitaru Akaibu Ippan Kokai no Kakaeru Kadai [Problems Involved with the Digital Libraries Open to Public]. IT News Letter **10**, 3–4 (2015)
15. Sugimoto, S.: Digital Archives and Metadata as Critical Infrastructure to Keep Community Memory Safe for the Future – Lessons from Japanese Activities. Archives and Manuscripts **42**, 61–72 (2014)
16. Yonemoto, Y., Kurihara, R.: Shimin Degitaru Akaibu Katsudo no Jittai to Henka [Activities and Changes of Digital Archives Organized by Citizens]. Journal of Joho Media Center **11**, 40–42 (2010)
17. Ministry of Internal Affairs and Communications.: Chiiki Jumin Sanka-gata Degitaru Akaibu no Suishin ni Kansuru Chosa Kento-kai Hokokusho [Survey Study on Group Report on the Promotion of Local Community Participation Type Digital Archives], pp. 1–88 (2010). http://www.soumu.go.jp/soutsu/kanto/stats/data/chosa/chosa21_1.pdf
18. Shimizu, H., Miyahara, N.: Cultural Heritage Online Plan and Regional Digital Archives. Electronic Intellectual Property and Social Infrastructure **121**, 7–12 (2003)
19. Kansai Institute of Information System.: Kyoto ni okeru Degitaru Akaibu no Suishin [Promotion of Digital Archives in Kyoto]. http://www.kiis.or.jp/salon/kikansi/kiis113/113htm/kyoto1.htm
20. Bunka, Sangyobukai [Culture, Industry Section Second Meeting].: Gijiroku [Minutes], July 30, (2004). Kyoto Prefecture Web Site, http://www.pref.kyoto.jp/it/10500009.html
21. Ministry of Internal Affairs and Communications.: Heisei 15 nen Joho Tsushin Hakusho, Dai 1 Shou Tokushu [The 2003 Government Report on Information Telecommunications, Chapter 1 Special 18. Issue "Aiming to be a New IT Society."] (2003). http://www.soumu.go.jp/johotsusintokei/whitepaper/ja/h15/html/F1401200.html
22. National Diet Library.: Bunka · Gakujutsu Kikan ni okeru Degitaru Akaibu tono Unei ni Kansuru Chosa Kenkyu, Dai 1 Chosa Repoto [A Survey Study on the Administration of Cultural, Academic Digital Archives, the 1st Survey Report.], pp. 1–11 (2003). http://current.ndl.go.jp/files/research/2009/1st_survey_report.pdf
23. Shimizu, H.: The Establishment of Kyoto Digital Archives and its Commercial Use. JinMonCon Proceedings, pp. 1–8 (2001)
24. Shimizu, H.: Kyoto Degitaru Akaibu no Seika to Kongo no Kadai [The Kyoto Digital Archives, Success and Challenge for the Future]. Learning Resources and Information **191**, 41–44 (2006)
25. Japan Association of Graphic Arts Technology.: Degitaru Akaibu wa Yoko no Hirogari e [Digital Archives Expanding Horizontally]. http://www.jagat.or.jp/past_archives/story/3077.html

Analyzing Users' Trust for Online Health Rumors

Alton Y.K. Chua[✉] and Snehasish Banerjee

Wee Kim Wee School of Communication and Information,
Nanyang Technological University, Singapore, Singapore
{altonchua,snehasis002}@ntu.edu.sg

Abstract. This paper analyzes users' trust for online health rumors as a function of two factors: length and presence of image. Additionally, two types of rumors are studied: pipe-dream rumors that offer hope, and bogie rumors that instil fear. A total of 102 participants took part in a 2 (length: short or long) x 2 (presence of image: absent or present) x 2 (type: pipe-dream or bogie) within-participants experiment. A repeated-measures analysis of variance suggest that pipe-dream rumors are trusted when they are short and do not contain images whereas bogie rumors are trusted when they are long and contain images.

Keywords: Online health information · Rumor · Virality · Trust

1   Introduction

Users widely seek health information on the Internet. One in every three American adults seeks online health information, while almost half of them rely on such sources to decide if they need medical attention [1]. Seeking online health information often elevates tension, which creates a fertile breeding ground for rumors [2]. Some rumors turn out to be true, while others are eventually busted. However, regardless of their veracity, rumors influence public opinion [3]. In the context of health, repercussions can be serious if the basis of users' trust for rumors is not judicious.

Prior studies suggest that rumors must be short to become viral [2]. However, overly sketchy information could thwart trustworthiness [4]. Additionally, rumors with images could inspire greater confidence than text-only entries [5]. However, the advent of sophisticated image editing software complicates the situation [6]. Moreover, rumors are of two types depending on whether they offer hope or instil fear. They are known as pipe-dream rumors and bogie rumors respectively [2], [7]. The former mirrors optimism, as in *"You can cure cancer by taking Vitamin C,"* whereas the latter reflects pessimism, as in *"You can get cancer by using a microwave"* [8]. Analyzing nuances in users' trust for pipe-dream and bogie rumors as a function of length and presence of image has not attracted much scholarly attention thus far.

Therefore, this paper seeks to investigate the extent to which the length of rumors and presence of image in the entries are related to users' trust. To delve deeper, the investigation is carried out for pipe-dream rumors and bogie rumors separately. In particular, rumors in the context of health information are used as the test case for investigation. The significance of the results is highlighted thereafter.

© Springer International Publishing Switzerland 2015
R.B. Allen et al. (Eds.): ICADL 2015, LNCS 9469, pp. 33–38, 2015.
DOI: 10.1007/978-3-319-27974-9_4

2   Literature Review

This paper is motivated by signalling theory [9] and warranting theory [10]. Signalling theory—originally developed in the disciplines of economics [11] as well as biology [12] and later extrapolated to social networking sites [9]—explains the role of signals as indicators of trustworthiness. Given that any human interaction entails motivation for deception, the theory suggests that the cost of being deceived determines the use of signals as cues for trustworthiness. Seeking online health information clearly is a task in which the cost of being deceived is substantial. Therefore, the length of information may serve as a signal to inform users' willingness to trust.

Warranting theory suggests that individuals reduce uncertainty in determining information trustworthiness by relying on cues that are difficult to manipulate [10]. In validating the theory, [13] found that auctions containing product images not only attract high bidding interest but also receive high sales price in websites such as eBay.com. Perhaps product images promote trust intention among bidders. In the context of health-information seeking, it therefore seems that presence of image in rumors might prompt users to trust the entries.

Even though length and the presence of images could apparently shape trust, prior research has not yet widely investigated how these two factors are related to users' perception of online health rumors. With respect to rumor length, two contrasting viewpoints exist. The first suggests that short rumors are more likely to be trusted than long ones [2]. This is because the prospect of a rumor becoming viral is constrained by human memory [14]. However, the Internet minimizes reliance on human memory for rumors to permeate. This leads to the second viewpoint, which suggests that lengthy rumors are trusted more than short ones. Lengthy information could serve to signal trustworthiness, thereby inspiring confidence [9]. Sketchy information, however, might thwart trustworthiness [4], especially in the context of health [8].

Additionally, images in rumors could warrant their veracity. This is because images are perceived by users as cues that are difficult to manipulate [10], [15]. This is a vestige of images' iconicity—ability to depict real objects and individuals by assigning them a documentary value [5], [16]. However, the advent of sophisticated image editing software facilitates creating realistic fictitious images blurs the lines between truth and fiction [6], [17]. Therefore, investigating how the presence of images in health rumors relates to users' trust intention is a significant scholarly undertaking.

Regardless of length and presence of images, rumors are of two types: pipe-dream and bogie [7]. Mirroring hopes and optimism [2], pipe-dream rumors invoke anticipated consequences. They are often trusted arising from the wish that they would be materialized [18]. In contrast, reflecting fears and pessimism [2], bogie rumors invoke disappointing consequences. They are often trusted with the fear that the most horrific claims are likely to be translated into reality [18]. In an offline setting, bogie rumors were found more abundant and more likely to be trusted than pipe-dream rumors [7]. This sets an interesting context to study differences in users' trust for the two types of rumors in an online setting.

3   Methods

A 2 (length: short or long) x 2 (presence of image: absent or present) x 2 (type: pipe-dream or bogie) within-participants web-based experimental design was used to study users' trust for online health rumors. The experimental stimuli included a total of eight rumors (2 x 2 x 2), in which, the three independent factors were induced.

For designing the experimental stimuli, entries were drawn from liuyanbaike.com, a Chinese website that contains some 800 health rumors. Randomly-selected entries from the website were coded as either pipe-dream or bogie, and translated into English by three research associates who were graduate students of Information Systems and effectively bilingual in English and Chinese. All translated entries were jointly checked to ensure accuracy. A few rounds of random-selection followed by coding and translation yielded an initial pool of 24 rumors uniformly distributed across the three independent factors. Thereafter, from each set of three, one rumor was randomly selected to obtain a total of eight entries evenly spread across the three independent factors—length, presence of image, and type of rumor.

These eight entries were further pre-tested to confirm the induction of length, presence of image, and rumor type. For this purpose, 10 participants were selected based on convenience sampling. Five of them were graduate students while the rest were working adults. All of them agreed with three induction checks. Therefore, these rumors were finalized as the experimental stimuli.

The length of the short rumors ranged from 25 words to 70 words. In contrast, the length of the long rumors ranged from 126 words to 145 words. While rumors with images contained colored pictorial illustrations, those without images contained only text. The pipe-dream rumors offered hope whereas the bogie rumors instilled fear.

A total of 102 participants took part in the main study. They were identified based on convenience sampling, and recruited upon meeting two eligibility criteria. First, their age was between 21 to 35 years. After all, individuals within this age range are likely to read and browse online health information [19]. Second, all participants had actual experiences of reading online health information in the recent past. Thus, they were appropriate for the context of this paper.

The participants were provided the URL for the web-based experiment. After obtaining informed consent, the experiment comprised two parts. The first presented the stimuli of the eight rumors arranged in a random sequence. Each rumor was accompanied by a question asking if participants trusted the information (Yes/No). The second part of the experiment asked demographics questions such as gender and age group. Of the 102 participants, 54 were female. Participants were requested not to surf the Internet to access other materials during their participation.

The extent to which length (short or long), presence of image (absent or present), and rumor type (pipe-dream or bogie rumors) influenced trust (1 = Yes, 0 = No) was tested using three-way repeated-measures factorial analysis of variance (ANOVA) [20]. Since no independent factor had more than two levels, the sphericity assumption was not violated, thereby obviating Greenhouse-Geisser correction.

4   Results

Table 1 presents the descriptive statistics of the dataset. The three-way repeated-measures factorial ANOVA indicated a statistically significant interaction (Wilks' Lambda= 0.83, $F(1, 101) = 20.95$, $p < 0.001$, partial $\eta^2 = 0.17$). The underlying two-way interactions—length x presence of images (Wilks' Lambda= 0.68, $F(1, 101) = 48.42$, $p < 0.001$, partial $\eta^2 = 0.32$), length x rumor types (Wilks' Lambda= 0.54, $F(1, 101) = 86.76$, $p < 0.001$, partial $\eta^2 = 0.46$), and presence of images x rumor types (Wilks' Lambda= 0.57, $F(1, 101) = 75.28$, $p < 0.001$, partial $\eta^2 = 0.43$)—were also statistically significant. Even though the simple effect of rumor types was statistically significant (Wilks' Lambda= 0.95, $F(1, 101) = 5.79$, $p = 0.018$, partial $\eta^2 = 0.05$), those of length and presence of images were non-significant.

Table 1. Descriptive statistics (Mean ± SD) of users' trust for rumors

Rumor Types	Length	Images Absent	Images Present
Pipe-dream rumors	Short	0.86 ± 0.35	0.27 ± 0.45
	Long	0.27 ± 0.45	0.35 ± 0.48
Bogie rumors	Short	0.14 ± 0.35	0.27 ± 0.48
	Long	0.39 ± 0.49	0.72 ± 0.45

To better understand the significant relationships, Fig. 1 presents the interaction plots for pipe-dream rumors and bogie rumors as a function of length as well as presence of image. It suggests that short pipe-dream rumors without images, and long bogie rumors with images substantially triggered users' trust.

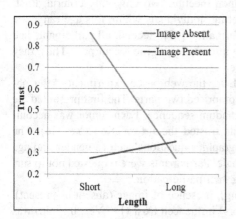 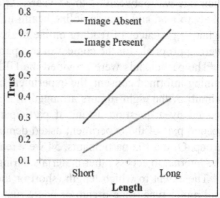

Fig. 1. Trust for pipe-dream rumors (left) and bogie rumors (right) as a function of length as well as presence of image

5   Discussion and Conclusion

This paper gleans three findings from the results presented in Section 4. First, pipe-dream rumors are trusted the most when they are short and without images. This is ironic, since sketchy information thwarts trustworthiness [4]. Moreover, rumors without images are often deemed less realistic than those with images [5]. Users seem likely to trust pipe-dream rumors when the entries are cognitively easy to process. Reading long entries with images might have required users to pay closer attention than processing short entries without images.

Second, bogie rumors are trusted the most when they are long and with images. This is consistent with both signalling theory and warranting theory. Since the cost of being deceived by a bogie health rumor is substantial, users seem to believe that information volume would correlate with trustworthiness [9]. Also, they perhaps view images as cues that are difficult to manipulate. Arising from the property of iconicity [16], images could be perceived as cues that warrant trustworthiness [10].

Third, length and presence of images enhanced users' trust for bogie rumors but not for pipe-dream rumors. Reading long entries supported with images conceivably requires more cognitive efforts than reading sketchy textual entries. Driven by the "*better safe than sorry rationale*" [21], users perhaps find it worthwhile to invest substantial cognitive efforts for reading bogie rumors but not pipe-dream rumors. This is not too surprising because bogie rumors have often been found to be viewed more seriously compared with their pipe-dream counterparts [7], [21].

This paper is significant on two counts. First, it empirically examines signalling theory [9] and warranting theory [10] in the context of online health rumors. Although the theories suggest that length and presence of image could promote trust, this paper finds non-significant simple effects for both. These two factors significantly informed users' trust intention only when their interplay with rumor types—pipe-dream or bogie—was taken into consideration.

Second, this paper has implications for health professionals on ways to share online health information with the youth. Hopeful information might be packaged so that it is easy to process. In contrast, gloomy information could be made detailed with adequate use of visual cues. Additionally, digital libraries could maintain a database of rumors trawled from the Internet. Information professionals together with the user community might be engaged to help ascertain rumor veracity as promptly as possible.

This paper has two major limitations that future research could address. First, since participants were selected using convenience sampling, it is important to exercise caution in generalizing the results. Additionally, more individual differences could have been taken into account. Second, even though the paper analyzed trust, it did not examine users' intention to share rumors. Such a study might have shed greater light on what makes rumors viral.

Acknowledgements. This work was supported by the Ministry of Education Research Grant AcRF Tier 2 (MOE2014-T2-2-020). The authors would like to thank Ang Han Guan, Liew Jun Xian, and Peng Peng for their help in the data collection.

References

1. Fox, S., Duggan, M.: Health Online 2013 (2013). http://www.pewinternet.org/2013/01/15/health-online-2013/ (retrieved April 20, 2015)
2. Knapp, R.H.: A Psychology of Rumor. Public Opinion Quarterly **8**(1), 22–37 (1944)
3. Doerr, B., Fouz, M., Friedrich, T.: Social networks spread rumors in sublogarithmic time. In: Proceedings of the ACM Annual Symposium on Theory of Computing, pp. 21–30. ACM (2011)
4. Mudambi, S.M., Schuff, D.: What Makes a Helpful Review? A Study of Customer Reviews on Amazon.com. MIS Quarterly **34**(1), 185–200 (2010)
5. Ball, M.S., Smith, G.W.H.: Analyzing Visual Data. Sage, Newbury Park (1992)
6. Faltesek, D.: Golden Tweet Camera Raw. Visual Communication Quarterly **20**(3), 159–167 (2013)
7. Rosnow, R.L., Yost, J.H., Esposito, J.L.: Belief in Rumor and Likelihood of Rumor Transmission. Language & Communication **6**(3), 189–194 (1986)
8. DiFonzo, N., Robinson, N.M., Suls, J.M., Rini, C.: Rumors about Cancer: Content, Sources, Coping, Transmission, and Belief. Journal of Health Communication **17**(9), 1099–1115 (2012)
9. Donath, J.: Signals in Social Supernets. Journal of Computer-Mediated Communication **13**(1), 231–251 (2007)
10. Walther, J.B., Parks, M.R.: Cues filtered out, cues filtered in: computer-mediated communication and relationships. In: Knapp, M.L., Daly, J.A. (eds.) Handbook of Interpersonal Communication, pp. 529–563. Sage, Thousand Oaks (2002)
11. Spence, M.: Job Market Signaling. Quarterly Journal of Economics **87**(3), 355–374 (1973)
12. Zahavi, A.: Mate Selection—a Selection for a Handicap. Journal of Theoretical Biology **53**(1), 205–214 (1975)
13. Van Der Heide, B., Johnson, B.K., Vang, M.H.: The Effects of Product Photographs and Reputation Systems on Consumer Behavior and Product Cost on eBay. Computers in Human Behavior **29**(3), 570–576 (2013)
14. Barlett, F.C.: Remembering. Cambridge University Press, Cambridge (1932)
15. Lambert, A.: Intimacy and friendship on Facebook. Palgrave Macmillan, New York (2013)
16. Messaris, P.: Visual Persuasion: The Role of Images in Advertising. Sage, Thousand Oaks, CA (1997)
17. Gupta, A., Lamba, H., Kumaraguru, P., Joshi, A.: Faking sandy: characterizing and identifying fake images on twitter during hurricane sandy. In: Proceedings of the International Conference on World Wide Web Companion, pp. 729–736. ACM (2013)
18. Rosnow, R.L.: Inside Rumor: A Personal Journey. American Psychologist **46**, 484–496 (1991)
19. Berger, M., Wagner, T.H., Baker, L.C.: Internet Use and Stigmatized Illness. Social Science & Medicine **61**(8), 1821–1827 (2005)
20. Lunney, G.H.: Using Analysis of Variance with a Dichotomous Dependent Variable: An Empirical Study. Journal of Educational Measurement **7**(4), 263–269 (1970)
21. DiFonzo, N.: The Watercooler Effect: A Psychologist Explores the Extraordinary Power of Rumors. Penguin, New York (2008)

Adaptive Web Crawling Through Structure-Based Link Classification

Muhammad Faheem[1,2] and Pierre Senellart[1,3(✉)]

[1] LTCI, CNRS, Télécom ParisTech, Université Paris-Saclay, Paris, France
pierre@senellart.com
[2] University of Ottawa, Ottawa, Canada
[3] IPAL, CNRS, National University of Singapore, Singapore, Singapore

Abstract. Generic web crawling approaches cannot distinguish among various page types and cannot target content-rich areas of a website. We study the problem of efficient unsupervised web crawling of content-rich webpages. We propose ACEBot (Adaptive Crawler Bot for data Extraction), a structure-driven crawler that uses the inner structure of the pages and guides the crawling process based on the importance of their content. ACEBot works in two phases: in the *learning* phase, it constructs a dynamic site map (limiting the number of URLs retrieved) and learns a traversal strategy based on the importance of *navigation patterns* (selecting those leading to valuable content); in the *intensive crawling* phase, ACEBot performs massive downloading following the chosen navigation patterns. Experiments over a large dataset illustrate the effectiveness of our system.

1 Introduction

A large part of web content is found on websites powered by content management systems (CMSs) such as vBulletin, phpBB, or WordPress [1]. The presentation layer of these CMSs use predefined templates (which may include left or right sidebars, headers and footers, navigation bars, main content, etc.) for populating the content of the requested web document from an underlying database. A study [1] found that 40–50% of web content, in 2005, was template-based; this order of magnitude is confirmed by a more recent web technology survey [2], which further shows that one specific CMS, WordPress, is used by 24% of websites, giving it 60% of CMS market share. Depending on the request, CMSs may use different templates for presenting information; e.g. in blogs, the *list of posts* type of page uses a different template than the *single post* webpage that also includes comments. These template-based webpages form a meaningful structure that mirrors the implicit logical relationship between web content across different pages within a website. Many templates are used by CMSs for generating different types of webpages. Each template generates a set of webpages (e.g. list of blog posts) that share a common structure, but differ in content. These templates are consistently used across different regions of the site. More importantly, for a given template (say, a list of posts), the same links usually lead to the same

R.B. Allen et al. (Eds.): ICADL 2015, LNCS 9469, pp. 39–51, 2015.
DOI: 10.1007/978-3-319-27974-9_5

kind of content (say, individual posts), with common layout and presentation properties.

Due to limited bandwidth, storage, or indexing capabilities, only a small fraction of web content can actually be harvested by web crawlers. This is true for archival crawlers of institutions with limited resources (e.g. the national library of a small country). This is even true for a company such as Google, that, as of June 2013, had discovered more than a trillion unique URLs [3], but indexed around 40 billion webpages. This suggests a need to develop a crawling strategy that not only effectively crawls web content from template-based websites, but also efficiently minimizes the number of HTTP requests by avoiding non-interesting webpages.

A generic web crawler performs inefficient crawling of websites. It crawls the web with no guarantee of content quality. An ideal crawling approach should solve the following three problems: What kind of webpages are *important* to crawl (to avoid redundant and invalid pages)? Which *important* links should be followed? What *navigation patterns* are required on the website?

We introduce in this article an intelligent crawling technique that meets these criteria. We propose a *structure-driven* approach that is more precise, effective, and achieves a higher quality level, without loss of information. It guides the crawler towards content-rich areas: this is achieved by learning the best traversal strategy (a collection of important navigation patterns) during a learning phase, that ultimately guides the crawler to crawl only content-rich webpages during an intensive crawling phase.

Our structure-driven crawler, ACEBot, first establishes connections among webpages based on their root-to-link paths in the DOM tree of the pages, then ranks paths according to their importance (i.e. root-to-links paths that lead to content-rich webpages), and further learns a traversal strategy for bulk-downloading of the website. Our main claim is that structure-based crawling not only clusters webpages which require similar crawling actions, but also helps to identify duplicates, redundancy, and boilerplates, and plays as well an important role in prioritizing the *frontier* (the list of URLs left to crawl).

After discussing related work in Section 2, we present our model in Section 3. The algorithm that ACEBot follows is then presented in detail in Section 4, followed by experiments in Section 5. Due to space constraints, some material (proofs of results, additional experiments, examples) could not be included but can be found in [4].

2   Related Work

In [5], Liu et al. proposed an algorithm, called *SEW*, that models a website as a hypertext structure. SEW relies on a combination of several domain-independent heuristics to identify the most important links within a webpage and thus discover a hierarchical organization of navigation and content pages. Kao et al. [6] have addressed a similar problem, and propose a technique to distinguish between pages containing *links* to news posts and the pages containing those news items.

Compared to our approach, both techniques above only cluster the webpages into two predefined classes of pages: navigational and content pages. In addition, Kao et al. [6] focus on pages of a specific domain. In contrast, we have proposed a system that performs unsupervised crawling of websites (domain-independent) without prior assumption on the number of classes.

[7,8], aim to cluster webpages into different classes by exploiting their structural similarity at the DOM tree level, while [9] introduces crawling programs: a tool that listens to the user interaction, registers steps, and infers the corresponding intentional navigation. This approach is semi-supervised as it requires human interaction to learn navigation patterns to reach the content-rich pages. A web crawler is generally intended for a massive crawling scenario, and thus semi-automatic approaches are not feasible in our setting. Therefore, in our proposed approach, we have introduced the learning phase which learns navigation patterns in an unsupervised manner.

Another structure-driven approach [10] has proposed a web crawler that requires minimum human effort. It takes a sample page and entry point as input and generates a set of navigation patterns (i.e. sequence of patterns) that guides a crawler to reach webpages structurally similar to the sample page. As stated above, this approach is also focused on a specific type of webpage, whereas our approach performs massive crawling at web scale for content-rich pages.

Several domain-dependent *web forum* crawling techniques [11,12] have been proposed recently. In [11], the crawler first clusters the webpages into two groups from a set of manual annotated pages using Support Vector Machines with some predefined features, and then, within each cluster, URLs are clustered using partial tree alignment. Furthermore, a set of ITF (index-thread-page-flipping) *regular expressions* are generated to launch a bulk download of a target web forum. The iRobot system [12], that we use as a baseline in our experiments, creates a sitemap of the website being crawled. The sitemap is constructed by randomly crawling a few webpages from a given website. After sitemap generation, iRobot obtains the structure of the web forum. The skeleton is obtained in the form of a directed graph consisting of vertices (webpages) and directed arcs (links between different webpages). A path analysis is then performed to learn an optimal traversal path which leads the extraction process in order to avoid redundant and invalid pages. A web-scale approach [13] has introduced an algorithm that performs URL-based clustering of webpages using some content features. However, in practice, URL-based clustering of webpages is less reliable in the presence of the dynamic nature of the web.

Our previous work [14] proposes an adaptive application-aware helper (AAH) that crawls known CMSs efficiently. AAH is assisted with a knowledge base that guides the crawling process. It first tries to detect the website and, if detected as a known one, attempts to identify the kind of webpage given the matched website. Then, the relevant crawling actions are executed for web archiving. This approach achieves the highest quality of web content with fewer HTTP requests, but is not fully automatic and requires a hand-written knowledge base that prevents crawling of unknown websites.

3   Model

In this section, we formalize our proposed model: we see the website to crawl as an directed graph, that is rooted (typically at the homepage of a site), and where edges are labeled (by structural properties of the corresponding hyperlink). We first consider the abstract problem, before explaining how actual websites fit into the model.

Formal Definitions. We fix countable sets of *labels* $\mathscr{L}$ and *items* $\mathscr{I}$. Our main object of study is the graph to crawl:

Definition 1. *A* rooted graph *is a 5-tuple* $G = (V, E, r, \iota, l)$ *with* V *a finite set of vertices,* $E \subseteq V^2$ *a set of directed edges,* $r \in V$ *the* root; $\iota : V \to 2^{\mathscr{I}}$ *and* $l : E \to \mathscr{L}$ *assign respectively a set of* items *to every vertex and a label to every edge.*

Here, items serve to abstractly model the interesting content of webpages; the more items a crawl retrieves, the better. Labels are attached to hyperlinks between pages; further on, we will explain how we can use the DOM structure of a webpage to assign such labels. We naturally extend the function ι to a set of nodes X from G by posing: $\iota(X) := \bigcup_{u \in X} \iota(u)$. We introduce the standard notion of paths within the graph:

Definition 2. *Given a rooted graph* $G = (V, E, r, \iota, l)$ *and vertices* $u, v \in V$, *a* path *from* u *to* v *is a finite sequence of edges* $e_1 \ldots e_n$ *from* E *such that there exists a set of nodes* $u_1 \ldots u_{n-1}$ *in* V *with:* $e_1 = (u, u_1)$; $\forall 1 < k < n, e_k = (u_{k-1}, u_k)$; $e_n = (u_{n-1}, v)$.
The label *of the path* $e_1 \ldots e_n$ *is the word* $l(e_1) \ldots l(e_n)$ *over* $\mathscr{L}$.

Critical to our approach is the notion of a *navigation pattern* that uses edge labels to describe which paths to follow in a graph. Navigation patterns are defined using the standard automata-theory notion of *regular expression* (used here as *path expressions*):

Definition 3. *A* navigation pattern *p is a regular expression over* $\mathscr{L}$. *Given a graph* $G = (V, E, r, \iota, l)$, *the result of applying* p *onto* G, *denoted* $p(G)$, *is the set of nodes* u *with a path from* r *to* u *that has for label a prefix of a word in the language defined by* p. *We extend this notion to a finite set of navigation patterns* P *by letting* $P(G) := \bigcup_{p \in P} p(G)$.

Note that we require only a *prefix* of a word to match: a navigation pattern does not only return the set of pages whose path from the root matches the path expression, but also intermediate pages on those paths. For instance, consider a *path* $e_1 \ldots e_n$ from r to a node u, such that the navigation pattern p is the path expression $l(e_1) \ldots l(e_n)$. Then the result of executing navigation pattern p contains u, but also all pages on the path from r to u; more generally, p returns all pages whose path from the root matches a prefix of the expression $l(e_1) \ldots l(e_n)$. Navigation patterns are assigned a score:

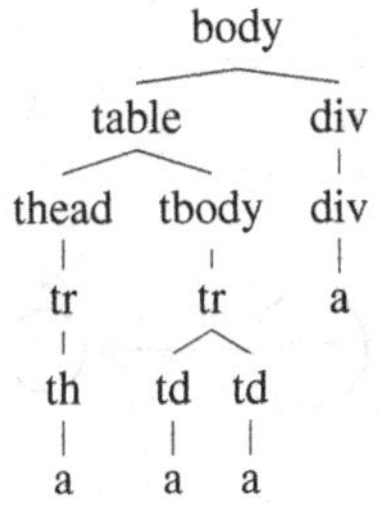

```
            body
         ┌────┴────┐
       table      div
      ┌──┴──┐      │
   thead  tbody   div
     │      │      │
     tr     tr     a
     │    ┌─┴─┐
     th  td  td
     │    │   │
     a    a   a
```

l_1 body/table/tbody/tr/td/a
l_2 body/table/thead/tr/th/a
l_3 body/div/div/a

NP #2-grams		score
l_1	5107	2553.5
$l_1 l_4$	7214	2404.7
l_3	754	754.0
l_2	239	239.0

Fig. 1. Partial DOM tree representation   **Fig. 2.** Root-to-link paths   **Fig. 3.** Navigation patterns with score

Definition 4. *Let $G = (V, E, r, \iota, l)$ be a rooted graph. The* score *of a finite set of navigation patterns P over G, denoted $\omega(P, G)$ is the average number of distinct items per node in $P(G)$: $\omega(P, G) := \frac{|\iota(P(G))|}{|P(G)|}$.*

In other words, a navigation pattern has a high score if it retrieves a large number of items in a relatively low number of nodes. The crawling interpretation is that we want to maximize the amount of useful content retrieved, while minimizing the number of HTTP requests made.

We can now formalize our problem of interest: given a rooted graph G and a collection of navigation patterns $\mathscr{P}$ (that may be all path expressions over $\mathscr{L}$ or a subclass of path expressions over $\mathscr{L}$), determine the set of navigation patterns $P \subseteq \mathscr{P}$ of maximal score over G. We can show (see [4] for proofs):

Proposition 1. *Given a graph G and a collection of navigation patterns $\mathscr{P}$, determining if one finite subset $P \subseteq \mathscr{P}$ has maximal score over G is a coNP-complete problem.*

Thus, there is no hope of efficiently obtaining an optimal set of navigation patterns. In this light we will introduce in Section 4 a non-optimal greedy approach to the selection of navigation patterns, that we will show in Section 5 still performs well in practice.

Model Generation. We now explain how we consider crawling a website in the previously introduced abstract model. A website is any HTTP-based application, formed with a set of interlinked webpages that can be traversed from some base URL, such as http://icadl2015.org/. The base URL of a website is called the entry point of the site. For our purpose, we model a given website as a directed graph (see Definition 1), where the base URL becomes the root of the graph. Each vertex of the graph represents a distinct webpage and, following Definition 1, a set of items is assigned to every vertex.

In our model, the items are all *distinct 2-grams* seen for a webpage. A 2-gram for a given webpage is a contiguous sequence of 2 words within its HTML representation. The set of 2-grams has been used as a summary of the content of a webpage [14]; the richer a content area is, the more distinct 2-grams. It also corresponds to the classical ROUGE-N [15] measure used in *text summarization*:

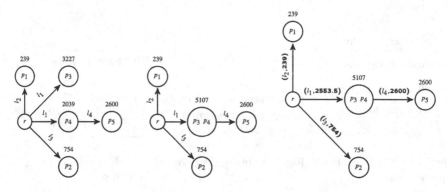

Fig. 4. Before clustering   **Fig. 5.** After clustering   **Fig. 6.** After scoring

the higher number of 2-grams a summary shares with its text, the more faithful the summary is. The set of items associated to each vertex plays an important role in the scoring function (see Definition 4), which eventually leads to select a set of webpages for crawling.

A webpage is a well-formed HTML document, and its Document Object Model (DOM) specifies how objects (i.e. texts, links, images, etc.) in a webpage are accessed. Hence, a *root-to-link* path is a location of the link (i.e. <a> HTML tag) in the corresponding DOM tree. Fig. 1 shows a DOM tree representation of a sample webpage and Fig. 2 illustrates its *root-to-link* paths.

Following Definition 1, each edge of the graph is labeled with a *root-to-link* path. Assume there is an edge $e(u, v)$ from vertex u to v, then a label $l(e)$ for edge e is the *root-to-link* path of the hyperlink pointing to v in vertex (i.e. webpage) u. Navigation patterns will thus be (see Definition 3) path expressions over root-to-link paths.

Two webpages reachable from the root of a website with paths p_1 and p_2 whose label is the same are said to be *similar*.

Consider the scoring of a navigation pattern (see Definition 4). We can note the following: the higher the number of requests needed to download pages comprised by a navigation pattern, the lower the score; the higher the number of distinct 2-grams in pages comprised by a navigation pattern, the higher the score.

4   Deriving the Crawling Strategy

Simple Example. Consider the homepage of a typical web forum, say http://forums.digitalspy.co.uk/, as the entry point of the website to crawl. This webpage may be seen as a two different regions. There is a region with headers, menus and templates, that are presented across several webpages, and is considered as a non-interesting region from the perspective of archiving the main content of the website. The other region at the center of the webpage is a content-rich area which should be archived. Since pages are generated by a CMS (vBulletin here), the underlying templates have a consistent structure across similar webpages. Therefore the links contained in those pages obey regular formating rules. In our example website, the links leading to blog posts and the messages within an individual post have some layout and presentational similarities.

Fig. 1 presents a simplified version of the DOM tree of the example entry point webpage and its *root-to-link* paths are shown in Fig. 2. Fig. 4 shows a truncated version of the generated graph for the corresponding site. Each vertex represents a unique webpage in the graph. These vertices are connected through directed edges, labeled with *root-to-link* paths. Each vertex of the graph is assigned a number of distinct 2-grams seen for the linked webpage (e.g. 3,227 distinct 2-grams seen for p_3). Furthermore, the set of webpages (i.e. vertices) that share the same path (i.e. edge label) are clustered together (see Fig. 5). The newly clustered vertices are assigned a collective 2-gram set seen for all clustered webpages. For instance, the clustered vertex $\{p_3, p_4\}$ has now 5,107 distinct 2-gram items. After clustering, all possible navigation patterns are generated for the graph. This process is performed by traversing the directed graph. Table 3 exhibits all possible navigation patterns. Afterwards, each navigation pattern (a combination of *root-to-link* paths) is assigned a score. The system does not compute the score of any navigation pattern that does not lead the crawler from the entry point to an existing webpage. Once all possible navigation patterns are scored then the navigation pattern with highest score is selected (since the highest score ensures the archiving of the core contents). Here, the navigation pattern l_1 is selected. The process of assigning the score to the navigation patterns keeps going after each selection for navigation patterns not selected so far. Importantly, 2-gram items for already selected vertices are not considered again for non-selected navigation patterns. Therefore, in the next iteration, the navigation pattern $l_1 l_4$ does not consider items from webpages retrieved by the l_1 navigation pattern. The process of scoring and selecting ends when no interesting navigation pattern is left.

Detailed Description. ACEBot mainly consists of two phases: learning and intensive crawling. The aim of the learning phase is to first construct the sitemap and cluster the vertices that share a similar edge label. A set of crawling actions (i.e. best navigation patterns) are learned to guide massive crawling in the intensive crawling phase.

Algorithm 1 gives a high-level view of the navigation pattern selection mechanism for a given entry point (i.e. the home page). Algorithm 1 has six parameters. The entry point r is the home page of a given website. The Boolean value of the parameter d specifies whether the sitemap of the website should be constructed dynamically. The argument k defines the depth (i.e. level or steps) of navigation patterns to explore. The Boolean *expDepth* specifies whether to limit the expansion depth of navigation patterns to a fixed value of 3; this is typically used in webpages with "Next" links. The argument a passes the set of attributes (e.g. id and class) that should be considered when constructing navigation patterns. cr sets the completion ratio: the selection of navigation patterns ends when this criterion is met.

Input: entry point r, dynamic sitemap d, navigation pattern expansion depth
       $expDepth$, navigation-step k, a set of attributes a, completion ratio cr
Output: a set of selected navigation patterns SNP
$siteMap \leftarrow generateSiteMap(r,d)$;
$clusteredGraph \leftarrow performClustering(siteMap)$;
$navigationPatterns \leftarrow getNavigationPatterns(r, clusteredGraph, k, expDepth, a)$;
$NP \leftarrow updateNavigationPatterns(navigationPatterns)$;
while *not* cr **do**
$\quad$| $topNP \leftarrow getTopNavigationPattern(NP, SNP)$;
$\quad$| $SNP \leftarrow addToSelectedNP(topNP)$;
$\quad$| $NP \leftarrow removeSubNavigationPatterns(topNP)$;

Algorithm 1. Selection of the navigation patterns

The goal of the learning phase is to obtain useful knowledge for a given website based on a few sample pages. The sitemap construction is the foundation of the whole crawling process. The quality of sampled pages is important to decide whether learned navigation patterns target the content-rich part of a website. We have implemented a double-ended queue (similar to the one used in [12]), and then fetched the webpages randomly from the front or end. We have limited the number of sampled pages to 3,000, and detailed experiments (see Section 5) show that the sample restriction was enough to construct the sitemap of any considered website. The *generateSiteMap* procedure takes a given entry point as parameter and returns a sitemap (i.e. site model).

The procedure *performClustering* in Algorithm 1 clusters the vertices with similar edge labels. It performs breadth-first traversal over the graph, starting from each root till the last destination vertex. For instance, in Fig. 5, vertex p_3 and p_4 share the label l_1 and thus are clustered together. The 2-gram measure is also computed for each clustered vertex. More precisely, similar nodes are clustered when cluster destination vertices share an edge label, such as a list of blog posts where the label l_2 is shared across vertices. Assume vertex v' has an incoming edge from vertex v with label l_1, and also vertex v' has an outgoing edge to vertex v'' with similar label l_1. Since v' and v'' share an edge label, these vertices will be clustered. For instance, page-flipping links (e.g. post messages that may exist across several pages) usually have the same *root-to-link* path. These types of navigation patterns end with a + (for example /html/body/div [contains(@class,"navigation")])+), that indicates the crawling action should be performed more than once on similar webpages during intensive crawling.

Once the graph is clustered, *getNavigationPatterns* extracts all possible navigation patterns for each root vertex $r \in R$. The procedure takes three parameters *clusteredGraph*, r, and k as input. The procedure generates the navigation patterns using a depth-first traversal approach where depth is limited to k (i.e. number of navigation-steps). node. Hence, a set of navigation patterns are generated, starting from the root vertex (i.e. the navigation patterns that do not start with the root vertex are ignored) and counting the k number of navigation-steps. This step will be performed for each root vertex and *updateNavigationPatterns* will update the set of navigation patterns NP accordingly.

The *getTopNavigationPattern* procedure returns a top navigation pattern on each iteration. The procedure takes two parameters NP (a set of navigation patterns), and SNP (a set of selected navigation patterns) as input. This procedure applies the subset scoring function (see Definition 4) and computes the score for each navigation pattern. *items*(NP) is computed by counting the total number of distinct 2-grams words seen for all vertices that share the navigation pattern NP. The size of the navigation pattern NP (i.e. *size*(NP)) is the total number of vertices that shares the NP. The SNP parameter is passed to the procedure to ensure that only new data rich areas are identified. More precisely, assume the $l_1 l_2$ navigation pattern is already selected. Now the scoring function for navigation pattern $l_1 l_2 l_3$ does not take into account the score for navigation pattern $l_1 l_2$, but only the l_3 score will play a role in its selection. Eventually, it guarantees that the system always selects the navigation patterns with newly discovered webpages with valuable content. The *removeSubNavigationPatterns* procedure removes all the sub navigation patterns. For instance, if navigation pattern $l_1 l_4 l_5$ is newly selected, and there already exists the navigation pattern $l_1 l_4$ in SNP, then $l_1 l_4$ will be removed from SNP.

The selection of navigation patterns ends when all navigation patterns from the set NP are selected or when some other criterion is satisfied (e.g. *completion ratio cr* condition reached). Then, the system will launch the intensive crawling phase and feed the selected navigation patterns to the crawler for massive crawling.

5   Experiments

In this section, we present the experimental results of our proposed system. We compare the performance of ACEBot with AAH [14] (our previous work, that relies on a hand-written description of given CMSs), iRobot [12] (an intelligent crawling system for web forums), and GNU wget[1] (a traditional crawler), in terms of efficiency and effectiveness. Though wget is relatively simple software as far as crawlers are concerned, we stress that any other traditional crawler (e.g. Heritrix) will perform in the same way: as no structure analysis of the website is executed, the website will be exhaustively downloaded.

Experimental Setup. To evaluate the performance of ACEBot at web scale, we have carried out the evaluation of our system in various settings. We first describe the dataset and performance metrics and different settings of our proposed algorithm. We have selected 50 websites from different application domains (totaling nearly 2 million webpages) with diverse characteristics, to analyze the behavior of our system for small websites as well as for web-scale extraction with both wget (for a full, exhaustive crawl), and our proposed system. To compare the performance of ACEBot with AAH, 10 websites (nearly 0.5 million webpages) were crawled with both ACEBot and AAH (note that AAH only works on selected CMS which prevents a comparison on the larger dataset).

---

[1] http://www.gnu.org/software/wget/

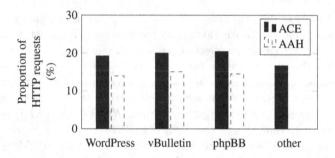

Fig. 7. Total number of HTTP requests (excluding overhead), in proportion to the total size of the dataset

In the learning phase, the site map of a given website is constructed either from the whole mirrored website or from a smaller collection of randomly selected sample pages, as detailed previously. We found that ACEBot requires a sample of 3,000 pages to achieve optimal crawling quality on large websites, comparable to what was done for iRobot [12] (1,000 pages) and a supervised structure driven crawler [10] (2,000 pages).

We consider several settings for our proposed Algorithm 1. The additional parameters d, cr, k, and a form several variants of our technique: The sitemap d may be dynamic (limiting to 3,000 webpages; default if not otherwise specified) or complete (whole website mirror). The completion ration cr may take values 85%, 90%, 95% (default). The level depth k is set to either 2, 3 (default), or 4. The attributes used, a, will be set to *id*.

We have compared the performance of ACEBot with AAH and GNU wget by evaluating the number of HTTP requests made by these crawlers vs the number of useful content retrieved. We have considered the same performance metrics used by AAH [14], where the evaluation of number of HTTP requests is performed by simply counting the requests. In the case of ACEBot, we distinguish between the number of HTTP requests made during the intensive downloading phase (or that would have made during this phase but were already done during that phase) and the *overhead* of requests made during the learning phase for content not relevant in the massive downloading phase (which is bounded by the sample size, i.e., 3,000 in general). Coverage of useful content is evaluated by the proportion of 2-grams in the crawl result of three systems, as well as by the proportion of external links (links to external websites) retrieved.

Crawl Efficiency. We have computed the number of pages crawled with ACEBot, AAH, and GNU wget, to compare the crawl efficiency of the three systems (see Fig. 7). Here, wget (or any other crawler not aware of the structure of the website) obviously crawls 100% of the dataset. ACEBot makes 5 times fewer requests than a blind crawl, and slightly more than AAH, the latter being only usable for the three CMS it handles. The numbers in Fig. 7 do not include overhead, but we measured the overhead to be 8% of the number of useful requests made by ACEBot on a diversified sample of websites, which does not significantly change

Table 1. Performance of ACEBot for different levels with dynamic sitemap for the whole data set

Level	Requests	Content (%)	External Links (%)	Completion ratio (%)
	376632	95.7	98.6	85
2	377147	95.8	98.7	90
	394235	96.0	99.1	95
	418654	96.3	99.2	85
3	431572	96.6	99.3	90
	458547	96.8	99.3	95
	491568	96.9	99.4	85
4	532358	97.1	99.4	90
	588512	97.2	99.4	95

the result: this is because the considered websites were generally quite large (on average 40,000 pages per site, to compare with the sample size of 3,000, which means that on the total dataset the overhead cannot exceed 7.5%).

The results shown in Fig. 8 plot the number of seen 2-grams and HTTP requests made for a selected number of navigation patterns. The numbers of HTTP requests and discovered 2-*grams* for a navigation pattern impact its score, and thus its selection. Therefore a navigation patterns with one single page, but with many new 2-*grams* may be selected ahead of a navigation pattern with many HTTP requests. Fig. 8 elaborates that prospect, where the 10th selected navigation pattern crawls a large number of pages but this navigation pattern was selected only because of a higher completion ratio.

Crawl Effectiveness. ACEBot crawling results in terms of coverage of useful content are summarized in Fig. 1 and 9. The coverage of useful content and external links for different navigation steps (levels) is shown in Fig. 1. Limiting the navigation patterns to level $k = 2$ or 3 results in fewer HTTP requests, and a performance of 96% content with $cr = 95\%$ completion ratio. However, level 3 performs better across many websites in terms of effectiveness, as important contents exist at link depth 3. Once the learned navigation patterns achieve the 95% coverage of 2-*grams* vs whole blind crawl, they will be stored in a knowledge base for future re-crawling. The proportion of external link coverage by ACEBot is also given in Table 1. Since ACEBot selects the best navigation patterns and achieves higher content coverage, over 99% of external links are present in the content crawled by ACEBot for the whole dataset.

Fig. 9 depicts the performance of ACEBot for different completion ratios for 10 selected websites, each with 50,000 webpages. The selection of navigation patterns ends when the completion ratio has been achieved. The experiments have shown that a higher (and stable) proportion of 2-*grams* is seen with a completion ratio of over 80%.

Comparison to AAH. The experiments of AAH [14] are performed for 100 websites. To compare ACEBot to AAH more globally, we have crawled 10 of the same

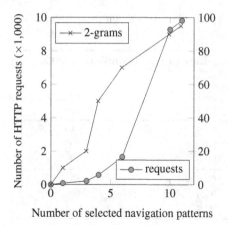
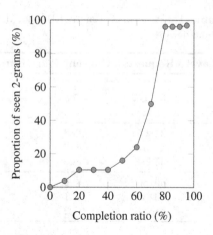

Fig. 8. HTTP requests and proportion of seen 2-grams for 10 websites

Fig. 9. Proportion of seen 2-*grams* for different completion ratios for 10 websites

websites (nearly 0.5 million webpages) used in AAH [14]. ACEBot is fully automatic, whereas the AAH is a semi-automatic approach (still domain dependent) and thus requires a hand-crafted knowledge base to initiate a bulk downloading of known web applications. Over 96 percent crawl effectiveness in terms of *2-grams*, and over 99 percent in terms of external links is achieved for ACEBot, as compared to over 99 percent content completeness (in terms of both *2-grams* and external links) for AAH. The lower content retrieval for ACEBot than for AAH is naturally explained by the 95% target completion ration considered for ACEBot. However the performance of AAH relies on the hand written crawling strategy described in the knowledge base by a crawl engineer. The crawl engineer must be aware of the website structure for the crawled website, to effectively download the important portion, as contrasted to our fully automatic approach, where one does not need to know such information for effective downloading and the crawler automatically learns the important portions of the website. The current approach makes 5 times fewer HTTP requests as compared to 7 times for AAH (See Fig. 7).

Comparison to iRobot. We have performed the comparison of our approach with the iRobot system [12]. iRobot is not available for testing because of intellectual property reasons. The experiments of [12] are performed just for 50,000 webpages, over 10 different forum websites (to compare with our evaluation, on 2.0 million webpages, over 50 different websites). To compare ACEBot to iRobot, we have crawled the same web forum used in [12]: http://www.tripadvisor.com/ForumHome (over 50,000 webpages). The completeness of content of the our system is nearly 97 percent in terms of *2-grams*, and 100 percent in terms of external links coverage; iRobot has a coverage of *valuable content* (as evaluated by a human being) of 93 percent on the same website. The number of HTTP requests for iRobot is claimed in [12] to be 1.73 times less than a regular web crawler; on the http://www.tripadvisor.com/ForumHome web application, ACE-Bot makes 5 times fewer requests than wget does.

6 Conclusions

We have introduced an Adaptive Crawler Bot for data Extraction (ACEBot), that relies on the inner structure of webpages, rather than on their content or on URL-based clustering techniques, to determine which pages are important to crawl. Extensive experiments over a large dataset have shown that our proposed system performs well for websites that are data-intensive and, at the same time, present regular structure.

Our approach is useful for large sites, for which only a small part (say, 3,000 pages) will be crawled during the learning phase. Further work could investigate automatic adjustment of the number of pages crawled during learning to the size of the website.

References

1. Gibson, D., Punera, K., Tomkins, A.: The volume and evolution of web page templates. In: WWW (2005)
2. Q-Success: Usage of content management systems for websites (2015). http://w3techs.com/technologies/overview/content_management/all
3. Alpert, J., Hajaj, N.: We knew the web was big (2008). http://googleblog.blogspot.co.uk/2008/07/we-knew-web-was-big.html
4. Faheem, M.: Intelligent Content Acquisition in Web Archiving. PhD thesis, Télécom ParisTech (2014)
5. Liu, Z.-H., Ng, W.-K., Lim, E.: An automated algorithm for extracting website skeleton. In: Lee, Y.J., Li, J., Whang, K.-Y., Lee, D. (eds.) DASFAA 2004. LNCS, vol. 2973, pp. 799–811. Springer, Heidelberg (2004)
6. Kao, H.Y., Lin, S.H., Ho, J.M., Chen, M.S.: Mining web informative structures and contents based on entropy analysis. IEEE Trans. Knowl. Data Eng. (2004)
7. Crescenzi, V., Merialdo, P., Missier, P.: Fine-grain web site structure discovery. In: WIDM (2003)
8. Crescenzi, V., Merialdo, P., Missier, P.: Clustering web pages based on their structure. Data Knowl. Eng. **54**(3) (2005)
9. Bertoli, C., Crescenzi, V., Merialdo, P.: Crawling programs for wrapper-based applications. In: IRI (2008)
10. Vidal, M.L.A., da Silva, A.S., de Moura, E.S., Cavalcanti, J.M.B.: Structure-driven crawler generation by example. In: SIGIR (2006)
11. Jiang, J., Song, X., Yu, N., Lin, C.Y.: Focus: Learning to crawl web forums. IEEE Trans. Knowl. Data Eng. (2013)
12. Cai, R., Yang, J.M., Lai, W., Wang, Y., Zhang, L.: iRobot: an intelligent crawler for web forums. In: WWW (2008)
13. Blanco, L., Dalvi, N.N., Machanavajjhala, A.: Highly efficient algorithms for structural clustering of large websites. In: WWW (2011)
14. Faheem, M., Senellart, P.: Intelligent and adaptive crawling of web applications for web archiving. In: Daniel, F., Dolog, P., Li, Q. (eds.) ICWE 2013. LNCS, vol. 7977, pp. 306–322. Springer, Heidelberg (2013)
15. Lin, C.Y., Hovy, E.: Automatic evaluation of summaries using n-gram co-occurrence statistics. In: HLT-NAACL (2003)

Investigating the Antecedents of Playing Games for Crowdsourcing Location-Based Content

Dion Hoe-Lian Goh[✉], Ei Pa Pa Pe-Than, and Chei Sian Lee

Wee Kim Wee School of Communication and Information,
Nanyang Technological University, Singapore, Singapore
{ashlgoh,ei1,leecs}@ntu.edu.sg

Abstract. Human Computation Games (HCGs) are games that harness human intelligence to tackle computational problems. Put differently, they are a means of crowdsourcing via games. Due to this entertainment-output generation duality, perceived enjoyment and perceived quality of outputs are potentially important determinants of HCG usage. This study adopts a multidimensional view of perceived enjoyment and output quality to investigate their influence on intention to use HCGs. This is done using SPLASH, our developed mobile HCG for crowdsourcing location-based content. Since SPLASH comprises various gaming features, we further study how the different dimensions of enjoyment vary across them. Using a survey of 105 undergraduate and graduate students, findings validated the multidimensionality of perceived enjoyment and output quality and showed their differing influence. As well, the different gaming features elicited different perceptions of enjoyment. Our results thus suggest that HCGs can be used for crowdsourcing tasks if they can fulfill enjoyment and assure output quality.

Keywords: Human computation games · Crowdsourcing · Location-based content · Mobile devices · Enjoyment · Output quality

1 Introduction

The popularity of social computing and proliferation of user-generated content have facilitated the crowdsourcing phenomenon. Essentially, crowdsourcing harnesses large groups of online users to address specific problems [1]. In the area of user-generated content, examples may include metadata generation (e.g. tags), and content creation (e.g. text and images). Platforms for facilitating crowdsourcing projects have also emerged, with Amazon Mechanical Turk (AMT) being a prominent one.

Despite the potential of crowdsourcing, a couple of conundrums exist. In particular, participants need to be motivated to perform their assigned tasks, which can be tedious. Consider an image tagging task where people sift through huge collections of images, generating descriptive tags for each. For some crowdsourcing platforms, the motivations of the volunteers are mostly intrinsic [2] and they are dependent on individuals' willingness to devote their time and effort to such a project. Other platforms, such as AMT, offer monetary payments to participants, but this limits crowdsourcing

© Springer International Publishing Switzerland 2015
R.B. Allen et al. (Eds.): ICADL 2015, LNCS 9469, pp. 52–63, 2015.
DOI: 10.1007/978-3-319-27974-9_6

projects to those backed with adequate funding [3], and does not guarantee the accuracy and truthfulness of the generated outputs [4].

Games have thus been investigated as an alternative means to motivate people to participate in crowdsourcing. Known variously as crowdsourcing games, games with a purpose or human computation games (HCGs, which this paper will adopt), they generate useful outputs as byproducts of gameplay [5]. HCGs are a promising approach to crowdsourcing because they capitalize on people's desire for entertainment [6]. In the context of digital libraries, HCGs may be employed for tasks such as metadata generation or content creation. Examples include ontology building, music tagging, sentiment analysis, and contributing of images [7,8], [6].

Understanding individuals' behavioral intention to use HCGs is an important step in the quest to create better games [9]. Since HCGs blend gaming with output creation, prior work suggests that enjoyment and output quality would be candidate antecedents for influencing usage intention [10,11]. However, the unique entertainment-output generation duality of HCGs [5] makes them different from purely hedonic or utilitarian-oriented systems. Thus, results obtained in these broader contexts may not be directly applicable to HCGs.

The present study addresses the following gaps in HCG research. First, the nature of HCGs suggest that individuals would perceive them differently from other types of systems. Consequently, an examination of the antecedents influencing usage intention is timely. Second, enjoyment and output quality have been treated as unidimensional in prior work (e.g. [9]) although there are studies suggesting that such constructs are multifaceted [12]. Treating such constructs as unidimensional may overlook the importance of specific facets that are only related to the phenomenon of interest [12]. Finally, there are limited studies on perceptions of HCG players [13], [7], and none have examined how different genres could influence such perceptions, even though there is evidence that genres could influence perception outcomes [14].

The present study comprises two parts, First, we employ multidimensional models of enjoyment and output quality to investigate usage intention of SPLASH (Seek, PLAy, SHare), our mobile HCG for crowdsourcing location-based content. Second, we delve deeper into the HCG by studying how perceptions of enjoyment vary across its different gaming features. Findings from our work will provide a better understanding of why people play HCGs, and in doing so, better design decisions can be made with the aim of improving players' experience during gameplay.

2   Human Computation Games

2.1   Related Systems

Put succinctly, HCGs are dual-purpose applications which generate computation through crowdsourcing and offer entertainment at the same time. As such, enjoyment and computation are prominent features of HCGs. This characteristic distinguishes HCGs from pure entertainment games in which enjoyment is considered to be the single most important goal [12].

HCGs initially emerged as web-based casual games. One well-known example is the ESP Game [15], which embeds the image labeling task into gameplay. The game rule is that a player has to guess the words that might be used by his/her partner to describe a given image and then enter their guesses in the form of labels; both players will be rewarded when their labels match. Players of the ESP Game produce labels as byproducts of gameplay that can later be used to improve image search engines. Other examples include HCGs for harvesting text annotation to improve natural language processing, building ontologies, and tagging music [2], [8]. On mobile platforms, HCGs have been primarily used in content generation, and examples include Indagator [16] and Eyespy [13] for sharing photos and texts of geographic locations, and Hidden View Game [17] for keeping maps and street views up-to-date.

2.2   SPLASH: A Mobile HCG for Location-Based Content Sharing

For the purpose of this study, we developed and employed SPLASH (Seek, PLAy, SHare), an Android-based multiplayer mobile HCG designed to facilitate creating, sharing, and accessing location-based content through gaming. SPLASH's content is known as "comments", comprising titles, tags, descriptions, media (e.g., photos) and ratings (Figure 1). Players can contribute comments about arbitrary geographic areas that are termed as "places" in SPLASH. Places can be further divided into "units" which hold associated comments. For instance, if a school is a place, a library inside the school will be considered to be a unit that contains comments.

SPLASH consists of three major gaming features or genres. Content sharing is achieved through a virtual pet game in which players "feed" location-based content to virtual pets (Figure 2). Pets represent units and live in apartments (explained later) within "mushroom houses" that represent places. The pet's appearance is influenced by four content attributes (Figures 4). A pet's size relates to the amount of content fed, while the ratings affect its color. Next, new content would make a pet look younger while older content would cause pets to age. Finally, pets fed with content that is generally positive in sentiment are happier, while those fed with content that is negative will appear sadder. Mushroom houses are visualized on a map interface for navigation and access to the respective content (Figure 3). Similar to the pets, the mushroom houses change in appearance according to the amount (size), quality (wall color), recency (roof color) and sentiment (weather) of the content (Figure 5). This appearance is based on the overall values of the content attributes belonging to all the pets inside the house.

SPLASH also provides a platform to foster social interaction. Players may visit each pet's apartments (virtual rooms) within the mushroom houses. These rooms are extensions of physical spaces (Figure 6) and players can decorate them with items purchased from a virtual game store. One such item is an arcade machine operating different types of mini-games which are casual in nature; they can be for pure entertainment such as puzzles and shooting, information-based games that harness the surrounding content to provide awareness of one's vicinity, or mini-HCGs for players to perform useful computations. Others include utility items such as chairs, tables, and musical instruments. The decoration of virtual rooms requires various amounts of in-game currency depending on the item type. To gain currency, players will need to feed pets or rate comments. There is also a comment board for players to chat.

Fig. 4. A pet's appearances

Fig. 1. SPLASH's comment.   Fig. 2. SPLASH's virtual pet.   Fig. 3. SPLASH's map view.   Fig. 5. A house's appearances.

Fig. 6. SPLASH's virtual room.   Fig. 7. SPLASH's avatar personalization page.

Finally, each SPLASH player has a customizable avatar (Figure 7). This allows for players to experience deeper levels of emotional attachment to the game. Players are able to choose hairstyles, hair color, clothes and other accessories. While the basic items are available at no cost, more attractive items have to be purchased using the in-game currency acquired by interacting with virtual pets. Players can show off their avatars by putting them on their profile page, as well as visiting the pets' apartments which display the avatars of current visitors.

3   Related Work and Hypotheses Development

3.1   Perceived Enjoyment

Perceived enjoyment (PE) is defined as the extent to which performing an activity is considered enjoyable in its own right, aside from performance consequences [18]. PE is known to be a salient factor driving behavioral intention to use online games [9] and information sharing systems [11].

As HCGs are of form of entertainment, PE is likely to be significant in determining intention to play them (INT). Although prior research treats enjoyment unidimensionally as a positive affective response [18], recent studies suggest that enjoyment is a complex construct [12], [19]. As suggested by [20], PE can be captured with three dimensions: perceived affective enjoyment (PAE) focuses on the emotional experiences in response to gameplay; perceived cognitive enjoyment (PCE) centers on the evaluative judgments in response to gameplay such as being interesting and worthy; perceived behavioral enjoyment (PBE) refers to the level of deep involvement or immersion during gameplay. As a HCG is a type of game, PE is likely derived from multiple sources. We thus postulate the following research hypotheses:

H1: PE is positively related to INT.

H1a: PAE, PCE, and PBE are antecedents of PE in HCGs.

Further, prior research on entertainment-oriented games suggests that players' in-game experiences affect PE [21]. Different game types comprise specific game mechanics that would afford particular gameplay experiences. For instance, games with virtual pets (VP) could evoke a sense of emotional attachment and nurturing relationship, whereas virtual rooms (VR) could create more immersive gameplay [22]. As well, avatar customization of player profiles (PP) provides a sense of ownership and self-expression [21]. Hence, this study aims to investigate whether PE differs across HCG feature types, and asks the following research question:

RQ1: What are the differences in PAE, PCE, and PBE across three types of HCG features (VP vs. VR vs. PP)?

3.2   Perceived Output Quality

Perceived output quality (POQ) is defined as an individual's perception of the quality of output provided by an information system [18]. It has been found to have substantial impact on adoption and usage of various online and mobile information-oriented systems [11], [23]. Since HCGs, in the context of our work, deal with the task of information creation [6], the quantity and quality of information contributed by players is an important concern. Thus, it is likely that individuals will continue using an HCG when they are satisfied with the quality of its information.

POQ is known to be a multidimensional construct [24]. In particular, perceived accuracy (PAC), completeness (PCO), relevancy (PRE), and timeliness (PTI) are regarded as important quality dimensions in the user-generated content context [23]. With the focus on information creation in our study, the above-mentioned aspects could be important in HCGs. Hence, the following hypotheses are proposed:

H2: POQ is positively related to INT.

H2a: PAC, PCO, PRE, and PTI are antecedents of POQ in HCGs.

4   Methodology

4.1   Participants and Data Collection Procedure

Participants were 105 undergraduate and graduate students recruited from universities in Singapore. There were 51 females and 54 males, with ages ranging from 19 to 41 with an average of 26 years. Approximately 52% of participants had a background in computer science, information technology or related disciplines, while the other 48% came from diverse disciplines such as arts, social sciences or business. About 62% of the participants played online games. All participants reported that they understood the concept of location-based information sharing, while about 51% reported that they had previously used the location check-in features of social networking applications.

Participants were recruited through advertisements via email, pamphlets and posters, and were given a modest incentive of $5 for their effort. The study was conducted across separate sessions, each of which consisted of a minimum of three and a maximum of ten participants to facilitate a multiplayer experience. Each session began with the researcher explaining the purpose of the study, including information about SPLASH and its features. Next, the participants were loaned Android mobile phones with SPLASH preloaded and asked to test the game and its features. Once the participants familiarized themselves with the game, a usage scenario was presented. This scenario required the participants to perform a series of tasks which included using SPLASH to (a) find places on the map, (b) feed pets, (c) rate comments, (d) visit a pet's apartment, (e) customize avatars, and (f) view the leaderboards. Upon completion of the given tasks, a questionnaire (described next) was administered. The entire study took approximately 40 minutes.

4.2   Measures Used

A questionnaire was developed to elicit participants' perceptions of the study's constructs. The measurement of each construct was developed by modifying existing scales to fit the target HCG context – perceived enjoyment (PE) [10], perceived output quality (POQ) [24], and intention to play (INT) [16]. In particular, PE was assessed using 12 items, with three sets of four questions evaluating affective, cognitive, and behavioral enjoyment derived from the gameplay. Next, POQ was measured with 12 items, and the four sub-dimensions were measured with three items each. Finally, three questions measured INT, that is, how likely players intend to play HCGs for content sharing, rating, and viewing.

As we aimed to measure players' enjoyment of the three different SPLASH features (VP, VR and PP), separate sets of items were included. Consequently, the final questionnaire consisted of 63 items for the study's main constructs. A pilot test was conducted using three graduate students, and items were modified based on feedback form the participants. The question items were measured using a 5-point Likert scale ranging from 1 (strongly disagree) to 5 (strongly agree).

5   Results

The collected data was analyzed using structural equation modeling (SEM), and one-way ANOVAs, using AMOS and SPSS. First, a confirmatory factor analysis (CFA) was performed. The results reveal that the lowest item loading of this study was 0.77, and the composite reliability (CR) and average variance extracted (AVE) were 0.90 and 0.70 respectively. Table 1 shows the results of the CFA.

Table 1. Results of confirmatory factor analysis.

Constructs	Items	Item reliability	Cronbach's Alpha	AVE
PAC	PAC1	0.89	0.92	0.80
	PAC2	0.95		
	PAC3	0.84		
PCO	PCO1	0.79	0.90	0.75
	PCO2	0.90		
	PCO3	0.90		
PRE	PRE1	0.85	0.89	0.74
	PRE2	0.85		
	PRE3	0.87		
PTI	PTI1	0.85	0.86	0.70
	PTI2	0.79		
	PTI3	0.82		
PAE	PAE1	0.81	0.92	0.76
	PAE2	0.92		
	PAE3	0.91		
	PAE4	0.83		
PCE	PCE1	0.79	0.89	0.70
	PCE2	0.81		
	PCE3	0.90		
	PCE4	0.77		
PBE	PBE1	0.82	0.91	0.73
	PBE2	0.89		
	PBE3	0.89		
	PBE4	0.83		
INT	INT1	.91	0.94	0.80
	INT2	.93		
	INT3	.88		
	INT4	.86		

Table 2 shows that the variances extracted by the constructs are greater than any squared correlations them. This implies that the constructs are empirically distinct. Hence, the measurement model showed adequate reliability as well as convergent and discriminant validity. The CFA also indicated good fit with the data, with all of the model-fit indices exceeding their respective common acceptance levels (X2/df = 1.56, AGFI = 0.75, NFI = 0.85, CFI = 0.94, RMSEA = 0.07 and IFI = 0.94).

Second, a SEM analysis was carried out. Comparison of six common fit indices with their corresponding recommended values provided evidence of a good model fit (X2/df = 1.62, AGFI = 0.75, NFI = 0.85, CFI = 0.93, RMSEA = 0.07 and IFI = 0.93). The hypothesized paths from POQ ($\beta = 0.48$, $p < 0.001$) and PE ($\beta = 0.67$, $p < 0.001$) were significant in predicting intention to play (INT) HCGs, hence hypotheses 1 and 2 were supported. Compared to POQ, PE exerted a stronger effect on INT. The proposed model accounted for 68% of the variance in predicting INT.

Table 2. Results of discriminant validity analysis.

	PAC	PCO	PRE	PTI	PAE	PCE	PBE	INT
PAC	0.894							
PCO	0.666	0.866						
PRE	0.526	0.774	0.857					
PTI	0.655	0.791	0.759	0.821				
PAE	0.482	0.529	0.451	0.413	0.870			
PCE	0.475	0.591	0.573	0.568	0.619	0.823		
PBE	0.257	0.358	0.326	0.363	0.596	0.538	0.856	
INT	0.613	0.661	0.659	0.545	0.693	0.677	0.581	0.894

Further, our results showed that PAE ($\lambda = 0.82$, $p = 0.001$), PCE ($\lambda = 0.77$, $p = 0.001$), and PBE ($\lambda = 0.74$, $p = 0.001$) were antecedents for PE. Here, PAE and PCE were slightly stronger in predicting PE than PBE. Similarly, the results revealed that PAC ($\lambda = 0.77$, $p = 0.001$), PCO ($\lambda = 0.88$, p = 0.001), PRE ($\lambda = 0.88$, $p = 0.001$), and PTI ($\lambda = 0.86$, $p = 0.001$) were predictive of POQ in the context of HCGs. Among all dimensions, PCO, PRE and PRI were relatively stronger determinants of quality. Therefore, hypotheses 1a and 2a were supported. A pictorial summary of the results of our SEM analysis is shown in Figure 8.

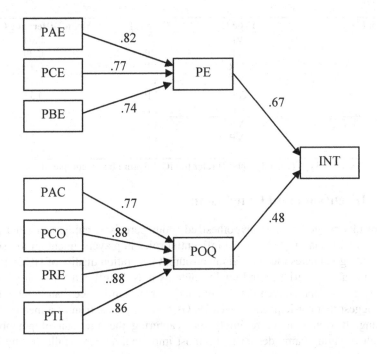

Fig. 8. Summary of the SEM analysis with all part coefficients significant at p < 0.001.

Finally, one-way ANOVAs were performed to address RQ1. Table 3 shows the means and standard deviations of participants' perceptions of the three game feature types. Significant differences were found in two enjoyment dimensions (cognitive and behavioral). Post-hoc comparisons using Tukey's test were then conducted. First, participants perceived HCG features as providing cognitive enjoyment differently $[F(2,312) = 14.20, p < .01]$. Both VP and VR performed better than PP. There was no difference in inducing cognitive enjoyment between VP and VR. Second, perceptions of behavioral enjoyment displayed a similar pattern of findings as that of cognitive enjoyment $[F(2,312) = 6.94, p = .001]$. That is, both VP and VR were viewed similarly and both were also rated higher than PP. These results are shown in Table 4.

Table 3. Means and standard deviations for perceptions of enjoyment (N=105).

Variable	Type of HCG feature / Mean (SD)		
	Virtual Pet (VP)	Virtual Room (VR)	Player Profile (PP)
Affective	3.22 (0.71)	3.10 (0.71)	2.91 (0.82)
Cognitive*	3.50 (0.68)	3.33 (0.73)	2.97 (0.79)
Behavioral*	3.14 (0.76)	3.13 (0.61)	2.81 (0.78)

*Statistically significant differences between the three applications at p<0.05.

Table 4. Comparisons between participants' perceptions of enjoyment across HCG feature type (N=105).

Variable	Type (1)	Type (2)	Mean Difference (1)–(2)
	VP	VR	0.04
Affective	VP	PP	0.20
	VR	PP	0.16
	VP	VR	0.17
Cognitive	VP	PP	0.53*
	VR	PP	0.36*
Behavioral	VP	VR	0.01
	VP	PP	0.33*
	VR	PP	0.32*

Note: *p<0.05. Type (1) and Type (2) refer to HCG feature being compared.

6   Discussion and Conclusion

Our results suggest that as hypothesized, both perceived enjoyment (PE) and perceived output quality (POQ) have influential roles in players' intention to use HCGs. This finding validates the entertainment-output generation duality of HCGs [5] in that both enjoyable experience and quality outputs must be offered for such games to be used by participants. Given that PE exerted a greater influence than POQ, our results also suggest that participants viewed HCGs first as games, than as a means of crowdsourcing. It would therefore imply that capturing the attention of potential users through engaging game design is the most important strategy, followed by ensuring that mechanisms are in place to produce quality outputs.

Within PE, all components, perceived affective enjoyment (PAE), cognitive enjoyment (PCE) and behavioral enjoyment (PBE), were important determinants. Although PAE and PCE had stronger coefficients than PBE, the differences were small. In the context of our work, this demonstrates that PE is not a monolithic construct as assumed by prior research, but is a complex interplay between one's emotions (PAE), value judgments (PCE) and gameplay involvement (PBE) [20].

In terms of PAE, players likely experienced various emotions through interacting with SPLASH's game elements, consistent with prior work [9]. The ease of creating potentially useful information and the nurturing of the virtual pet also enhanced this emotional experience. Likewise, PCE could be derived from players recognizing the value of SPLASH in crowdsourcing information, and therefore they were intrinsically motivated to participate. This was supported by SPLASH's ratings feature, which allowed players to ascertain the value of information contributed. With PBH, our findings suggest that SPLASH could create an absorptive experience for players so that they wanted to keep themselves engaged with the game [19]. This bodes well for SPLASH and other HCGs that are of the casual game genre since it means that players do not need to spend large amounts of time, as in multiplayer role-playing games, to feel a sense of immersion and engagement.

Like PE, POQ is multidimensional, as indicated by the results of our study. These include perceived accuracy (PAC), perceived completeness (PCO), perceived relevancy (PRE) and perceived timeliness (PTI). Although PAC had a slightly weaker coefficient than the other dimensions, the differences were small. Thus, our results suggest that in terms of assessing the quality of outputs in HCGs, our participants adopted a holistic judgment that factored in multiple attributes.

Consequently, while it is important that HCGs provide an enjoyable experience for their users, features for supporting the four output quality dimensions need to be present. In the case of SPLASH, this is in part achieved through the visualization of the virtual pets. For example, the size of the pet reflects the amount of information provided at a specific location, suggesting completeness of coverage (PCO). The age of the pet reflects the recency of contributed information and hence influences PTI. Finally, content and sentiment ratings, as depicted by the pet's color and demeanor, indicates relevancy and accuracy. These attributes may then be verified by the users themselves when the information is viewed. With regards to the latter, the ease of accessing location-based information through the map is therefore deemed important.

Probing deeper, our investigation of RQ1 showed that source of PE likely arose from the virtual pet (VP) and virtual room (VR) features of SPLASH since these were perceived to be more cognitively (PCE) and behaviorally (PBE) enjoyable than the avatar customization of player profiles (PP). There were no differences in PAE across the three features. The poor reception of the PP feature was surprising since the ability to customize one's avatar allows a player to express himself/herself and evokes a sense of ownership in the game. One possible explanation is that unlike the VP and VR features which had both gaming and crowdsourcing components, the PP feature only had the former. Consequently, this lesser role may have caused participants to feel less cognitively and behaviorally engaged. Nevertheless, the support for self-expression likely resulted in a sense of emotional attachment to the avatar and hence

PAE was similar across all features. Taken together, this finding suggests the need for a focused game design approach in HCGs, in that features should help players concentrate on the main objective at hand, which is to serve a crowdsourcing purpose during gameplay. Non-essential stimuli may distract players from this objective.

In conclusion, this study contributes to both research and practice. Our research argues for the multidimensionality of perceived enjoyment and output quality in the context of HCGs. This leads to a more nuanced understanding of how to sustain engagement among HCG players. In particular, HCG game designers should pay attention to the dimensions of PE and POQ to augment the user experience. Taken together, our work suggests that digital libraries and other information intensive environments could employ HCGs in crowdsourcing contexts such as metadata generation and content creation. These platforms should address the affective, cognitive and behavioral dimensions of enjoyment, as well as the quality of content in terms of accuracy, completeness, relevance, and timeliness.

There are, however, limitations in our study that warrant consideration for future work. One, our results were obtained from a specific type of HCG within a specific computational domain of mobile content creation. It would be helpful for future research to replicate this study with different HCG genres and computational domains for the purposes of generalizability. Two, participants in our study were primarily undergraduate and graduate students. HCG usage could span other user types and it would therefore be helpful to conduct follow-up studies with diverse age groups or educational backgrounds. Finally, use of other data collection methods such as observations, interviews and application logs would be valuable to triangulate our findings and provide a better idea of the factors influencing intention to use HCGs.

Acknowledgements. This work was supported by MOE/Tier 1 grant RG64/14.

References

1. Doan, A., Ramakrishnan, R., Halevy, A.Y.: Crowdsourcing systems on the World-Wide Web. Commun. Acm. **54**, 86–96 (2011)
2. Brabham, D.C.: Moving the crowd at Threadless: Motivations for participation in a crowdsourcing application. Inform. Commun. Soc. **13**, 1122–1145 (2010)
3. Fort, K., Adda, G., Cohen, K.B.: Amazon Mechanical Turk: Gold mine or coal mine? Comput. Linguist. **37**, 413–420 (2011)
4. Huck, S., Kübler, D., Weibull, J.: Social norms and economic incentives in firms. J. Econ. Behav. Organ. **83**, 173–185 (2012)
5. Goh, D.H., Ang, R.P., Lee, C.S., Chua, A.Y.K.: Fight or unite: Investigating game genres for image tagging. J. Am. Soc. Inf. Sci. Tec. **62**, 1311–1324 (2011)
6. von Ahn, L., Dabbish, L.: Designing games with a purpose. Commun. Acm. **51**, 58–67 (2008)
7. Goh, D.H., Lee, C.S.: Perceptions, quality and motivational needs in image tagging human computation games. J. Inf. Sci. **37**, 515–531 (2011)
8. Krause, M., Takhtamysheva, A., Wittstock, M., Malaka, R.: Frontiers of a paradigm: exploring human computation with digital games. In: ACM SIGKDD Workshop on Human Computation, pp. 22–25. ACM Press, New York (2010)

9. Wu, J., Liu, D.: The effects of trust and enjoyment on intention to play online games. Journal of Electronic Commerce Research **8**, 128–140 (2007)
10. Fang, X., Zhao, F.: Personality and enjoyment of computer game play. Comput. Ind. **6**, 342–349 (2010)
11. Kim, B., Han, I.: The role of trust belief and its antecedents in a community-driven knowledge environment. J. Am. Soc. Inf. Sci. Tec. **60**, 1012–1026 (2009)
12. Mekler, E.D., Bopp, J.A., Tuch, A.N., Opwis, K.: A systematic review of quantitative studies on the enjoyment of digital entertainment games. In: SIGCHI Conference on Human Factors in Computing Systems, pp. 927–936. ACM Press, New York (2014)
13. Bell, M., Reeves, S., Brown, B., Sherwood, S., McMillan, D., Ferguson, J., Chalmers, M.: Eyespy: supporting navigation through play. In: SIGCHI Conference on Human Factors in Computing Systems, pp. 123–132. ACM Press, New York (2009)
14. Johnson, D., Gardner, J.: Personality, motivation and video games. In: 22nd Conference of the Australian Computer-Human Interaction Special Interest Group, pp. 276–279. ACM Press, New York (2010)
15. von Ahn, L., Dabbish, L.: Labeling images with a computer game. In: SIGCHI Conference on Human Factors in Computing Systems, pp. 319–326. ACM Press, New York (2004)
16. Lee, C.S., Goh, D.H.-L., Chua, A.Y.K., Ang, R.P.: Indagator: Investigating perceived gratifications of an application that blends mobile content sharing with gameplay. J. Am. Soc. Inf. Sci. Tec. **61**, 1244–1257 (2010)
17. Lee, J., Kim, J., Lee, K.: Hidden view game: designing human computation games to update maps and street views. In: 22nd International Conference on World Wide Web companion, pp. 207–208 (2013)
18. Davis, D., Bagozzi, P., Warshaw, R.: Extrinsic and intrinsic motivation to use computers in the workplace. J. Appl. Psychol. **22**, 1111–1132 (1992)
19. Weibel, D., Wissmath, B.: Immersion in computer games: The role of spatial presence and flow. International Journal of Computer Games Technology **6** (2011)
20. Nabi, R.L., Krcmar, M.: Conceptualizing media enjoyment as attitude: implications for mass media effects research. Commun. Theor. **14**, 288–310 (2004)
21. Trepte, S., Reinecke, L., Behr, K.: Avatar creation and video game enjoyment: effects of life-satisfaction, game competitiveness, and identification with the avatar world. In: Preconference, Humans and Avatars, ECREA (2010)
22. Richter, G., Raban, D.R., Rafaeli, S.: Studying gamification: the effect of rewards and incentives on motivation. In: Reiners, T., Wood, L.C. (eds.) Gamification in Education and Business, pp. 233–251. Springer International Publishing (2015)
23. Schaal, M., Smyth, B., Mueller, R.M., MacLean, R.: Information quality dimensions for the social web. In: International Conference on Management of Emergent Digital EcoSystems, pp. 53–58. ACM Press, New York (2012)
24. Lee, Y.W., Strong, D.M., Kahn, B.K., Wang, R.Y.: AIMQ: A methodology for information quality assessment. Inform. Manage. **40**, 133–146 (2002)

Formal Acknowledgement of Citizen Scientists' Contributions via Dynamic Data Citations

Jane Hunter[✉] and Chih-Hsiang Hsu

The University of Queensland, Brisbane St Lucia, QLD 4072, Australia
j.hunter@uq.edu.au, chih.hsu@uqconnect.edu.au

Abstract. Data citation provides a valuable method for rewarding citizen scientists by formally acknowledging the contributions that they make to valuable scientific datasets. The difficulty is that citizen science databases that comprise volunteer-generated observations are highly dynamic and contain data contributed by a very large number of volunteers. Moreover, the scientists re-using the citizen science data often only want to cite a small sub-set of the entire database, as it existed at a specific date and time. The majority of data citation approaches assume that the dataset is static, owned by a single agent and the entire dataset is being cited (not just a subset). This paper describes, implements and evaluates an innovative approach to dynamic data citation that potentially overcomes many of the challenges associated with citing sub-sets of constantly changing citizen science datasets and thus enables formal recognition of the volunteers who contributed the data.

Keywords: Dynamic data citation · Scalable · Citizen scientist · Recognition

1 Background

Data citation is the practice of providing a formal, structured reference to data in the same way that scholars provide bibliographic references to relevant, existing publications. Significant effort has been focused on data citation recently because of the important role that research data plays in providing evidence to support scholarly claims. Global initiatives have been focusing on Data Citation Principles [1], data citation standards [2,3] and unique persistent identifiers [4,5] to enable data to be treated as a first class research output and to support data citation.

Within the context of many citizen science datasets, data citation potentially provides a valuable method for rewarding and retaining citizen scientists by formally acknowledging and attributing the contributions that they make to scientific datasets. Hence, data citation can potentially help to attract and retain volunteers [6], an issue that many citizen science projects struggle with.

However, most existing data citation efforts assume that datasets being cited are static, owned by a single agent or organization and the entire dataset is being cited (not just a subset). The reality is that many citizen science datasets comprise: data that is generated by large online communities; data that is constantly changing and expanding; and scientists/authors who are re-using the data but who only want to cite a small sub-set of the data.

R.B. Allen et al. (Eds.): ICADL 2015, LNCS 9469, pp. 64–75, 2015.
DOI: 10.1007/978-3-319-27974-9_7

Recently, the Dynamic Data Citation Working Group within the Research Data Alliance (RDA) [7] proposed an approach to solve the problem of precisely citing subsets of large scale databases that are changing and growing over time. The proposed approach involves two main principles: (i) the underlying database must be versioned and support time stamping of changes or additions; (ii) the Persistent Identifier (PID) to the citable data comprises a query to the dataset and a timestamp. Within this context, retrieving a precise subset of data involves re-running the query on the dataset as it existed at that date and time.

2 Objectives and Challenges

The principle aim of this paper is to evaluate the applicability of the dynamic data citation approach proposed by the RDA's Dynamic Data Citation Working Group [7,8] in the context of evolving datasets generated by citizen scientists. The goal is to streamline the generation of data citations for scientists who are re-using specific subsets of large volunteer-generated datasets and who want to acknowledge the re-use of the data and provide attribution to the volunteers who collected it. The focus of this paper is primarily on citizen science datasets that comprise observations or measurements of the environment (e.g., species observations, climate observations, air or water quality measures) that have been captured and uploaded by volunteers. The size of this problem is significant and growing because citizen science projects, in which volunteers collect data for conservation or scientific investigation, are the most common category of citizen science projects [9,10].

The other main category of citizen science projects, identified by Wiggins & Crowston [10], is the "virtual" project, such as Galaxy Zoo, in which volunteers perform online classification tasks. This type of citizen science project is interesting because it presents a different set of challenges associated with formal acknowledgement of annotations, but it is out of the scope of this paper.

In this paper, we are primarily interested in scenarios in which as scientist wants to cite specific sub-sets of large citizen science (observational) databases. For example, imagine a scientist who wants to cite all of the observations in the eBird Reference Dataset 3.0 [11] of a particular bird species "saltmarsh sharp-tailed sparrow" that occurred in Maryland between 2005-2010.

In order to comply with recommended best practice in data citation [1],[12], the scientist needs a Web service capable of generating:

- a unique persistent Digital Object Identifier (DOI) [5] to the dataset of interest;
- a set of metadata that ideally complies with the DataCite Metadata Schema [3];
- a landing page that displays the associated metadata and a link to the dataset;
- a citation string that can be pasted into the references of publications that use this dataset. For example, in the DataCite format: *Creator(s), (Publication Year), Title. Publisher. Identifier.*

Below is an example of such a data citation string:

F.Andrews, A.Brown, C.Jones, D.Smith, D.White, E.Wilson, (2005-2010), *"Observa-tions of Saltmarsh Sharp-tailed Sparrow in Maryland from 2005-2010"*. Avian Know-ledge Network, eBird Reference Dataset 3.0.   doi:10.1594/GBIF.726855.

3   Methodology

In order to implement and evaluate the proposed dynamic data citation approach, the Avian Knowledge Network's eBird 3.0 reference dataset [13],[11] (that contains more than 2 million observations by over 20,000 registered users) was downloaded to use as the testbed dataset. A sub-set of the eBird 3.0 dataset (an Excel file) was then up-loaded into a relational (MySQL) database.

The MySQL database was further extended by adding two additional tables to record: time-stamping of all additions, deletions and modifications of records in the database; data citation query strings, timestamps and associated metadata fields.

Next, a browser-based user interface was developed to enable users to query the underlying testbed dataset. Users can search and retrieve records based on: date or place of observation, species of bird observed, or the last name of the volunteer. The retrieved subset is displayed as a list of records that match the search term, in chrono-logical order of the date of the observation.

Thirdly, a data citation service was developed, based on the Dynamic Data Citation approach [15,16], which automatically generates: a persistent ID (PID) to a time-stamped query string which can retrieve the dataset, a set of metadata compliant with the DataCite Standard [3], and a data citation string for incorporation as a reference in a publication. Where possible, the metadata and data citation string are automatically generated by parsing the result set. For example, the value in the *Creator* metadata field is automatically derived by: parsing the result set for the names of all of the con-tributors/volunteers, removing any duplicates, and listing the volunteers' last names in alphabetical order. For those metadata fields that can't be automatically derived (e.g., the *Title*), a user interface is also provided to allow the person creating the citation to manually input their own preferred values. After the metadata fields and associated citation are satisfactory and complete, they are saved in the *QueryCitation* Table in the repository.

Finally, a series of tests were performed to evaluate the performance of the Dy-namic Data Citation approach and its application to citizen science datasets (com-pared with storing the cited sub-sets as CSV files). A set of limitations and issues requiring further research are also identified.

The remainder of the paper is structured as follows: Section 4 describes Related Work; Section 5 describes the design and implementation of the prototype Dynamic Data Citation service; Section 5 describes the results of the evaluation phase; and Section 6 outlines open issues and provides concluding remarks.

4   Related Work

Over the past two years, the Research Data Alliance (RDA) Data Citation Working Group has proposed a scalable approach that allows scientists to create, reference, cite and reuse subsets of any size and complexity, by applying requirements for dynamic data citation to different types of data storages.

The approach that the RDA Working Group on Data Citation (WGDC) adopts [16] is to:

- Ensure that the data is stored in a versioned and timestamped manner
- Identify subsets of the data as it existed at a particular time, by storing timestamped queries that can be re-executed against the timestamped data store and assigning persistent identifiers (PIDs) to the queries.

The implementation of database systems that support time-stamping of transactions is not a new idea [17]. However the adoption of time-stamped databases in the context of: the global trend towards data citation and new data citation standards such as Data Cite, time-stamped persistent and uniquely identifiable queries as recommended by the RDA WGDC, and observational citizen science databases such as eBird, is an original and potentially valuable combination of technologies that has the potential to enhance the re-use of community-generated data and provide formal recognition to the volunteers who generated it.

Since this proposal, a number of Use Cases or Pilot projects have been evaluating the RDA WGDC approach in the context of their data repositories and users' citation needs [18].

In [14], Proll and Rauber present a use case involving the monitoring of large concrete dams used for hydroelectric power generation. More than 30 different sensor types gather data such as rainfall, water levels, temperature, humidity and many other factors. Complexity, volume, coverage and data collection frequency vary considerably, and all of the sensor data is collected in a central database.

Other examples of projects that are evaluating RDA's Data Citation WG's approach include: the TIMBUS[1] and SCAPE[2] EU projects; UK Natural Environment Research Council Data Centres; ESIP (Earth Science Information Partners); the CLARIN project (Field Linguistics Transcriptions) and the Virtual Atomic and Molecular Data Centre[3].

So although numerous groups worldwide have been and are currently evaluating the Scalable Dynamic Data Citation approach in the context of a wide variety of scientific disciplines, data types and underlying databases and repositories, as far as we are aware, no one has evaluated this approach in the context of citations to formally recognize contributions to citizen science observational databases.

---

[1] http://timbusproject.net/
[2] http://www.scape-project.eu/
[3] http://portal.vamdc.eu/portal/home.seam

5   Design and Implementation

5.1   Architectural Design

This section describes how the prototype was developed, the technologies employed and it also provides a brief overview of the system structure. Figure 1 shows the high level system architecture.

The Web-based user interface (UI) was developed using HTML 5 and CSS. Users can search and browse the records in the local repository using JQuery. JQuery acts as a controller for each web page and all the user interaction activities are captured and processed by it. Screen shots of the user interface are shown in the next section. After an HTTP request is made, JSP (Java Server Pages) then capture the request from users and determine which action to take based on the request parameter(s). After a decision is made, it then calls the backend to process the data. The backend (Java Database Programing) has two main responsibilities: (i) to process the query and retrieve the data; and (ii) to generate a persistent DOI and data citation.

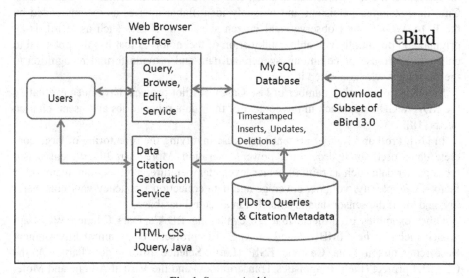

Fig. 1. System Architecture

The local repository comprises a My SQL 5.6 database running on a Dell Power-edge R710 2U Rack Server. The database stores a subset (2010-12-01 to 2011-01-31 in America) of the eBird 3.0 collection [11]. The MySQL database has been extended to support two additional tables.

The *History* Table is required so the database at the time of the original query can be recreated. It stores:

- Timestamps for all INSERT, UPDATE and DELETE statements
- The history of all inserts, updates and deletes with the original values

The *QueryCitation* Table stores the data required to re-run the queries and dynamically retrieve the cited data sub-set. Hence it stores:

- SELECT query strings that correspond to queries that identify subsets of data that need to be persistent and citable
- The PID assigned to each query which serves as identification for the citation record
- The timestamp of the query – so it can be re-executed against the database as it existed at that time

When a User clicks on a PID to a QueryCitation, the query is re-executed against the database as it existed at that timestamp. The result set is retrieved and cached temporarily. It is then parsed to extract those DataCite Schema metadata fields that can be automatically generated: DOI/Identifier, Creator(s), Title, Publisher, PublicationYear, ResourceType. Finally, a Landing Page to the cited dataset is presented to the user which displays all of the metadata fields and values, as well as a link to the actual temporarily cached dataset, which can be saved or downloaded. Users can manually input/update metadata fields if necessary before saving the citation to the repository.

5.2   User Interface

The Web browser-based user interface enables users to search records/observations based on: *Species*, *State*, *Contributor's last name* and *DateRange*. Figure 2 shows the user interface for the query: all sightings of "Albert's Towhee" within the State of "California".

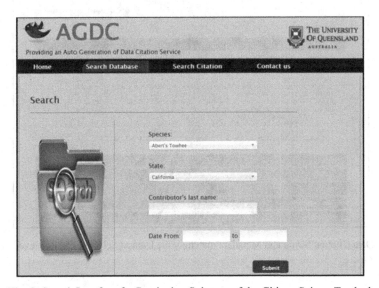

Fig. 2. Search Interface for Retrieving Sub-sets of the Citizen ScienceTestbed

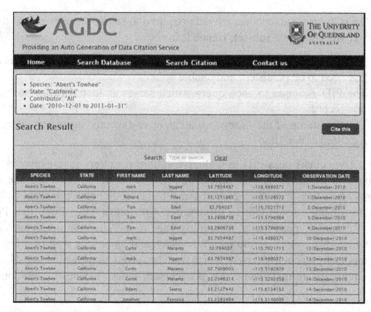

Fig. 3. Display of Citizen Science Observation Records that match the Query entered in Fig. 2

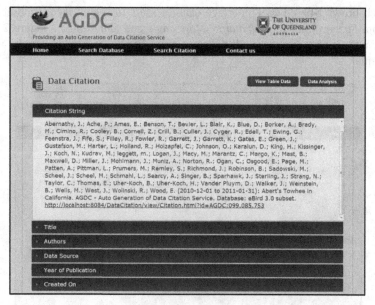

Fig. 4. Data Citation String and Metadata matching the Dataset Selected and Retrieved in Fig.3

Figure 3 illustrates the display of records/observations that have been retrieved from the underlying MySQL database, that match the query illustrated in Figure 2. Once the required dataset has been selected, users can click on the "Cite this" button (top RHS of Figure 3). A popup window will then be displayed asking users to specify a *Title* and *CitationType* (Query String or CSV file) for this citation. (CSV files are only supported so that the Dynamic Data Citation/Query approach can be compared against storing the citable sub-sets as CSV files.)

The data is then parsed to generate a list of author names (in alphabetical order) and a date range. A citation string and persistent identifier is also generated. The dataset is then saved either as combined query string or as a CSV file in a repository, depending on the citation type users specified earlier. The interface also allows users to add additional metadata to the data citation, prior to it being saved in the QueryCitation Table (which was described in Section 5.1).

6   Evaluation

6.1   Comparative Analysis

In order to evaluate the Dynamic Data Citation approach (which stores and re-runs time-stamped queries), we also implemented the conservative approach for comparison. The "conservative" approach involves saving each extracted and citable dataset as a CSV file, together with metadata describing it. This also provides us with the original sub-set or ground truth for validating and verifying that the time-stamped query retrieves the precise sub-set specified by the DOI.

Storing extracted data sub-sets is advantageous in that it does not require the support and maintenance of time-stamped, versioned databases, but this approach has numerous disadvantages in terms of storage, discovery, performance and conducting statistical analyses for citation. Both of these approaches will face performance issues when dealing with very large relational databases (> 1 million records). However, with proper optimization of database queries, the time-stamped query approach is likely to perform better than the duplicate CSV files approach. For example, Lomet et al. [19] demonstrated how transaction time database support can be built into the SQL Server engine, without impairing performance when executing historical queries.

According to [20], the number of eBird observations is growing exponentially (30-40%) every year, and tends to peak in May each year. For example, in May 2013, over 5 million observations were submitted [21]. In addition, all observations go through a semi-automated quality control process that adds further updates to the underlying database. Given the scale and frequency of updates to the eBird database, which is built on Oracle servers and data storage systems, it is likely that a commercial solution such as Oracle's Flashback technology[4] would be capable of supporting the required database time-stamping and versioning in a scalable manner.

---

[4] http://www.oracle.com/technetwork/database/features/availability/flashback-overview-084412.html

Storing large numbers of query strings could also potentially cause performance is-sue(s) due to the large volume of HTTP requests made to the server whenever users wish to view the extracted dataset associated with the citation. A recent paper on e-Bird [21] stated that "in the past decade, more than 90 peer-reviewed publications either used eBird data or studied aspects of the eBird project". However [20] also stated that "over the past year, more than 1100 individuals from 40 countries have requested eBird data, making more than 3400 downloads representing ca. 2.6 terabytes of data". These figures indicate that the number of eBird data downloads greatly exceeds the number of publi-cations that use the eBird data. Supporting 90 data citations corresponding to related publications over 10 years is the highest priority, and would not present performance challenges. However, supporting >3400 data citations (and associated query strings) per year would be more challenging but of lower priority.

On the other hand, saving 3400 datasets per year as CSV files will face the same issues when users want to download the file from the server. If there are lots of con-current download requests from users, the Internet bandwidth could be fully used and the server may be unable to deliver the requests or may be slow in responding.

6.2   Evaluation of Query-based Citations on a Changing Dataset

A number of tests were also performed to check that the retrieved data sub-set was precisely the same as the original version, even after multiple *insertions, updates* and *deletions* were performed on the MySQL database.

This test process comprised firstly executing the example query in Figure 1, then saving the retrieved results both as a dynamic data citation (a DOI to a time stamped query string) as well as a CSV file.

Next, a number of new records were inserted that also matched the original query. Running the original query via the user interface indicated that these new records were included in the result set. However, selecting the original PID for the data cita-tion before the new records were inserted, did not include these records in the re-trieved dataset.

Similarly, the dataset retrieved using the original data citation DOI did not change even after performing a number of deletions and updates on the database that affected the results of the original query.

6.3   Discussion

The evaluation of the prototype testbed described above revealed a number of advan-tages associated with the Dynamic Data Citation approach, including:

- There is no need to save explicit overlapping copies of data subsets, hence by citing only the query instead of the whole data set, the aim is to achieve scal-able data citation and save on storage and metadata;
- The proposed approach works for both dynamic, changing datasets as well as static datasets and for both small and large datasets;
- It enables volunteers to be individually recognized and attributed by a for-mal, machine-processable method.

On the other hand, the implementation and evaluation described above also revealed a number of limitations and disadvantages, associated with the proposed approach:

- The need to add timestamping and versioning to the relational database;
- Scalability of the system over time has not been adequately tested – if there are numerous and frequent changes to the database and numerous frequent fine-grained data citations, performance may degrade;
- When there are very large numbers of volunteers/data creators, the generated citation strings may become unmanageable and not easily incorporated within a publication's reference section;
- Nested or complex/composite queries have not yet been evaluated;
- Citizen science databases that are not relational DBMSs – for example, XML, Linked Open Data, RDF Triple stores and NoSQL databases;
- Citizen science observations that comprise not just records/rows comprising text strings and numeric values but other data types - raster data, image, video and audio datasets, have not yet been evaluated.

7   Future Work and Conclusion

The primary aim of the system described here is to evaluate the feasibility of the Dynamic Data Citation approach (as proposed by Pröll and Rauber [14,15] and the RDA Data Citation WG [7,8]) in the context of citing sub-sets of citizen science databases to provide formal attribution to voluntary citizen scientists.

Although the prototype developed here demonstrates the feasibility of the Dynamic Data Citation approach, it has not fully implemented the recommendations of the RDA Data Citation Working Group [8]. More specifically, there are three aspects that have not yet been implemented but which we plan to implement in the future:

- Detecting identical queries – queries should be written in a normalized form (so that identical queries can be detected) and a checksum of the normalized query computed, to efficiently detect identical queries and to avoid the multiple assignment of new PIDs to identical queries;
- Stable Sorting: an unambiguous sorting of the records in the data set should be ensured;
- Result Set Verification: a checksum (hash key) of the query results should be computed and stored to enable verification of the correctness of a result upon re-execution.

Other areas that have been identified as also requiring further investigation include:

- Data citation metrics – determine those subsets of the data that are most reused by analysing overlaps between data citation query results plus citation metrics associated with publications that cite the datasets;
- Notifying volunteers when their data has been cited and analysing the impact of data citations on volunteer retention rates and frequency of participation;
- Recording provenance after download – what happens to the data, what is it aggregated with, how is it analysed, what is derived from it?

To conclude, this paper describes the application and evaluation of a dynamic data citation approach to a changing citizen science database to automatically generate data citations for subsets of data. The service has been investigated as a means of providing attribution to the volunteers who contributed those sub-sets. Previous surveys of citizen science communities [10] indicate that volunteers are more likely to participate in citizen science projects and to continue to actively participate for extended periods if they receive feedback that details how their data is having an impact by being re-used by scientists to advance scientific research. The research in this paper demonstrates that dynamic data citation using time-stamped queries provides a scalable, efficient approach for formally recognizing the contributions of volunteers to citizen science databases. Hence, it offers a socio-technical solution to help overcome the challenge of attracting and retaining citizen scientists.

References

1. CODATA-ICSTI Task Group on Data Citation Standards and Practices: Out of Cite, Out of Mind: The Current State of Practice, Policy, and Technology for the Citation of Data. Data Science Journal **12**, 1–75 (2013)
2. DataCite. http://www.datacite.org/
3. DataCite Metadata Schema. http://schema.datacite.org/meta/kernel-3/
4. Wilson, B.E., Cook, R.B., Beaty, T.W., Lenhardt, W., Grubb, J., Hook, L.A., Sanderson, C.: Enhancing The Recognition, Reusability, And Transparency Of Scientific Data Using Digital Object Identifiers (2010)
5. Paskin, N.: Digital Object Identifier (DOI) System. Encyclopedia of Library and Information Sciences **3**, 1586–1592 (2010)
6. Piwowar, H.A., Vision, T.J.: Data Reuse and the Open Data Citation Advantage. PeerJ **1**, e175 (2013)
7. RDA Working Group on Data Citation: Making Data Citable. https://rd-alliance.org/groups/data-citation-wg/wiki/scalable-dynamic-data-citation-rda-wg-dc-position-paper.html
8. RDA Working Group on Data Citation: Scalable Dynamic Data Citation Approaches, Reference Architectures and Applications, RDA WG Data Citation Position Paper, Draft Version (2015). https://www.rd-alliance.org/groups/data-citation-wg/wiki/scalable-dynamic-data-citation-rda-wg-dc-position-paper.html
9. Citizen Scientists: Linking People with Science to Understand and Protect Ecosystems. http://www.citizenscientists.com/examples/
10. Wiggins, A., Crowston, K.: From conservation to crowdsourcing: a typology of citizen science. In: 2011 44th Hawaii International Conference on System Sciences (HICSS), pp. 1–10. IEEE (2011)
11. EBird. http://ebird.org/
12. Martone, M. (ed.): Data Citation Synthesis Group: Joint Declaration of Data Citation Principles. FORCE11, San Diego (2014). https://www.force11.org/datacitation
13. Munson, A., Webb, K., Sheldon, D., Fink, D., Hochachka, W.M., Iliff, M., Riedewald, M., Sorokina, D., Sullivan, B., Wood, C., Kelling, S.: The eBird Reference Dataset, Version 3.0. Cornell Lab of Ornithology and National Audubon Society, Ithaca (2011)
14. Pröll, S., Rauber, A.: Scalable data citation in dynamic, large databases: model and reference implementation. In: IEEE International Conference on Big Data (2013)

15. Pröll, S., Rauber, A.: Citable by design - a model for making data in dynamic environments citable. In: 2nd International Conference on Data Management Technologies and Applications (DATA 2013), Reykjavik, Iceland (2013)
16. Rauber, A., Asmi, A., van Uytvanck, D., Pröll, S.: Data Citation of Evolving Data: Recommendations of the Working Group on Data Citation (EGDC) (2015). https://rd-alliance.org/system/files/documents/RDA-DC-Recommendations_150924.pdf
17. Jensen, C.S., Lomet, D.B.: Transaction timestamping in (temporal) databases. In: VLDB, pp. 441–450 (2001)
18. Lomet, D., Barga, R., Mokbel, M.F., Shegalov, G., Wang, R., Zhu, Y.: Immortal DB: transaction time support for SQL server. In: Proceedings of the 2005 ACM SIGMOD International Conference on Management of Data, pp. 939–941. ACM (2005)
19. RDA Data Citation Working Group, Dynamic Data Citation Use Cases (2015). https://rd-alliance.org/groups/data-citation-wg/wiki/collaboration-environments.html
20. Kelling, S., Gerbracht, J., Fink, D., Lagoze, C., Wong, W.K., Yu, J., Gomes, C.: A Human/Computer Learning Network to Improve Biodiversity Conservation and Research. AI Magazine **34**(1), 10 (2012)
21. Sullivan, B.L., Aycrigg, J.L., Barry, J.H., Bonney, R.E., Bruns, N., Cooper, C.B., Kelling, S.: The eBird Enterprise: An Integrated Approach to Development and Application of Citizen Science. Biological Conservation **169**, 31–40 (2014)

Searching for Health Information Online for My Child: A Perspective from South East Asia

Anushia Inthiran[1(✉)] and Ireneous Soyiri[2]

[1] School of Information Technology, Monash University Malaysia,
Jalan Lagoon Selatan, Bandar Sunway, Selangor, Malaysia
anushia.inthiran@monash.edu
[2] Centre of Population Health Sciences, The University of Edinburgh,
Teviot Place, Edinburgh EH8 9AG, UK
isoyiri@exseed.ed.ac.uk

Abstract. Research studies investigating online health information searching behavior are abundant. While there is research pertaining to the online health information seeking behavior of parents in developed countries, similar information for countries with developing economies in the South East Asia region is not available. In this research study, we focus on information searching behavior of parents with children under the age of eighteen. This study describes the information searching behavior of 50 parents. Results indicate participants are motivated to search for information online for doctor visit and non-doctor visit purposes. Google is the most popular search engine used. Results provide insights on the information searching behavior of parents in South East Asia.

Keywords: Children · Information searching · Online health · Parents · South East Asia

1 Introduction

Survey results indicate that searching for health information online is popular among citizens of developed nations [1]. Non-expert online health information seekers are generally categorized as general consumers, caregivers and patients. Caregivers are unique because they take on a different role when performing a search [2]. A parent is the primary caregiver for children with an illness [2]. Taking care of the health needs of a child is different to those of an adult [3]. Parents' information searching behavior for their child has been well researched in countries with developed economies since the early 2000's. However, there is limited understanding of this for South East Asian countries that fall under the classification of countries with developing economies (SEADE) [4]. While knowledge on parents' online information searching behavior can be gleaned from studies in developed countries, the focus has been on specific illnesses [3], [5]. Our focus is on the online health search behavior of parents without reference to any particular illness. We focus on SEADE, as mothers in this region are forgoing traditional media and have turned to online means to obtain information [6]. In addition, governments in these countries have plans to encourage online health searching [7,8].

© Springer International Publishing Switzerland 2015
R.B. Allen et al. (Eds.): ICADL 2015, LNCS 9469, pp. 76–81, 2015.
DOI: 10.1007/978-3-319-27974-9_8

Our research aim is to describe the online health information searching behavior of parents from SEADE on behalf of their child. The following research questions will be explored: RQ1) Why do parents search for health information online? (motivation) and RQ2) What sources are used to perform the search?

2   Related Work

With the exception of three research studies [9,10,11] online health information searching focusing on SEADE countries is scarce. In developed countries, parents of children with chronic multisystem diseases and parents with children with a pre-existing health condition [3], [5], [12] search for information online. A child's condition is a motivating factor to perform a search. A warranted visit to the emergency room also triggers a search [13,14]. In other cases, the lack of information given by physicians motivated parents to search for information online [14]. Human and work condition factors such as time constraints during the consultation process or personal and emotional dynamics also prompted the search process [14]. Results indicate that there needs to be a trigger for parents to search for health information online. We postulate that parents in SEADE continuously search for health information for well-being and general healthcare due to poor health literacy [15].

In developed countries, Google remains the preferred search engine over the years [3], [14], [12]. However, parents are also using Web 2.0 type domains [15], [17]. Parents also seek sites that provide personal accounts and experiences [20]. Similarly, parents played an active role by contributing their experiences and knowledge online [15], [17]. Given that typical health information searching in an SEADE country is primarily conducted on Google [11], we postulate SEADE parents rarely use Web2.0 domains and are only consumers of health information due to low health literacy [15].

3   Methodology

A purposeful homogenous sampling technique was used. Participants were recruited via call for participation notice. Participants contacted the researcher and an appointment was set. Participants must be of 18 years and above and have at least one child under the age of 18. Participants must be a citizen and residing in an SEADE country, must not be from the healthcare or allied healthcare profession and must have performed an online health search for their child prior to participating in this study.

3.1   Data Collection and Procedure

A semi-structured face to face interview and questionnaire was used. The English language was the medium used to conduct the interview. The questionnaire collected socio-demographic details and information about the health search experience. We used a previous research study [13] as the base of the interview questions. The interview was audio recorded. A pilot test was conducted prior to the main experiment.

As a result of the pilot test, interview questions were fine-tuned. The main experiment took place after the pilot test. Participants were informed of the purpose of the research study via explanatory statements and consent forms. On average the interview took 20 minutes.

3.2   Data Analysis

Results from the questionnaire were analyzed using descriptive statistics. The audio recording was transcribed verbatim. This was to allow close links to be created between the data and the researcher [18]. Open coding was used and coding categories were derived inductively from the audio recording to fit the grounded theory approach [18]. A master list of codes was first created based on induction. These codes were revisited after every third participant. These codes were then reduced to themes using the constant comparative method. The first author conducted the transcription and derivation of codes. The second author cross checked the transcription, codes and themes based on the audio recording.

3.3   Participants

There were 50 participants. The participants' average age was 36 years (SD=4.7). There were 30 female and 20 male participants. Participants' educational qualifications ranged from a diploma to a PhD. Participants were professionals in fields such as business, engineering, information technology, administration, consultants and business owners. Participants had an average health search experience (for their child) of 4.6 years (SD=2.6). Participants consisted of the following nationalities: Malaysian (40%), Indonesian (24%), Thai (20%) and Cambodian (16%). The age range of participants' children was between 5 months and 16 years old.

4   Results

SEADE parents perform an online health search for two reasons: a doctor visit and a non-doctor visit purpose. 40 participants only performed doctor visit searches, while remaining participants performed both types of search. Searches performed for non-doctor visits are for the purpose of general wellbeing, awareness and to seek peer advice and experience.

Participant S: I want to obtain information and experience from mothers all over the world. I want to take different views under consideration...

The doctor visit category can be further categorized into pre-visit and post- visit needs. Among pre-visit needs are to determine if there is a need to visit the doctor, to search for immediate remedy, to have a better understanding of a child's health situation and to make better decisions.

Participant L3: He was having a lot of gas in the tummy, we thought we needed to take him to the clinic, but then we found out that this is something very normal so we realized we can help him at home without going to the doctor, if you seek medical help the doctor won't be able to give much help in this situation anyway....

Participant L2: my baby had something growing on his skin, we quickly referred to some Internet resources before going to the doctor...

Post visit needs are to determine side effects of medication and to find out if there are natural or traditional remedies available. The two reasons for a post visit need search is because participants felt the doctor did not furnish them with all the information required due to limited consultation time. The second reason is to verify information given by the doctor.

Participant M3: if it matches with information from the doctor then I am happy...

Participants use various sources to perform a health search. Google is the favored search engine used, with forty five participants solely performing the search on this domain. Remaining participants solely used specialized health type websites such as Boots, Mumsnet, Babycenter.com, Babycenter.uk and Babycentre.my. Participants who use the sites mentioned above are subscribed to receive emails from these sites. Participants indicate not opening these emails as diligently as before but not deleting them, either.

Participant M: I do not open these emails as regularly maybe once in three months...

Participants E2: I have a folder to keep all these emails...

Participants also indicate searching on Chinese, Taiwanese, Malay and Indonesian traditional medicine websites.

Participant E: I am Chinese and sometimes we believe in Chinese Medicine, Boots is western medicine, sometimes there are traditional rules of what to eat and what not to eat when a child has chickenpox, the western doctor says the child can eat anything...

5 participants indicate being members of Facebook communities and child healthcare social networks. 5 participants indicate that for untreatable conditions where nothing can be done but 'to wait it out', support group sites are preferred rather than reading medical information. These 5 participants indicate that they were active on the site (as consumers) during the period of the untreatable condition and became less active as the untreatable condition passed. All participants indicate they are only consumers of health information.

5   Discussion

Our contributions indicate participants perform a search for doctor and non-doctor visit purposes. We note that participants who were first time parents and had children under the age of 3 years performed doctor and non-doctor visit searches. As first time parents with newborns and young children, parents wanted to be equipped with health related information, peer advice and experience. Results also indicate doctor visit purpose can be further categorized into pre and post visit searches. Our research study shows some similarities with previous studies conducted in developed countries [3], [5] where the lack of information and time constraints [14], [16] triggered the search. None of the participants report discussing information found with the doctor. This coincides with results of previous research studies where the doctor-patient relationship in SEADE is affected by social-economic distance, healthcare setting, medical education and cultural characteristics [19]. This does not encourage SEADE parents to partake in the process of patient centered healthcare and decision making.

Similar to results of previous research studies [3], [5], [12], our results indicate Google is the favored search engine to perform a search. Few participants use health specific websites or Web2.0 type sites. We postulate participants were not aware of medical specific sites, and thus resorted to using the most popular search engine in South East Asia [20]. Parents also searched for traditional medication on traditional medicine websites. Citizens in SEADE have strong cultural heritage and traditions passed down from the elders. Thus, it is not surprising for participants to turn to alternate or traditional remedies for the purpose of wellbeing. Traditional medication was used prior to the arrival of western medicine in South East Asia. While citizens from Indonesia and Malaysia are most active on social networks in Asia [20] this trend did not translate to using social networks for the purpose of a health search. There are publicly available government health portals in SEADE, yet participants do not use these portals. Apparently, citizens are unaware of the availability of these portals, which contain authoritative and country-specific health information.

6   Conclusion and Future Work

Our results provide preliminary theoretical contributions on how SEADE parents perform online health information searching for their child. While our results cannot be generalized, we provided information on search motivation and sources used. In future work we intend to describe search collaboration activities in a large scale study.

References

1. Fox, S.: Health Fact Sheet, Pew Research Centre. http://www.pewinternet.org/fact-sheets/health-fact-sheet/
2. Fox, S., Duggan, M., Purcell, K.: Family caregivers are wired for health, Part 1 Health Information Specialist. http://www.pewinternet.org/2013/06/20/part-1health-information-specialists/

3. Khoo, K., Bolt, P., Babi, F.E., Jury, S., Goldman, R.D.: Health information seeking by parents in the Internet age. Journal of Paediatrics and Child Health **44**, 419–423 (2007)
4. International Monetary Fund: World Economic Outlook: Recovery Strengthens, Remains Uneven. www.imf.org/external/pubs/ft/weo/2014/01/pdf/text.pdf
5. Tuffrey, C., Finaly, F.: Use of the Internet by parents of paediatric outpatients. Arch. Dis. Child. **87**, 534–536 (2002)
6. Huang, E.: How are mothers in South East Asia using the Internet. https://sg.news.yahoo.com/mothers-southeast-asia-using-internet-080016075.html
7. Association of Southeast Asian Nations: ASEAN ICT Masterplan (2015). http://www.scribd.com/doc/111870071/ASEAN-ICT-Masterplan-2015
8. Wee, J.: Online health portal Tanya Dok wins Indonesia Satellite Award. http://e27.co/online-health-portal-tanyadok-wins-indonesia-satellite/
9. Saad, A.B.: Online health information seeking behavior among employees at two selected company, business engineering and industrial applications colloquium (BEIAC). In: 2013 IEEE (2013)
10. Kitikannakorn, N., Sitthiworanan, C.: Searching for health information on the Internet by undergraduate students in Phitsanulok, Thailand. International Journal of Adolescent Medicine and Health **21**(3), 313–318 (2014)
11. Inthiran, A., Alhashmi, S.M., Ahmed, P.K.: Online Consumer Health: A Malaysian Perspective. International Federation Information Processing, (IFIP). W9.4 Newsletter. http://www.iimahd.ernet.in/egov/ifip/jun2013/inthiran.htm
12. D'Alessandro, D.M., Kreiter, C.D., Kinzer, S.L., Peterson, M.W.: A randomized controlled trial for an information prescription for pediatric patient education on the Internet. Archives of Pediatric and Adolescent Medicine **158**(9), 857–862 (2004)
13. Kostagiolas, P., Martzoukou, K., Georgantzi, G., Niakas, D.: Information seeking behaviour of parents paediatric patients for clinical decision making the central role of information literacy in a participatory setting. Information Research **18**(3) (2013)
14. Gage, E.A., Panagakis, C.: The devil you know parents seeking information online for paediatric cancer. Sociology of Health and Illness **34**(2), 444–458 (2012)
15. Chen, S.F., Tsai, T.I., Wang M.H.: Health literacy and impact factors of the Southeast Asian immigrant women in Taiwan, Honor Society of Nursing, Sigma Theta Tau. In: International 24th International Nursing Research Congress. http://www.nursinglibrary.org/vhl/bitstream/10755/304306/1/Chen_HealthLiteracy.pdf
16. Wade, S.L., Wolfe, C.R., Pestian, J.P.: A web-based family problem solving intervention for families of children with traumatic brain injury. Behavioural Resource Methods Instrument Computing **36**(2), 261–269 (2004)
17. Bouwman, M.G., Teunissen, Q.G.A., Wijburg, F.A., Linhorst, G.E.: 'Doctor Google' ending diagnostic odyssey in lysosomal storage disorders parents using internet search engines as an efficient diagnostic strategy in rate diseases. Arch. Dis. Child. **95**, 642–644 (2010)
18. Strauss, A., Corbin, J.: Basics of Qualitative Research: Techniques and Procedures for Developing Grounded Theory, 2nd edn. Sage Social, Thousand Oaks (1998)
19. Claramita, M., Nugraheni, M.D.F., van Dalen, J., van der Vleuten, C.: Doctor– patient communication in Southeast Asia: a different culture? Adv. Health Sci. Educ. Theory Pract. **18**(1), 15–31 (2013)
20. Samarajiva, R.: More Facebook users than Internet users in South East Asia?. Lirneasia.net. http://lirneasia.net/2014/08/more-facebook-users-than-internetusers-in-south-east-asia/

Evaluation of a General-Purpose Sentiment Lexicon on a Product Review Corpus

Christopher S.G. Khoo[✉], Sathik Basha Johnkhan, and Jin-Cheon Na

Wee Kim Wee School of Communication & Information,
Nanyang Technological University, Singapore, Singapore
chriskhoo@pmail.ntu.edu.sg, {sathik,TJCNa}@ntu.edu.sg

Abstract. This paper introduces a new general-purpose sentiment lexicon called the WKWSCI Sentiment Lexicon and compares it with three existing lexicons. The WKWSCI Sentiment Lexicon is based on the *6of12dict* lexicon, and currently covers adjectives, adverbs and verbs. The words were manually coded with a value on a 7-point sentiment strength scale. The effectiveness of the four sentiment lexicons for sentiment categorization at the document-level and sentence-level was evaluated using an Amazon product review dataset. The WKWSCI lexicon obtained the best results for document-level sentiment categorization, with an accuracy of 75%. The Hu & Liu lexicon obtained the best results for sentence-level sentiment categorization, with an accuracy of 77%. The best bag-of-words machine learning model obtained an accuracy of 82% for document-level sentiment categorization model. The strength of the lexicon-based method is in sentence-level and aspect-based sentiment analysis, where it is difficult to apply machine-learning because of the small number of features.

Keywords: Sentiment lexicon · Sentiment analysis · Sentiment categorization

1 Introduction

Digital libraries increasingly contain user-contributed content in the form of user comments and reviews on the digital library materials. Some digital libraries, especially those of cultural heritage materials, contain crowdsourced content [1]. User-contributed materials are more likely to contain subjective content and sentiment expressions. It will become desirable to be able to categorize, analyze and summarize the subjective and sentiment content of digital libraries.

This paper introduces a new general-purpose sentiment lexicon called the Wee Kim Wee School of Communication & Information (WKWSCI) Sentiment Lexicon, and reports an evaluation of its effectiveness in document-level and sentence-level sentiment categorization of a product-review corpus. The sentiment lexicon is not derived from a particular corpus, and is not specific to a particular domain. It is based on the *12dicts* common American English word lists compiled by Alan Beale from twelve source dictionaries—eight English-as-a second-language dictionaries and four "desk dictionaries" [2]. Specifically, we make use of Beale's *6of12* list comprising 32,153 American English words common to 6 of the 12 source dictionaries. This

© Springer International Publishing Switzerland 2015
R.B. Allen et al. (Eds.): ICADL 2015, LNCS 9469, pp. 82–93, 2015.
DOI: 10.1007/978-3-319-27974-9_9

reflects the core of American English vocabulary. Currently, the WKWSCI Sentiment Lexicon comprises adjectives, adverbs and verbs. Sentiment coding of nouns is in progress.

The project started three years ago when, dissatisfied with the sentiment lexicons that were available on the Web, we decided to systematically develop our own general-purpose sentiment lexicon. Since then, however, other researchers have developed their own sentiment lexicons, and a new version of SentiWordNet has been published.

This paper compares the WKWSCI lexicon with three comparable sentiment lexicons available on the Web:

1. General Inquirer[1]
2. MPQA (Multi-perspective Question Answering) lexicon[2]
3. Hu & Liu Lexicon[3]

We compare the effectiveness of the four lexicons in an automatic sentiment categorization task, using an Amazon product reviews dataset. In the experiments, we applied each lexicon to predict the document-level sentiment polarity (i.e. the overall rating assigned by the reviewer, converted to binary values of positive/negative), as well as sentence-level sentiment polarity.

There are two main approaches to automatic sentiment categorization: the machine learning approach and the lexicon-based approach.

A machine learning approach builds a sentiment categorization model using a training corpus. This approach basically selects words (or assigns weights to words) that are useful in distinguishing between positive and negative documents, based on a set of training documents that have been annotated with the sentiment category to predict (i.e. positive or negative). Usually, individual words in the documents are used as features in the model, and hence it is referred to as a bag-of-words approach. The most commonly-used machine learning methods in sentiment analysis are the Support Vector Machine (SVM) [3,4] and the Naïve Bayes method [5]. Wang and Manning [6] found the Naïve Bayes method to be more effective for snippets or short reviews, whereas SVM was more effective for longer documents or full-length reviews.

A sentiment lexicon-based approach uses a general-purpose or domain-specific sentiment dictionary, comprising a list of words, each word tagged as positive, negative or neutral (and sometimes with a value reflecting the sentiment strength or intensity). The lexicon may be developed manually [7,8], automatically using word associations with known "seed words" in a corpus [9,10], or semi-automatically deriving sentiment values from resources such as WordNet [11,12]. To predict the overall sentiment of a document, a formula or algorithm is needed to aggregate the sentiment values of individual words in the document to generate the document-level sentiment score.

Sentiment categorization models developed using machine learning are expected to be more accurate than a general-purpose sentiment lexicon, if the training corpus is

---

[1] http://www.wjh.harvard.edu/~inquirer/spreadsheet_guide.htm
[2] http://mpqa.cs.pitt.edu/lexicons/subj_lexicon/
[3] http://www.cs.uic.edu/~liub/FBS/sentimentanalysis.html#lexicon

sufficiently large. A model developed using machine learning is customized to the vocabulary of the corpus and the writing style of the genre. The machine learning approach has the disadvantage that a sufficiently large training corpus that has been annotated with the target sentiment category must be available or has to be constructed. With the proliferation of product review sites with user comments and ratings, there is an abundance of such annotated documents on the Internet. A machine learning approach is not feasible when there is no readily available annotated corpus.

A machine learning approach is also more appropriate for document-level sentiment categorization, where there are more textual features (i.e. words) to make sentiment category predictions. To perform finer sentiment analysis at the sentence or clause level, a sentiment lexicon is needed. Fine-grained sentiment analysis includes aspect-based sentiment analysis (identifying the writer's sentiment towards various aspects of a product or topic, rather than the overall sentiment) [13], multi-perspective sentiment analysis (identifying the sentiment of various stakeholders or roles) [14], and identifying the type of sentiment (rather than just positive or negative sentiment polarity) [15].

The disadvantage of lexicon-based methods is that words can have multiple meanings and senses, and the meaning and sense that is common in one domain may not be common in another. Furthermore, words that are not generally considered sentiment-bearing can imply sentiments in specific contexts. However, when a domain specific lexicon is not available, a good general-purpose sentiment lexicon will be useful, and can give acceptable results. Taboada et al. [8] developed a Semantic Orientation Calculator for computing the sentiment polarity and strength of words and phrases based on a manually-built sentiment lexicon, and showed that such a method is robust and can give reasonably good results across domains.

2   WKWSCI Sentiment Lexicon: Overall Characteristics

The WKWSCI Sentiment Lexicon was manually coded by 12 undergraduate students in the Bachelor of Communication program at the Wee Kim Wee School of Communication & Information, Nanyang Technological University, Singapore. Second-year and third-year undergraduate students were recruited to do the coding in the summer of 2013 and 2014. Students who responded to an email recruitment advertisement were given a coding test, and in each year, six students with the highest scores in the test were recruited. Each word list was coded by three coders. The sentiment coding was carried out in two phases:

- Phase 1: the coders coded the words as positive, neutral or negative. They were instructed to follow their first impression without agonizing over their coding, and to select "neutral" when in doubt. The codings that were not unanimous among the three coders were reviewed by the first author, who made the final decision. The implication of this approach is that some slightly positive and slightly negative words are coded as neutral.

- Phase 2: the words that were coded as positive in Phase 1 were subjected to a second-round coding by 3 coders into 3 subcategories: slightly positive (sentiment value of 1), positive (2) and very positive (3). Another 3 coders coded the negative words into slightly negative (-1), negative (-2) and very negative (-3). Again, the words that did not obtain unanimous sentiment values from the 3 coders were reviewed by the first author.

Nearly 16,000 words, comprising approximately 7,500 adjectives, 2,500 adverbs and 6,000 verbs, have been coded with sentiment values. Table 1 lists the number of adjectives, adverbs and verbs coded with the different sentiment values. There are 2,334 positive words, 4,384 negative words and 9,206 neutral words. It is noted that there are almost twice as many negative words as positive words in the lexicon. In contrast, there are usually more instances of positive words than negative words in a text corpus. Few words in the lexicon are very positive or very negative.

Looking at the distribution of verbs: there are many more negative verbs (1,284) than positive verbs (269). Furthermore, sentiment verbs tend to have weak sentiment strength: there are more than twice as many slightly negative verbs than negative and very negative verbs, and three times as many slightly positive verbs than positive and very positive verbs.

Some words have multiple parts-of-speech:

- 474 words occur as both adjectives and verbs
- 374 words occur as both adjectives and adverbs
- 83 words occur as both adverbs and verbs
- 65 words occur as adjectives, adverbs and verbs.

There are 177 words with multiple parts-of-speech that have conflicts in their sentiment score for the different parts-of-speech. Most of the conflicts involve a positive or negative sentiment for one part-of-speech, and neutral sentiment for another part-of-speech. There are two exceptions: "keen" and "smart" have positive sentiment as adjectives, but negative sentiment as verbs.

Table 1. Frequency of words in the WKWSCI lexicon, with various parts-of-speech and sentiment values

Sentiment Polarity	Positive			Negative			Neutral	Total
Sentiment Score	3	2	1	-3	-2	-1	0	
Adjective	60	686	735	34	1031	1318	3656	7520
Adverb	5	316	243	12	429	276	1091	2392
Verb	4	63	202	12	400	872	4459	6012
Total	2334			4384			9206	15924

3   Comparison with Other Sentiment Lexicons

We compared our lexicon with three other comparable sentiment lexicons available on the Internet. We excluded SentiWordNet[4] from the study as we did not find the lexicon effective enough in identifying sentiment polarity in an earlier project [13]. This was possibly because the use of SentiWordNet requires effective word sense disambiguation, which we did not attempt. However, a new version of SentiWordNet 3.0 has been published, which we shall evaluate in the future.

The General Inquirer [7] has 11,789 word senses (some words have multiple senses), grouped into 182 categories. In this study, we analyzed only those words in the categories Postiv (1915 words) and Negativ (2291). Furthermore, we compared only the words tagged Modif (which are mainly adjectives, with a few adverbs and verbs) and SUPV (which are mostly verbs). We analyzed the conflicts in sentiment coding between General Inquirer and WKWSCI Lexicon. The main conflicts are between neutral words in the WKWSCI lexicon which are coded as positive or negative in General Inquirer.

The MPQA Subjectivity Lexicon has 8,222 words: 2719 positive, 4914 negative and 591 neutral words. It includes adjectives, adverbs, verbs, nouns and "anypos" (any part-of-speech). This study compares the adjectives, adverbs and verbs with our WKWSCI lexicon, ignoring the nouns. The lexicon was aggregated from a variety of sources, including manually developed and automatically constructed sources. A majority of the entries were collected in a project reported by Riloff and Wiebe [16].

As with the General Inquirer, most of the conflicts are between neutral codings in WKWSCI and positive/negative codings in MPQA. There are 45 words that appear in both lexicons but with opposite polarity (i.e. ignoring neutral codings in WKWSCI lexicon). 22 positive words in MPQA are coded negative in WKWSCI, and 23 negative words coded positive in WKWSCI. The main reason for the conflicting polarities is multiple senses of words: a word can have a positive sense and a negative sense. Examples are *gritty, accountable, comical, dogged, edgy, eternal, expedient, formidable, imposing, rigorous, sharp, sober, sympathetic, uneventful, unobserved,* and *zealous.* These are coded "1" (slightly positive) in WKWSCI lexicon and negative in MPQA.

The sentiment coding in some cases depends on the narrow or broader context being considered. For example, to "commiserate" and to "empathize" are polite gestures (positive) in a narrow context, but they indicate a broader context of misfortune for the person being commiserated or empathized with. The coding in WKWSCI is biased towards the narrow context. Of the 173 neutral words (of any part-of-speech) in WKWSCI that match with words in MPQA, 47 are coded positive in MPQA and 47 coded negative. The MPQA coding looks reasonable. As the coders for the WKWSCI lexicon had been instructed to code a word as neutral when in doubt, they were quite conservative in assigning sentiment polarity.

The Hu & Liu lexicon [12] has 6,790 words with no part-of-speech tags: 2006 positive words and 4783 negative words. This lexicon was generated automatically using

---

[4] http://sentiwordnet.isti.cnr.it/

machine learning techniques based on customer reviews from various domains compiled over several years. Again, most of the conflicts with the WKWSCI lexicon involve neutral words in WKWSCI coded as positive or negative in the Hu & Liu Lexicon.

4   Evaluation Experiments and Results

4.1   Evaluation Corpus

The sentiment categorization experiments made use of a subset of an Amazon product review corpus, downloaded from http://www.cs.uic.edu/~liub/ FBS/sentimentanalysis.html. The corpus was constructed by Jindal and Liu [17] for their study of opinion spam (fake review) detection. They noted that the corpus can be used for sentiment analysis experiments. The dataset has 25 product categories, each with up to 1000 positive and 1000 negative reviews. Each review is labelled as positive if the user rating score is 4 or 5, and negative if the user rating score is 1 or 2. We randomly selected 5 product categories out of 10 categories that have 1000 positive and 1000 negative reviews. The selected product categories are: apparel, electronics, kitchen & housewares, sports and outdoors, and video. For developing and evaluating machine learning models, we randomly selected 700 positive and 700 negative reviews from each product category to form the training set, and used the rest as the test set. This evaluation study made use of the review texts and the sentiment polarity (positive/negative). The review texts were lemmatized and tagged with part-of-speech tags using the Stanford core NLP parser [18].

We carried out the evaluation both at the document level and sentence level. For the sentence level evaluation, we randomly selected 50 positive and 50 negative reviews for each topic (500 reviews in all), and hired undergraduate students to code the sentences. Natural language toolkit 3.0 sentence tokenizer [18,19] was used to segment the review texts into sentences. Each sentence was coded by two coders, and conflicts were reviewed by the first author, who made the final decision.

It is important to note that three of the lexicons in the study were not constructed specifically for analyzing product reviews, whereas the Hu & Liu lexicon was developed based on product review texts. We were particularly interested to find out whether general-purpose sentiment lexicons can be applied with reasonable results to another domain.

4.2   Evaluation of Document-Level Sentiment Categorization

Two baseline experiments were carried out:

- Method 1a: Machine learning using bag-of-words, using Support Vector Machine (SVM) and Naïve Bayes method
- Method 1b: Lexicon-based method using *number of positive words – number of negative words.*

The SVM and Naive Bayes packages in the Scikit Learn Library [20] were used to develop the sentiment classifiers. The default parameters were used for both packages, with the SVM kernel set to polynomial.

Method 1a: Baseline machine learning method using bag-of-words. SVM and Naïve Bayes classifiers were built using the training dataset. Two weighting schemes were used: term frequency (tf) and term frequency*inverse document frequency (tf*idf). The results are given in Table 2. It can be seen that the results are about the same for tf and tf*idf weighting schemes, and for SVM and Naïve Bayes models. The accuracy rate is generally 81%; the highest accuracy is 82% for Naïve Bayes model using tf*idf weighting.

Table 2. Evaluation of Baseline SVM and Naïve Bayes models

	SVM (*tf* weighting)		SVM (*tf*idf* weighting)	
	Positive	Negative	Positive	Negative
Precision	0.807	0.808	0.789	0.836
Recall	0.809	0.807	0.848	0.773
F1 Score	0.808	0.807	0.818	0.803
Accuracy	0.808		0.811	
	Naïve Bayes (*tf*)		Naïve Bayes (*tf*idf*)	
	Positive	Negative	Positive	Negative
Precision	0.825	0.794	0.875	0.782
Recall	0.784	0.834	0.751	0.892
F1 Score	0.804	0.814	0.808	0.833
Accuracy	0.810		0.822	

Method 1b: Baseline lexicon-based method. The lexicon-based baseline method calculates sentiment scores for the reviews using the simple formula: *number of positive words - number of negative words*. The reviews are then ranked in decreasing score, and the top half of the reviews are categorized as positive, and the bottom half negative.

The results are given in Table 3. It can be seen that the WKWSCI lexicon (excluding slightly positive and slightly negative words) performed slightly better than the Hu & Liu lexicon, and clearly better than MPQA and General Inquirer. The WKWSCI lexicon obtained an accuracy rate of 72%, even though the lexicon is not derived from product review texts and does not include nouns.

Table 3. Accuracy of document-level sentiment categorization using baseline scoring method of counting positive and negative words

Lexicon	Accuracy
WKWSCI	0.694
WKWSCI (excluding slightly positive and slightly negative words)	0.723
Hu & Liu lexicon	0.710
MPQA	0.682
General Inquirer	0.634

Method 2: Lexicon-based method using logistic regression to determine the weights for different categories of words. Instead of just counting the number of positive and negative words, this method assigns different weights to different categories of words: each category is a combination of part-of-speech and sentiment strength (i.e. very positive, positive, etc.). Each word category then represents a feature whose value is the number of words of that category found in the document, normalized by dividing by the length of the review (i.e. review word count). Logistic regression (in the SPSS statistical package) is applied to the training dataset to determine the appropriate weights for each word category.

The logistic regression model for the WKWSCI lexicon indicates that the baseline score (using the baseline formula of Method 1b) should be combined with a normalized version of the baseline score (by dividing by the length of the review). The model also suggests that a higher number of adverbs indicates a negative review. For the WKWSCI lexicon, the accuracy improved from 0.723 for the baseline model (Model 1b) to 0.755 (see Table 4).

The logistic regression model for the Hu & Liu lexicon (not listed due to space constraints) indicates that the normalized version of the baseline score gives better results than the baseline score. In addition, the number of positive words have a significant impact on the accuracy of the sentiment categorization. The accuracy of the logistic regression model improved from 0.71 for the baseline model to 0.733 (see Table 4), which is still a little worse than the WKWSCI lexicon.

However, both models are substantially worse than bag-of-words machine learning models, which easily obtained accuracies of above 80%. The accuracy of the best machine-learning model probably represents the upper bound of what can be achieved using sentiment lexicons. The strength of sentiment lexicons is that training is not absolutely necessary, as the baseline scoring method still gives reasonable results of above 70%.

Table 4. Results of the logistic regression models for WKWSCI lexicon compared with the Hu & Liu lexicon on the test set

	WKWSCI lexicon	
	Positive reviews	**Negative reviews**
Precision	0.771	0.739
Recall	0.742	0.768
F1 Score	0.756	0.753
Accuracy	0.755	
	Hu & Liu lexicon	
	Positive reviews	**Negative reviews**
Precision	0.744	0.723
Recall	0.711	0.755
F1 Score	0.727	0.739
Accuracy	0.733	

4.3   Evaluation of Sentence-Level Sentiment Categorization

50 positive and 50 negative reviews were randomly sampled from each of the five topics, to make up 500 reviews in all. 1840 sentences were extracted from the 250 positive reviews, and 1528 sentences were extracted from the 250 negative reviews. They were coded by two coders into positive, negative and neutral/indeterminate sentiment polarity. Only unanimous codings were accepted as positive and negative sentences. There were 869 clearly positive sentences, and 964 clearly negative sentences. 24 reviews did not have any positive or negative sentences, and were dropped from the evaluation dataset.

To find out how important sentence-level sentiment is in determining the overall sentiment of a review, we calculated a sentiment score for each review using the formula: *number of positive sentences − number of negative sentences*. The reviews with a score of 0 and above were categorized as positive, and reviews with a score of -1 and below were categorized as negative. This obtained an accuracy rate of 0.937—for predicting the overall sentiment polarity of a review based on the number of positive and negative sentences. This indicates that accurate sentence-level sentiment categorization can improve the accuracy of document-level sentiment categorization.

Method 3: Baseline lexicon-based method for sentence categorization. The lexicon-based baseline method calculates sentiment scores for sentences using the simple formula: *number of positive words - number of negative words*. The accuracy of the sentence-level sentiment categorization is summarized in Table 5. Hu & Liu lexicon had the highest accuracy of 0.732, with WKWSCI obtaining the second highest accuracy of 0.716.

Table 5. Accuracy of sentence-level sentiment categorization using baseline scoring method

Lexicon	Accuracy
WKWSCI	0.716
WKWSCI (excluding slightly positive and slightly negative words)	0.692
Hu & Liu lexicon	0.732
MPQA	0.702
General Inquirer	0.669

Method 4: Lexicon-based method but using logistic regression to determine the weights for different categories of words. Stepwise logistic regression was applied to the training dataset to determine the appropriate weights for the number of positive words in the sentence, number of negative words, number of negation words, and the interaction variables—number of negation words multiplied by each of the other variables. The results of applying the logistic regression models for the four lexicons to the test dataset are given in Table 6. The accuracy for the Hu & Liu lexicon improved from 0.732 for the baseline model to 0.774 for the logistic regression model. The accuracy for WKWSCI lexicon improved from 0.716 to 0.758, which is a little worse than the results for Hu & Liu lexicon.

Table 6. Results for sentence-level sentiment categorization using logistic regression models for the four sentiment lexicons

	Polarity	Precision	Recall	F1-Score	Accuracy
WKWSCI	Positive	.772	.695	.732	**.758**
	Negative	.748	.815	.780	
MPQA	Positive	.732	.707	.719	.738
	Negative	.744	.767	.755	
General Inquirer	Positive	.700	.737	.718	.726
	Negative	.751	.715	.733	
Hu & Liu	Positive	.838	.650	.732	**.774**
	Negative	.737	.886	.805	

4.4   Error Analysis

We carried out an error analysis of the false positive and false negative errors that had been predicted with high probability of above 0.70 by the logistic regression model. 27 sentences were incorrectly predicted by the model to be negative with high probability, and 22 sentences were incorrectly predicted to be positive with high probability.

The biggest source of error is the need for common sense inferencing to identify a review as positive or negative. This is especially true in the case of false positives. Several of the cases involve long, complex sentences in reviews of videos. Users also tend to use sarcasm or hyperbole to express negative sentiments. Inferencing is difficult to model using lexicon-based methods or bag-of-words machine-learning models.

The second major source of the error for false negatives is the incorrect handling of negation words. Our regression models do take into consideration the presence of negation words in the sentence, but they are handled as an independent negation feature and as interactions with the sentiment features. In other words, we did not consider the position of the negation word—whether it immediately precedes a senti-ment-bearing word. From our observation, the negation word usually precedes the sentiment-bearing word that it modifies, but there can be up to 2 words in between. Surprisingly, negation handling did not appear to be a major problem in false positive predictions.

Sentiment-bearing phrases is the third source of error. They include: *be careful, do not bother, just like any other, hard to go wrong,* and *cannot beat it.* This can be addressed by reviewing 2 or 3-word sequences associated with positive or negative reviews, and compiling a list of such sentiment phrases.

We also examined the 74 sentences that do not have any word matches with the four lexicons. The majority of the cases (37) require commonsense inferencing, though some of these can be handled using domain-specific cue phrases that indicate negative features or sentiments. 15 of the cases contained the words "do not buy", "never ever buy", "never buy", or "not buy". 5 cases involve colloquial sentiment expressions such as "dorky", "wtf", "this movie rocks", "what a crock" and "yikes".

5   Conclusion

We have described the characteristics of the WKWSCI sentiment lexicon in comparison with three other comparable lexicons. The WKWSCI lexicon currently covers adjectives, adverbs and verbs from the *6of12dict* lexicon. The sentiment coding was carried out by undergraduate students in the Bachelor of Communication program. Each word was reviewed by 3 coders, and assigned a sentiment strength on a 7-point scale. Sentiment-bearing nouns are currently being coded.

From direct comparisons between the WKWSCI lexicon and the other lexicons, it was found that the WKWSCI lexicon is weaker in the category of slightly positive and slightly negative words, as the coders were instructed to assign the neutral category in cases of doubt. We thus recommend that the WKWSCI lexicon be supplemented with a list of words with the same sentiment polarity in both MPQA and the Hu & Liu Lexicon.

The four lexicons were used to perform document-level sentiment categorization on an Amazon product reviews dataset, as well as sentence-level sentiment categorization of sentences from a subset of the reviews. For document-level sentiment categorization, the WKWSCI lexicon performed slightly better than the Hu & Liu lexicon, whereas Hu & Liu performed slightly better for sentence-level sentiment categorization. The WKWSCI lexicon obtained an accuracy of 72% using a simple count of positive and negative words. The accuracy increased to 75% when the weights for the various counts were determined using logistic regression. For sentence-level sentiment categorization, the WKWSCI lexicon also obtained an accuracy of 75% when the weights were determined using logistic regression. However, the Hu & Liu lexicon did better this time, obtaining 77% accuracy.

Both WKWSCI lexicon and the Hu & Liu lexicon are clearly better than MPQA and General Inquirer. The Hu & Liu lexicon was derived from product review texts and is thus customized for the domain. It also does not have part-of-speech tags and thus includes nouns in the lexicon. In contrast, the WKWSCI lexicon is general-purpose and currently does not include nouns. Sentiment coding of nouns is in progress.

Bag-of-words machine-learning categorization models were developed using Support Vector Machine and Naïve Bayes machine learning methods. These models obtained an accuracy of about 82% for document-level sentiment categorization. This probably represents the upper bound of what can be achieved using a lexicon-based method. The strength of the lexicon-based method is in sentence-level and aspect-based sentiment analysis, where it is difficult to apply machine-learning because of the small number of features. For document-level sentiment categorization, sentiment lexicons can obtain reasonable results in different domains using simple counts of positive and negative words, without training. However, more work is needed to confirm this across a variety of domains and text genres.

References

1. Oomen, J., Aroyo, L.: Crowdsourcing in the cultural heritage domain: opportunities and challenges. In: Proceedings of the 5th International Conference on Communities and Technologies, pp. 138–149. ACM, June 2011
2. Dicts introduction. http://wordlist.aspell.net/12dicts-readme/

3. Cortes, C., Vapnik, V.: Support-Vector Networks. Machine Learning **20**(3), 273–297 (1995)
4. Vapnik, V.N.: Statistical Learning Theory. John Wiley and Sons, New York (1998)
5. Zhang, H.: The optimality of Naive Bayes. In: Proceedings of the Seventeenth Florida Artificial Intelligence Research Society Conference, pp. 562–567. The AAAI Press (2004)
6. Wang, S., Manning, C.D.: Baselines and bigrams: simple, good sentiment and topic classi-fication. In: Proceedings of the 50th Annual Meeting of the Association for Computational Linguistics, pp. 90–94. Association for Computational Linguistics (2012)
7. Stone, P.J., Dunphy, D.C., Smith, M.S., Ogilvie, D.M.: The General Inquirer: A Computer Approach to Content Analysis. MIT Press, Cambridge (1966)
8. Taboada, M., Brooke, J., Tofiloski, M., Voll, K., Stede, M.: Lexicon-Based Methods for Sentiment Analysis. Computational Linguistics **37**(2), 267–307 (2011)
9. Hatzivassiloglou, V., McKeown, K.: Predicting the semantic orientation of adjectives. In: Proceedings of 35th Meeting of the Association for Computational Linguistics, pp. 174–181 (1997)
10. Turney, P., Littman, M.: Measuring Praise and Criticism: Inference of Semantic Orienta-tion from Association. ACM Transactions on Information Systems **21**(4), 315–346 (2003)
11. Esuli, A., Sebastiani, F.: SentiWordNet: a publicly available lexical resource for opinion mining. In: Proceedings of 5th International Conference on Language Resources and Evaluation (LREC), pp. 417–422 (2006)
12. Hu, M., Liu, B.: Mining and summarizing customer reviews. In: Proceedings of the ACM SIGKDD International Conference on Knowledge Discovery and Data Mining (KDD–2004), pp. 168–177. ACM, New York (2004)
13. Thet, T.T., Na, J.C., Khoo, C.: Aspect-Based Sentiment Analysis of Movie Reviews on Discussion Boards. Journal of Information Science **36**(6), 823–848 (2010)
14. Wiebe, J., Wilson, T., Cardie, C.: Annotating Expressions of Opinions and Emotions in Language. Language Resources and Evaluation **39**(2–3), 165–210 (2005)
15. Khoo, C., Nourbakhsh, A., Na, J.C.: Sentiment Analysis of News Text: A Case Study of Appraisal Theory. Online Information Review **36**(6), 858–878 (2012)
16. Riloff, E., Wiebe, J.: Learning extraction patterns for subjective expressions. In: Proceed-ings of the 2003 Conference on Empirical Methods in Natural Language Processing (EMNLP–2003), pp. 105–112. Association for Computational Linguistics (2003)
17. Jindal, N., Liu, B.: Opinion spam and analysis. In: Proceedings of the 2008 International Conference on Web Search and Data Mining, pp. 219–230. ACM, New York (2008)
18. Manning, C.D., Surdeanu, M., Bauer, J., Finkel, J., Bethard, S.J., McClosky, D.: The stan-ford CoreNLP natural language processing toolkit. In: Proceedings of 52nd Annual Meet-ing of the Association for Computational Linguistics: System Demonstrations, pp. 55–60 (2014)
19. Bird, S., Loper, E., Klein, E.: Natural Language Processing with Python. O'Reilly Media (2009)
20. Pedregosa, F., et al.: Scikit-learn: Machine learning in Python. The Journal of Machine Learning Research **12**, 2825–2830 (2011)

Exploring Context-Sensitive Query Reformulation in a Biomedical Digital Library

Erin Hea-Jin Kim[1], Jung Sun Oh[2], and Min Song[1(✉)]

[1] Department of Library and Information Science, Yonsei University, Seoul, Korea
{erin.hj.kim,min.song}@yonsei.ac.kr
[2] School of Information Sciences, University of Pittsburgh, Pittsburgh, USA
jsoh@pitt.edu

Abstract. We propose a novel semantic query expansion technique that enables inference of contextual information in queries and user information. In the present study, we detect and map bio entities such as gene, protein, and disease in a query to concept tuples, and incorporate user context data based on the PubMed query logs and user profile into the algorithm. In objective evaluation, we can see a concept tuple aided with UMLS concepts adds semantic information to the initial query. In subjective evaluation, we find that in a context-enabled search environment, where context terms that the users are interested in are combined into their initial search terms, users tend to assign higher relevance scores to the retrieval results by these queries.

Keywords: Biomedical digital libraries · Biomedical informatics · Information retrieval · Query expansion · User study · Unified medical language system meta-thesaurus

1   Introduction

Searching for biomedical information is an integral part of daily activities in biomedicine. Unfortunately, current search tools are unable to satisfy a diverse range of biomedical researchers with their unique search goals since these systems yield cookie-cutter results for all users regardless of context [1]. While information needs and behaviors of users vary considerably by contextual factors, traditional search systems employ content-based approaches without considering individual differences and contextual information. This causes, from a user's point of view, irrelevant results to be displayed alongside relevant results. Examining these challenges, we find an opportunity to improve search effectiveness.

One of the fundamental problems in information retrieval (IR) is the mismatch between the words in a user's query and the words in documents used to describe the same concept. Although numerous query expansion techniques attempt to solve this problem, there remains a gap between the query space and the document space. This is because, at least in part, these proposed query expansion techniques employ a one-size-fits-all approach that treats all users and all situations the same way. In other

© Springer International Publishing Switzerland 2015
R.B. Allen et al. (Eds.): ICADL 2015, LNCS 9469, pp. 94–106, 2015.
DOI: 10.1007/978-3-319-27974-9_10

words, traditional query expansion techniques ignore contextual information in queries and user-specific information, leading to a failure to satisfy a broad range of user query needs nuanced by such contextual information.

Thus, for bridging the gap between what the user wants and what the formulated queries find, we posit that not only the key conceptual terms but also the peripheral terms hinting at the user's context and intention should be considered in the query expansion process. In this paper, we introduce a novel semantic query expansion where an ontology-based concept expansion is supplemented with contextual terms to improve the ordering of the displayed results. Our approach finds and maps conceptual terms in a query to concept tuples derived from a domain ontology. In addition, the proposed approach incorporates user context data based on PubMed query logs and user profiles into its algorithm. From a usability standpoint, the proposed system is particularly suited to the challenges resulting from the diversity of potential users of the system in terms of their background and biomedical knowledge.

This paper is structured as follows: we begin with a discussion of related works and background information of user context in section 2. Section 3 presents a detailed description of our approach. In section 4, we analyze the experiment results followed by discussion in section 5.

2 Related Work

2.1 Ontology-Based Approach

Although corpus-wide statistical analysis is broadly used, this method has some drawbacks. Co-occurrence terms are often too general and consume a considerable amount of computing resources [2-3]. Some studies have found that expansion terms from domain-specific knowledge sources are more effective than those provided by corpus-based analysis methods [4-5]. In the study, we present an ontology-based approach for query expansion.

Srinivasan [6] utilizes retrieval feedback, inspired by relevance feedback, for ontology-based query expansion using MeSH concepts. Although retrieval feedback shows significant performance improvement [6], in the present paper, instead of relevance feedback, we adopt term re-weighting, concept-based mapping, and the semantic relation techniques to make the query expansion algorithm less human involved and increase contextual accuracy in an automatic manner.

For optimal term weighting, Matos et al. [7] suggest user-definable weights for the classes of concepts utilized in the query expansion. Their method performs a concept-oriented query expansion, but it allows users control over the weights of different concepts. A concept-based query expansion discovers concepts in a query or a document and links them to one another [7-9]. To discover concepts, MeSH or the Metathesaurus, a component of the Unified Medical Language System (UMLS), is commonly employed [4], [6], [10-12] in biomedical retrieval systems.

Semantic query expansion techniques exploit a semantic network constructed from knowledge sources [13-14]. These systems rely on domain knowledge of healthcare professionals to endorse semantic relations among the suggested medical concepts for higher success rates. To overcome this issue, we assign class labels compiled from the lists of classes based on the domain-specific taxonomies to the concept tuple which is one of three elements of our approach for detection of concepts in a query.

2.2   Approach Based on User Profile and Query Logs

Current tools such as PubMed do not incorporate the user's context into the searching and mining process of biological discovery [15]. To make systems truly context-enabled, along with a user's input, the system should be able to automatically extract information about the context in which documents are consulted during the mining process.

Among others, a promising approach to mining user context is to use user query logs or past queries [16-19]. Fonseca et al. [19] displayed a concept-based query expansion technique by generating concepts from query logs. Their approach needs extra effort from users in selection of the concept related to the current query. This forces the user to choose one concept, the most related to the query. Unlike this approach, our query expansion technique automatically determines the semantically related terms in context term index built by PubMed query logs using the Random Indexing (RI) algorithm to reduce human involvement in the query expansion process.

3   Method

In this section, we describe the proposed query expansion approach including the mining techniques for incorporating relevant conceptual and contextual information

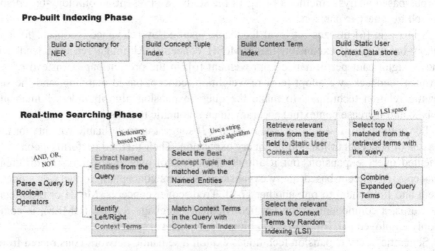

Fig. 1. The proposed system architecture.

into an expanded query. The proposed approach requires several data sources pre-built: a bio-entities dictionary, a concept tuple index, a context term index, and a user profile. We will explain these sources more in depth in this section. Figure 1 shows the system architecture of the proposed approach. The details of each phase are explained in the subsequent sections.

3.1 Incorporating Inference of User Intent into Query Expansion

In order to infer the user contextual information in a query, we presume a query contains two parts; conceptual terms, called named entities in our experiment and context terms. Figure 2 below shows an example of a decomposed user query.

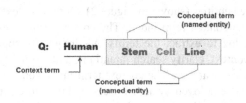

Fig. 2. Decomposed user query by detecting named entities.

Building a Dictionary for NER and Concept Tuple Index. We detect named entities for conceptual terms in a query with the dictionary-based Name Entity Recognition (NER) technique. We adopt a dictionary-based NER instead of a supervised learning approach because the supervised learning-based NER typically takes a long sequence of words such as a sentence, but a query consists of one or two terms in most cases, which makes it impractical in detecting named entities in a query. We constructed the dictionary with Unified Medical Language System (UMLS). A dictionary entry is a concept tuple that consists of {UMLS concept, semantic type, class}. The concept in a tuple is a noun, a noun phrase, or a combination of adjective and noun extracted from UMLS and converted to a singular form to eliminate word variations. The semantic type for each concept is also drawn from UMLS. The third component of our concept tuple, class, is the top level concept for a concept entry. Since UMLS does not provide class information, we compiled the lists of classes based on the taxonomies by Fan and Friedman [20] and Bodenreider and McCray [21] and assigned relevant class label to each concept to complete the tuple. The total number of tuples is 452,825. In order to select the best concept tuples that match the named entities in a query, we used an approximate string matching algorithm.

Table 1 shows the sample entries of a concept tuple. If the bio entity portion of a user query is found in a concept tuple, we add the semantic type of the concept tuple to the query.

Table 1. Sample entries of concept tuple.

Concept	Semantic Type	Class
(131)I-Macroaggregated Albumin	Amino Acid, Peptide, or Protein	gene_protein
1,4-alpha-Glucan Branching Enzyme	Amino Acid, Peptide, or Protein	gene_protein
1-Carboxyglutamic	Acid Amino Acid, Peptide, or Protein	gene_protein
1-Sarcosine-8-Isoleucine	Angiotensin II Amino Acid, Peptide, or Protein	gene_protein

Building Context Term Index. We define a context term of a query as a term that is not part of the named entities (shown in Figure 2). Once a context term is identified, it is compared with the context term index. The context term index is built by mining the PubMed query log to extract the terms that frequently appear near conceptual terms to establish context, clarify search intentions, and/or qualify the meaning of the concepts in biomedical searches. The context term index contains an aggregated collection of query terms employed by actual users, and therefore supplements the ontology-based concept tuples. The National Library of Medicine (NLM) makes a part of PubMed query log data publicly available for research. It consists of 3 million queries. To build a context term index, we treat each session as a document unit and the queries that the respective user used during the session as a bag of words in a document. We built the index with the Lucene indexing software (http://lucene.apache.org/core/). To determine whether the context portion of a query is matched with the context term index, we employ a Random Indexing (RI) algorithm [22].

Building Static User Context Data. Here, we assume that users have registered the subjects or topics of their interest in their profile, and incorporate the user profiles data into query expansion. Top N terms relevant to subject terms that a user needs to supply in the user profile are compared with a query. If there is a good match (based on string similarity) between a profile term and a query term, we assign a higher weight to the matched query term(s), and also add the profile terms that have a similarity score higher than our threshold to the expanded query. To find the profile terms related to the current query, we use a semantic similarity score based on Jiang and Conrath's algorithm [23]. The algorithm combines a lexical taxonomy structure with corpus statistical information.

3.2   Steps of the Proposed Approach

Our query expansion technique consists of three steps: applying the concept tuple from dictionary-based NER, adopting context terms from PubMed query logs and user profile, and reassigning weight. The details of these steps are as follows:

Step 1: Apply Concept Tuple. Once an original query is input by the user, the system breaks the query into chunks by Boolean Operators such as 'OR', 'AND', and 'NOT'. For each chunk, the system detects named entities, and finds the best concept tuple for each named entity using Language Model based weighting. The semantic type of a concept from the matching concept tuple is added to the query in this step.

Step 2: Apply Context terms from Query Logs and User Profile. Next, the system locates context terms besides extracted named entities, and selects the best context terms from the context term index built from the PubMed query log (in space of LSI). In addition, Top N terms relevant to subject terms in the user profile are compared with a query.

Step 3: Assign Weight. Term weight is determined by whether a portion of a query is a concept tuple or a context term. The higher the weight given a term, the more significant it becomes when using the ranking module. We set weights by trial and error. The supplement bio entity detected in the user query is assigned the weight of 1.5, whereas the weight 2 is assigned to core bio entities such as gene or disease. If terms except for bio entity terms are matched with the context term index, we assign a 1.2 weight to the terms. If terms in the bio entity or the context term category are matched with the user profile, the highest weight is reassigned to them. Additional terms added during query expansion process are given a weight of 1. For instance, we assign weights to terms in the query "the developmental regulator pax6 is essential" as follows:

$$"development"^{1.2}"regulator"^{1.5}"pax6"^{2}"essential"^{1} \qquad (1)$$
$$"Amino\ Acid, Peptide, or\ Protein"^{1}$$

For two bio entity terms, 'regulator' is given 1.5 and 'pax6' are given a weight of 2. Since the term 'pax6' has the matched concept tuple, {pax6.1 protein, Amino Acid, Peptide, or Protein, gene_protein} with a high probability, we add the corresponding semantic type 'Amino Acid, Peptide, or Protein' for query expansion. 'development' is found in the context term index so is set to 1.2. Term 'essential' (an adjective) is not assigned weight, and the rest of terms are excluded in the processing of stopwords removal. Upon completion of the three steps for all query terms, the system combines the expanded query terms and the assigned weights to reformulate the query.

4 Evaluation

To evaluate the performance of our technique, we conducted two different sets of experiments. The first experiment provides an objective comparison of our approach against the golden standard answer sets. The objective evaluation is a traditional evaluation method in IR. The other is a subject-based test, designed to evaluate the proposed technique as a whole, consisting of concept tuples, context terms, and user profiles, for its ability to provide context-sensitive query expansion. Through the subject-based evaluation, we intend to measure the performance from an angle of the real user's seeking behavior. This subjective evaluation is crucial because the ultimate judgment on the effectiveness of query expansion is to be made by the users themselves, especially when it involves user profiles and mining of search contexts as in our technique. The results of each experiment show a different aspect of the usefulness and effectiveness of the proposed system.

4.1   Objective Evaluation

Data Collection. We used the OHSUMED data collection that consists of 348,566 references from MEDLINE including titles and/or abstracts from 270 medical journals over a five-year period (1987-1991). It was created to assist information retrieval research specifically geared to and used for medical text retrieval research [24]. The test set contains 106 queries, each comprising patient information and information request. Each query represents a need for medical information, and is associated with a number of documents in the collection.

Evaluation Method. As the measures for the objective evaluation, we use recall, precision, and F-measure. Recall and precision are two most well-received evaluation methods in information retrieval. Recall is a measure of the ability of a system to present all the relevant records. Precision is a measure of the ability of a system to present only relevant records. F-measure is a single evaluation method combining recall and precision scores. Our primary interest in evaluation is to investigate whether adding concepts, semantic types, and context terms to query expansion improves the performance.

Objective Evaluation Results. In this evaluation, we compare the concept-tuple part of the proposed technique against a baseline system that uses the Language Model (LM) based ranking algorithm. LM is a popular ranking algorithm that achieves high accuracy [25]. In LM-based ranking, documents are ranked based on Bayes' rule; The score of document D with respect to query Q, score (Q,D), is defined as the conditional probability $P(Q|\theta_D)$ where θ_D is a language model estimated based on document D.

For the basic comparison, we used two different sets of document units: 'title only' and 'title plus abstract'. We compare the performance of concept tuples to the popular LM above. Upon investigation of the results by queries, it was found that 37 out of 106 queries return no results at an initial search in the 'Title only' condition, and 22 out of 106 queries in the 'Title+Abstract' condition. Since these queries retrieved no relevant documents at baseline, we changed the objective evaluation setting and divided the sample queries into two groups; Group 1 (no-initial-resulted queries) and Group 2 (ordinary baseline). We intend to distinguish the performance of query expansion on how the concept tuple infers user intent from no-resulted queries more precisely. The results of the first experiments are presented in Table 2-3. We also show the percentage of improvement when we apply our query reformulation strategy; according to paired-samples t-test, there is a statistically significant difference in measured performance between the baseline and the proposed approach (2-tailed, $p < .001$).

Table 2. The comparison of precision, recall, and F-score of Group 1

	Baseline LM		Concept tuple	
	Title only	Title+Abstract	Title only (% increase)	Title+Abstract (% increase)
Avg. Precision	-	-	0.16 (new)	0.24 (new)
Avg. Recall	-	-	0.32 (new)	0.43 (new)
F-score	-	-	0.18 (new)	0.28 (new)

Table 3. The comparison of precision, recall, and F-score of Group 2 (ordinary baseline).

	Baseline LM		Concept tuple	
	Title only	Title+Abstract	Title only (% increase)	Title+Abstract (% increase)
Avg. Precision	0.17	0.18	0.25 (49.70%)	0.32 (80.87%)
Avg. Recall	0.39	0.41	0.42 (5.47%)	0.43 (5.94%)
F-score	0.21	0.22	0.28 (34.04%)	0.34 (50.09%)

Tables 2 and 3 show how concept tuple affects query performance. For queries in Group 1, where the baseline did not yield any result, our query expansion applying concept tuple led to retrieval of relevant documents in all cases, with the average recalls of 0.32 and 0.43 (Title only and Title+Abstract conditions, respectively). For queries in Group 2, concept tuple achieved a superior performance in precision, recall, and F-measure, with a drastic 50.09% increase of F-measure and 80.87% increase of precision in the Title+Abstract condition.

This type of evaluation is not suitable for a personalized search since contextual terms are weighted by incorporating user profile terms; that is, it is very hard to measure the system performance while reflecting individual differences of users into the system performance. Thus, we conduct a subjective evaluation to examine the effectiveness of the proposed approach from the user's perspective.

4.2   Subjective Evaluation

To conduct a subjective evaluation involving human assessment of the results, we recruited 37 students majoring in Biomedical Engineering or related fields at New Jersey Institute of Technology. Prior to performing the user task, participants were asked to fill out a pre-task survey.

User Task. A user task includes multiple actions, or steps, to be considered by an information requester, or seeker, for a particular goal. Each participant was randomly given one of the two task assignments described below. The two tasks are comparable in their complexity in terms of search requirements and steps. Users were not asked to collaborate when completing their information seeking tasks.

> *User Task 1:* OHSUMED MeSH Q1 (Calcimycin)
> *User Task 2:* OHSUMED MeSH Q2 (Abdomen)

Each participant took about 10-15 minutes to work on the task. They were then asked to fill out a post-task survey. The total amount of time to complete the experiment was about 30-35 minutes.

Rotation of Conditions and Tasks. There are four combinations of tasks and system conditions, with the above two tasks rotated between two system conditions – the proposed approach and the baseline. Our approach consists of concept tuples, context terms, and a user profile. The baseline is the language model-based IR technique which was used for the objective evaluation. In order to evenly distribute task assignments with different systems, we randomly divided all participants into four groups in advance. Figure 3 illustrates how these combinations of task assignment and system conditions were randomized. With this rotation design of user tasks and system conditions, potential threats to validity associated with a within-subjects design can be eliminated.

The participants were asked to follow the assignment introduction sent by email to perform the assigned task using the two system conditions in their home. After completing the task, they were asked to send back their results via email and fill out the post-task survey. The participants were told to ask any questions should they arise during the experiment by contacting us via email.

Task Rotation		×	System Conditions	
Q1 (Calcimycin)	Q2 (Abdomen)		ConseQE	Baseline
Q2 (Abdomen)	Q1 (Calcimycin)		Baseline	ConseQE

Fig. 3. Rotation of user's tasks and system conditions.

Participants' Background. 23 male and 14 female participants aged between 20 and 35 completed the experiment. Most of them are master's students. Only 5 participants are PhD students and one participant is an undergraduate student. On a 7-point Likert scale, with 1 as least experienced and 7 as most experienced, most of the 37 participants considered themselves very skillful with the mean of 6.297 in using internet search engines. However, their experience in using digital libraries such as Scopus, ACM and IEEE was very slim with the mean of 3.486.

Subject-based Evaluation Results. After finishing their tasks using the baseline and our approach, each subject was required to fill out a submission template. They wrote down the titles and rankings of relevant documents they found in the search results. The document rankings by users were compared with the answer sets provided as part of the OHSUMED collection. In information retrieval evaluations, subjects usually are unable to examine the entire set of retrieved documents to judge the relevance of each and every document, due to the typically large volume of the retrieval set. Instead, subjects are often instructed to save a certain number of documents that they find relevant. Veerasamy and Belkin [26] proposed the use of interactive recall and precision, which compares the documents saved by subjects with the Golden Standard (GS) answer set that includes documents marked as relevant by an assessor. Interactive precision and recall are defined as follows:

$$Interactive\ recall = \frac{Number\ of\ GS\ relevant\ answer\ sets\ saved\ by\ user}{Number\ of\ GS\ relevant\ documents\ in\ the\ corpus} \quad (2)$$

$$Interactive\ precision = \frac{Number\ of\ GS\ relevant\ documents\ saved\ by\ the\ user}{Total\ number\ saved\ by\ the\ user} \quad (3)$$

In addition to interactive recall and interactive precision, we use Mean Average Precision (MAP) to compare the overall performances of two system conditions. Because of the *within-subject* experimental design, each participant worked on one task in a treatment condition (using the proposed approach) and the other task in the baseline condition (using baseline) for the same task (query). Mean Average Precision (MAP) used this information to objectively compare the two systems. MAP is used for a set of queries and defines the mean of the average precision scores for each query. The formula is shown as below:

$$MAP(Q) = \frac{1}{|Q|}\sum_{j=1}^{|Q|}\frac{1}{m_j}\sum_{k=1}^{m_j}Precision(R_{jk}) \quad (4)$$

where R_{jk} is the set of ranked retrieval results including top k documents and mj is the number of relevant documents in search results.

23 of all received submission templates met the requirements specified for the assignment, 12 for Q1 and 11 for Q2. From each template containing the documents saved by the respective user, we counted those documents that are also in the Golden Standard set. The number of retrieved documents for each query was stored in database.

A paired-samples t-test was conducted to compare the performance when using the baseline versus our approach. There was a significant difference in performance between two conditions: $T=7.579$, $p< .001$ for interactive precision of Q1, $T=3.455$, $p< .001$ for interactive recall of Q1, T=8.028, $p< .001$ for interactive precision of Q2, and $T=7.103$, $p< .001$ for interactive recall of Q2 (df=46, 2-tailed).

Table 4. Subject-based Evaluation Results

		Interactive precision	Interactive recall	MAP
Proposed Technique	Q1	0.329	0.288	0.797
	Q2	0.322	0.655	
Baseline	Q1	0.203	0.083	0.586
	Q2	0.196	0.545	

As shown in Table 4, our approach utilizing user contextual information inferred from concept tuple, query logs, and user profile obtains higher scores in each performance measure than baseline. To be specific, the result of MAP improves from 0.586 to 0.797, which shows 36.0% increase in performance. The experimental results indicate that the queries enriched by automated inference of contextual information yield better retrieval results for users.

5   Discussion and Conclusion

In this paper, we have presented a context-sensitive query expansion technique that integrates inference of user preferences into an ontology-base query expansion. The proposed technique first uncovers concepts from ambiguous queries submitted to search engines by detecting named entities based on concept tuple, and leverages contextual information to deliver better search results. The main advantage of our approach is that, while aiming at personalized searches, it reduces human involvement in the retrieval process by harnessing existing or prebuilt resources with several text mining techniques. Techniques for mining contextual cues used in previous search sessions from query logs, and for incorporating user profiles into query expansion are introduced in this paper as part of the proposed approach.

In order to assess the impact of proposed query expansion on retrieval performance, we conducted two experiments. The results of the objective evaluation show that the concept tuples pull up the overall search performance by adding relevant concepts not present in the initial query. The subject-based evaluation further demonstrates the merits of our approach incorporating contextual information in addition to conceptual information. It was found that, in general, the context-enriched queries achieve better retrieval performance. Another valuable finding is that in a context-enabled search environment, where context terms reflecting user interests and search intents are combined into their initial search terms, users tend to assign higher relevance scores to the results retrieved by such queries. The results of our experiments show that our approach achieves a substantial improvement on the performance compared to a baseline technique in both objective and subject-based evaluations with statistically significant difference, however, the results of retrieval effectiveness vary across queries.

We acknowledge limitations of the proposed technique. For query expansion, original queries are mapped to UMLS concepts by detecting bio-entities via NER. We have not considered term relationships such as synonyms, hypernyms, or hyponyms in our QE algorithm because we assume that they are covered via the semantic type of a concept tuple. This assumption needs to be confirmed in a follow-up study.

Acknowledgements. This work was supported by the National Research Foundation of Korea Grant funded by the Korean Government (NRF-2012S1A3A2033291) and (in part) by the Yonsei University Future-leading Research Initiative of 2015.

References

1. Bai, J., Nie, J.Y., Bouchard, H., Cao, G.: Using query contexts in information retrieval. In: ACM SIGIR Conference on Research and Development in Information Retrieval, pp. 15–22 (2007)

2. Greenberg, J.: Optimal query expansion (QE) processing methods with semantically encoded structured thesauri terminology. J. Am. Soc. Inf. Sci. Technol. **52**(6), 487–498 (2001)

3. Shamim Khan, M., Sebastian, S.: Enhanced web document retrieval using automatic query expansion. J. Am. Soc. Inf. Sci. Technol. **55**(1), 29–40 (2004)

4. Stokes, N., Li, Y., Cavedon, L., Zobel, J.: Exploring criteria for successful query expansion in the genomic domain. Inf. Retr. Boston **12**(1), 17–50 (2009)

5. Xu, X., Zhu, W., Zhang, X., Hu, X., Song, I.Y.: A comparison of local analysis, global analysis and ontology-based query expansion strategies for bio-medical literature search. In: IEEE International Conference on Systems, Man and Cybernetics (SMC 2006), vol. 4, pp. 3441–3446 (2006)

6. Srinivasan, P.: Query expansion and MEDLINE. Inf. Process. Manag. **32**(4), 431–443 (1996)

7. Matos, S., Arrais, J.P., Maia-Rodrigues, J., Oliveira, J.L.: Concept-based query expansion for retrieving gene related publications from MEDLINE. BMC Bioinformatics, **11**, 212 (2010)

8. Leroy, G., Chen, H.: Meeting medical terminology needs-the ontology-enhanced medical concept mapper. IEEE J. Biomed. Health. Inform. **5**(4), 261–270 (2001)

9. Yang, Y., Chute, C.G.: An application of least squares fit mapping to text information retrieval. In: ACM SIGIR conference on Research and Development in Information Retrieval, pp. 281–290 (1992)

10. Aronson, A.R., Rindflesch, T.C.: Query expansion using the UMLS metathesaurus. In: Proc. AMIA. Symp., pp. 485–489 (1997)

11. Díaz-Galiano, M.C., Martín-Valdivia, M.T., Ureña-López, L.A.: Query expansion with a medical ontology to improve a multimodal information retrieval system. Comput. Biol. Med. **39**(4), 396–403 (2009)

12. Lu, Z., Kim, W., Wilbur, W.J.: Evaluation of query expansion using MeSH in PubMed. Inf. Retr. Boston **12**(1), 69–80 (2009)

13. Jain, H., Thao, C., Zhao, H.: Enhancing electronic medical record retrieval through semantic query expansion. Information Systems and E-Business Management **10**(2), 165–181 (2012)

14. Zeng, Q.T., Crowell, J., Plovnick, R.M., Kim, E., Ngo, L., Dibble, E.: Assisting consumer health information retrieval with query recommendations. J. Am. Med. Inform. Assoc. **13**(1), 80–90 (2006)

15. Mosa, A.S.M., Yoo, I.: A study on PubMed search tag usage pattern: association rule mining of a full-day PubMed query log. BMC Med. Inform. Decis. Mak. **13**(1), 8 (2013)

16. Billerbeck, B., Scholer, F., Williams, H.E., Zobel, J.: Query expansion using associated queries. In: Proc. ACM Int. Conf. Inf. Knowl. Manag., pp. 2–9 (2003)

17. Cui, H., Wen, J.R., Nie, J.Y., Ma, W.Y.: Probabilistic query expansion using query logs. In: Proc. Int. World Wide Web Conf., pp. 325–332 (2002)

18. Huang, C.K., Chien, L.F., Oyang, Y.J.: Relevant term suggestion in interactive web search based on contextual information in query session logs. J. Am. Soc. Inf. Sci. Technol. **54**(7), 638–649 (2003)

19. Fonseca, B.M., Golgher, P., Pôssas, B., Ribeiro-Neto, B., Ziviani, N.: Concept-based interactive query expansion. In: Proc. ACM Int. Conf. Inf. Knowl. Manag., pp. 696–703 (2005)

20. Fan, J.W., Friedman, C.: Semantic classification of biomedical concepts using distributional similarity. J. Am. Med. Inform. Assoc. **14**(4), 467–477 (2007)

21. Bodenreider, O., McCray, A.T.: Exploring semantic groups through visual approaches. J. Biomed. Inform. **36**(6), 414–432 (2003)
22. Cohen, T., Schvaneveldt, R., Widdows, D.: Reflective Random Indexing and indirect inference: a scalable method for discovery of implicit connections. J. Biomed. Inform. **43**(2), 240–256 (2010)
23. Jiang, J.J., Conrath, D.W.: Semantic similarity based on corpus statistics and lexical taxonomy. In: International Conference on Research in Computational Linguistics (1997). arXiv preprint cmp-lg/9709008
24. Hersh, W.R., Buckley, C., Leone, T.J., Hickam D.H.: OHSUMED: an interactive retrieval evaluation and new large test collection for research. In: ACM SIGIR conference on Research and Development in Information Retrieval, pp. 192–201 (1994)
25. Liu, X., Croft, W.B.: Statistical language modeling for information retrieval. Annual Review of Information Science and Technology **39**, 2–32 (2005)
26. Veerasamy, A., Belkin, N.J.: Evaluation of a tool for visualization of information retrieval results. In: SIGIR on Research and Development in Information Retrieval, pp. 85–92 (1996)

An Approach to Document Fingerprinting

Yunhyong Kim[1,2](✉) and Seamus Ross[2,1]

[1] University of Glasgow, Glasgow, UK
yunhyong.kim@glasgow.ac.uk, seamus.ross@utoronto.ca
[2] University of Toronto, Toronto, Canada

Abstract. The nature of an individual document is often defined by its relationship to selected tasks, societal values, and cultural meaning. The identifying features, regardless of whether the document content is textual, aural or visual, are often delineated in terms of descriptions about the document, for example, *intended audience, coverage of topics, purpose of creation, structure of presentation* as well as relationships to other entities expressed by *authorship, ownership, production process, and geographical and temporal markers.* To secure a comprehensive view of a document, therefore, we must draw heavily on cognitive and/or computational resources not only to extract and classify information at multiple scales, but also to interlink these across multiple dimensions in parallel. Here we present a preliminary thought experiment for fingerprinting documents using textual documents visualised and analysed at multiple scales and dimensions to explore patterns on which we might capitalise.

Keywords: Text analysis · Natural language processing · Patterns · Readability

1 Introduction

The usefulness and potential of automating appraisal and selection for archival and records management and digital library management has been examined earlier([7], [13]). These and other studies emphasise the availability of multiple classes of metadata if these processes are to be automated ([14]). Further, the process often involves answering a range of questions about the document, addressing information such as *intended audience, coverage of topics, purpose of creation, structure of presentation* as well as relationships to other entities expressed by *authorship, ownership, production process,* as well as *geographical and temporal markers.* Improving mechanisms for automating these processes has significant implications for the construction of digital libraries and the development of information discovery and access services to support both human and machine users.

In 2013, Kim and Ross ([9]), highlighted the potential of bringing together a variety of language processing approaches in a parallel processing workflow as a

---

For proper interpretation of images, colour coding is required. This is available in the electronic version of the proceedings at http://dx.doi.org/10.1007/978-3-319-27974-9_11

© Springer International Publishing Switzerland 2015
R.B. Allen et al. (Eds.): ICADL 2015, LNCS 9469, pp. 107–119, 2015.
DOI: 10.1007/978-3-319-27974-9_11

means of assessing selection and appraisal criteria[1] such as those suggested by the Digital Curation Centre (DCC). The discussion, however, was limited to a very high level consideration of potential with little exploration as to how this might be done and how parallel processing of multiple information classes could benefit selection and appraisal. Each of the document characteristics that come into focus, however, draw heavily on cognitive and/or computational resources to extract, making precise guidelines for a comprehensive extraction framework difficult to implement. Here we step back, to visualise and explore multi-scale multi-dimensional profiles of documents, a *document fingerprint*, that would allow automatically deriving answers to complex questions such as those asked in relation to appraisal and selection in digital preservation.

Typical formulations of document analysis focus on three aspects: form, content, and relationship to other documents. These are usually interlinked and inseparable. To understand the nature of documents, however, it can be useful to attempt independent examination of these layers in parallel. For example, by taking a step back, initially, from the content of the textual language to access content-free form of the text, focus can be redirected to structural and stylistic patterns, just the same as we might study the techniques of a painter divorced from the subject of their painting. Salient features of content (for example, semantic annotation such as general and domain specific named entities) can be explored afterwards and/or in parallel, supported by language specific concepts (e.g., part-speech, chunking, parsing), as can the document's relationship to other information outwith the document itself, to situate it within its temporal and spatial context.

Here we briefly examine the *content-free* form of text that makes explicit structural organisation and the kinds of information to be derived from such analyses. The aim is to move away from document analysis methods that immediately rely heavily on content analysis. This approach aligns with recent efforts to build language identification approaches that do not rely on access to content ([1], [10]). The structural examination is intended to complement the limitations of the bag-of-words model (e.g. the Okapi model [8]) in document analysis, returning to the original discussion of language as not merely a bag-of-words ([6]).

The paper emphasises the potential of examining form, content and relationships in parallel. The argument for carrying out several tasks in parallel for mutual improvement is not new [3]. The consideration of content-free form as a driving factor in information processing, while not new, has had less attention. It is the contention of this paper that automated appraisal can only be made viable by processing tasks to reflect form, content, and document relationship in parallel. Here we propose new first steps towards achieving this goal.

---

[1] http://www.dcc.ac.uk/resources/how-guides/appraise-select-data

2   Analysing Text Structure

There are two immediate ways to divorce content from form when dealing with textual information: the statistical analysis of features common to a wide range of documents and languages, and the transformation of the document to a medium which obscures direct access to content as text. We employ both methods in this paper to demonstrate how they can be used to make transparent document structure. We use the NLTK toolkit[2] to segment text and the Stanford NLP tools[3] to annotate text. The text is then transformed to an image based on the segmentation and annotation.

The document structure presented here uses, among other elements, white space to delimit words and fullstops to delimit sentences. The existence of these delimiters are language dependent characteristics, but the concept of segmentation is present in most human languages, implying that similar types of examination can be applied more widely. For example, while it is well known that white space is not used to delimit words in Chinese, the concept of word segmentation is still in operation and, accordingly, tools have been developed to accommodate this (e.g., the Stanford Word Segmenter[4]).

This discussion depends on two assumptions about the target text:

- Text can be extracted from the object of interest without substantial encoding/decoding problems; and,
- There exist conceptual segmentation of the language into related blocks.

In this discussion, we limit the examination to English texts. English texts typically consist of blocks of text which in turn consist of smaller blocks of text (for example, chapters, followed by paragraphs, followed by sentences). Some types of text adhere to this hierarchy more strictly than others (e.g., plays, for instance, do not). Typically, however, the basic text in English might be considered to have a three-story architecture with the notion of words at the basement of the structure. These words are organised into sentences to form the ground floor of the structure. Sentences, in turn, are organised into additional first-floor data structures (chapters, sections, themes, paragraphs), the most simple structure being line changes or blank lines to enforce block layout.

The structural examination presented is agnostic of identities of textual elements: it focuses on notions of lengths, sizes, and distributions. The length of each word can be measured by the number of characters in the word, the length of each sentence measured by the number of words in the sentence, and the lengths of paragraphs, in turn, can be measured by sentences and/or lines. Theoretically speaking, we could start with characters measured by binary bits rather than starting with words (e.g. a method used in [1] and [10] for language identification). The discussion here, however, is limited to structures designed to be accessible to human perception.

---

[2] http://www.nltk.org/
[3] http://nlp.stanford.edu/software/corenlp.shtml
[4] http://nlp.stanford.edu/software/segmenter.shtml

The computational approach described here is not intended to be perfectly faithful to the concepts of written languages that inspired them. The data are expected to be noisy: the focus is on the potential of numerical patterns in describing textual structure, in particular, those that might help determine higher level concepts mentioned earlier (such as intended audience). For example, sentence lengths and word lengths (often measured by syllables) already play a central role in determining readability[5] (reading ease in relation to your target audience). Understanding structure, could expand this to determine the relationship between structure and readability, which is less understood.

Text segmentation in this paper was carried out with the Python[6] programming language using wordpunct_tokenizer, sent_tokenizer, line_tokenizer, and blankline_tokenizer, as provided by the NLTK toolkit. These tokenizers segment text, constructed with the aim of extracting words (separated from punctuation), sentences, Text separated by new lines, and text blocks separated by blank lines (suggestive of paragraphs). These tools will be applied hierarchically: application of higher level tokenisation followed by lower level tokenization. We will take a brief look at the distribution of text block (words, sentences, paragraphs) sizes, and the structural patterns are further presented in a visualisation to make relationships explicit, a process to be explained further in Section 3.

A brief look at two types of named entity recognition and part-of-speech tagging will be included, to show how document structure (and its relationship to genre such as song lyrics and wikipedia articles), named entity recognition, and part-of-speech tagging can be brought together to diagnose errors. A lot of the language processing tools perform at a reasonable standard already on known types of data (often performing at greater than 90% accuracy). Enhancing overall performance across heterogeneous data requires something new. Some suggest correcting training data ([12]). The argument here suggests that parallel processing to capture different types of information (e.g. document structure, syntax, and named entity), could result in improvement of all processes.

3   From Text to Image

In the first instance, the examination is limited to wikipedia articles, poetry, lyrics, and a tagged PubMed[7] MEDLINE abstracts used in the BioNLP/NLPBA 2004 named entity recognition task[8]. Including an article from the dataset of an information extraction task may seem odd. This article, however, is a great example of structured text. The numbers in Table 3 reflects the number of text blocks extracted using the NLTK tokeniser blankline_tokenize, line_tokenize, sent_tokenize, and, wordpunct_tokenize. The last row of the table presents the number of sentences extracted if the text is not segmented first using lines and blank lines. There is a clear discrepancy between the number of sentences

---

[5] https://en.wikipedia.org/wiki/Readability
[6] https://www.python.org/
[7] http://www.ncbi.nlm.nih.gov/pubmed
[8] http://www.nactem.ac.uk/tsujii/GENIA

extracted using the two methods, and, in the case of the poem, lyrics, and dataset article, the difference is enormous. This confirms what we already know as being common practice: new lines are used everywhere to format these latter types of documents. In Figures 1, 2 and 3, we present, respectively, the graphs for the Epic Poem, Wikipedia article 2, and the abstract from the BioNLP 2004 dataset, showing the number of sentences (y-axis) for a given length measured by the number of words (x-axis). The epic poem has been truncated to the first 171 sentences to make it more comparable to the article in the BioNLP 2004 dataset. The figures suggest that a poem is, in some ways, more similar to an abstract tagged and structured to be part of a dataset than it is to Wikipedia article written in prose. This is not too surprising, especially since the poem in this example is a blank verse, i.e., poetry expressed in regular metrical unrhymed lines, almost always iambic pentameter. In fact, the regularity of sentence length distribution in the poem is clear in Figure 4, a graph produced based on an analysis of the entire 96,827 words. In Figures 5 & 6, we have presented a more comprehensive visualisation of the article Wikipedia 1 and the Epic Poem revealing the three-

Table 1. Number of blocks, lines, sentences, words in each document

Segment	Wikipedia 1	Wikipedia 2	Epic Poem	Lyrics 1	Lyrics 2	BioNLP dataset abstract
blankline	55	49	29	5	5	5
line	133	115	10,572	20	33	166
sentence	404	347	11,266	20	44	171
word punct	9,022	10,128	96,827	143	188	416
sentence (from raw)	363	306	1835	6	12	6

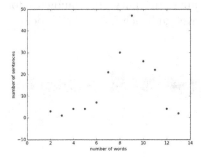

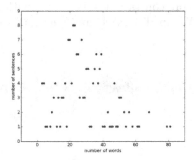

Fig. 1. Epic Poem: graph showing number of sentences (y-axis) for a given length in number of word s (x-axis).

Fig. 2. Wikipedia 2: graph showing number of sentences (y-axis) for a given length in number of word s (x-axis).

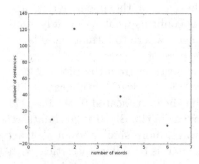 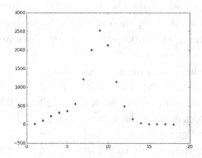

Fig. 3. Tagged Medline abstract: graph showing number of sentences (y-axis) for a given length in number of word s (x-axis).

Fig. 4. Epic Poem: graph showing number of sentences (y-axis) for a given length in number of word s (x-axis) for the entire poem.

story architecture described in Section 2. On the top, we have words represented as lines, their lengths reflecting the number of characters in the words. In the middle, we have sentences represented as rectangles, their widths representing the number of words in the sentences. Finally, on the bottom, we have paragraphs represented, again by rectangles, their widths mirroring the number of sentences in the paragraph. The representation is only based on the first 2,000 words. The figures illustrate immediately that, word lengths vary more widely in the Wikipedia article than they do in the epic poem (maximum word lengths are twenty-one and sixteen, respectively). The situation is similar for sentences. It is, however, also noticeable that paragraphing is used regularly throughout the Wikipedia article, whereas, there are hardly any paragraphs in the epic poem. In fact, there are fifty-five blocks of text separated by a blank line in the Wikipedia article consisting of less than 10,000 words compared to twenty-nine blocks in the epic poem across more than 96,000 words. The lack of basement structure poses barriers to readability: for example, the Flesh-Kincaid readability score contrasts the two texts with a beginning university grade audience for the Wikipedia article and a graduate school level audience for the epic poem.

Fig. 5. Wikipedia 1: structural representation of the article with words on the top (lengths of lines corresponding to number of characters), sentences in the middle (size of rectangles reflect number of words in the sentence), and paragraphs on the bottom.

Fig. 6. Epic Poem: structural representation of the poem with words on the top (lengths of lines corresponding to number of characters), sentences in the middle (size of rectangles reflect number of words in the sentence), and paragraphs on the bottom.

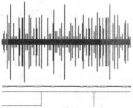

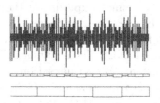

Fig. 7. Visualisation of article from the BioNLP 2004 dataset (top row: words, middle row: sentences, bottom row, paragraphs).

Fig. 8. Visualisation of song lyrics (top row: words, middle row: sentences, bottom row: paragraphs).

For comparison, in Figure 7 & 8, we present similar visualisation for the MEDLINE article from the BioNLP 2004 dataset (tagged with named enties and structured as trainging data), and song lyrics[9], respectively. The visualisation of words show the MEDLINE article to be very regular with short words and longer words alternating from one extreme to the other as if by rule. There is a frequent stream of short words throughout forming the dark belt in the middle. The lyrics, in contrast, has a wider variety of word lengths, with wavelike hills in many places as words get longer and shorter in increasing steps. Both visualisations show a fair amount of regularity at the sentence and paragraph level, where lines are more regular for the article from the dataset while paragraphs are more regular for song lyrics. The visualisation for the words in natural language text are reminiscent of sound waves, but not so much so for the dataset. By translating the frequency of different lengths into sound frequencies after recalibrating to allow a frequency of one to be 20Hz, this stream can be played as music. The result produces a repeated beat stream, including a constant beat just at the edge of the human hearing range. This is representative of the frequent short length words prominent in the image of Figures 5 & 6 as a black band in the middle.

---

[9] Five verse version of "Twinkle Twinkle Little Star".

4   Adding Some Colour

So far, in our discussion we have ignored specific document content and/or classes. Named entity recognition is one way of enriching message understanding. Named entities can be generic, for example, labelling words as instances of location, date, time, person and organisation, or specific to a specialist subject area (e.g. biomedical named entities). So, depending on the recogniser it could provide the reader with a quick summary of topics covered by a document and/or a list of possible candidates to be attributed with authorship, ownership, and geographic and temporal markers.

Just as a small experiment, the first 100 sentences of the article Wikipedia 1 and the Epic Poem were tagged using the Stanford named entity tagger[10] to distinguish four biomedical named entities (DNA, RNA, PROTEIN, CELL TYPE, and CELL LINE). The results are displayed in Figures 9 & 10 as coloured lines in the document word visualisation. The first 100 sentences of the Wikipedia article contained 2013 words, and 0.028% were tagged as biomedical entities, while the first 100 sentences of the poem contained 864 words and 0.0007% of these were returned as instances of biomedical entities. Most of the entities (96.5%) in the Wikipedia article were in the second half of the text, and selected paragraphs seemed to be densely populated with the entities, while 66.6% of words tagged as entities in the poem were in the first half of the poem and seemed to be distributed uniformly across the first half of the text.

Fig. 9. Wikipedia 1: named entity visualisation (blue: DNA, red: RNA, green: protein, magenta: cell type, and yellow: cell line).

Most likely the words tagged as entities in the poem[11] were incorrectly labelled as biomedical entities (in fact, the words were *Eden, Man* and *God*[12] all labelled as PROTEIN). While there are incorrect labels in the Wikipedia article[13] (e.g. "economic elements" labelled as protein; proteins labelled as DNA and vice versa), there were also plenty of correct labels (e.g. amyloid precursor protein labelled correctly as PROTEIN). This little experiment suggests that: 1) knowing the genre of the document (for example, poem versus article) can help us predict the accuracy of named entity recognition; and, 2) the way the named entity recogniser labels the document (number of entities returned; the

---

[10] http://nlp.stanford.edu/software/CRF-NER.shtml
[11] John Milton's "Paradise Lost", available from Project Gutenberg.
[12] Capitals retained from original text.
[13] A page on "Alzheimer's disease."

Fig. 10. Epic Poem: named entity visualisation (blue: DNA, red: RNA, green: protein, magenta: cell type, and yellow: cell line).

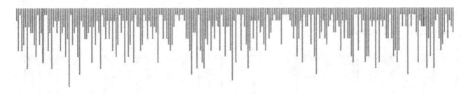

Fig. 11. Wikipedia 1: named entity visualisation (blue: PERSON, red: ORGANISA-TION, green: TIME, magenta: LOCATION, and yellow: DATE).

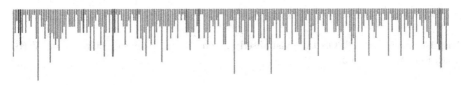

Fig. 12. Epic Poem: named entity visualisation (blue: PERSON, red: ORGANISA-TION, green: TIME, magenta: LOCATION, and yellow: DATE).

distribution of entities), even if the labelling is inaccurate could inform us about document type.

In Figures 11 & 12, we present a visualisation of generic named entity tagging (for LOCATION, PERSON, ORGANIATION, DATE, and TIME) on the same data. With this tagging the tables are turned on the two texts: only 0.006% of the words in Wikipedia 1 are returned with a named entity tag in the first 100 sentences, while, 0.023% of words in the poem are retuned as a named entity. Despite the change in percentage, the labels on the Wikipedia article still appear to be more plausible (53.8%) than that on the poem (20%). This is most likely because the training data for named entity tagging is almost never a set of poems. This raises the conjecture that precision of tagging performance could be boosted by considering genre coverage in training data[14]. Using the taggers in tandem could also improve the performance of both taggers. For example, closer examination shows that the two types of named entity taggers labelled the same entity APP as DNA and as ORGANISATION, respectively. Since an entity is

---

[14] Lack of cross-genre applicability in the literature also observed by Nadeau, D. and Sekine, S. A survey of named entity recognition and classification. phLingvisticae Investigationes, 30 (1): 3–26, 2007.

Fig. 13. Wikipedia 1: POS tags visualised (green: Noun, blue: adjective, pink: Verb, gold: Personal Pronouns).

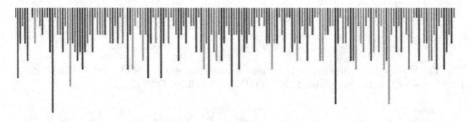

Fig. 14. Epic Poem: POS tags visualised (green: Noun, blue: adjective, pink: Verb, gold: Personal Pronouns).

unlikely to be both DNA and ORGANISATION, this suggests immediately that one or both of the taggers has labelled the entity incorrectly (in fact, the former is correct: APP on its own stands for Amyloid Precursor Protein, hence a type of protein but, here, it is used to denote the gene that encodes the protein). Likewise, in the poem, the two independent taggers (incorrectly) tagged Eden as PROTEIN and ORGANISATION, respectively, again signalling probable error.

In addition to named entities, syntactic tagging and text chunking can provide valuable information in identifying salient concepts. Chunks identify linguistic constituents, and could, potentially be used to re-assess reliability of named entity labelling processes, by making explicit which parts of the sentence can belong together in a phrase to specify conceptual entities. The Stanford POS tagger was used to tag the first 100 sentences of the article Wikipedia 1 and Epic Poem, respectively (Figure 13 & 14). There seem to be differences in relative numbers of words in each class distinguishing the two textual classes (the poem seems to have more pronominal tags). This would need further study to validate but other studies have suggested a relationship between genre and POS tags [5]. The tags can be used to identify the longest adjective (blue), noun (green) and verb (pink). For the article, these were neurodegenerative, disorientation, and understood, respectively. For the poem, these were adventurous, disobedience, and unattempted. Combining structural elements (such as size and location) with functional elements (such as POS tag information) can serve to offer a more comprehensive understanding of topical coverage. More immediately, however, analysing part-of-speech tagging errors can assist simultaneously with resolving errors in named entity recognition. For example, in the poem, *Heavenly* was tagged as a proper noun and ORGANISATION, suggesting the same features can lead to concurring errors.

5   Conclusion

In this research we took a brief look at document structure based on a three-layered architecture consisting of words, sentences and paragraphs. A parallel visualisation of these three levels was explored (in Section 3 above) to highlight possible correlations with document presentation structure, genre, and readability. A substantial amount of information can be gleaned from the documents without analysing their content, which could potentially complement other information extraction tasks, for example, by providing genre information to boost named entity recognition. This analysis has given us confidence to pursue more detailed investigation of the conjecture that many errors resulting from automated content labelling are correlated to document structure and genre. Simple numbers from sentences, words and paragraphs can reveal characteristics of selected text types, such as poems, articles and data structure to enable the first step.

A proper understanding of document structure is only possible by moving away from the bag-of-words model to an approach that considers multiple structures and processes it in parallel. Document structure is integral to understanding document genre, and determining the purpose of creation and use. The changing structure over time tells a story of its own about purpose (e.g., Jane Austen's *Emma* will exhibit a different structure depending on whether it is an edition intended for human consumption or it is part of a computational linguistics corpus).

At the same time named entity recognition captures candidate entities that identify authorship, ownership, affiliations and geographical and temporal markers. Used with entities of specialist domains, named entity recognition can provide a description of document topics. In this paper we saw that tags from one tagger could potentially assist another tagger in *self-assessing* possibility of error. Further, errors can concur around the same area with respect to independent taggers. The system can identify areas of text that might pose an increased level of difficulty for taggers by having access to the performance of several taggers.

The visualisation for the words is reminiscent of sound waves and so it should be because document content is no different from other signals of information. By translating the frequency of different lengths into sound frequencies, this stream can be played as music to reveal a repeating background beat with no specific melody. As a poetic twist we might even conjecture that it is the content analysis that introduces melody to text; characterising textual melodiousness might provide a new metric for genre classification.

6   Next Steps

This research illuminates the potential of visualising and analysing multi-scale and multi-dimensional document characteristics in parallel. These results show that more research will be required if a clear path for document fingerprinting is to be established. Our underlying research is limited to aspects that might lead to answering questions related to document characteristics (e.g., intended audience, geographical markers) discussed in Section 1, and, even in this we only examine some of the information presentation, extraction and classification issues that might be involved; going forward a wider range should be explored.

The discussion is further limited to textual documents. The general concepts, however, are likely to apply equally well to non-textual content as long as it has a natural hierarchical segmentation (e.g. in the case of images, "components" that form "objects" that form "scenes"). The discussed features (e.g. intended audience, topic coverage, authorships) still apply in aural, visual contexts. This would clearly be one of the next targets for research and may unearth further patterns across document types on which we might capitalise.

This research is intended as ground work for multiple other applications. Effective pipelining of automation and the application of multiple techniques in tandem provides the most viable method for addressing resource management in archival and records-based digital libraries. A variety of approaches have been proposed to support this automation and our own investigations have in the past focused on document analysis. Here we have shown that other methods have potential to enhance the precision and recall of these processes.*Document fingerprinting* has implications for areas such as author attribution([4]), near duplicate detection ([11]), and plagiarism detection ([2]). These, however, will also depend on the scalability and efficiency of the approach, suggesting the necessity for testing performance on larger datasets.

Acknowledgement. This research was supported in part by the Universities of Glasgow and Toronto, and the European Commission through Blogforever (FP7-ICT-2009-6-269963). We benefited from insightful observations by anonymous ICADL2015 reviewers.

References

1. Baldwin, T., Lui, M.: Language identification: the long and the short of the matter. In: Human Language Technologies: The 2010 Annual Conference of the North American Chapter of the Association for Computational Linguistics, HLT 2010, pp. 229–237. Association for Computational Linguistics, Stroudsburg (2010). http://dl.acm.org/citation.cfm?id=1857999.1858026
2. Barrón-Cedeño, A., Vila, M., Martí, M., Rosso, P.: Plagiarism meets paraphrasing: Insights for the next generation in automatic plagiarism detection. Comput. Linguist. **39**(4), 917–947 (2013). http://dx.doi.org/10.1162/COLI_a_00153

3. Cohen, H., Crammer, K.: Learning multiple tasks in parallel with a shared annotator. In: Ghahramani, Z., Welling, M., Cortes, C., Lawrence, N.D., Weinberger, K.Q. (eds.) NIPS, pp. 1170–1178 (2014). http://dblp.uni-trier.de/db/conf/nips/nips2014.html#CohenC14

4. Donais, J.A., Frost, R.A., Peelar, S.M., Roddy, R.A.: A system for the automated author attribution of text and instant messages. In: Proceedings of the 2013 IEEE/ACM International Conference on Advances in Social Networks Analysis and Mining, ASONAM 2013, pp. 1484–1485. ACM, New York (2013). http://doi.acm.org/10.1145/2492517.2500308

5. Fang, A.C., Cao, J.: Enhanced genre classification through linguistically fine-grained pos tags. In: Otoguro, R., Ishikawa, K., Umemoto, H., Yoshimoto, K., Harada, Y. (eds.) PACLIC, pp. 85–94. Institute for Digital Enhancement of Cognitive Development, Waseda University (2010)

6. Harris, Z.: Distributional structure. Word **10**(23), 146–162 (1954)

7. Harvey, R.: Appraisal and selection. In: Curation Reference Manual. Digital Curation Center (2007). http://www.dcc.ac.uk/resources/curation-reference-manual/completed-chapters/appraisal-and-selection

8. Jones, K.S., Walker, S., Robertson, S.E.: A probabilistic model of information retrieval: development and comparative experiments - part 1. Inf. Process. Manage. **36**(6), 779–808 (2000). http://dblp.uni-trier.de/db/journals/ipm/ipm36.html#JonesWR00

9. Kim, Y., Ross, S.: Closing the loop: assisting archival appraisal and information retrieval in one sweep. In: Proceedings of the 76th ASIS&T Annual Meeting: Beyond the Cloud: Rethinking Information Boundaries, ASIST 2013, pp. 16:1–16:10. American Society for Information Science, Silver Springs (2013). http://dl.acm.org/citation.cfm?id=2655780.2655796

10. Lui, M., Lau, J.H., Baldwin, T.: Automatic detection and language identification of multilingual documents. TACL **2**, 27–40 (2014)

11. Manku, G.S., Jain, A., Das Sarma, A.: Detecting near-duplicates for web crawling. In: Proceedings of the 16th International Conference on World Wide Web, WWW 2007, pp. 141–150. ACM, New York (2007). http://doi.acm.org/10.1145/1242572.1242592

12. Manning, C.D.: Part-of-speech tagging from 97% to 100%: is it time for some linguistics? In: Gelbukh, A.F. (ed.) CICLing 2011, Part I. LNCS, vol. 6608, pp. 171–189. Springer, Heidelberg (2011). http://nlp.stanford.edu/manning/papers/CICLing2011-manning-tagging.pdf

13. Oliver, G., Ross, S., Guercio, M., Pala, C.: Report on automated re-appraisal: Managing archives in digital libraries (2008). https://www.academia.edu/10963951/Report_on_Automated_re-Appraisal_Managing_Archives_in_Digital_Libraries_Deliverable_6.10.1_

14. Oliver, G., Kim, Y., Ross, S.: Documentary genre and digital recordkeeping: red herring or a way forward? Archival Science **8**, 295–305 (2008)

A Linked Data Model to Aggregate Serialized Manga from Multiple Data Providers

Senan Kiryakos[✉] and Shigeo Sugimoto

Graduate School of Library, Information and Media Studies,
University of Tsukuba, Tsukuba, Japan
Senank@gmail.com, Sugimoto@slis.tsukuba.ac.jp

Abstract. Many different institutions create bibliographic data for manga, a style of Japanese comic. These institutions typically describe the same resources, but in ways that differ depending on their institution type. The sharing of this data would result in a more complete bibliographic data landscape for manga; the majority of this data, however, exists in isolation from other institutions. In seeking to combine this data, this paper presents a Linked Data model for the aggregation of bibliographic data for manga. The Europeana Data Model was used as the basis for the aggregation functions, while the Dublin Core and BIBFRAME vocabularies were used for bibliographic description. Data from Monash University's JSC Manga Library, the Media Arts Database from the Japanese Agency for Cultural Affairs, and Web resources was collected, and records suitable for aggregation were identified. The result is a conceptual model that enables the aggregation of bibliographic data for manga, creating a more complete bibliographic data landscape for manga.

Keywords: Metadata · Europeana Data Model · BIBFRAME · Comics · Metadata aggregation · Popular culture database · Bibliographic data for manga

1   Introduction

Manga, a type of Japanese comic, is increasing in popularity worldwide. As recreational and academic interest in manga grows, so too does the need for various institutions to better describe their manga collections for the benefit of their users. A wealth of descriptive data already exists, created by special institutions, libraries with a focus on manga, or by hobbyists on the Web, and can be found in varying levels of detail and across different languages. Different institutions are typically describing the same manga resources, so the exchange of data would be useful for enriching the data of all parties involved. As most bibliographic data for manga exists in isolated "silos," however, this data exchange is not currently taking place.

In an attempt to bring together these various descriptions about similar manga resources, this paper presents a conceptual model for the aggregation of bibliographic data for manga in Linked Data (LD) formats using Semantic Web technologies. Bibliographic data sourced from Monash University's Japanese Studies Centre (JSC) Manga Library (MML) and the Media Art Database (MAD) for the Japanese Agency

© Springer International Publishing Switzerland 2015
R.B. Allen et al. (Eds.): ICADL 2015, LNCS 9469, pp. 120–131, 2015.
DOI: 10.1007/978-3-319-27974-9_12

for Cultural Affairs, created by Toppan Printing Co. Ltd., along with Web data from Wikipedia, was examined. Metadata schemas using Dublin Core (DC), Europeana Data Model (EDM), and BIBFRAME vocabularies were then applied to the data to facilitate their application to the aggregation model. Using OpenRefine software and leveraging information from DBpedia, related manga resources within the different datasets were identified as available for aggregation within the model. The final result is a conceptual LD model that enables the aggregation of institutional metadata for manga, connecting data across institutions for both individual manga volumes, and higher-level, conceptual FRBR Work level manga resources, while providing the basis for possible future Semantic Web applications, such as a manga data Web portal or manga authority resource.

The remainder of the paper is organized as follows. Section 2 outlines the current landscape for bibliographic data for manga, and discusses the study's research goals. Section 3 examines related works, and Section 4 presents the aggregation model and details its contents and functions. Section 5 examines how available bibliographic data for manga works within the model and how resources are identified as available for aggregation. Lastly, Section 6 discusses and concludes the results.

2   Background

2.1   Overview

Different institution types describe Manga in different ways. These descriptions differ depending on what bibliographic properties an institution chooses to describe, as well as to what level of granularity. In addition, different "levels" for manga can be described, namely Work and Item, referring to two different entities within the Functional Requirements for Bibliographic Records (FRBR) model. Institutions with records for individual volumes of manga are describing the resource in terms resembling the FRBR "Item" entity. At this level, one is able to not only describe broader properties such as author or main title, but also aspects such volume summaries, chapter titles, physical dimensions, and others. Cataloguing an entire manga series as a single record more closely resembles the FRBR "Work" level, which can describe a resource more broadly and in terms agnostic of specific publications or volumes. With these differences in mind, the following section details how different institution types handle bibliographic description of manga, and what level of description they focus on.

2.2   Bibliographic Data for Manga

Bibliographic Data for manga exists in various locations and typically comes from one of three data provider types. First, institutions traditionally responsible for bibliographic description, i.e. libraries, may collect some manga or specialize in it entirely. Many US academic library collections such as Stanford, Cornell, Ohio State, et al., contain manga. Internationally, special libraries dedicated entirely to manga also exist, such as Kyoto Manga Museum or Monash University's Japanese Studies Centre (JSC) Manga Library MML. Data here may be at the Work or Item level, dependent on cataloguing practices; a general series record is closer to the Work entity, while the inclusion of publisher or volume specific information means the data is describing manga at the Item level. These institutions may have strong authority data, but typically lack granular information about manga that fans of pop culture resources are quite interested in [1].

The second provider type is organizations that deal with manga from the role of a business or manufacturer and may keep bibliographic databases for manga as a part of larger cultural resource data project. An example of this is the Media Art Database (MAD) hosted by Agency for Cultural Affairs of the Japanese Government, which contains databases for Manga, Anime, Games and other Media Art, development of which was carried out by Toppan Printing Company. In this paper, MAD-M will be used to refer to the manga-focused databases. Depending on the size and data keeping practices of the organization, these databases can be excellent sources of granular bibliographic data for manga. As these databases are normally kept for business purposes, however, they are usually private or unpublished, so the data can be difficult to access. Originally this was the case with the MAD-M, though it has recently been published online at http://mediaarts-db.jp/. Depending on organization practices, data from these providers may be at the Work or Item level, but typically Item level or both. The MAD-M, for example, keeps separate files on entire manga series, as well as individual volumes of manga. While, similar to libraries, the data here may be authoritative, this is dependent on the organization and typically varies from source to source. The level of granularity here is typically higher than that of libraries, but is again dependent on the organization. One involved in printing and distribution may record data on specific date and price originally published, for example.

The last common data provider type is hobbyist-oriented Web resources. These can be general-purpose resources that contain some manga data, such as Wikipedia, or dedicated manga fan-sites such as www.manga-updates.com. As they exploit the dedication of the fan-base and do not have to serve a specific function such as serving library patrons or cataloguing business needs, Web resources can contain a lot of unique bibliographic data for manga. Like many user-editable sources, however, the authority may be questionable. Similar to the previous data providers, the data here can be either at the Work or Item level. General Wikipedia articles that describe an entire manga series are Work level resources, while articles specific to certain manga volumes are Item level resources. Like the second provider type, this information is more granular than libraries, but the information is not organization-centric and includes data typically absent from the other provider types, such as plot summaries or character biographies.

2.3   Models for Bibliographic Description and Aggregation

While the different data providers may be describing the same manga resources, they typically do so using different models of bibliographic description. For libraries, data may be described using formal or informal models. Formal models here refer to traditional bibliographic description models and methods for libraries, such as those based on MARC, AACR2, RDA, etc. Recently, the US Library of Congress has proposed a new LD model and vocabulary for library bibliographic description called BIBFRAME, short for Bibliographic Framework. As a LD model that is aimed primarily but not solely at libraries, BIBFRAME may be an interesting option to investigate as a LD-capable bibliographic description model for non-library institutions that create bibliographic descriptions similar to those produced by libraries. The informal models in this space are institution-specific and are used by smaller, specialized manga libraries. Monash's JSC Manga Library is an example of this; their holdings are stored and accessed through spreadsheet files rather than ILS and OPAC, so the data model and vocabulary used are simply the column headers within the spreadsheet.

This is also the case with the second provider type, organizations that maintain project-based or activity-based databases. These databases are typically not based on standard bibliographic description models, but instead are uniquely developed and designed to serve the organizational needs that the database is meant to support. Librarians or professional cataloguers may assist in the creation of the database, as is the case with the MAD-M, but the end result is a tabular database with institution-specific column headers rather than a standard data model for bibliographic description.

Web resources creating bibliographic data for manga may do so according to formal, semi-formal, or informal models, depending on the data provider. Fan-sites such as manga-updates do not use a formal data model and simply create HTML pages containing bibliographic data for manga. Wikipedia functions similarly, though a structured data version of Wikipedia exists as DBpedia. One can consider DBpedia's data to be semi-formal, as their pages are structured as LD, but the content itself is editable data sourced from Wikipedia.

Separate from these bibliographic description models are aggregation models used to aggregate data from multiple providers for related resources. The most popular aggregation model is the Europeana Data Model (EDM), which is the underlying data model that serves the Europeana cultural heritage portal. Designed to collect information from various European cultural heritage institutions, EDM is a method of collecting, connecting, and enriching metadata [2]. While EDM typically deals with museums and artwork rather than libraries, organizations, and manga, the core function of aggregating data from multiple providers for the same resource make investigating EDM for use with manga worthwhile.

2.4   Research Goals

As mentioned in Section 2.2, different provider types commonly maintain data of different granularity. While ideally, the data between these professional and hobbyist institution types could be shared and exchanged to improve the granularity of all bibliographic records, most of the data discussed currently exists in isolated "silos."

In seeking to address this issue, this study aims to improve the current bibliographic landscape for manga by bringing together data from different providers for related manga resources, creating more comprehensive bibliographic records. To achieve this, records from different data providers will be applied to an aggregation model, allowing single manga resources to be described by different institutions, from different points of view, and of differing levels of granularity. To facilitate this, LD models will be applied to bibliographic data for manga, allowing the data to not only work within the LD aggregation model, but to encourage the exchange and reuse of the data on the Semantic Web. The aggregation of data from multiple provider types on the Semantic Web will hopefully improve the granularity of these resources, which will better serve the needs of both hobbyists and professionals, be it on the Web or within institutions.

Apart from the users' interest in minutiae, manga differs from other serials in that the key relationship is one of succession between volumes, as the story content within manga typically requires sequential, volume-to-volume reading to be understood, rather than the hierarchical relationship that exists between article and journal. These factors justify the exploration of a model unique to manga, rather than attempting to satisfy the medium's needs with a generalized serial model.

3   Related Works

Southwick's [3] project looked at the transformation of digital collections metadata from the University of Nevada, Las Vegas, into LD. The author lists the motivations for the project as the desire to break up the isolated data silos in which the digital collections metadata resides, to interconnect their data to data from other providers, and improved search capabilities of relevant data no matter its origin. Though the intended use differs, similarly to this study Southwick used both OpenRefine and EDM, making this a particularly valuable project to examine.

In a discussing the benefits and challenges for the adoption of LD in libraries, Gonzales [4] sees BIBFRAME as a way to connect library bibliographic materials with other resources on the web. The challenges to BIBFRAME's adoption, such as a current lack of large cooperative effort towards implementation, are discussed, but the author views BIBFRAME as having the potential to allow libraries integrate their authoritative data with user-generated data from the web, a similar goal to one presented in this study.

Zapounidou, Sfakakis, and Papatheodorou have authored two related papers of particular relevance to this study, as both discuss the use of BIBFRAME within EDM. Central to both papers is the mapping of BIBFRAME core classes to EDM to ensure interoperability when using both models. The initial paper [5] contains a single base mapping of the BIBFRAME core classes to the EDM core classes. In the following work [6] the authors extend the former by mapping to different paradigms, namely a 2012 EDM library metadata alignment report, and an EDM-FRBRoo (FRBR-object oriented) profile. This second paper uses the ore:Proxy class in EDM, which allows for different institutional descriptions of the same ProvidedCHO. While both works focused mainly on monographs and not serials, the core ideas behind the mappings were nonetheless influential in the formulation of the model used in this study.

He, Mihara, Nagamori, & Sugimoto used Wikipedia articles for manga, accessed using DBpedia, as a method of identifying FRBR Works using Linked Open Data (LOD) resources [7]. The authors used DBpedia as a pseudo-authority in order to identify Work entities of manga housed in the Kyoto Manga Museum's catalogue. This study seeks to build on the ideas of multi-level manga entities and the leveraging of LD resources put forth in these works, in particular the use of LD resources for identifying Work level resources available for aggregation.

4   Model for the Aggregation of Bibliographic Data for Manga

Based on the aforementioned research goals, this section presents an aggregation model that seeks to perform various functions. The model aggregates data for manga resources from multiple data providers at both the Work and Item levels, while also expressing both hierarchical and successive relationships between manga resources. The remaining portions of this section will detail these functions within the model.

Figure 1 shows an overview of the aggregation model defined in this study based both on EDM and BIBFRAME. Groups 1 and 2 represent data and functional components to be used for aggregating Item level, or individual manga volume data, from multiple providers. Groups 5 and 6 are similar, but instead represent manga at the Work level. The group 3 and 4 represent EDM components required to describe Item and Work-level Expressions, as well as establish relationships between related manga resources.

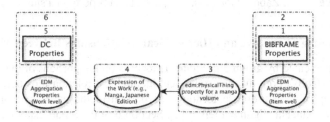

Fig. 1. Simplified overview of the full aggregation model

4.1   Aggregation for Bibliographic Data

Figure 2 provides a detailed look at groups 1 and 2. These groups include all of the core classes of the EDM model, plus the ore:Proxy property that is required for maintaining unique data provided by different institutions, along with bibliographic description properties from an institution, represented by the BIBFRAME Properties node. In this figure, the edm:ProvidedCHO represents an example single volume of manga, labeled "Manga Volume 2;" in group 6, this would instead be the Work entity representing the entire manga intellectual property, e.g. "One Piece."

Figure 2 is an example of a single institution's data being attached to a single manga volume, represented by edm:ProvidedCHO. Additional institutions replicate this group of properties for their own data, which is then also attached to the edm:ProvidedCHO. Unique institutional bibliographic data, represented by groups 1 and 5, is attached to their own respective ore:Proxy properties, rather than the ProvidedCHO itself. This allows for separate institutions to describe the same volume of manga, or ProvidedCHO, from their respective point of views, without data being overridden, conflicting, etc.

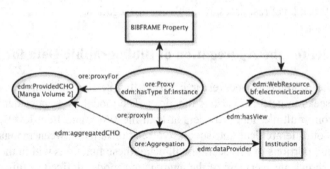

Fig. 2. Bibliographic data from a single provider and EDM properties required for aggregation

The bf:hasAnnotation property labels the edm:WebResource as a bf:electronic-Locator according to EDM's mandatory requirement of edm:WebResource property. As a URI representing the ProvidedCHO is an allowed form of a WebResource, it was decided that the use of the bf:electronicLocator property, which represents an electronic location from which the resource is available,[1] would be the most consistently available WebResource to use; Zapounidou et al. [5,6] used this property in a similar role.

4.2 Modeling Successive and Hierarchical Relationships Between Manga

Figure 3, represented by group 3 in Figure 1, focuses on the portions of the aggregation model that establish both the successive and hierarchical relationships between manga resources. Information useful in forming this portion of the model was found in the EDM library metadata alignment report [8]. Section 6 of the report examined the use of EDM for serials, with a focus on journals and their articles, and modeled two types of serial relationships – hierarchical relationships using the property dcterms:isPartOf, and successive relationships, using edm:isNextInSequence. This model uses both, with edm:isNextInSequence connecting successive volumes of manga, and dcterms:isPartOf connecting all available volumes to their respective Work level resource.

The use of edm:PhysicalThing in this model is unique and was not used a similar way, by Zapounidou et al. [5,6] or Angjeli [8]. The author felt the use of edm:PhysicalThing was necessary to distinguish between the different levels of FRBR entities. Instead of using the broad class edm:InformationResource (see http://onto.dm2e.eu/edm#InformationResource), edm:PhysicalThing is used to represent the manga at the volume, or Item level. The edm:InformationResource property is instead used with FRBR Work level descriptions.

---

[1] http://bibframe.org/vocab/electronicLocator.html

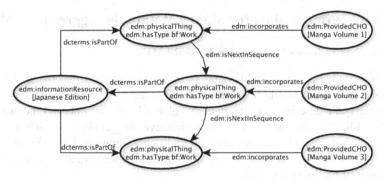

Fig. 3. Successive and hierarchical relationships within the model

4.3   Work Entity and Related Resources

The edm:InformationResource property labeled [Japanese Edition] in Figure 4 represents the Japanese manga, and, like Wikipedia entries, the main conceptual Work of the resource. In order to describe the Work level using bibliographic data, an instance of edm:ProvidedCHO is attached. This Work level entity represents the conceptual Work in a way that resembles a general Wikipedia entry.

This portion also features additional example edm:InformationResource properties that represent how related non-manga resources can be connected to manga instances within the model. The examples used are an English translation of the manga, and an anime adaptation. As the Work level in the model is similar to the FRBR Work entity, the high level Work instance can represent various media formats belonging to the same manga series. Using Wikipedia data to describe this high level Work instance is also valid because, as mentioned, the Wikipedia entries for manga act as umbrella articles for related non-manga works in the series.

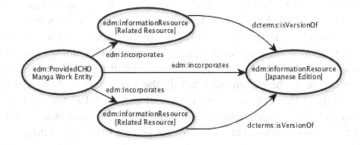

Fig. 4. The Work level entity and example related, non-manga resources

5   Bibliographic Data for Manga Within the Aggregation Model

5.1   Manga Volumes Described in BIBFRAME

After an examination of available datasets, it was determined that the BIBFRAME model and vocabulary would be suitable for use in the aggregation model in performing bibliographic description at the Item or volume level. Not only did the properties of the BIBFRAME vocabulary allow for a high level of granularity, which is required at this level, but the lack of dependence on traditional library technologies meant that BIBFRAME was useful for non-library institutions that also wanted to describe granular levels of bibliographic data.

To test the use of BIBFRAME in the model, the MAD-M and MML databases were used for a single manga volume. Separate BIBFRAME-based mappings were created based on the properties available in each dataset's tabular files, which were then applied to the data using the OpenRefine software and its RDF extension, transforming the tabular data into RDF data, a requirement to work within the LD aggregation model. Once applied to the model, each dataset provides unique data for individual manga volumes, thus increasing the granularity for manga resources.

For sample data applied to the aggregation model, 13 properties from MML and 23 properties from MAD-M were used in describing single volumes of manga. Apart from properties common to both datasets, data from MML was useful for its English translations and transliterations of Japanese titles, while the MAD-M provided original Japanese data, as well as a lot of granular publication information, thanks to Toppan's role in the publication and printing of manga. BIBFRAME was successful both at maintaining the original granularity of both of these datasets and enabling the data to work within the LD aggregation model.

5.2   Manga Volumes Described in EDM and DC

While BIBFRAME was used for the bibliographic description at the Item level, bibliographic data for the Work level was described using Dublin Core terms found in the EDM library metadata alignment report [8]. As bibliographic data for the Work level in this study is coming from the Web, using a common Web ontology like DC is more straightforward than BIBFRAME. As it can be difficult to enable multi-level bibliographic models from libraries to work within the LD space, as discussed by Baker, Coyle, and Petiya [9], using an aggregate model that uses DC for existing Web resources may provide an alternative. In addition, the data at the Work level tends to focus on general information such as creator names and titles, rather than more granular data belonging to specific mediums, such as publication information for manga. Therefore, general DC terms provide an adequate level of granularity at the Work level that can be applied to any Expression of the manga Work, no matter the medium, and more granular information that is needed for specific media format instances can be described elsewhere in the model using different vocabularies, as is done with BIBFRAME in this study.

5.3   Identifying Related Manga Resources

In order to aggregate bibliographic manga data, related resources across datasets need to be identified. Similar to He et al. [7], DBpedia was leveraged in identifying Work level resources present in the available data. Comparing MML and MAD-M title data to DBpedia produced URLs representing the Work level entity, which were then compared across datasets to find matching data to be aggregated. While a fully automated method of identifying related data was not completed, the use of OpenRefine software was used in aiding with identifying related bibliographic data for manga. OpenRefine features a Reconciliation function to link and extend data with various webservices. This function matches a column from tabular data against a Web service of the user's choosing. Once a match is found, the table cell will contain a hyperlink to the Web resource, which in this study, is the relevant DBpedia page.

This reconciled URL signifies the same Wikipedia entry that represents the Work level edm:ProvidedCHO and is used for finding matching data across datasets. Once Reconciliation is performed on multiple datasets, the DBpedia URL can be used as a way to find matching resources. The DBpedia URL is more reliable for finding related resources than simply using the title, as Reconciliation produces the same DBpedia URL for variations, including titles of different languages, thanks to DBpedia properties such as dbpprop:jaKanji. In other words, performing Reconciliation with DBpedia on the MAD-M data with the title 鉄腕アトム will produce the same DBpedia URL as MML data titled "Astro Boy," because both the English and Japanese titles appear in DBpedia; a more simple text matching method performed on the title fields would not produce a match. It is worth noting that typically, only the English versions of Wikipedia pages will contain English and Japanese titles for manga, with the Japanese pages only containing Japanese. Thus, Reconciliation in this study was performed using English DBpedia.

While matching general Work level properties, such as title, is suitable for matching Item resources to their Work entity, Item-to-Item level aggregation requires that the publication instance be the same, so one must also match publisher, editions, volume, etc. OpenRefine lets one find matching records across datasets, as discussed in the example above, to find matching DBpedia URLs across datasets. To the author's knowledge, however, this can only be done one column at a time; it does not appear possible to create single expression to match multiple columns at once, such as title, volume number, and publisher, which is needed for matching specific Item entities. An automated way of matching volume data remains to be investigated, but would help greatly with aggregation at the Item level.

6   Discussion and Conclusions

The motivation of this study was to improve the granularity of bibliographic data for manga using existing resources. To achieve this, an aggregation model based on EDM was developed. In order to work within the EDM-based model, as well as encourage data reuse and exchange on the Semantic Web, manga records from Monash's JSC Manga Library and the MAD-M database were transformed into a BIBFRAME-based

RDF schema using OpenRefine. The use of the BIBFRAME vocabulary supported bibliographic data of differing levels of detail and languages to describe manga volumes within a LD model, while EDM enabled the aggregation of this data, as well as establishing relationships between related manga resources. OpenRefine and DBpedia were leveraged in identifying related manga resources across datasets, which were then aggregated within the model. The use of multiple data providers to describe manga resources from different points of view, in various levels of detail, and in different languages, resulted in an increased level of bibliographic description granularity for manga.

Using three datasets – MML, MAD-M, and Wikipedia – created a more complete bibliographic description for manga resources. Aggregating data for manga from multiple data providers both increased the granularity of bibliographic records for manga, and provided a greater number of access points for users by including data in multiple languages. In addition, the model established important successive and hierarchical relationships, connecting related manga volume instances to each other and to the Work entity to which they belong. If related, non-manga materials are made to work within the model (see Section 4.3), the hierarchical relationship would link manga volumes to related Anime, Video Games, and other media types, providing an even more complete bibliographic landscape for these resources.

While the data contents were not discussed in detail in this paper, there are some points to note. The model allows for aggregation at the Work level, similar to the Item level, but only a single source was used in this study, i.e. Wikipedia. Wikipedia's manga information is generally quite thorough, and as bibliographic data at the Work level is generic (e.g. title, author information), including more sources here is unlikely to contribute any unique or new properties not already present in Wikipedia.

The aggregation of MML and the MAD-M data did result in increased granularity, particularly in terms of incorporating data from multiple languages; some interesting data, such as chapter titles and volume summaries from Wikipedia, was not included. The data exists in Wikipedia pages, but is not structured in a way that makes it as accessible through LD means using DBpedia. Future investigation on how to include this information, as well related, non-manga resources within the model, would contribute to the goal of increasing granularity for manga resources.

Acknowledgments. The authors express our thanks to Mitsuharu Nagamori and other members of our laboratory for their useful comments. We thank Monash JSC, Agency for Cultural Affairs, and Toppan Printing Co. Ltd. for contributing data. This research is supported in part by JSPS KAKENHI Grant Number Grant No. 25240012 and collaborative research project with Infocom Corporation.

References

1. Fee, W.T.: Where Is the Justice... League?: Graphic Novel Cataloging and Classification. Serials Review **39**(1), 37–46 (2013)
2. EDM Factsheet. http://pro.europeana.eu/share-your-data/data-guidelines/edm-documentation

3. Southwick, S.B.: A Guide for Transforming Digital Collections Metadata into Linked Data Using Open Source Technologies. J. Lib. Metadata **15**(1), 1–35 (2015)
4. Gonzales, B.M.: Linking Libraries to the Web: Linked Data and the Future of the Bibliographic Record. ITAL **33**(4) (2014)
5. Zapounidou, S., Sfakakis, M., Papatheodorou, C.: Integrating library and cultural heritage data models. In: Proceedings of the 18th Panhellenic Conference on Informatics, PCI 2014. ACM, Athens (2014)
6. Zapounidou, S., Sfakakis, M., Papatheodorou, C.: Library data integration: towards BIBFRAME mapping to EDM. In: Studer, R., Garoufallou, E., Sicilia, M.-A., Closs, S. (eds.) MTSR 2014. CCIS, vol. 478, pp. 262–273. Springer, Heidelberg (2014)
7. He, W., Mihara, T., Nagamori, M., Sugimoto, S.: Identification of works of manga using LOD resources. In: Proceedings of the 13th ACM/IEEE-CS Joint Conference on Digital Libraries, JCDL 2013, pp. 253–256. ACM, Indianapolis (2013)
8. Angjeli, A., et al.: D5.1 Report on the alignment of library metadata with the Europeana Data Model (EDM) (2012)
9. Baker, T., Coyle, K., Petiya, S.: Multi-entity models of resource description in the Semantic Web. Library Hi Tech **32**(4), 562–582 (2014)

Instagram This! Sharing Photos on Instagram

Chei Sian Lee[✉], Nur Alifah Binte Abu Bakar,
Raudhah Binti Muhammad Dahri, and Sei-Ching Joanna Sin

Wee Kim Wee School of Communication and Information,
Nanyang Technological University, Singapore, Singapore
{leecs,w130004,raudhah001,joanna.sin}@ntu.edu.sg

Abstract. Sharing behavior is a major element in understanding the influence of social networking services. The aim of the present study is to examine the motivations driving users to share photos on Instagram, a popular photo-sharing social networking service. This study applied the uses and gratifications approach to determine Instagram members' reasons for sharing photos. Data (N=115) were collected from an online survey. A principal component factor analysis indicated that there were four motives for sharing photos: informativeness, community support, status-seeking, and self- representation. We also conducted correlation and regression analyses. Our results indicate that age, number of followers and number of followings on Instagram are related to the gratifications users seek on Instagram. Further, we found that users' photo sharing was mainly motivated by the need for self-representation and status-seeking. Implications of our work are also discussed.

Keywords: Photo-sharing · Photo social network services · Motivations

1   Introduction

Over the last few years, photo-sharing social networking services (PSNS) such as Instagram, Flickr, and Pinterest have seen significant increases in the proportion of adults sharing photos on these sites. Indeed, sharing photos on PSNS is becoming a daily routine for many people [1,2]. PSNS offer easy sharing directly from mobile phones and enable individuals to communicate with large groups of distributed people through an image. Even though the use of PSNS has been integrated into the daily social networking activities of many adults, the motivations driving them to share these photos on PSNS are not well understood.

Conventional studies concerned with information sharing have identified some motivational factors that predict sharing behavior. For example, both social (e.g., maintain/create social relationships, information exchange) and personal (e.g., entertainment, status-seeking, prior experiences) reasons were found to be related to users' sharing behavior in social media [1], [3,4]. Other researchers explained that content sharing activities in social and mobile media can be personally and emotionally satisfying [3], [5]. Different people may also interpret a photo differently depending on their backgrounds and personal experiences [1], [4]. Indeed, the gratifications people seek in social networking services (SNS) may differ among people

© Springer International Publishing Switzerland 2015
R.B. Allen et al. (Eds.): ICADL 2015, LNCS 9469, pp. 132–141, 2015.
DOI: 10.1007/978-3-319-27974-9_13

from different demographic profiles. For instance, [6] reported that younger users were more willing to share personal information in SNS. Further, it was reported that women were more likely than men to use SNS to seek community support during difficult times [5]. Hence, individual differences are likely to influence the gratifications sought in SNS.

Due to the popularity of SNS, there is an expanding body of research related to their use. However, most of the studies focus on widely adopted SNS such as Facebook and Twitter [7,8] and not solely on photo-sharing. Indeed, research on PSNS is limited and results obtained from general SNS may not be directly applicable to PSNS. Past works on PSNS (e.g. Pinterest, Flickr) largely focused on platform features and tools [9,10,11]. Research on the social and psychological aspects of photo-sharing is only in its nascent stage. For example, there is some evidence of demographic differences in the motivations for SNS usage in general (including, but not limited to Flickr users) [12]. It is as yet unclear whether there are demographic differences in the motivations for using PSNS in particular. Since different SNS have different focuses, attract different populations and promote different activities, research on the other less studied PSNS platforms will be insightful [13].

To fill this research gap, this study examines the gratifications driving the use of a PSNS, Instagram, which is currently the one of the most popular and important PSNS platforms [14,15,16]. The objectives of the present study are two-fold. First, our study draws from the uses and gratifications theory (U&G) to investigate the gratification factors that influence user's photo sharing behavior on Instagram. Second, this study aims to examine the relationship between the demographic profiles of Instagram users and the gratifications sought from sharing photos. This theory is appropriate in the current study because it explains the social and psychological needs that motivate individuals to select particular media channels [3].

In sum, the present study aims to investigate the following research questions: *1) What are the gratification factors that influence users to share photos on Instagram? 2) What are the associations between gratifications sought from photos sharing and the demographic profiles of Instagram users?*

2 Literature Review

2.1 Overview of Instagram

Instagram was launched in October 2010 and hit the 150 million user mark within a short span of 3 years, gaining 128 million new users after being acquired by Facebook in 2012 [14]. As of 2015, Instagram has more than 300 million users worldwide with more than 80 million pictures shared daily. Instagram is a free photo and video-sharing SNS that can be easily accessed on smartphones of different operating systems as well as personal computers. Users can take photos within the application or share existing photos.

Three unique features of Instagram will be elaborated here. First, Instagram caters for self-expression, which is not surprising as visual images have become synonymous with self-expression. Specifically, users can create, edit, and contribute photos and short videos. Second, Instagram enables the editing of photos through the use of photographic filters. This function allows users to choose different 'filters' that can enhance the photo and provides a creativity outlet for users. Third, like other SNS, Instagram is based around the concept of social connections. On the user's profile page, besides the username and profile picture, users are able to track the number of uploaded photos, followers and followings. Instagram users can also connect their Instagram account to other SNS, such as Facebook and Twitter.

2.2   Uses and Gratifications Theory

The uses and gratifications theory attempts to explain what social and psychological needs motivate audiences to select particular media channels and content [17], [3]. This theory has been widely applied to investigate audience's gratifications in a variety of media channels and content, including mobile gaming applications [18], and specific information such as news content [19]. From a uses and gratifications perspective, selecting a media channel is an actively involved procedure in which audiences evaluate the potential benefits of media usage.

In addition, past research has provided evidence to suggest that the gratifications people seek in SNS may differ among people from different demographic profiles (e.g. age, gender, educational background). For instance, it was reported that men and women have different information behaviors in SNS. Past research reported that individual differences (e.g. gender, age, number of connections) significantly influence why people use SNS [17].

2.3   Seeking Gratification Through Photo Sharing on Instagram

In this study we argue that the act of sharing photos can be gratifying to the sharer. The use of photos has fundamentally changed due to digitization. Specifically, photos are no longer about preserving special memories and are fast becoming chronicles of the fleeting moments of an individual's everyday life [20]. Social media, in particular PSNS, allow users to share their photos and document their daily lives. Instead of sharing photos in thick albums on special occasions, photos are being uploaded online regularly to be shared with family and friends, regardless of geographical boundaries.

Prior studies on mobile content-sharing applications have shown that people are able to anticipate theirs or others' potential information needs and share content in order to facilitate future information seeking [4]. This means that social media can help users to seek information and satisfy future information needs. In other words, users may share photos to provide relevant and timely information to meet potential information needs. This gratification factor is known as the informativenesss gratification. Next, [21] examined photo contribution on Facebook and found that postings lead to interactions with the online community and ultimately garnering support from them. This means that continued participation and content contribution from members are crucial for the ongoing success of social interaction and gathering support in online communities. In this case, sharing photos is a means for users to get community support. Third, it has been recognized that users share information to obtain peer recognition [22]. Likewise in the case of Instagram, users share photos because they enjoy the feeling of being important and looking outstanding among other Instagram users. Thus, we propose that users share photos to seek status. Last but not least, photos are a way of self-expression and present the information individuals would like to convey to others [4]. Social media in general has enabled users to create an online persona separate from their real selves. The creation of such a persona can be viewed as a form of self-representation [23]. On Instagram, users create this self-representation through the types of photos they share. Hence, sharing photos on Instagram is a form of creating and experimenting with identities and allows users to create impressions of themselves in the minds of others. Here we term this as the self-representation gratification.

3   Methodology

3.1   Sample

A self-administered online questionnaire was developed to collect data. The sample consisted of adult Instagram users (>21 years old) in Singapore. Snowball sampling was used to recruit respondents, as members of the Instagram population were difficult to locate [24]. In this study, Instagram users were contacted through emails, Facebook messages and Instagram Direct messages which included a link to the online survey. A total of 129 survey responses were collected, with 115 usable ones. The demographic profiles of the respondents are summarized in Table 1.

Table 1. Sample demographics (N=115)

Demographic variables		N	%
Gender	Men	39	33.91
	Women	76	66.01
Educational Level	Junior College/Polytechnic	44	38.26
	Bachelor's Degree	64	55.65
	Master's Degree and above	3	2.60
	Others	4	3.48
Age	21-30	82	71.30
	31-40	32	27.83
	41-50	1	0.87
No. of Followers	1-50	47	71.30
	51-100	14	12.17
	101-150	18	15.65
	>150	29	25.00
	Missing values	7	6.09
No. of Followings	1-50	43	37.39
	51-100	13	11.30
	151-200	10	8.70
	>200	20	16.14
	Missing values	5	4.35

3.2   Operational Measures

Photo sharing is operationalized by asking users to indicate the frequency with which they use Instagram to share photos as well as their intention to continue to share photos on Instagram [18,19]. The measurements assessing gratifications were drawn from previous U&G studies [17], [3]. Factors including informativeness, community support, status-seeking, and self-representation were incorporated into the survey instrument to explore potential predictors of photo sharing on Instagram. A total of 24 questions were developed to assess the different gratification dimensions and were measured using a 5-point Likert scale with a range of 1 (Strongly disagree) to 5 (Strongly agree). The entire set of 24 items was analyzed by a principal component factor analysis using Varimax rotation. Two items were dropped due to low factor loadings and two items were dropped due to high cross factor loadings.

The remaining 20 items fell into four groups representing the four gratification factors: informativeness, community support, status-seeking and self-representation (see Table 2). We also used Cronbach's alpha as an indicator to test for reliability and all factors exhibited adequate reliability requirement ($\alpha > .7$).

- "Informativeness" describes the extent to which photos shared on Instagram can provide other users with relevant and timely information.
- "Community Support" measures the extent to which sharing photos on Instagram makes users feel part of a community.
- "Status-seeking" describes how sharing photos helps one to attain status among peers.
- "Self-representation" measures the extent to which sharing photos on Instagram is a form of creating and experimenting with identities.

Table 2. Factor Analysis Results (N=115)

	Factors				Alpha (α)
Informativeness					.88
To share tips on photography.	.81	.08	-.14	.07	
To provide situational awareness. (e.g. earthquake region)	.80	-.15	.10	-.08	
To communicate with people from all over the world.	.76	.32	-.10	-.01	
As a form of encouragement to others.	.74	.05	.22	.04	
To provide first-hand accounts of events to others.	.71	.13	.34	-.30	
To participate in photo competitions/contests.	.65	.04	.19	-.07	
Because I can link it to other social networking sites, e.g. Facebook/Twitter.	.63	-.20	.31	-.13	
To get anonymous feedback about my photos.	.61	.18	-.14	.33	
So that my followers will post content as well.	.57	.07	.11	.50	

Table 2. (*continued*)

Self-Representation					.86
To express myself as an individual.	.06	**.85**	.26	.19	
To contribute my own experience.	.08	**.80**	.07	.03	
To express my creativity.	.18	**.79**	.14	.13	
To tell stories about my life.	-.09	**.74**	.34	.13	
Community Support					.86
Because I think my followers will like the photos.	.24	.25	**.78**	.20	
Because it makes me happy when others comment on my photos.	.05	.26	**.75**	.31	
Because I feel like people can understand me through my photos.	.13	.35	**.74**	.19	
To feel a part of a community.	.37	.04	**.50**	.40	
Status-Seeking					.74
Because it helps me feel important when sharing content.	-.17	.15	.20	**.82**	
So that my followers will not be disappointed with my lack of updates.	.14	.00	.06	**.70**	
Because it helps me look good.	-.05	.22	.32	**.62**	
Eigenvalue	7.04	3.95	1.96	1.66	
Variance explained (%)	29.35	16.45	8.17	6.90	

4 Analyses and Results

First, we utilized regression analysis to examine the relationship between the four gratification factors and sharing of photos on Instagram (RQ1). The results are shown in Table 3. The regression analysis results show that self-representation and status-seeking were found to be significant and positive factors in predicting sharing of photos. However, community support and informativeness were not significant.

Table 3. Results from Regression Analysis (N=115)

Gratification factors	Standardized β	t-values
Informativeness	-.01	-.10
Community Support	.01	.09
Status-Seeking	.20	1.85*
Self-Representation	.23	2.13*
F (3.240)	28.60*	
Adjusted R Square	.11	

Note: a. Dependent Variable is Photo Sharing, b. * p < 0.05

Next, a correlational analysis was conducted to explore if there were any relationships between the gratifications sought and individual differences (RQ2). From Table 4, the results indicate that older respondents were more likely to share photos on Instagram to seek gratifications of informativeness, while younger respondents sought status. The number of followers was also associated with the types of gratifications sought. Respondents with more followers were more likely to seek status. However, the higher the number of people they followed, the more likely they were to seek both community support and status. There were no statistically differences in the gratifications sought between men and women Instagram users or among users with different educational levels.

Table 3. Results from Correlation Analysis (N=115)

Demographic Factors	Gratification Factors			
	Informativeness	Community Support	Status-Seeking	Self-Representation
Gender	.05	.15	-.01	.15
Age group	.41**	.08	-.27**	.08
Education level	-.13	-.07	.02	-.04
No. of followers	.07	.17	.27**	.09
No. of followings	.14	.29*	.31**	.08

Note: **. Correlation is significant at the 0.01 level (2-tailed).
      *. Correlation is significant at the 0.05 level (2-tailed)

5   Discussion and Conclusion

Drawing from the U&G perspective, the purpose of this research is to investigate the gratification factors driving users to share photos on Instagram. We found that Instagram users who shared photos were mainly motivated by self-representation and status-seeking. Our second objective is to examine individual differences' effect on the gratifications sought via photos shared in PSNS.

Overall, we found that self-representation was the strongest motivator driving users to share photos on Instagram. Instagram's filters and tools allow users to present the best photos to their followers [23], [15], which allow them to present and manage their online personas on the platform. It should be noted that a search on Instagram with the hashtag "#selfportrait" returned 2 million hits, indicating the proliferation of self-representation images on Instagram. The other two gratification factors were likely not significant in our study because other well-established SNS, such as Facebook and Twitter, were able to gratify the needs for informativeness and community support. Indeed, many respondents indicated the use of several other SNS concurrently.

To shed light on the sharing behaviors of adult users, the focus of this study was restricted to adults who are twenty-one years and above. Our results suggest that younger adults share photos for status and self-representation, while older users are more motivated by information exchange. Young adults, especially those who are in the early 20s, are in the midst of exploring and finding their own identities, and hence their use of Instagram reflects their developmental goals. With regards to the influence of the number of online connections, we also identified that users with a larger number of followers were more motivated to seek status. On the other hand, users with more followings were more motivated by both community support and status-seeking. It should be noted that on many SNS platforms, more connections in terms of more followers and followings may result in information overload because of the constant stream of updates posted online. The information overloading problem may be of a lesser concern for sharers on PSNS such as Instagram, as the content shared are photos, images and videos.

The present study contributes to SNS research in several aspects. Our findings provide insights on the features that PSNS should include (e.g. features for self- expression, content-related features for older users) as sustained participation and content contribution from users are critical for the viability and success of any SNS. Second, our findings on the effects of age and the gratifications sought have major implications for the business use of Instagram, especially for marketing of products and services. In terms of contribution to libraries, this study provided insights on how to motivate library users to contribute content since Instagram is one of the latest platforms that libraries are experimenting with. Specifically, this platform allows libraries to introduce a little more fun into their online profiles and interact with users in new ways. Ultimately, the findings from this study will benefit photo digital libraries (e.g. PhotoGeo) as well as libraries and higher educational institutions as they move towards the direction of building a collaborative digital library to enable their users to share a variety of content including photographs to participate on their collaborative platform.

There are some limitations in the present study. First, we investigated the usage of one photo-sharing social networking site, which may limit the generalizability of our findings. Indeed, different PSNS platforms have distinct features, which may be used to satisfy different user gratifications [9]. Future studies need to include different PSNS. We acknowledge the limitation of the snowball sampling used in the current study. Specifically, snowball samples should not be considered to be representation of the population being studied. However, as members of the Instagram population were difficult to locate at the point of data collection, snowballing sampling is an alternate means to recruit respondents [24]. In addition, the respondents of the present study were from Singapore and there may exist cultural and national differences in the use of PSNS which may limit the generalizability of our findings to users in other countries. This warrants future investigation. Nonetheless, despite these shortcomings, the present study contributes to a better understanding of photo-sharing behavior on Instagram.

References

1. Ames, M., Naaman, M.: Why we tag: motivations for annotation in mobile and online media. In: Proceedings of the SIGCHI Conference on Human Factors in Computing Systems, pp. 971–980. ACM, San Jose (2007)
2. Bakhshi, S., Shamma, D.A., Gilbert, E.: Faces engage us: photos with faces attract more likes and comments on instagram. In: Proceedings of the SIGCHI Conference on Human Factors in Computing Systems, pp. 965–974. ACM Press, Toronto Ontario Canada (2014)

3. Ruggiero, T.E.: Uses and gratifications theory in the 21st century. Mass Comm. and Soc. **3**(1), 3–37 (2000)
4. Goh, D.H.-L., Ang, R.P., Chua, A.Y., Lee, C.S.: Why we share: a study of motivations for mobile media sharing. In: Liu, J., Wu, J., Yao, Y., Nishida, T. (eds.) AMT 2009. LNCS, vol. 5820, pp. 195–206. Springer, Heidelberg (2009)
5. Lee, C.S.: Exploring Emotional Expressions on YouTube through the Lens of Media System Dependency Theory. New Media and Soc. (2012)
6. Boyle, K., Johnson, T.J.: MySpace is your space?: Examining self-presentation of MySpace users. Comput. in Hum. Behav. **26**, 1392–1399 (2008)
7. Boyd, D.M., Ellison, N.B.: Social Network Sites Definition, History, and Scholarship. J. of Comp-Mediated Commun. **13**, 210–230 (2007)
8. Urista, M.A., Dong, Q., Day, K.D.: Explaining why young adults use MySpace and Facebook through Uses and Gratifications Theory. Hum. Commun. **12**, 215–229 (2009)
9. Herrema, R.O.N.: Flickr, communities of practice and the boundaries of identity: a musician goes visual. Visual Studies **26**, 135–141 (2011)
10. Nov, O., Naaman, M., Ye, C.: What drives content tagging: the case of photos on Flickr. In: Proceeding of the Twenty-Sixth Annual SIGCHI Conference on Human Factors in Computing Systems, pp. 1097–1100. ACM, Florence (2008)
11. Taylor, C.A., Anicello, O., Somohano, S., Samuels, N., Whitaker, L., Ramey, J.A.: A framework for understanding mobile internet motivations and behaviors. In: Proceedings of the SIGCHI Conference on Human Factors in Computing Systems, pp. 2679–2684. ACM (2008)
12. Oh, S., Syn, S.Y.: Motivations for sharing information and social support in social media: A comparative analysis of Facebook, Twitter, Delicious, YouTube, and Flickr. J. Am. Soc. Inf. Sci. Tec. (2015)
13. Hargittai, E.: Whose space? Differences among users and non-users of social network sites. J. of Comp. of Mediated Commun. **13**, 276–297 (2008)
14. Burnham, K.: Instagram hits 150 million users, plans ads. Information Week. http://www.informationweek.com/infrastructure/networking/instagram-hits-150-million-users-plans-ads/d/d-id/1111465
15. McCune, Z.: Consumer Production in social media networks: A Case Study of the Instagram iPhone App. Master Dissertation. University of Cambridge (2011)
16. Milanovic, R.: The World's 21 Most Important Social Media Sites and Apps in 2015. http://www.socialmediatoday.com/social-networks/2015-04-13/worlds-21-most-important-social-media-sites-and-apps-2015
17. Park, N., Kee, K.F., Valenzuela, S.: Being immersed in social networking environment: Facebook groups, uses and gratifications, and social outcomes. CyberPsychology & Behav. **12**, 729–733 (2009)
18. Lee, C.S., Goh, D.H.-L., Chua, A.Y.K., Ang, R.P.: Indagator: Investigating perceived gratifications of an application that blends mobile content sharing with gameplay. J. Am. Soc. Inf. Sci. Tec. **61**, 1244–1257 (2010)
19. Ma, L., Lee, C.S., Goh, D.H.: That's news to me: the influence of perceived gratifications and personal experience on news sharing in social media. In: Proceeding of the 11th Annual International on Digital Libraries, JCDL 2011, pp. 141–144. ACM/IEEE, Ottawa, Canada (2011)

20. Murray, S.: Digital images, photo-sharing, and our shifting notions of everyday aesthetics. J. of Vis. Culture **7**, 147–163 (2008)
21. Burke, M., Marlow, C., Lento, T.: Feed me: motivating newcomer contribution in social network sites. In: Proceedings of the SIGCHI Conference on Human Factors in Computing Systems, pp. 945–954. ACM Press, Boston (2009)
22. Hew, K.F., Hara, N.: Knowledge sharing in online environments: A qualitative case study. J. Am. Soc. Inf. Sci. Tec. **58**, 2310–2324 (2007)
23. Huang, C.L., Yang, S.C.: Study of online misrepresentation, self-disclosure, cyber- relationship motives, and loneliness among teenagers in Taiwan. J. of Educational Comput. Res. **48**, 1–18 (2013)
24. Baltar, F., Brunet, I.: Social research 2.0: Virtual snowball sampling method using Facebook. Internet Research **22**, 57–74 (2012)

Comparing Network Structures of Different Versions of a Book: A Case Study of the Bible

Keeheon Lee[✉]

Department of Library and Information Science, Yonsei University, Seoul, South Korea
keeheon4research@gmail.com

Abstract. A book can be written in different versions even if their languages are the same. Or they can be published in different languages with the same message. Different versions can be represented as a co-word network or a co-topic network. In this study, I posit that different versions of a book may have similar but different topologies which imply slightly various interpretations. Two English versions of the Bible are used as a case study. Co-word networks and co-topic networks for topology comparison show that the King James Version and New International Version cover similar topics but have slightly different emphases in terms of network structure. This study shows that the comparisons among different versions of a book can be done through network analysis. Future work will be performed with domain experts. For example, with the Bible, experts in theology are required to connect network structural features to the present theology.

Keywords: Bible · Book · Co-word network · Co-topic network · Digital humanities · Network structure · Translation · Versions

1   Introduction

A book can be written in different versions or different languages but its message, the main theme an author wants to deliver, is the same. Different versions of a book may exist due to additional editions, various classes of readers, and diverse publishers. The King James Version (KJV) is an English translation of the Bible published by King James the First in 1611. The New International Version (NIV) is a modern English translation of the Bible, which was published in the 1970s and updated in 1984 and 2011. There are many other versions of the Bible such as Darby, the New American Standard Bible, the New King James Version, and Webster. A book is published in different languages to introduce and disseminate the message of the book to international readers. For example, the Bible has been translated into 100 different languages [1]. However, a book, in general, has one message with assorted contents although versions may differ.

In this study, I investigate whether different versions of a book have different knowledge structural properties. Here, a knowledge structure is a network of knowledge entities comprising a message of the book. A knowledge entity is an element that specifies or distinguishes the message. It can be any part of speech in English.

© Springer International Publishing Switzerland 2015
R.B. Allen et al. (Eds.): ICADL 2015, LNCS 9469, pp. 142–152, 2015.
DOI: 10.1007/978-3-319-27974-9_14

For example, in the Bible, words such as "LORD", "God", "Jesus", and "said" are knowledge entities. "said" is also a knowledge entity since it implies an action of speech. The associations among the words form a knowledge structure of the Bible.

The knowledge structure can be represented as a co-occurrence network of words or topics. A co-word network is an example of a knowledge structure. Basically, its nodes are knowledge entities in words and its edges are associations between the co-occurring knowledge entities within a range of terms in a book. It is a lower level representation of a knowledge structure whose knowledge entities are terms. A co-topic network is another example. A topic is a concept representing a group of associated terms. It is labeled with a vocabulary generalizing the terms by several experts. It is a higher-level representation of a knowledge structure since its knowledge entities are topics. And the co-topic network represents associations of concepts extracted from a book. Two co-word networks can be compared based on central words, important edges, and subnetworks. In case of co-topic network, rather than central words, I compare the central topics of one co-topic network to another. In particular, I choose the Bible as a case study. The Bible is a collection of books having one message. I build co-word networks and co-topic networks of two English versions of the Christian Bible, KJV and NIV. Their publication years are different and their English versions are altered.

The Bible is one of the most wide-spread books online, and books will be published in different versions rapidly in digital era. Computational network analysis of the Bible can not only enrich our understanding of the Bible, but also help us prepare to analyze digital books in a new way. In particular, machine-based translation of a document from one language to another language may benefit from computational network analysis. Also, we may discover translation differences caused by translator, place, and time without knowing history. This can be done by quantifying and examining numbers in a structural form such as a network.

The rest of this paper is organized as follows. Section 2 explains the methodology of co-word network and co-topic network analyses. Section 3 shows the result of this study in perspectives of nodes, edges, and modules. Section 4 concludes findings and future works.

2   Related Work

2.1   The History of Christian Bible Translation

The Bible was first written in Greek manuscripts and translated into many languages. Later, the Roman Catholic Church allowed only the Latin version of Bible. However, some scholars realized the need for the Bible for ordinary people and began to translate Greek manuscripts into English. Thanks to printing and distribution systems, the English Bible became widespread and different versions and translations were published for accurate but culturally acceptable Bibles.

Table 1 shows a brief history of different versions of English Christian Bible with an exemplary verse of John 3:16. As we may easily discover uninterpretable terms, we can confirm the evolution of English over time. In the exemplary verse, Tyndale's version and the NIV used loveth and love while the others applied lufode, loued, and loueth as the first verb in the verse. In the original version or Latin version of Bible, the corresponding verb means 'charity' rather than 'love'. 'Charity' matches to love between friends (i.e., philia) and love that serves unconditionally (i.e., agape). But the Tyndale version and the NIV used 'love' because the meaning of 'charity' had been restricted to generosity and 'love' can be well-understood by ordinary people.

The Anglo-Saxon Proto-English version was the initial English version of Bible. However, the Wycliff version was the first hand-written English Bible manuscript, produced in 1380. The Tyndale version was the second complete Bible, printed in English in 1534 for ordinary people. The Great Bible was the first authorized English Bible published in 1539. The Geneva version was the first Bible to annotate numbered verses to the chapters, extensive notes and references in 1560. The Douai-Reims version was the translation of the Church of Rome published in 1582.

The KJV was published in 1611 to fulfill the demand for a Standard English Bible, which influenced English Language and Literature until now. The NIV is a conversational version after the New American Standard Version Bible (NASB). The NASB is known as a modern English Bible that translates the original Greek and Hebrew scriptures accurately by word-for-word translation. For better reading and understanding, the NIV was written by phrase-for-phrase translation and became the best-selling modern English Bible.

Table 1. The history of English Christian Bible Translation with an exemplary verse

Version name (year of publication)	Example (John 3:16)
Anglo-Saxon Proto-English (995)	God lufode middan-eard swa, dat he seade his an-cennedan sunu, dat nan ne forweorde de on hine gely ac habbe dat ece lif.
Wycliff (1380)	for god loued so the world; that he gaf his oon bigetun sone, that eche man that bileueth in him perisch not: but haue euerlastynge liif
Tyndale (1534)	For God so loveth the worlde, that he hath geven his only sonne, that none that beleve in him, shuld perisshe: but shuld have everlastinge lyfe.
Great Bible (1539)	For God so loued the worlde, that he gaue his only begotten sonne, that whosoeuer beleueth in him, shulde not perisshe, but haue euerlasting lyfe
Geneva (1560)	For God so loueth the world, that he hath geuen his only begotten Sonne: that none that beleue in him, should peryshe, but haue euerlasting lyfe
The Douai-Reims (1582)	For so God loued the vvorld, that he gaue his only-begotten sonne: that euery one that beleeueth in him, perish not, but may haue life euerlasting
KJV (1611)	For God so loued the world, that he gaue his only begotten Sonne: that whosoeuer beleeueth in him, should not perish, but haue euerlasting life.
NIV (1973)	For God so loved the world, that he gave his only begotten Son, that whosoever believeth in him should not perish, but have everlasting life.

2.2   Computational Analysis in Translation Studies

Translation studies involve a systematic view on the theory and the application of translation including localization. Quantification and numerical analysis based on computational power has been widely applied to translational studies. One known name for a study using such analysis is corpus-based translation studies. Hu (2012) applied unsupervised learning to Proverbs and Psalms. His result not only matched the findings by Biblical scholars, but he also added new findings that could not dis-covered by traditional methods [2]. Miyake et al. [3] used web-based software to ex-amine many problems from differences in interpretation in biblical research. Current-ly, papers on a certain topic are often examined by computational network analysis to discover new knowledge from the present literature [4]. However, such analysis on digital books is limited. Carron and Kenna [5] analyzed the properties of networks built on mythological narratives. Books are not free to conduct computational me-thods, e.g., topic modeling, on them yet.

3   Methodology

3.1   Dataset

In this study, I choose the English Bible as a case since it is the most well-known, well-studied, well-spread humanities publication in the world. I collected 2 versions of English Bible, the King James Version (KJV) and the New International Version (NIV). A gap of 400 years exists between the publication years of the two versions. Certainly, the KJV and NIV are different not only in language but also in their in-tended readers. As the name indicates, the KJV was made for people who lived in England 400 years ago. The NIV was published for modern international people.

3.2   Co-word Network Construction

A co-word network links words occurring concurrently within a range. In this study, the range is a sentence. Every word of Bible is extracted and stop words such as ar-ticles and prepositions are eliminated. The extracted words are linked by co-occurrence. The association or edge is weighed by the frequency of co-occurrence as its importance. Co-occurrence does not guarantee explicit relations but ensures impli-cit relations between words.

For example, in the KJV, Roman 8:38-39 states that "For I am persuaded, that nei-ther death, nor life, nor angels, nor principalities, nor powers, nor things present, nor things to come, nor height, nor depth, nor any other creature, shall be able to separate us from the love of God, which is in Christ Jesus our Lord." In the NIV, the same verses are written as "For I am convinced that neither death nor life, neither angels nor demons, neither the present nor the future, nor any powers, neither height nor depth, nor anything else in all creation, will be able to separate us from the love of God that is in Christ Jesus our Lord." Figure 1 shows the corresponding co-word net-works of KJV and NIV without removing stopwords.

3.3   Co-topic Network Construction

To extract topics from texts, the topic modeling technique is applied. Topic modelling assumes that a document is a probabilistic combination of different topics. In particu-lar, Latent Dirichlet Allocation (LDA) is used [6]. LDA allocates each term of a doc-

ument to a topic when the number of topics is given by a user. Each topic has a distribution of terms representing the topic semantically. I build a co-topic network by
connecting two topics whose member terms occur in the same document. The weight
of an edge reflects the frequency of co-occurring member terms in two different topics. That is, it represents how strong the two topics are interrelated implicitly. Compared to a co-word network, it has a small number of nodes that enhances viewers to
understand the knowledge structure of a subject, the Bible in this case, easily on a
conceptual level.

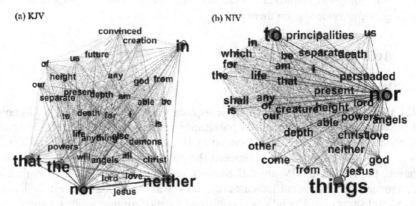

Fig. 1. An example of co-word network of Rome 8:37-38 in (a) KJV and (b) NIV

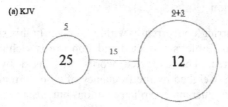

Rome 8:37   persuaded-12 death-12 life-12 angels-12 principalities-12 powers-12 things-12 present-12 things-12

Rome 8:38   height-25 depth-25 creature-25 separate-25 love-12 god-12 christ-12 jesus-12 lord-25

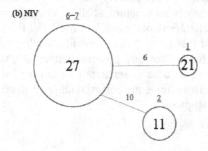

Rome 8:37   convinced-27 death-27 life-27 angels-27 demons-21 present-27 future-27 powers-27

Rome 8:38   height-11 depth-11 creation-27 separate-27 love-27 god-27 christ-27 jesus-27 lord-27

Fig. 2. An example of co-topic network of Rome 8:37-38 in (a) KJV and (b) NIV

Figure 2 shows the corresponding co-topic networks of Figure 1. Namely, the terms in the verses are assigned to certain topics after deleting stop words such as "nor", "not", and "to". In Figure 2, the red-colored parts of the network is the representation of the red-colored "term-topic" list of Rome 8:37. And then, the blue-colored parts of the network are constructed. Thus, in the KJV, two topics, 12 and 25, are represented as nodes with the sizes of 5 and 12. The sizes are the frequencies of the topics. The number of the combination of the co-occurring topics is 15 and it is the weight of the edge between topics 12 and 25. In the NIV, two topics are made in Rome 8:37 and two topics are generated in Rome 8:38. Since two verses share one same topic, three nodes are created.

3.4 Network Comparison

The co-word networks of the KJV and the NIV as well as the co-topic networks of the KJV and the NIV are compared by centralities of nodes, weights of edges, and elements of modules or topics. The centralities are degree, weighted degree, closeness, and betweenness [7]. Degree represents the local popularity of a node, weighted degree stands for the local popularity of a node regarding associating nodes, closeness reflects the reachability of a node from all the other nodes, and betweenness is the degree to which a node plays the role of a mediator. The weight of an edge is the degree of a pairwise relation between two nodes. A module is detected by a community detection algorithm that distinguishes similar nodes as the members of a group from the others [8]. The algorithm calculates the similarity between nodes not by semantic meanings but by co-occurring density between nodes. That is, a node is assigned to a module if adding the node does not drop the density of the module under a certain threshold, such as 0.9. The density can be thought of as the clustering degree of a module. Similarly, using LDA with 1.0 and 0.01 for two parameters of alpha and beta in [6], a topic is a probability distribution of terms representing a concept. Also, in co-topic networks, a module can be induced by grouping similar nodes (i.e., topics). And thus, the modules of a co-word network are groups of terms while those of a co-topic network are clusters of topics. Topics may share terms but modules do not share terms or topics.

This network comparison based on the centralities of nodes, the one-to-one relationships of nodes (i.e., edges), and the group relationships of nodes (i.e., modules or communities) enables us to understand lexical differences depending on co-occurring terms. In a co-word network, central terms, term-to-term relationships, and term clusters may differ. In a co-topic network, central topics, topic-to-topic relationships, and topic clusters may be different. When a person develops opinions or thoughts, the person chooses terms carefully in order to deliver a clear message. There can be nuance according to chosen terms even if the message is the same.

4   Result

The co-word network of the KJV consists of 13,037 nodes and 607,574 edges. That of the NIV is composed of 16,300 nodes and 688,165 edges. 7994 nodes are in common. On the other hand, the co-topic networks have 30 nodes and 29 edges for each node. In this study, I restricted the number of topics for each version to 30 and the number of terms for each topic to 150. The size of topics can be altered but 30 topics have sufficient topic variety and are not large enough to make the network complex.

The following co-word networks and co-topic networks of the KJV and NIV were performed under a Java 1.8 environment.

4.1   Co-word Network Results

Table A.1 [9] shows nodes for perspectives of degree, weighted degree, closeness, and betweenness. The top 10 nodes in each co-word network and are similar. The top 10 nodes in the KJV co-word network are LORD, thy, God, said, king, man, Israel, son, people, and house, in perspectives of degree, weighted degree, closeness, and betweenness. The orders were almost the same. The top 10 nodes in NIV co-word network are "LORD", "who", "God", "said", "king", "son", "people", "Israel", "man" ("men"), and "land". "son" rose from 8th to 3rd in perspective of betweenness. That is, "son" is important in mediating other terms as well as in linking them directly. However, "Jesus" was ranked 32nd in the KJV and above 20th in the NIV. On the other hand, "children" was in the top 30 nodes in the KJV but below 90th in the NIV.

Second, the relationship between two nodes, i.e., edge, is investigated. Table A.2 [9] shows the top 20 ranked edges according to the weight (i.e., the frequency of co-occurrence) of an edge in co-word networks of the KJV and NIV. They are similar in that "God-Lord", "said-LORD", "LORD-Israel", "LORD-says/saith" and similar relations are the main. That is, both versions of the Bible tell us that God is LORD and LORD said something many times. To be specific, LORD is associated with Israel. This is consistent with the knowledge that the Bible is the word of God. However, the KJV has edges of "house-LORD" and "hand-LORD" while the NIV has "son-king" and "declares-LORD" edges

Third, the modules of the KJV co-word network (Table A.3 [9]) and NIV co-word network (Table A.4 [9]) are examined. The number of modules were 20 and 34 for the KJV and NIV co-word networks respectively. Two people who have read the Bible for more than 30 years labeled a concept for each module and the featured words of each module are listed next to the concept. The featured words have high centralities. In both networks, modules such as {Zeeb, Oreb}, {Zalmunna, Zebah}, {Abiram, Dathan}, {harps, cymbals, lyres}, {Meschach, Shadrach, Abednego}, {thorns, briers}, {Anah, Zibeon} are detected in common. The first two modules are the heads of Midian who were opponents of Israel and killed by Kideon. Both modules are known for God's support. The third module represents the rebels in Israel in the time of Moses. The fourth module stands for instruments used for praising God. The fifth module implies the friends of Daniel who were distinguished in the province of Babylon. The sixth module is thorns and briers, often used for symbolizing evil. The last common module stands for Edom, which is a tribe rooted from Esau, the older brother of Jacob. The Edom always had trouble with Jacob and Israel. In addition, in both the KJV and NIV, there are similar concepts such as obscenity, kings, uncleanness, Jesus Christ, and the elected (elitism) with slightly different terms in modules. The similarities show the two versions share sins such as uncleanness and obscenity, the events when God helped His elected people, Israel, and Jesus Christ regardless of their time difference.

However, the differences of the KJV and NIV in modules show that the KJV discusses concepts such as awake, judge, respect, circumcision, and Judas Iscariot while the NIV discloses concepts such as lamentation, hell, foreigners, foreign town, ordinance, servant, waist belt, Jacob's wits, marriage, oath, attack, feast of tabernacles, and Jubilee. This implies that the KJV focuses on legal issues and the NIV concentrates on human behaviors in front of God.

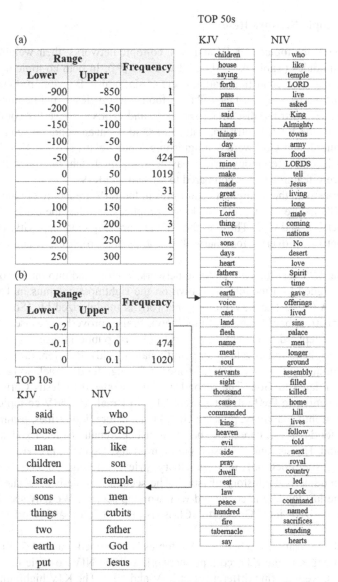

Fig. 3. The differences of (a) degree centrality and (b) betweenness centrality between KJV and NIV terms and the corresponding lists

Figure 3 (a) shows the distribution of differences between degree centralities of two versions. For example, "said" may have degree centrality of 50 in KJV and 30 in NIV. Then, "said" has a difference of 20 and is assigned to the range of [0, 50] which will increase the corresponding frequency. This difference implies the position change of the term in two networks. Figure 3 (b) is similar to Figure 3 (a) but betweenness instead.

4.2   Co-topic Network Results

I first explore the topics of KJV and NIV co-topic networks, their weighted degrees, and their modules (Table A.5 [9] and Table A.6 [9]). In both co-topic networks, Solomon's prosperity, contrition, battle, cycle of sin, praise, Babylon, prophecy, exodus, injustice, proverbs, kings, tribes, offering, food, harvest, Jesus' public ministry, Israel, gospel, gospel doctrine, disciples, sanctuary, and captivity were the common topics. However, in the KJV, contrition, nature of God, Canaan conquest, cleanse, wilderness, shepherd, and God were distinguishing topics relative to the NIV. In the NIV, nature, idol, psalm, ceremony, priest, payment, repair, Judah, foreigner, land, and His servants were featured topics compared to those in the KJV.

The topics with the 11 highest centralities in the KJV are nature of God (new), captivity, God's nature (old), proverbs, kings, prophecy, exodus, the cycle of sin, praise, gospel doctrine, and God. Those in the NIV are praising God, captivity, His servants, gospel doctrine, proverbs, food/harvest, priest, psalm, prophecy, Israel, and the cycle of sin.

Both the KJV and the NIV co-topic networks are divided into three modules. Each topic is assigned to a module, as shown on the rightmost columns in Table A.5 [9] and Table A.6 [9]. The KJV co-topic network is modularized by {Solomon's prosperity, contrition, battle, nature of God(new), Praise, proverbs, cleanse, food, wilderness, God, shepherd, sanctuary, captivity}, {Jesus' public ministry, gospel doctrine, gospel, disciples}, and {cycle of sin, God's nature (old), Babylon, prophecy, exodus, Canaan conquest, injustice, David, tribes, offering, food, Israel, kings}. The first module is related to God. The second module is related to Jesus Christ. The third module is similar to the first, but more related to Israel. The NIV co-topic network is decomposed into {captivity, praising God, kings, nature, idol, tribes, psalm, prophecy, Babylon, food/harvest, ceremony, battle, injustice, repair, Israel, Exodus, Judah, foreigner, land, His servants}, {Jesus' public ministry, payment, proverbs, cycle of sin, disciples, gospel doctrine}, and {sanctuary, priest, offering, Solomon's prosperity}. The first module is the history of Israel. The second module is associated with Jesus Christ. The last module is connected with worship service. We may see the KJV and NIV summarized into God-Jesus Christ-Israel (People) and God-Jesus Christ-Worship.

Second, the relationship between two topics is examined. Table A.7 [9] lists the top 10 ranked edges in the KJV co-topic network and the NIV co-topic network. Under these edges, we may find differences in KJV and NIV. The KJV highlights the nature of God in The Old Testament and The New Testament associated with captivity the most. And it stresses the words of God, such as proverbs and prophecy. Interestingly, wilderness in captivity is also emphasized. However, the NIV underlines praising God. It also accentuates His servants and gospel doctrine. This implies that the KJV pays more attention to who God is and how sinful humans are. There, King (David) is spotlighted. This may be because the KJV was published during a time when kings ruled countries. The NIV not only stresses who God is, but emphasizes the gospel and how God works through His servants.

5   Discussion and Conclusion

This study applies co-word network and co-topic network analyses to two versions of Bible to compare network structural differences in different versions of a digitized book. The result shows that the two versions are similar but have differences. The analyses enable us to compare two books not only in terms of lexicons but also in terms of concepts. We accumulate knowledge in texts but may not know or remember all the texts. Increasing knowledge cannot be all scanned by a human being, and a supporting tool is required to analyze not only various books but also books in different versions easily. The digital era spurs the demand for such tool. In this study, I explore the different versions of Bible with their central lexicons in relation to a network of lexicons or topics. I could easily confirm that the two versions share the theme that God is speaking but highlighting topics may differ.

For example, in terms of co-word networks, "Jesus", "Jerusalem", "father" were more central in NIV than in KJV evidently. And, "children" was more central in KJV than in NIV. I may guess that, 400 years later in NIV, the translators of NIV emphasized "Jesus" and New Testament. "thy" was more popular in KJV than NIV while "who" was more popular in NIV than KJV. It implies the lexical and grammatical difference between KJV and NIV in terms of writing. Both versions commonly state that God is LORD and LORD said something many times. LORD is associated with Israel. It is consistent with the knowledge that the Bible is the word of God. However, the KJV has edges of "house-LORD" and "hand-LORD" while the NIV has "son-king" and "declares-LORD" edges. With this observation, I may guess that the KJV focuses on how Lord treated the house (i.e., Israel) while the NIV concentrates on Jesus, who is king and the son of God. The modules are more diverse in the NIV than the KJV with the same threshold for community detection algorithm. This entails that the NIV may be of clear and specific terms relative to the KJV. In terms of co-topic networks, the KJV and NIV are summarized into God-Jesus Christ-Israel (People) and God-Jesus Christ-Worship with the same number of modules. However, in the KJV, the first module is related to God. The second module is related to Jesus Christ. The third module is similar to the first, but more related to Israel. In the NIV, the first module is the history of Israel. The second module is associated with Jesus Christ. The last module is connected with worship service. From the analysis on top edges of co-topic networks, KJV focuses on God's nature, sinners, and kings while NIV concentrates on God's nature and works as well as gospel.

Although these analyses give us easy summarization of different versions of a book for comparison, there still are issues to address. The number of topics that distinguishes a book should be examined. However, for each book, it will be different and the number would not matter for comparison if it is not too small. The labelling process and implications may be advanced with the help of scholars who study theology. Yet, common concepts rest in ordinary people may be acceptable to label a popular representative term for each topic. By comparing the results of this study with existing biblical scholarship and a historical contextualization of the translations, a better conclusion may be developed. Domain experts in theology are required for in-depth analyses. Applying this approach to Old Testament and New Testament separately would also result in verifying the perspectives of two versions on Old and New Testaments. There are also several advanced text mining techniques and methods to improve the comparison quantitatively.

Acknowledgements. This work was supported by the Yonsei University Future-leading Research Initiative of 2015.

References

1. Christodouloupoulos, C., Steedman, M.A.: Massively parallel corpus: The Bible in 100 languages. Lang. Resour. Eval. **49**(2), 375–395 (2014)
2. Hu, W.: Unsupervised Learning of Two Bible Books: Proverbs and Psalms. Sociology Mind **2**(3), 325 (2012)
3. Miyake, M., Akama, H., Sato, M., Nakagawa, M., Makoshi, N.: Tele-synopsis for biblical research: development of NLP based synoptic software for text analysis as a mediator of educational technology and knowledge discovery. In: Proceedings of the IEEE International Conference on Advanced Learning Technologies, 2004. IEEE, pp. 931–935 (2004)
4. Song, M., Kim, S.Y.: Detecting the knowledge structure of bioinformatics by mining full-text collections. Scientometrics **96**(1), 183–201 (2013)
5. Mac Carron, P., Kenna, R.: Universal properties of mythological networks. EPL **99**(2), 28002 (2012)
6. Blei, D.M.: Probabilistic topic models. Communications of the ACM **55**(4), 77–84 (2012)
7. Freeman, L.C.: Centrality in social networks conceptual clarification. Soc. Networks **1**(3), 215–239 (1979)
8. Blondel, V.D., Guillaume, J.L., Lambiotte, R., Lefebvre, E.: Fast unfolding of communities in large networks. J. Stat. Mech. Theor. Exp. **10**, P10008 (2008)
9. http://informatics.yonsei.ac.kr/tsmm/kh_lee.html

Data Transfer Between Discovery Services and Library Catalogs: A Case Study at the University of the Fraser Valley

Hongfei Li[✉] and Diane Cruickshank

University of the Fraser Valley, Abbotsford, Canada
{hongfei.li,diane.cruickshank}@ufv.ca

Abstract. This case study explores the challenges and successes that the University of the Fraser Valley had with bibliographic/holding data transfer and other customizations between their ILS (SirsiDynix Symphony) and EBSCO Discovery Service. Two sets of data transfer will be considered: the identification and transfer of deleted ILS MARC records to the EDS, and the inclusion of a dynamic location map from UFV's library catalogue in the EDS layer. Technical details are included.

Keywords: Web-Scale discovery interface · EBSCO Discovery Service · Integrated Library Systems (ILS) · Library catalog · MARC record · Bibliographic data · Holding data

1 Introduction

The Web-Scale Discovery interface is becoming commonplace within academic libraries. Diverse library resources with various platforms and the need to improve ease of use for library users are leading to this adoption. Previously, resource management and discovery were in the realm of Integrated Library Systems (ILS) vendors. If data transfer problems arose, the ILS vendor could come up with a solution as the discovery tool was their own. However, there has been a technological direction change where resource management has been separated from resource discovery, and online catalog modules of Integrated Library Systems (ILS) are no longer being updated. Instead, the focus is on developing independent discovery tools [1,2]. Currently, the three dominant discovery service vendors are Serials Solutions' Summon, EBSCO Discovery Service (EDS), and OCLC WorldCat Discovery. With these Discovery Service providers, libraries are finding themselves once again struggling with issues of synchronizing their ILS holding data with the discovery service.

Discovery services require the bibliographic and holdings data of each individual library to be loaded remotely onto the discovery service's server. Furthermore, the library must update these records whenever changes are made in the local library system. In August 2012, the University of the Fraser Valley (UFV) implemented the Web-Scale discovery system with EBSCO's EDS. The initial data loading of MARC

© Springer International Publishing Switzerland 2015
R.B. Allen et al. (Eds.): ICADL 2015, LNCS 9469, pp. 153–157, 2015.
DOI: 10.1007/978-3-319-27974-9_15

records in the EDS went smoothly, but very soon the ILS data updates became an issue. It was difficult to keep the EDS records accurate, and deleted and discarded items continued to be found by students using the discovery layer. Grand Valley State University and Eastern Michigan University Library had similar issues with their discovery layer [3,4].

EBSCO Customer Support advised us to do a refresh loading weekly. However, doing so took 4 hours manually, with a net result of the changes only being reflected in the EDS interface a week later. With many items (physical and e-books) being added and removed weekly, the discrepancy between real time searches of the catalogue and the EDS were significant.

A solution was found when the UFV library developed a method which captured all changes in the library catalog by creating MARC records with all additions and deletions in one single file. The data, using FTP, was sent to the EDS daily.

To explore the other end of the data transfer, we also will cover how the EDS helped us to integrate one of the features we had in our library catalog, a dynamic location map, into the EDS search layer.

2   Literature Review

There are not many case studies focused on data transfer between discovery services and library catalogs. A consortium of colleges in North Carolina (NC-PALS) writes about updating records daily in Ex Libris Primo Discovery Service. They used three scripts, run once a day. The first daily script extracts added or updated authority records, the second extracts catalog keys for any items that have been deleted, and the final script extracts any added or modified MARC records [5]. However, the paper does not provide the technical details of how the discovery service knew which records should be deleted or changed.

No detailed case studies were found specifically for libraries using SirsiDynix ILS and the EBSCO Discovery Service. In the book by Popp and Dallis, Indiana University reports that their data was sent to the EDS and updated weekly [6], the same situation that UFV initially found itself in.

3   Methods and Processes

3.1   Daily Holdings Updates

Shortly after we loaded our catalog data with the EBSCO Discovery Service, we decided to give up the weekly complete loading update. It was too time consuming and ineffective. Instead, we focused on resolving the asynchronous Bibliographic data match between library catalog and EDS. This could be done with a daily update.

SirsiDynix ILS contains a delivered API script, which can extract all records added and changed daily. For newly added book titles or copies, this script can successfully catch and create the MARC records. However, difficulties arise because the API script cannot identify the deleted or shadowed records. When the EDS receives the data file, these records are not highlighted for removal; the result is students finding items in the EDS that no longer exist.

Manually editing our MARC records with a "delete" was, again, too time consuming. Instead, UFV needed to find a way to identify the record to be deleted, and mark it automatically with a "d." We created a data flow task of four separate parts: extracting the deletion records; changing the character in Leader 05 to "d" (to indicate a deleted file); merging addition/deletion changes all into one file, and; using a cron job to FTP the data to the EDS.

All the items that needed to be deleted in the EDS were selected using a modified SirsiDynix API script. The original API script needed MARC records. Unfortunately, some of the items we needed to be deleted no longer had MARC records available in the ILS. It was therefore not possible to create a proper record for the EDS to read. UFV found, though, that if we searched the ILS transaction logs and captured the catalog keys for deleted records, we could then create "fake" MARC records which the EDS processing program would cross-check and delete.

The deletion files were extracted from the ILS transaction logs, and converted into a text based file. The text file was read, using a PERL script, to identify the start of each record. Then, the position of the leader 05 was located, and replaced with a 'd'. Fortunately, it didn't matter whether the rest of the MARC fields were completed or not. The next step was to merge all updated records together into one file, and then FTP to the EDS. All processes were run automatically, daily, without using staff time.

The strategy was implemented under Oracle Solaris 10 with SirsiDynix Symphony 3.3.1. We used the SirsiDynix API script to catch the records changed, and PERL script to find catalog keys for deleted records in transaction logs. We also used PERL script to locate and replace the leader 05 for all EDS deletion records. Korn Shell commands were used to merge the "fake" MARC records and other holdings data into one ready-to-send file. Figure 1 shows the data flow.

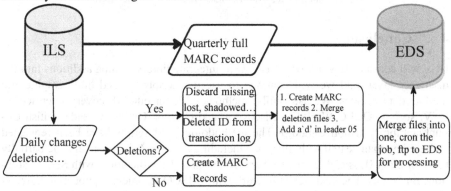

Fig. 1. Data processing and transfer from UFV's ILS to EBSCO's Discovery service

After introducing this method for EDS daily update, the mismatch between the library catalog and the EDS interface disappeared. We should mention that it is not truly synchronous, as there is a one-day delay for the EDS processing program to update the changes in the EDS.

3.2   Customizing the EDS Layer with UFV's Dynamic Map

UFV has a dynamic map in the library catalog which shows users a book's position on the shelf. It is a script based on item location and call number [7]. The dynamic map display has received positive feedback, so we wanted to add this feature into both the results list and detail page in the EDS.

EBSCO technical support created a hypertext link "Floor Map" for the searched item, which redirects the request to a layer program housed on a Linux server at UFV. This program is designed to receive the catalog key from EDS interface, query the ILS for the call number/location, and generate dynamic maps for the selected book title. A pop-up window opens, displaying the dynamic map. The program uses PHP 5.3.3 script and a pre-created base floor map database. Figure 2 shows the data flow.

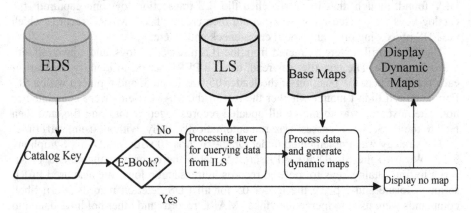

Fig. 2. Data transfer from EBSCO Discovery Service to ILS

4   Conclusion

UFV will continue to work with EBSCO to integrate library catalog additions into the discovery layer, and we will continue to use our scripts to send bibliographic and holding data updates. We use similar methods with our other discovery interfaces at UFV, such as OCLC WorldCat Discovery, and Outlook Online (Canada British Columbia Library Union Catalog). The methodology and scripts have been requested and used by many SirsiDynix libraries, including those in Asia. It can also be partially used for other ILSs and Discovery Services, such as III Millennium with Serials Solutions Summons. The next step is to work with EBSCO technical support to remove e-Books directly purchased from vendors. These e-Book deletion records are directly from the book vendors, not from the ILS, therefore have no catalog keys on which the whole automation process is based. Possibly, a second record ID, such as OCLC number, could be used for identifying the existing records in EDS. With the emergence and popularity of Web-Scale discovery services in the library world, the issue of synchronicity between library catalogs and Discovery interfaces will continue to pose challenges. Fortunately, scripts and technical solutions are being developed and documented for future improvements.

References

1. Breeding, M.: The State of the Art in Library Discovery 2010. Computers in Libraries **30**(1), 31–34 (2010)
2. Breeding, M.: Looking Forward to the Next Generation of Discovery Services. Computers In Libraries **32**(2), 28–31 (2012)
3. Daniels, J., Roth, P.: Incorporating Millennium Catalog Records into Serials Solutions' Summon. Technical Services Quarterly **29**(3), 193–199 (2012)
4. Wrosch, J., Rogers-Collins, K., Barnes, M., Marino, W.: Search Me: Eastern Michigan University's Journey through the Highs and Lows of Implementing the Summon Discovery Tool. College & Undergraduate Libraries **19**(2–4), 367–386 (2012)
5. Mortimore, J., Dunn, L., McNaughton, D., Novicki, E., Wade, E., Whittington, C.: Smoke Gets in Your Eyes: Trials and Triumphs of Implementing the Ex Libris Primo Discovery Service in a Small Regional Consortium. College & Undergraduate Libraries **19**(2–4), 344–366 (2012)
6. Popp, M.P., Dallis, D.: Planning and Implementing Resource Discovery Tools in Academic Libraries. IGI Global, Hershey (2012)
7. Li, H., Deng, S.: Linking Location and Shelf Mapping from OPAC Search Results: With Reference to Wichita State University. New Library World **109**(3/4), 107–116 (2008)

Enhancing Subject Metadata with Automated Weighting in the Medical Domain: A Comparison of Different Measures

Kun Lu[1(✉)], Jin Mao[2], and Gang Li[2]

[1] School of Library and Information Studies, University of Oklahoma,
Norman, OK 73019, USA
kunlu@ou.edu
[2] Center for the Studies of Information Resources, Wuhan University, Wuhan, China
danveno@163.com, imiswhu@aliyun.com

Abstract. Subject metadata has an important role in supporting subject access to information resources in digital libraries. Existing subject indexing systems generally produce binary outcomes (either assign or not assign a subject descriptor) that do not adequately reflect the extent to which a document is associated with the assigned subject descriptors. An automated weighting mechanism for subject descriptors is needed to strengthen the role of the subject metadata field. This study compares five measures for automated weighting subject descriptors in documents. The performance of the measures is evaluated according to their ability to discriminate major descriptors from non-major ones. Experiments on a medical collection with 348,566 articles suggest that all the measures are able to rank the major descriptors significantly higher than the non-major ones. Jaccard coefficient, Cosine similarity, and KL Divergence showed better performance than Mutual Information and Log Likelihood Ratio. The findings of this study contribute to the development of weighted subject indexing systems that have direct applications for aiding users' information seeking and improving knowledge organization in digital libraries.

Keywords: Weighted subject indexing · Relatedness measures · MeSH terms · Experiments

1 Introduction

Metadata is an essential component of digital libraries. Among different metadata fields, subject metadata has a most important role in supporting subject access to information resources. Subject indexing is the process of generating subject metadata, which generally consists of conceptual analysis and index term assignment [1]. There have been lengthy discussions on subject indexing. Most research focuses on how to determine the subjects of a document or how to construct effective thesauri to describe the subjects, while the importance of assigned subject terms (descriptors) to a document has been rarely researched. It has been well noted that a piece of work may cover multiple concepts and the importance of these concepts should be different.

© Springer International Publishing Switzerland 2015
R.B. Allen et al. (Eds.): ICADL 2015, LNCS 9469, pp. 158–168, 2015.
DOI: 10.1007/978-3-319-27974-9_16

However, most existing systems do not make a distinction among the assigned subject descriptors. Some systems adopt preliminary weighting systems only to differentiate between primary and secondary descriptors, such as the Medical Subject Headings of the National Library of Medicine (MeSH). On the other hand, term weighting is prevalent in free-text indexing and is the key to its success. A more sophisticated weighting system is needed for subject metadata.

The ability to reveal the extent to which a document is about the subject descriptors will strengthen the role of the subject metadata field. However, term weighting methods for free-text terms may not be directly applicable to subject descriptors, as there are fundamental differences between free-text terms and subject descriptors. For example, the term frequency method, an essential component of term weighting for free-text terms, assumes repeated terms in a document are more important. This is not applicable to subject metadata, since all descriptors occur once in the subject metadata field. To weight the descriptors in documents, we need to examine the semantic relatedness between a descriptor and the document to which it is assigned. Manually assigning weights to subject descriptors is possible but will add a considerable burden to indexers. A recent study by Lu and Mao [2] proposed an automatic approach to infer the weights of descriptors in documents based on weighted mutual information. However, as a first attempt to develop automated methods for weighted subject indexing, their study did not fully examine other possible measures. It is not clear whether there are better measures for this problem. This study compares five different relatedness measures that can be used to weight descriptors in a document, including the one used in Lu and Mao [2]. A thorough comparison of the different measures contributes to developing improved weighting methods for the subject metadata field.

2 Weighted Subject Indexing

The idea to distinguish the extent to which a document is about its index terms is not new. Wilson discussed at length the discrimination of the relative dominance and subordination of different elements of a document [3]. Maron described the problem of index term assignment as being to decide "whether or not (or to what degree) it (the index term) is to be assigned to a given document" (p. 39) [4], which evidently includes weighting as a part of the indexing process. Cooper and Maron [5] clearly discriminated binary indexing from weighted indexing, where binary indexing involves either assigning the index term or not, without any intermediate choices, and weighted indexing allows specifying numeric indicators of the strength of assignment. Kent et al. [6] carried out retrieval experiments with the idea of applying probabilistic weights to manual subject indexing. The indexing process of the well-known Cranfield tests incorporated manually weighted indexing to indicate the relative importance of each concept within the document [7].

Although well noted among the pioneers in the field, weighted subject indexing is largely absent in current indexing practice. A recent study by Zhang et al. [8] advocated the need for a systematic weighting mechanism for subject indexing and also pointed out the prohibitive cost for manually implementing weighted subject indexing systems. Lu and Mao proposed an automated approach to infer the weights of subject descriptors in documents according to their semantic relatedness [2]. Promising results were reported from their experiments on a test collection in the medical domain. Further studies in this direction are still needed to develop effective weighted subject indexing systems.

3   Method

3.1   Dataset

The data used in this study is the Ohsumed collection [9]. Ohsumed is a collection of 348,566 metadata records for articles in the medical domain from MEDLINE. Each record consists of seven metadata fields: title, abstract, MeSH descriptors, author, publication type, source, and record identifier, among which MeSH descriptors are subject metadata.

3.2   Preprocessing

Text Processing. All the documents in the collection were indexed by the Lemur toolkit[1]. Index terms were stemmed by the Krovetz stemmer and stop words were removed. Document representations and subject descriptor representations were built based on these index terms.

Descriptors with Multiple Qualifiers. MeSH uses qualifiers to describe different aspects of a concept. For example, for the MeSH descriptor "Psychotic Disorders/DT", "DT" is a qualifier that represents "Drug Therapy". Many MeSH descriptors are assigned with multiple qualifiers to represent different aspects of the concepts. For example, "Psychotic Disorders/*CO/DT/TH" can be split into "Psychotic Disorders/CO", "Psychotic Disorders/DT", and "Psychotic Disorders/TH". It is noted that the different aspects may have different importance for the article. Therefore, we infer the weights for different aspects separately.

NLM indexers assign asterisks to MeSH descriptors that represent the major topics of the articles. Among the above three split MeSH descriptors, "Psychotic Disorders/CO" is identified as a major topic as the qualifier "CO" was marked with an asterisk. Main subject headings can also be regarded as major ones, as asterisks can be assigned to those descriptors without qualifiers, e.g., "Psychotic Disorders/*".

Non-subject MeSH. NLM categories MeSH terms into five different types: Descriptors, Publication Types, Geographics, Qualifiers, and Supplementary Concept Records. Not all types are related to the subject content. The focus of this study is on the semantic relatedness between MeSH headings and articles. Non-subject related types, including Publication Types and Geographics, were removed.

---

[1] http://www.lemurproject.org

3.3 Subject Descriptor Representation

A prerequisite to measuring the relatedness between subject descriptors and documents is the subject descriptor representation. A subject descriptor can be considered a concept whose meaning is embodied in the documents to which the subject descriptor is assigned. Therefore, we represent a subject descriptor as a collection of documents to which it is assigned. More specifically, each subject descriptor is represented as a "bag-of-words" based on the documents to which it is assigned. TF-IDF (Term frequency – Inverse document frequency) weighting is used to discriminate the importance of terms that represent subject descriptors. Table 1 presents some examples of the subject descriptor representations. It's observed that the terms, especially the top ones, are related to the meaning of the MeSH descriptors. Take "Liver Circulation" as an example. The terms "liver" and "circulate" are ranked high, which are literally from this MeSH heading. The term "hepatic", a conjugate of "liver", also has a high weight. Other terms on the list also have strong semantic associations with the MeSH descriptor. It appears that the subject descriptor representation adopted in this study is reasonable.

Table 1. Examples of Subject Descriptor Representations.

Liver Circulation		Liver Circulation/DE		Ascitic Fluid/PA	
liver	0.0349	hepatic	0.0244	peritoneal	0.0223
hepatic	0.0285	flow	0.0181	ascitic	0.0150
portal	0.0260	liver	0.0171	endometriosi	0.0130
flow	0.0148	portal	0.0160	fluid	0.0127
circulate	0.0107	de	0.0105	cytology	0.0125
vein	0.0090	blood	0.0103	pa	0.0092

Another observation is that the subject descriptor representations can distinguish the MeSH descriptors with different qualifiers. This is evidenced by the differences in the representations for "Liver Circulation" and "Liver Circulation/DE" (Table 1).

It should be noted that the subject descriptor representation does not apply to Mutual Information and Log Likelihood Ratio as they measure the associations between subject descriptors and terms in documents directly as described below.

3.4 Semantic Relatedness Measures

Jaccard Coefficient (Jac). Jaccard coefficient measures the similarity between two sets based on their overlapping elements. In this study, Jaccard coefficient represents the ratio of overlapping terms from subject descriptor representations and documents. For a subject descriptor h and a document d, the Jaccard coefficient is defined as:

$$Jac(h, d) = \frac{|W_h \cap W_d|}{|W_h \cup W_d|} \tag{1}$$

where W_d denotes the set of terms in the document d and W_h denotes the set of terms in the subject descriptor representation of h.

Cosine (Cos). Cosine similarity is widely used to measure similarity among documents in Vector Space Model. Geometrically, it represents the angle between two document vectors. In this study, the Cosine similarity measures the similarity between the term vectors of subject descriptor representations and documents. It is calculated as follows:

$$Cos(h, d) = \frac{V_h \times V_d}{|V_h| \times |V_d|} = \frac{x_{1,h}x_{1,d} + \cdots + x_{k,h}x_{k,d} + \cdots}{\sqrt{x_{1,h}^2 + \cdots x_{k,h}^2 + \cdots}\sqrt{x_{1,d}^2 + \cdots x_{k,d}^2 + \cdots}} \tag{2}$$

where V_d is the term vector of the document d, $x_{k,d}$ represents the weight for the k-th term of V_d, V_h is the term vector of subject descriptor h, and $x_{k,h}$ represents the weight for the k-th term of V_d. TF-IDF was used for term weights.

Mutual Information(MI). Mutual information assesses the mutual dependence of two random variables. In this context, mutual information is used to measure the associations between subject descriptors and terms in documents. The mutual information between a term w and a subject descriptor h is defined as:

$$I(h; w) = p(w, h)log\frac{p(w, h)}{p(w)p(h)} \tag{3}$$

where the probabilities $p(w,h)$, $p(w)$ and $p(h)$ can be estimated by Maximum Likelihood Estimator (MLE) at the document level:

$$p(\iota) = \frac{df_\iota}{N} \tag{4}$$

where df_l is the document frequency of the item l (i.e. number of documents that contain l), and N is the number of documents in the collection. Then, the association between a subject descriptor h and a document d is calculated as:

$$I(h; d) = \sum_{w \in V_d} I(h; w) \tag{5}$$

where W_d is the term set in the document d.

Log Likelihood Ratio (LLR). Log Likelihood Ratio is a statistic adapted from Pearson's Chi-square test to measure word collocation through the co-occurrence counts and the mutual exclusive occurrence of word pairs. The relatedness between a subject descriptor h and a document d measured by Log Likelihood Ratio is defined as follows:

$$LLR(h, w) = log L(p_1, k_1, n_1) + log L(p_2, k_2, n_2) \\ - log L(p, k_1, n_1) - log L(p, k_2, n_2) \tag{6}$$

where $log L(p, k, n) = klogL(p) + (n - k)log(1 - p), p_1 = \frac{k_1}{n_1}, p_2 = \frac{k_2}{n_2}, p = \frac{k_1 + k_2}{n_1 + n_2}$, k_l is the number of documents where the descriptor h and the term w co-occur, n_l is the document frequency of the term w, k_2 is the number of documents where the descriptor h appears but not the term w, and n_2 is the number of documents where the term w does not occur. Then, the relatedness between the descriptor h and document d is obtained by:

$$LLR(h, d) = \sum_{w \in \theta_d} LLR(h, w) \tag{7}$$

where W_d is the set of terms in the document d.

KL Divergence (KL). KL divergence is widely used in language modeling to measure the relationships between two language models. In this study, a language model θ_h can be constructed for a subject descriptor h based on its representation. Then, the relationship between a document d and a descriptor h can be measured as:

$$KL(\theta_d||\theta_h) = \sum_w p(w|\theta_d)log\frac{p(w|\theta_d)}{p(w|\theta_h)} \tag{8}$$

where the term probabilities are estimated by MLE.

3.5   Evaluation

The performance of different measures is evaluated by their ability to rank major MeSH descriptors higher than the non-major ones. Each measure assigns scores to the list of MeSH descriptors in each document. We then rank the MeSH according to their scores in the document and compute the average ranks of the major MeSH and non-major MeSH produced by different measures. Measures that produce higher ranks for major MeSH indicate better performance.

4   Results

4.1   Overview of MeSH Descriptors

The Ohsumed collection has 3,696,239 assigned MeSH descriptors. After splitting descriptors with multiple qualifiers, 4,189,494 separate MeSH were obtained and 3,454,297 of them were identified as subject related. We only inferred the weights for these subject related MeSH descriptors. 1,027,427 major headings and 2,426,870 non-major headings are included in the subject related MeSH descriptors. The overview of MeSH descriptors in the Ohsumed collection is shown in Table 2. Descriptive statistics of the MeSH descriptors in the collection is provided in Table 3.

Table 2. Overview of MeSH descriptors in Ohsumed (after splitting multiple qualifiers).

No. of MeSH	No. of subject related MeSH	No. of subject related major MeSH	No. of subject related non-major MeSH
4,189,494	3,454,297	1,027,427	2,426,870

Note: Among all the subject related MeSH, those with asterisks are subject related major MeSH and those without asterisks are subject related non-major MeSH.

Table 3. Descriptive statistics of MeSH terms in Ohsumed.

Types of MeSH	Avg. # MeSH per doc	Std. # MeSH per doc	Min # MeSH per doc	Max # MeSH per doc
All	12.02	5.22	0	49
Subject related	9.91	4.54	0	47
Subject related major MeSH	2.95	1.37	0	13
Subject related non-major MeSH	6.96	4.13	0	41

4.2   Example of Weighted MeSH in a Document

With the subject descriptor representation and five semantic relatedness measures, we automatically assigned weights to MeSH descriptors in documents. An example of the weighted MeSH descriptors in a document (PubMed ID 87049559, titled "Postpartum thyroiditis--an underdiagnosed disease") is shown in Figure 1. The normalized weights were inferred by Cosine similarity. The original MeSH assigned by professional indexers are *Female, Human, Pregnancy, Propranolol/TU, Puerperal Disorders/*DI, Thyroiditis/*DI/DT,* and *Thyroxine/TU*. Among them, *Female* is not a subject related descriptor. The descriptor *Thyroiditis/*DI/DT* was split into two descriptors: *Thyroiditis/DI* and *Thyroiditis/DT*. The two major descriptors have the highest weights and the descriptor *Human* is given the lowest weight. In addition, the two descriptors that share the same main heading *Thyroiditis* but with different qualifiers (*DT* and *DI*) are assigned with different weights. The weight of the major aspect (*Thyroiditis/DI*) is slightly higher than the weight of the non-major aspect (*Thyroiditis/DT*). This is an example where inferred weights successfully rank the major descriptors higher than the non-major ones.

4.3   The Performance of Different Measures

The average ranks of major MeSH descriptors and non-major MeSH descriptors for the five semantic relatedness measures are provided in Figure 2. It can be observed that the average ranks of major MeSH descriptors are much higher than the average ranks of non-major MeSH descriptors for all five measures. A group of t-tests reveal that the differences of the average ranks between major MeSH descriptors and non-major MeSH descriptors are statistically significant (for all the five measures, df=9, p<0.001). This suggests that all the measures are able to rank major MeSH descriptors significantly higher than non-major ones.

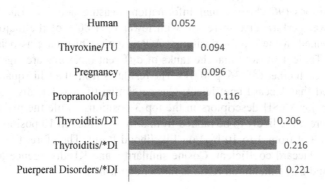

Fig. 1. The weighted MeSH descriptors for document # 87049559 (by Cosine similarity).

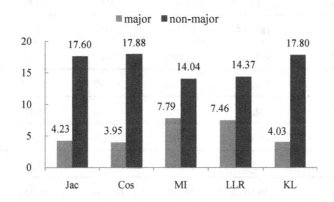

Fig. 2. Average ranks of the major subject descriptors and the non-major subject descriptors. (Smaller values indicate higher ranks)

Among all the measures, Cosine similarity achieves the best performance in terms of ranking major MeSH descriptors at the top. The average ranks of non-major MeSH descriptors also provide evidence for their performance: the average ranks of non-major MeSH descriptors for Jaccard coefficient, Cosine similarity, and KL Divergence are lower than the average ranks of non-major MeSH for Mutual Information and Log Likelihood Ratio.

To provide more details on their rankings, Table 4 lists the rank distributions of the major subject descriptors in the top 10 positions. The numbers in Table 4 represent how many times the major subject descriptors appear in that rank. Jaccard coefficient, Cosine similarity, and KL Divergence sorted more than 95% of the major MeSH descriptors within the top 10 positions, suggesting their high levels of performance in recall. KL Divergence placed the most major MeSH descriptors within the top 10 positions (96.1%). Mutual Information measure and Log Likelihood Ratio showed lower performance in recall, with fewer than 80% of the major MeSH descriptors ranked in the top 10 positions. A Pearson's Chi-square association test on the data in Table 4 showed that the ranks of different measures are significantly different from each other (df=36, p<0.01). The residuals from the Chi-square association test revealed that Jaccard coefficient, Cosine similarity, and KL divergence tend to place the major MeSH descriptors in the top 3 positions, while the major MeSH descriptors were more likely to be ranked from 5 to 10 in the top 10 positions by Mutual Information and from 4 to 10 by Log Likelihood Ratio. Therefore, the superior performance of Jaccard coefficient, Cosine similarity, and KL divergence to Mutual Information and Log Likelihood Ratio is further confirmed.

Table 4. The frequencies of major MeSH descriptors in each rank for the five measures. (Percentile represents the percentage of the major MeSH in the top ten positions out of all major MeSH)

Rank	Jac	Cos	MI	LLR	KL
1	187,318	219,922	7,992	7,215	201,390
2	177,758	194,060	42,468	47,521	188,329
3	154,889	158,753	77,897	89,074	159,539
4	127,110	122,635	98,316	109,147	126,903
5	99,802	91,437	106,226	113,483	97,652
6	77,929	67,399	106,422	110,399	73,373
7	59,006	49,781	102,019	102,551	54,222
8	43,716	35,838	94,007	92,365	39,170
9	31,693	25,627	84,066	80,593	27,656
10	22,246	18,757	72,756	67,851	19,449
In total	*981,467*	*984,209*	*792,169*	*820,199*	*987,683*
Percentile	*95.5%*	*95.7%*	*77.1%*	*79.8%*	*96.1%*

5   Discussion and Conclusion

Weighted subject indexing can strengthen the role of subject metadata in digital libraries. The development of automated weighting methods provides a cost-effective implementation for weighted subject indexing. This study evaluated five measures for weighting subject descriptors. A collection of 348,566 medical articles are used and the performance of different measures is evaluated according to their ability to discriminate major and non-major MeSH descriptors. All five measures are able to rank major descriptors significantly higher than non-major descriptors. Cosine similarity shows the best performance in terms of ranking major descriptors at the top, followed by KL divergence and Jaccard coefficient. The findings of this study contribute to a better understanding of the automated subject weighting problem.

Developing weighted subject indexing has direct applications for aiding users in information seeking and improving knowledge organization. With the ability to discriminate the importance of subject descriptors to a document according to the weights of subject descriptors, users will be able to rank search results beyond the simple Boolean search functions that are available in the subject metadata field of most existing systems. In addition, knowledge organization will benefit from such fine-grained subject indexing systems that distinguish the extent to which a document is about the subject descriptors.

Several limitations of the study need to be acknowledged. The findings of this study are drawn from the medical domain and may not be generalizable to other domains and/or thesauri. That is, depending on the different text patterns and vocabularies of different domains, different measures may better serve some domains than others. However, it is noted that the same methods should be applicable to other domains and thesauri to generate automated weightings for subject descriptors. Second, although the experiments revealed that Jaccard coefficient, Cosine similarity, and KL Divergence have better performance than Mutual Information and Log Likelihood Ratio in discriminating major and non-major descriptors, it is not completely clear why one measure is better or worse than another. An in-depth case study is needed to understand the underlying mechanisms. Third, the subject descriptor representations in this study are based on the "bag-of-words" model which has its limitations in ignoring the sequences of terms in texts. Future research will further investigate other possible representation methods and the underlying mechanisms of the performance differences. Extending the study to other domains is also another direction of future study.

Acknowledgements. The paper is supported by the Key Program of National Social Science Foundation of China under the project No. 13&ZD173 and National Natural Science Foundation of China under projects No. 71420107026 and No. 71373286.

References

1. Taylor, A.G.: The organization of information, 3rd edn. Libraries Unlimited, Westport (2008)
2. Lu, K., Mao, J.: Automatically infer subject terms and documents associations through text mining. In: Proceedings of ASIST 2013, pp. 1–3. Wiley, Montreal (2013)
3. Wilson, P.: Two kinds of power. An essay on bibliographic control. University of California Press, Berkeley (1968)
4. Maron, M.E.: On indexing, retrieval and the meaning of about. Journal of the American Society for Information Science 28(1), 38–43 (1977)
5. Cooper, W.S., Maron, M.E.: Foundations of probabilistic and utility-theoretic indexing. Journal of the ACM 25(1), 67–80 (1978)
6. Kent, A., Lancour, H., Daily, J.E.: Probabilistic or weighted indexing. In: Encyclopedia of Library and Information Science: Volume 24 – Printers and Printing: Arabic Printing to Public Policy: Copyright, and Information Technology. CRC Press (1978)
7. Cleverdon, C.W.: The significance of the Cranfield tests on index languages. In: Proceedings of the 14th ACM SIGIR, pp. 3–12. ACM, New York (1991)
8. Zhang, H., Smith, L.C., Twidale, M., Gao, F.H.: Seeing the wood for the trees: Enhancing metadata subject elements with weights. Information Technology and Libraries 30(2), 75–80 (2011)
9. Hersh, W., Buckley, C., Leone, T.J., Hickam, D.: OHSUMED: an interactive retrieval evaluation and new large test collection for research. In: Proceedings of SIGIR 1994, pp. 192–201. Springer London (1994)

Enhancing Digital Heritage Archives Using Gamified Annotations

Job King'ori Maina$^{(\boxtimes)}$ and Hussein Suleman

Department of Computer Science, University of Cape Town, Private Bag X3,
Rondebosch 7701, South Africa
j@kingori.co hussein@cs.uct.ac.za
http://www.cs.uct.ac.za

Abstract. Digital archives have focused on the collection of information and not on the collaborative capabilities digital heritage archives could have. In this study, we look at how we can add a collaborative element to an already existing digital heritage archive and incentivise users to engage with it more. Using *gamified annotations*, we show that gamification could play an important role in giving the participants an incentive to engage with the digital archive and guide them to contribute relevant content. We found that gamified annotations do affect the number and quality of annotations submitted. We believe successful implementation of a gamified annotation framework should go a long way to improve viewership, sharing, learning and debate around the content of heritage archives.

Keywords: Gamification · Heritage archives · Annotations

1 Introduction

The main reason digital collections are placed online is to invite students, researchers, teachers, and the public to explore and connect with our past. Historians, librarians, archivists, and curators who share digital collections and exhibits measure their success in moving toward this goal by how people use, reuse, explore and understand these objects [1]. However, digital heritage archives so far have primarily focused on the collection of information and not on the discussion that occurs around that information. As a result, they have largely become collections of work used by professionals in the domain that the digital archive is targeted towards. This has been fast-tracked by widespread digitisation.

While widespread digitisation is certainly a step in the right direction, it can pose an interesting problem going forward. These digital heritage archives have become highly specialised environments thus making it more difficult to instigate and enhance engagement with the archives by the viewers [2].

Genius[1], formerly and popularly known as Rap Genius, was at its conception a lyrics website with a focus on rap content. The site allows users to add

---

[1] http://genius.com

© Springer International Publishing Switzerland 2015
R.B. Allen et al. (Eds.): ICADL 2015, LNCS 9469, pp. 169–179, 2015.
DOI: 10.1007/978-3-319-27974-9_17

context and interpretations to text and images through an annotation system. The website has slowly grown to include other genres. Each annotation layers extra information on top of the content, enabling the reader to understand its context as they read. An annotation therefore is like a miniature Wikipedia page with constantly improving distillations of the combined wisdom of the users' submissions. As a result, Genius becomes a conversation built around texts and the interpretations of those texts. Users of Genius are incentivised to participate through a system of reputation and rewards. Each user can earn reputation in the form of *'IQ points'*[2] for various actions and reactions on the site, for example: writing an annotation, getting their annotation up-voted and moderating someone else's work [3].

According to Horowitz, Genius' approach of starting with rap, though not intentional, ended being the best choice [4]. The popular perception of rap as trivial, indecipherable, or too ethnic made it the perfect candidate for annotation. Horowitz argues that we need knowledge of the genre's particular culture, history, and people to fully understand the references in rap and so, to fully understand the content in rap lyrics, one needs to know the circumstances that form the setting for the event, statement, or idea covered by the referent.

Genius' application of gamified annotations could be adapted to digital heritage archives. Annotations seem to be the suitable technology layer that enables scholars to crowd-source the most correct interpretation or meaning of a heritage object without altering the content itself and gamification could be a catalyst to user engagement and participation.

2   Related Work

To better understand the needs of the viewers of digital collections, Sweetnam et al. break down these viewers into four distinct groups based on their communities of interest. These are professional researchers, apprentice investigators, informed users and the general public [5]. Despite their different interests, there is considerable overlap when it comes to basic user requirements. Some common requirements include the ability to perform accurate searches, add in-line annotations, bookmarks, have more visualised interactions with contents such as maps and so on. Each of these requirements is ultimately aimed to personalise the collection, enrich it or enhance their developing engagement with its contents.

In their study, it was noted that there was a transference and reliance of knowledge from the more expert users down to the average users. The professional researchers had the most specific and advanced requirements, followed by the apprentice investigators, informed users and finally the general public. The intermediate groups hoped to benefit from the exposed work carried out by the

---

[2] IQ points in the context of Genius do not represent the more commonly know *'intelligence quotient'*, a score derived from one of several standardised tests designed to assess human intelligence.

more knowledgable groups. The general public had very little contextual information about the collection and identified the need for accessible introductions to the collections that would explain the material they contain and its historical context [5]. The CULTURA project is an example of a project that aimed to use annotation as a tool to improve the interaction of non-specialist users and the general public with cultural heritage contents [6], [7].

At the beginning of the life of a digital heritage archive comes the collection and analysis of content. After the experts are done with the data, the general public gets access to the authoritative and complex hyperlinked content. Silberman suggests that one of the greatest contributions to the public understanding of the past is to go beyond this system [8].

3   The Annotated Digital Bleek and Lloyd Collection

The digital heritage archive of choice for this study was the Digital Bleek and Lloyd Collection[3]. It is an archive of Khoisan heritage formed from the digitised records of Lucy Lloyd and Wilhelm Bleek's notebooks.

While most digital libraries are traditionally implemented using complex database-powered infrastructure, the Digital Bleek & Lloyd archive took a different approach. It is implemented as a static and portable website. The XHTML pages are pre-generated from XML source data using XSLT. This conversion is not done client side as some browsers do not support client-side XSLT. Conversion is therefore done once and when complete the generated files form the collection. This collection can then be browsed like a typical webpage by clicking on hyperlinks that link up the various pages [9].

3.1   System Design

The approach used to add gamified annotations to the digital Bleek & Lloyd collection required minimal changes to its structure. The system consisted of two isolated parts:

1. **Annotation Engine**[4] — This is a remote JSON REST API based on the Annotator Store specification[5]. When a user creates, deletes, views or edits an annotation on the archive, those user interactions are converted into API requests that are transferred via HTTP to this engine. In addition to storage, the annotation engine is also responsible for authenticating users and enforcing permissions.
2. **Enhanced Digital Archive** — JavaScript libraries such as Annotator[6] and Annotorious[7] and some custom JavaScript were used on the digital heritage

---

[3] http://lloydbleekcollection.cs.uct.ac.za

[4] https://github.com/itsmrwave/annotator_store-gem

[5] http://docs.annotatorjs.org/en/v1.2.x/storage.html

[6] http://annotatorjs.org

[7] https://annotorious.github.io

archive to create widgets to support user interaction. They serialise user actions into API requests that the annotation engine can understand.

The only change required on the static site was to include a few lines of JavaScript to each page. In fact, since the Annotation Engine was separate from the archive itself, this meant that it could be used to add annotations to other archives at the same time.

3.2 Annotating Text

Involved selecting a portion of text, after which the user is presented with an annotation widget. The widget contains a text box where the user types out the content of the annotation. Once an annotation is created, it is marked by a yellow highlight.

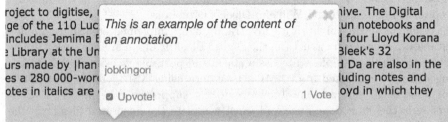

Fig. 1. Annotation widget used when viewing an annotation.

To view the annotations made, the user hovers the mouse over the yellow highlight to reveal the view widget. The view widget shows the content of the annotations, edit and delete buttons, the username of the annotator and up-vote information. The up-vote section has a checkbox for users to up-vote the annotation and also a count of the total number of up-votes that the annotation has received. See Figure 1.

3.3 Annotating Images

Follows a similar process to the one used when creating a text annotation. However, instead of selecting a portion of text, the user selects a portion of an image. The section of the image to be annotated is then represented as a bounding box. See Figure 2.

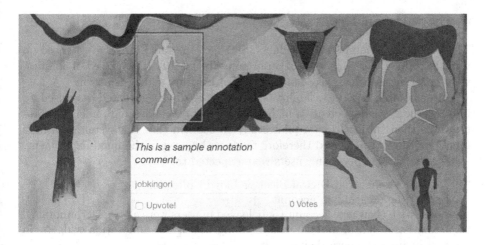

Fig. 2. Annotation widget used when viewing an image annotation.

3.4   Gamification Elements

To implement gamified annotations, a scoring system was created to serve as a measure of participation in the core activity and the quality of annotations. The scoring was based on the number of annotations a user made and the number of up-votes that their annotations received from other users. Each annotation and up-vote was ascribed a value of one point. The total score was calculated by summing up all the points from annotations and up-votes. A leaderboard was featured on the left of the digital archive showing a list of user's usernames and their respective total scores. This served as a ranking system for the users. See Figure 3.

Fig. 3. Leaderboard showing the usernames of different users and their respective scores, which were derived from totals of annotations and up-votes.

4   Evaluation Process

The U.S.E. Questionnaire (Usefulness, Satisfaction, and Ease of use), based on work by A.M. Lund, was used to evaluate usability [10]. It consisted of 30 questions covering usefulness, ease of use, ease of learning and satisfaction.

After completing the usability study, the feedback gathered was used to improve the system to create a high-fidelity prototype. This high-fidelity prototype was then subjected to a pilot study to confirm that the system was fully functional, free of bugs and therefore ready to be used in the main experiment.

For the main experiment, users were expected to:

1. Visit the Annotated Digital Bleek & Lloyd Collection.
2. Sign up by creating an account.
3. Login with their new account (only logged in users were allowed to annotate).
4. Browse the digital archive while making use of the annotation widgets on text or images where they saw fit.
5. Complete a system evaluation survey once they are done using the system.

As the users signed up, they were allocated to different groups: a *gamified* or *un-gamified* group. Each group's experience with the archive would be different. For the gamified group, they would be able to view and make use of the gamification elements while the un-gamified group would only be able to annotate.

5   System Usability

11 users participated in the usability evaluation. 8 had MSc. degrees as their last completed degrees while the rest had BSc. degrees. 9 of the participants were men and 2 women. 4 of the participants were between the ages of 25-29 years, 5 between 30-35 years and the 36-40 and 41-45 year bands each had 1 participant. It was deemed appropriate to use this pool of users as they were considered to be a source of an expert evaluation of the system because they were all computer science research students.

Based on the background information gathered through a pre-survey questionnaire, it was noted that each participant often participated in content consumption activities online. However, they hardly carried out any content generation activities such as commenting, uploading images, annotating and blogging.

Usefulness — All participants agreed that the system was useful. About 36.36% agreed that the tool met their need with an equal portion staying neutral. Almost half (45.45%), agreed that the tool did everything it was expected to do with 9.09% staying neutral and 27.27% disagreeing.

Ease of Use — 90.91% found that the system was simple and easy to use without any written instructions and without inconsistencies. 72.73% found the system user friendly with only 18.18% neutral and 9.09% disagreeing. 81.82% agreed that the system required the fewest steps possible to achieve the task they were supposed to complete.

Satisfaction — All participants agreed that it is a wonderful tool. 81.82% of the participants were satisfied with the system. 90.91% of them said they would recommend it to a friend.

Ease of Learning — All participants were able to learn how to use the tool quickly and easily and even remember how to use it. 90.91% agreed that they quickly became skilful at using it with only 9.09% who were found neutral.

6   Results and Observations

6.1   Task Analysis

Rank Annotating Users in Order of Total Annotations Submitted. Sorting the annotating participants in order of the total annotations they submitted reveals a majority of gamified users. Out of the 16 annotating participants on the list, 10 (62.50%) are gamified users while the remaining 6 (37.50%) are un-gamified users. 4 out of the 6 (66.67%) un-gamified users were found in the bottom half of the list and with counts lower than 5. This means that the gamified users dominated the top of the list and annotated more than the un-gamified users. See Table 1.

Table 1. Ranked list of the 16 users who annotated in order of their total count of annotations for text and image annotations.

User	Count	Text	Images	Mode	User	Count	Text	Images	Mode
19	80	4	76	Gamified	9	11	11	0	Gamified
40	36	31	5	Un-gamified	39	10	10	0	Gamified
22	33	27	6	Gamified	64	7	1	6	Gamified
58	21	19	2	Gamified	63	4	4	0	Un-gamified
11	17	14	3	Gamified	55	3	3	0	Un-gamified
46	15	0	15	Gamified	42	2	0	2	Un-gamified
32	15	14	1	Gamified	65	1	1	0	Un-gamified
8	11	11	0	Un-gamified	66	1	0	1	Gamified

Relevance of Annotation Content to Subject Matter. The annotations submitted could be categorised by content type into 2 groups: relevant and feedback annotations. 'Relevant' refers to those annotations whose annotation content was directly related to or is a comment on the subject matter of the digital archive. 'Feedback' refers to those annotations whose content was considered to be a message made to the owner of the digital archive to communicate appreciation, feature requests or comments on design aspects of the archive. See Table 2.

109 of the 117 (93.16%) image annotations were relevant to the subject matter. Text annotations had only 16 of the 150 (10.57%) annotations submitted

Table 2. Breakdown of 267 submitted annotation by content.

Category	Text			Images		
	Gamified	*Un-gamified*	*Total*	*Gamified*	*Un-gamified*	*Total*
Feedback	86 (64.2%)	48 (35.8%)	134	6 (66.7%)	3 (33.3%)	9
Relevant	14 (87.5%)	2 (12.5%)	16	104 (96.3%)	4 (3.7%)	108

having relevant content with the remaining 134 annotations (89.33%) used to provide feedback about the digital archive. While relevance of the annotation content seemed to be a factor of the type of annotation, it did not seem to be affected by gamification.

6.2 System Survey Responses: Motivation

Out of the 61 registered users, 20 took time to complete the system evaluation survey after using the final system. 12 were women and only 8 were men. The participants were all university students who came from diverse backgrounds with different degree levels, majors and year in which they joined university. The diversity of the users' backgrounds and interests was considered to be representative of the general public. For both the gamified and un-gamified groups, 80% of the users were not new to digital archives, however, for all the participants it was their first time using a digital heritage archive.

Four survey questions were targeted to find out what would contribute to each participants' motivations to view more, revisit the digital archive, contribute and share the digital archive with others. In each action, 7 features were presented to the user for them to give feedback on which ones they felt compelled them to perform a certain action. The 7 features are listed in Table 3. The results to the questions are shown in Figures 4 and 5.

Table 3. Survey questions to evaluate user motivations to viewing, contributing, revisiting and sharing the archive.

Code	Question
TQ1	Having content on the digital archive annotated with extra information
TQ2	Having only your annotations visible at a time when browsing
TQ3	Having everyone's annotations visible at the same time (including yours) when browsing
TQ4	Receiving and being able to view points awarded to you for annotating
TQ5	Being able to view other participant's scores (e.g. via visible scoreboard)
TQ6	Receiving achievement badges based on points you've accumulated (e.g. 'Top Contributor', 'User of the year')
TQ7	Being able to view achievement badges assigned to other users (e.g. 'Top Contributor', 'User of the year')

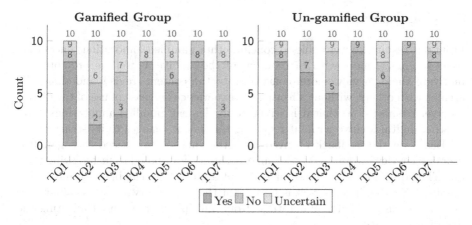

Fig. 4. User feedback on features that promote or motivate *viewing more of the archive*.

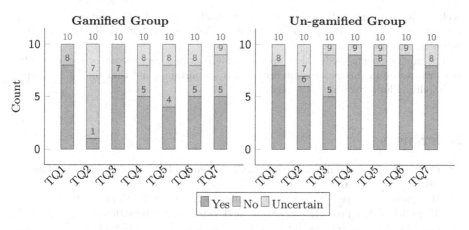

Fig. 5. User feedback on features that promote or motivate *sharing the archive with others*.

It was observed that the results showing user motivations to contribute more to the archive or revisit the archive had similar trends to the results showing user motivations to view more of the archive. See Figure 4.

In each instance, the results for *TQ1*, *TQ4*, *TQ5*, *TQ6*, and *TQ7* showed consistent and positive feedback from the majority of users for both gamified and un-gamified groups. These show that features highlighted by each question contributed to the users' motivations.

For *TQ2* and *TQ3*, the gamified and un-gamified groups had different results. Gamified users preferred viewing everyone's annotations at the same time while un-gamified users preferred viewing only their annotations. Investigation of this phenomenon was not within the scope of this study and therefore any attempt to explain this variation would have to be carried out in a future study.

7 Conclusion

From our results we were able to conclude that gamified annotations encourage users to engage more with the content of the archive as well as promote and motivate them to view more, contribute to the content, revisit and share the archive with others, without affecting the experience and ease of use of the digital archive. We also show that it is trivial to implement gamified annotations in an existing digital archive without requiring significant changes to its structure.

Based on the feedback received from the survey, we noticed that gamified users prefer viewing annotations from other users as opposed to just viewing their own. The question raised however is if that approach is scalable with increasing numbers of users. Therefore it is important that going forward, we evaluate the best approach to display annotations from multiple users without affecting the experience negatively.

Acknowledgements. This research was partially funded by the National Research Foundation of South Africa (Grant numbers: 85470 and 83998), University of Cape Town and Telkom SA Ltd.

The authors acknowledge that opinions, findings and conclusions or recommendations expressed in this publication are that of the authors, and that the NRF accepts no liability whatsoever in this regard.

References

1. Owens, T.: Digital cultural heritage and the crowd. Curator: The Museum Journal **56**(1), 121–130 (2013)
2. Hampson, C., Agosti, M., Orio, N., Bailey, E., Lawless, S., Conlan, O., Wade, V.: The CULTURA project: supporting next generation interaction with digital cultural heritage collections. In: Ioannides, M., Fritsch, D., Leissner, J., Davies, R., Remondino, F., Caffo, R. (eds.) EuroMed 2012. LNCS, vol. 7616, pp. 668–675. Springer, Heidelberg (2012)
3. Lehman, T., Zechory, I.: Introducing Genius.com. http://meta.genius.com/ Genius-founders-introducing-geniuscom-annotated (accessed: October 5, 2014)
4. Horowitz, B.: From Rap Genius to Genius - Ben's Blog. http://www.bhorowitz. com/from_rap_genius_to_genius (accessed: October 6, 2014)
5. Sweetnam, M.S., Agosti, M., Orio, N., Ponchia, C., Steiner, C.M., Hillemann, E.-C., Ó Siochrú, M., Lawless, S.: User needs for enhanced engagement with cultural heritage collections. In: Zaphiris, P., Buchanan, G., Rasmussen, E., Loizides, F. (eds.) TPDL 2012. LNCS, vol. 7489, pp. 64–75. Springer, Heidelberg (2012)
6. Agosti, M., Conlan, O., Ferro, N., Hampson, C., Munnelly, G.: Interacting with digital cultural heritage collections via annotations: the CULTURA approach. In: Proceedings of the 2013 ACM Symposium on Document Engineering, DocEng 2013, pp. 13–22. ACM, New York (2013)
7. Ferro, N., Munnelly, G., Hampson, C., Conlan, O.: Fostering interaction with cultural heritage material via annotations: the FAST-CAT way. In: Catarci, T., Ferro, N., Poggi, A. (eds.) IRCDL 2013. CCIS, vol. 385, pp. 41–52. Springer, Heidelberg (2014)

8. Silberman, N.A.: Beyond theme parks and digitized data: What can cultural heritage technologies contribute to the public understanding of the past? (2005)
9. Suleman, H.: Digital libraries without databases: the Bleek and Lloyd collection. In: Kovács, L., Fuhr, N., Meghini, C. (eds.) ECDL 2007. LNCS, vol. 4675, pp. 392–403. Springer, Heidelberg (2007)
10. Lund, A.M.: Measuring usability with the USE questionnaire. http://www.stcsig.org/usability/newsletter/0110_measuring_with_use.html (accessed: June 24, 2014)

AfriWeb: A Web Search Engine for a Marginalized Language

Nkosana Malumba, Katlego Moukangwe, and Hussein Suleman(✉)

Department of Computer Science, University of Cape Town, Private Bag X3,
Rondebosch, South Africa
n.malumba@gmail.com, katlego@moukangwe.com, hussein@cs.uct.ac.za

Abstract. isiZulu is a Bantu language spoken by approximately 9 million people, but with very few written documents available on the Internet. The lack of electronic documents and supporting infrastructure to store and retrieve documents in isiZulu is an additional threat for its survival as a written language. This paper documents an investigation into the creation of one such infrastructural element - a custom Web search engine - for isiZulu, where previously no such system was in existence. The focus of the search engine was on the language-specific elements of morphological parsing and statistical language modelling. Morphological parsing was shown to produce better results for isiZulu, an agglutinative language, than traditional affix-based stemming. Statistical language modelling was able to successfully separate isiZulu documents from others, thus enabling the use of a language-based focused crawler.

Keywords: isiZulu · Web search · Morphological analysis · Language modelling · Focused crawling

1 Introduction

IsiZulu is one of South Africa's 11 official languages. It is the most widely spoken home language in South Africa and is understood by more than 50% of South Africa's population of about 53 million people [1]. In spite of the prevalence of this language in South Africa, it is almost impossible to find information on the World Wide Web written in isiZulu i.e., submitting a query in IsiZulu to a popular search engine, such as Google, and getting results only or mostly in isiZulu.

One reason for this is that digital documents in Zulu are very rare; in October 2014, there were only 682 Zulu-Wikipedia documents [2]. However, the number of such documents has the potential to increase as more speakers of the language become digitally literate, more government documents are produced, more documents on the Web are translated and more books are produced for teaching, learning and popular consumption. Increasing the use of a written language requires a multi-pronged solution to motivate the creation of content.

© Springer International Publishing Switzerland 2015
R.B. Allen et al. (Eds.): ICADL 2015, LNCS 9469, pp. 180–189, 2015.
DOI: 10.1007/978-3-319-27974-9_18

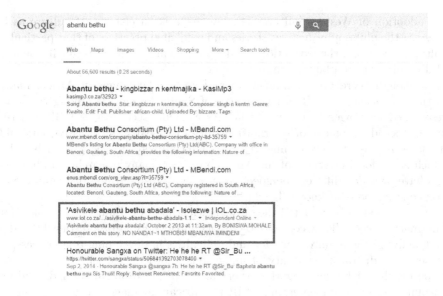

Fig. 1. Google search result for "abantu bethu"

Systems for storage and retrieval of documents are one aspect of this solution; if a document in isiZulu cannot be found on the Internet, there is little motivation to put it online.

As seen in Figure 1, a Google search for the word "abantu bethu" – meaning: our people – results in the first page with content written in IsiZulu being ranked fourth. The system appears to be biased towards English documents that contain those words surrounded by English content. The small amount of isiZulu content online means that it has little prominence in the networked community and will not be highlighted in link-based search results. Ali [3] showed experimentally how documents in languages other than English are automatically ranked lower because of differences in collection statistics when search engines ignore the language of documents. This anomalous behaviour applies to isiZulu as well.

Therefore, to increase the prominence and discoverability of isiZulu documents online, it is necessary to develop tools and algorithms that are specifically intended to, firstly, create a level playing field for all languages and, secondly, boost the visibility of a language for particular developmental reasons. This paper describes the AfriWeb project that investigated both aspects by testing the viability of search engine algorithms - specifically morphological analysis - for isiZulu and an isiZulu portal with documents crawled from the Web using a focused crawler.

2   Related Literature

Africa has 54 countries that use an estimated total of over 2000 languages. Some languages are endangered due to the assimilation of other dominant groups and the adoption of Western cultures [4]. Language is an element of culture as it presents the philosophy, history, stories and medicinal practices of that particular culture. Therefore, the extinction of a language will inevitably result in the loss of diversity within a larger community [4].

Although there are a large number of spoken languages in Africa, many of these, especially the Bantu languages of South Africa, are among the least researched languages in the world [5]. As a result, technologies that are crucial in the advancement of information retrieval research, such as corpora and dictionaries, are still either undeveloped or incomplete. In the case of IsiZulu, which is the focal language of the AfriWeb project, many researchers in linguistics have provided different perspectives that have resulted in a distributed and non-cohesive body of knowledge [6].

Cosijn et al. [7] conducted the only known study of isiZulu as a language for information access. They considered cross-language information retrieval (CLIR) and analyzed the requirements for and difficulties in developing text processing systems for digital accessibility of indigenous knowledge in isiZulu. Their critique concluded by showing that there are multiple problems and difficulties encountered when implementing CLIR for African languages, including : ambiguity, incorrect stemming, paraphrasing in translations, untranslatability and mismatching [7].

The morphology of African languages has been studied in the context of other languages. El-Khair [8] and Nwesri, et al. [9] highlighted the importance of understanding the characteristics of Arabic to create effective information retrieval systems, especially the need for morphological analysis to handle the highly inflected word forms. Similar morphological analysis approaches were explored successfully by Hurskainen [10] for kiSwahili and Tune et al. [11] for the Ethiopian Afaan Oromo language.

In order to obtain documents for this project, a focused crawler was used; its goal is to selectively seek out pages that are relevant to a pre-defined set of topics (in our case a language) and follow relevant links to crawl through the Web [12] [13]. A focused crawler is driven by a language identification algorithm, based on comparisons of language profiles. Generating a language profile involves breaking the text from the category sample into n-grams and counting the occurrence of each n-gram [14]. Kneser-Key smoothing [15] was used in this study. It provided an additional tuning of simple n-gram counts by smoothing the effect of unigrams with unduly high frequencies because of co-occurrences.

3   General Architecture

The general architecture of the system is indicated in Figure 2.

There are two main parts to the system: the indexing and retrieval of data, and the harvesting of Web pages and documents from the Web. An outline of the technologies that were employed in the development of the system are as follows:

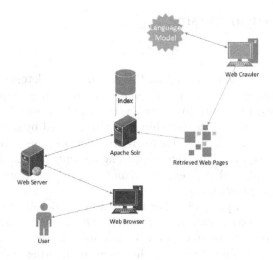

Fig. 2. General architecture of AfriWeb search system

- Web Server – required to host the AfriWeb Search Engine application.
- Search Engine Interface – the set of Web pages that the user is going to interact with, hosted on the Web server. Through this interface, a user can submit a query that is based on a particular information need and be able to view the results from the search engine.
- Apache Solr – an information retrieval toolkit, which will primarily be used to index and retrieve documents. SOLR was customized through plugins and alteration of the schema properties to ensure efficient indexing and retrieval of isiZulu documents.
- Focused Web crawler – an application that systematically browses the Web to index the contents of websites that are relevant to some constraint, in this case language of the content. Given a set of URLs as inputs, the crawler visits these URLs and, based on its set of rules, indexes the page and scans for other URLs within the same page, which it can visit next. The crawler was used for harvesting isiZulu text from the Web.
- Language model – a probabilistic model of a specific language, in this case isiZulu. Probabilities indicate an estimate of the likelihood of a given text being in a particular language. In this case, a language model was used to classify a Web page or parts thereof as being written in isiZulu or not.

Many of these components are standard Web search engine components. The language-specific components are the morphological parser that is needed by the SOLR indexer and the model-based language identification that drives the focused crawler. Each of those is discussed and evaluated in the sections that follow.

4 Morphological Parsing

4.1 Design

The relationship between a query and a document is determined to a large degree by the frequency of the query terms in individual documents. However, as documents have to adhere to language constraints, a single word may have morphological variants and the matching algorithms used by search engines will not match the possible variants. Therefore, by reducing the terms to their root form, the results returned by the search engine will have higher probability of relevance. Two algorithms were tested in this process: a prefix/suffix-based stemmer and a morphological parser.

There are two main principles that are used in the development of the stemming algorithm: iteration and longest-match. The iteration principle assumes that affixes are attached to stems in a certain order using a predefined class of affixes. The algorithm simply removes the affixes from either start to end or end to start, based on which class the detected affix matches. The second principle - the longest match - states that within any given class of endings, if more than a single ending provides a match, the longest one should be removed from the word. The affixes used in the development of the stemming algorithm included prefixes from the noun classification system and nominal suffixes. An example of a removed suffix is the diminutive 'ana' that is removed from 'abantwana'.

In the field of linguistics, the morphology of a language is the study of the word formation process in a language based on the parts of the language structure such as morphemes, affixes and other language phenomena that occur in the word formation process. Morphological analysis allows the breakdown of a word into various components that would have been overlooked by light stemming algorithms [16], such as the one described above. Once the semantic structure is obtained from morphological analysis, the parser is then able to apply predefined computations to the word to extract the root word.

The development of a morphological parser focused on the word formation rules that were described by Pretorius and Bosch [5]. The aim of using a morphological parser was to reverse word formation rules (such as ikhanda+ana transforming into ikhanjana) by detecting word patterns based on the affixes and word formation rules. In terms of the prefixal analysis, the scope focused on the noun classification and concordial systems. The noun classification system forms the basis of all prefixes and determines the types of concords that can be applied to a stem. These concords have different categories, which have different semantics that must be considered when analyzing a particular word. Figure 3 is the pseudo-code for the final analyzer that was used.

4.2 Evaluation

Two experiments were conducted.

The first experiment evaluated the accuracy of the morphological parser compared to the stemming algorithm given a language corpus. The experiment was

```
       Check the suffix category:
            If (word has a preprefix):
                 IF (consonant preprefix AND non-suffix category):
                      CHECK concord class:
                           IF possessive concord:
                                MARK as root
                           ELSE:
                                CHECK concord pattern
                                MARK and REMOVE concord
                                MARK word as root

                 ELSE IF (consonant preprefix AND simple-suffix
category):
                      CHECK concord class:
                           MARK and REMOVE concord
                           MARK word as root

                 ELSE IF (consonant preprefix AND special suffix
category):
                      CHECK formation rule for suffix:
                           REVERSE word formation
                           REMOVE prefix
                           MARK word as root

                 ELSE IF (vowel prefix and special suffix category):
                      CHECK preprefix class:
                           REVERSE word formation
                           MATCH prefix pattern
                           REMOVE prefix
                           MARK word as root

                 ELSE:
                      #word has no preprefix
                      MARK word as root

       RETURN root;
```

Fig. 3. Morphological parser algorithm for isiZulu

conducted using the Ukwabelana open source isiZulu corpus [17]. The corpus has a set of 10040 words that have been deconstructed into morphemes and roots. The morphological parser produced 48% accuracy in which the result contained the stem or root word, as compared to 42% produced by the stemming algorithm.

The second experiment required the pre-processing algorithms to be used in the search engine as a pre-processing step during indexing and retrieval of information. 12 Subjects who knew isiZulu were recruited. The purpose of the experiment was to measure if the relevance of the results of a user's query would increase using a morphological parser in comparison to a stemming algorithm. The use of a morphological parser in the indexing and querying of data resulted a in higher precision score as opposed to the stemming algorithm. The mean precision of the morphological parser was found to be 0.138, compared to the stemming algorithm's score of 0.102.

In both cases, the morphological parser resulted in a higher accuracy in the reduction of words, due to its sensitivity to the word formation rules and morphemes used in the derivation of inflected forms. This allows the morphological parser to better deconstruct words using a set of predefined morphemes. In the case of stemming, a brute force stripping of suffixes and prefixes may have resulted in a phenomenon called understemming or overstemming. These processes usually result in the word being incorrectly stemmed due to some of the morphemes either being incorrectly detected, or totally omitted by the algorithm.

5   Language Identification

5.1   Design

Supervised classification is choosing the right label for a given input. The language model was used to decide if a given string was isiZulu or non-isiZulu. Strings were used because documents online are seldom in isiZulu only. The language model was trained using the Ukwabelana sentence corpus [17]. Words in the training data were broken up into n-grams; n-grams such as 'ukw' and 'nhl' are indicative of isiZulu. The language model was also trained using the VariKN language modelling toolkit [18], which included support for Kneser-Key smoothing. Given the language model, a Bayesian classifier, written in Python, was then used to decide if a string belongs to isiZulu or not, by comparing the probabilities of the given text with those of isiZulu and English (as normative language). This language attribute was then used by the focused crawler in deciding whether a page as a whole was mostly isiZulu or not.

Figure 4 is the pseudo-code for the language analysis algorithm that was used.

5.2   Evaluation

The language identification method was tested on 4 datasets.

IsiZulu contained 29423 variable length sentences with 100% Zulu words. *PEnglish* contained 28000 variable length sentences with 100% English words. *PZplus* contained 25000 variable length sentences of which 40% was Zulu and 60% was English. *PItalian* contained 25215 variable length sentence with 100% Italian words.

The results from accuracy tests are shown in Table 1. The percentages indicated are for the number of words identified correctly as isiZulu or not (Y) and those identified incorrectly (N). Of the isiZulu documents, 98.4% were correctly identified. Most documents in English or Italian were correctly identified as non-isiZulu; Italian had understandably lower accuracy, as the system was trained with English n-grams. The mixed documents had 97.5% accuracy for the isiZulu subset.

Algorithm   IDENTIFYLANGUAGEWITHSMOOTHING(input)

global english-pdf,Zulu-pdf,english-dict,Zulu-dict
procedure LOADLANGAUGEMODEL(smoothedARPAfile)
  comment: pdf is a Python defaultdictionary

  pdf ← {}
  for each ngram ∈ smoothedARPAfile
    do pdf[ngram] ← ngram probability
  return (pdf)

procedure CALCULATEPROBABILITY(pdf,word)
  $p \leftarrow 1$
  for each ngram ∈ word
    do $p \leftarrow p$ *pdf[ngram]
  return (p)

main
  if input ∈ Zulu-dict **and** input ∈ english-dict
    then return (*non − Zulu*)
  if input ∈ Zulu-dict
    then return (*Zulu*)
  if input ∈ english-dict
    then return (*non − Zulu*)
  english-pdf ← LOADLANGAUGEMODEL(english-arpa-file)
  Zulu-pdf ← LOADLANGAUGEMODEL(Zulu-arpa-file)
  english-probability ← CALCULATEPROBABILITY(english-pdf)
  Zulu-probability ← CALCULATEPROBABILITY(Zulu-pdf)
  if |Zulu-probability−english-probability| ≤ 10₃
    then return (*non − Zulu*)
  if Zulu-probability < english-probability
    then return (non-Zulu)
    else return (Zulu)

Fig. 4. Language identification algorithm for isiZulu

Some Zulu words were classified as non-Zulu because they also appear in English (into, bake, etc.). A small number of words in the Zulu corpus were also found to be English words for which there was no equivalent in Zulu (e.g., assurance).

Table 1. Accuracy for language identification

Dataset	isiZulu(Y)	Non-isiZulu(N)	Non-isiZulu(Y)	isiZulu(N)
IsiZulu	98.4	1.6	0	0
PEnglish	0	0	98.8	1.2
PItalian	0	0	87.6	12.4
PZplus	97.5	2.5	98.3	1.6

6   Conclusions

This project centred on a Web search engine to support the development of content in a marginalized language – isiZulu. In attempting to meet this objective, language-specific algorithms were developed for morphological analysis of the language and for identification of the language within a focused crawler.

The morphological parser achieved an accuracy level of 48%, which surpassed the accuracy level of a typical affix-driven stemmer. However, there is clearly scope for further investigation on stemming in Bantu languages. The statistically-driven language identification was mostly successful, with isiZulu documents being separated from non-isiZulu documents with an accuracy greater than 90%. When used with a focused crawler, more than 60000 documents were successfully obtained.

The short supply of text resources, formal language grammars and foundational work in isiZulu computational linguistics made this project particularly difficult. However, it was shown that specific components of a Web search engine can be optimized for a marginalized language, with some success. It is hoped that the availability of such search engines can lead to greater interest in written documents in isiZulu, feeding back into the development of better language tools, in a cycle that ultimately promotes and preserves marginalized African languages. The number of speakers of isiZulu is not decreasing over time and there is greater recognition of national languages in South Africa so this work will support an expanding community of writers and readers of an important language.

Acknowledgement. This research was partially funded by the National Research Foundation of South Africa (Grant numbers: 85470 and 88209) and University of Cape Town. The authors acknowledge that opinions, findings and conclusions or recommendations expressed in this publication are that of the authors, and that the NRF accepts no liability whatsoever in this regard.

References

1. Statistics South Africa: Census 2011 (2012). http://www.statssa.gov.za/census2011/default.asp
2. Wikipedia: Ikhasi Elikhulu, Wikimedia Foundation (2014). http://zu.wikipedia.org/wiki/Ikhasi_Elikhulu

3. Mustafa, M., Suleman, H.: Mixed language Arabic-English information retrieval. In: Gelbukh, A. (ed.) CICLing 2015, Part II. LNCS, vol. 9042, pp. 427–447. Springer, Heidelberg (2015)

4. Mukami, L.: Africa's endangered languages. African Review (2013). http://www.africareview.com/Special-Reports/Africas-endangered-languages/-/979182/2008252/-/12yos0s/-/index.html

5. Pretorius, L., Bosch, S.E.: Finite-state computational morphology: An analyzer prototype for Zulu. Machine Translation 18(3), 195–216 (2003)

6. Madondo, L.M., Muziwenhlanhla, S: Some aspects of evaluative morphology in Zulu (2000)

7. Cosjin, E., Pirkola, A., Bothma, T., Jarvelin, K.: Information access in indigenous languages: a casestudy in Zulu. South African Journal of Libraries and Information Science 68(2), 94 (2002)

8. Abu El-Khair, I.: Arabic information retreival. In: Annual Review of Information Science and Technology, pp. 505–533. John Wiley and Sons, Egypt (2007)

9. Nwesri, A.F., Tahaghoghi, S.M., Scholer, F.: Answering english queries in automatically transcribed arabic speech. In: 6th IEEE/ACIS International Conference on Computer and Information Science (ICIS 2007). IEEE (2007)

10. Hurskainen, A.: Swahili Language Manager. Nordic Journal of African Studies 8(2), 139–157 (1999)

11. Tune, K.T., Varma, V., Pingali, P.: Evalutation of Oromo-English Cross Language Information Retrieval. Cross Language Evaluation Forum, Hyderabad, India (2007)

12. Chakrabarti, S., van der Berg, M., Dom, B.: Focused crawling: A new approach to topic-specific Web resource discovery. Computer Networks 31, 1623–1640 (1999)

13. Novak, B.: A survey of focused web crawling algorithms (2004)

14. Cavnar, W.B., Trenkle, J.M.: N-gram-based text categorization. In: 3rd Annual Symposium on Document Analysis and Information Retrieval (SDAIR 1994), pp. 161–175 (1994)

15. Chen, S.F., Goodman, J.: An empirical study of smoothing techniques for language modeling. Computer Speech & Language 13(4), 359–393 (1999)

16. McEnery, T.: Corpus linguistics: An introduction. Edinburgh University Press (2001)

17. Spiegler, S., Van Der Spuy, A., Flach, P.A.: Ukwabelana: an open-source morphological Zulu corpus. In: 23rd International Conference on Computational Linguistics. Association for Computational Linguistics (2010)

18. Siivola, V.: VariKn - Language modelling toolkit (2007). http://forge.pascal-network.org/docman/view.php/33/58/variKN_toolkit.html

Participatory Journalism, Blurred Boundaries: Introducing Theoretical IS Frameworks to Re-Orient Research Practices

Nora Martin[✉]

University of Technology - Sydney, Ultimo, Australia
`nora.martin@uts.edu.au`

Abstract. Social media now plays a pivotal role in how broadcast media engages with their audiences. This paper contemplates the nature of our digital media culture, the diversity of actors involved and how the role of the journalist has evolved. The methodology includes examining the findings of a pilot research study investigating journalists' information practices in the digital realm. Two theoretical frameworks from the discipline of Information Science are introduced to re-orient research practices. The findings reveal digital journalism facilitates richer and more expansive storytelling, with connectivity between experts, journalists and the public. The author posits that the citizen-informant is reconceptualised in the news milieu.

Keywords: Digital journalism · News-story verification · Social media

1   Introduction

In the digital world, the nature of news has fundamentally changed. This paper explores the impact of converging technologies on journalism practice in an age of digital social media. The discussion draws on the findings of pilot research study investigating journalists' information practices in the digital realm [1] and explores the application of theoretical frameworks from Information Science to re-orient research practices. This voyage of discovery will assist in navigating the blurred boundaries of our journalistic terrain, thereby seeing it with new eyes.

2   Research Methods

Interviews are widely used for exploring the sense-making of social actors, drawing out the rhetorical construction of their experience and perspective [2]. In journalism research, interviews have been employed in studies on networked journalism [3,4] and news-story verification [5,6].

This paper explores digital media using a qualitative framework [2]. The research methodology includes examining the findings of a pilot research study on the effect of social media on journalists' information practices [1]. The findings were based on

© Springer International Publishing Switzerland 2015
R.B. Allen et al. (Eds.): ICADL 2015, LNCS 9469, pp. 190–196, 2015.
DOI: 10.1007/978-3-319-27974-9_19

interviews with journalists employed in the Australian broadcast media sector. The researcher adopted a case study approach whereby in-depth interviews with nine semi-randomly selected participants were undertaken.[1]

The interviews were face-to-face, in informal settings where each participant worked. Qualitative semi-structured interviews using the Neutral Questioning technique [7] were conducted to ascertain how journalists verify and report on information originating in or reaching them via social media. Participants were asked in a general way for his/her views on how journalists discover, use and share information. This led to a discussion on how broadcast media professionals assess the credibility of new information and whether social media technologies are influencing the way journalists access and share information. These interviews were recorded with the consent of the participants.

No effort was made to define social media technologies, or any of the terms or phrases used during the interviews. This minimized bias from the researcher's thoughts or persuasions as much as possible. As the interviews were informal, each interview was more like a conversation. In this way, the researcher was able to elicit detailed answers from each participant. The interviews were transcribed in full, with the transcripts reviewed by the researcher to determine broad themes that suggested trends. Analysis was conducted on the data using Grounded Theory [8]. Participants were de-identified to ensure ethical practice.

3   Theories

3.1   Theory of Information Poverty

The Theory of Information Poverty [9] places information-seeking behavior within the framework of social norms in a bid to understand why individuals sometimes do not seek, ignore, or actively avoid information that could be useful. Chatman defines an impoverished information world as a dysfunctional one in which "a person is unwilling or unable to solve a critical worry or concern", in part because of their status as an insider or outsider [9]. Here, insiders are people who use their greater understanding of social norms to enhance their social roles, and outsiders are those who deviate from the norm. Chatman sees the insider-outsider conflict as the context for engagement in self-protective behaviors which influence how information is sought and used [10].

Chatman's characterisation of the insider-outsider conflict reflects the social status of so-called traditional journalists and their tech-savvy counterparts when it comes to technology. Journalists who do not use Twitter are regularly portrayed as falling short of the tech-savvy norm, concretising their status as outsiders [11]. For the 'traditional' reporter, a world which constantly privileges breaking news over investigative reporting could engender the deep distrust that Chatman suggests. It is possible that traditional

---

[1] In the initial pilot research study, two in-depth, qualitative semi-structured interviews were undertaken [1]. For this follow-up research, seven in-depth interviews were conducted with semi-randomly selected broadcast media professionals to collect further qualitative data.

journalists' acceptance or avoidance of technologies could be shaped by the insider-outsider conflict. Chatman's theory therefore has valuable applications in studies of technology acceptance pertaining to journalism in a socially networked world.

3.2   Suzanne M. Miller's Monitoring-and-Blunting Theory

Monitoring-and-Blunting (M&B) Theory seeks to explain people's information-seeking behavior during stressful situations. Miller suggests that, when faced with a stressful or aversive event, people differ in their preference for information [12]. 'Monitors' are people who seek information because 'knowing what is happening' helps to decrease their stress. 'Blunters' deal with unfavourable events by distracting themselves and avoiding information as a self-protective measure. M&B theory provides insight into information seeking as a coping mechanism, acknowledging that each individual is unique in his/her desire for information [12]. In doing so, Miller emphasizes the inextricability of users from their situational contexts.

Miller's approach presents very worthwhile concepts and recommendations for media researchers. The investigation of affective factors as motivators for information behavior can be usefully adapted to research in digital media culture and provides a sound basis for a holistic exploration of journalists use (or non-use) of social networks such as Twitter. When faced with a threatening situation, a journalist can respond by focusing on the threatening information ('monitoring') using Twitter as a newsfeed or by avoiding threatening information ('blunting') by choosing not to engage with, or otherwise use this medium.

To date few studies have examined the differences between categories of journalists in relation to social media use [13]. There is a need for more research which recognises the significance of emotion in driving human interaction with technology. Similarly, Olsson believes "the growth of social media opens up ideal territory to explore issues of the role of affective discourses in emerging virtual social spaces" [14].

4   Age of Participatory News

The shift to tablets and smartphones for communication, news and entertainment has dramatically changed the media terrain. A recent Nielsen report reveals that 56% of Australians read a newspaper via digital devices every month [15].

When asked whether social media is influencing the way journalists access and share information, here is one particular viewpoint:

I'm a believer that it's a tool and it doesn't replace anything that's already there. It's another tool in your tool kit, it's like you bought a new spanner, you know, that's a different size. It is changing things, I'm not saying it's not... it's just another way of accessing things (Z2).

In relation to Twitter, one participant underscored the fact that only once a reputable news source is associated with a story is it seen as having authority and credibility.

... something recently flashed up about Nairobi; that X number of people had been shot at, at that shopping centre in Nairobi, and the first flash came from someone whose name you don't recognise. But the minute you see a reputable news source, that news brand attaching their name to the story, that's when it becomes an important story to follow (A1).

The balance of power between news media and the audience has been irrevocably altered, with a power shift in the digital age from 'journalist as gatekeeper' to the citizen as editor. As Jarvis argues, "witnesses to events can now help report what they see and context and explanation can come from both journalists and the experts they quoted who can now also publish....I see that not as a competitive threat, but as a grand opportunity" [16].

4.1   BLUNTERS - We Verify Now and Publish Later

Verification is a routine part of journalistic information gathering activities. One participant, when discussing the use of Twitter, said:

So even though I might log onto Twitter regularly I won't pay much attention to individuals who are not attached to organisations which I respect. Individuals are just that, unless I can verify where they come from, where they are attached to and therefore how much weight I should give their opinions and thoughts (A1).

Equally, participants insisted that other motivations for conforming to this ideal ranged from the impact of an error on their credibility (A1, Z2, W6), on the reputation of their news brand (A1) or that of the journalistic profession as a whole (A1, Z2, X4). As one participant maintains:

It's my reputation and also you owe it to the story I think, because if you get something wrong, of course you can get sued and stuff like that if there's defamation and all those legalities (Z2).

Another participant points out that working in a deadline driven situation means it is imperative not to waste time on sources that could be doubtful:

It's very important that I don't waste time ... reading information that could be from a questionable source, and that doesn't attribute its facts and statistics to any organisation or entity that I can then research further ... it's all about verifying the original source (A1).

Evidence based practice is often at the core of journalistic endeavours, with "information gathered according to rigorous principles and presented in the formats of conventional science" [17]. This aligns with the research by Shapiro et al. in their Canadian study [6]. Their findings reveal substantial diversity in verification strategies employed by journalists, often mirroring social scientific methods such as 'source triangulation.'

4.2   MONITORS - We Publish Now and Correct Later

Networked journalism has created numerous challenges, with concerns about sourcing, authenticity and fairness due to "looser editing standards that often exist with a digital first policy stressing speed over verification", often without effective front-end checks and balances [18]. Various participants stressed the importance of being accurate in the 24/7 news environment, making statements attesting to this professional norm.

When discussing how to assess the credibility of new information, as one put it:

... I mean look it's a trap for all of us too you know, the very famous truism about assume makes an ass of you and me and it's something as journalists' who are striving to be accurate and known for that, we fall into that trap every single day potentially if we don't check, and it's not assuming (A1).

One participant thought a recent news story was published in a certain masthead. As it turned out, the story was published on another date and in a different paper. This matter was resolved after contacting a news researcher:

... you have to check and triple-check everything, I assumed it was in a certain publication ... there's a lot swilling in your head, you have to be accurate in this game, you have to be one-hundred percent accurate (A1).

Another participant emphasized the importance of familiarizing oneself with a subject, prior to commencing more in-depth research:

The first basis is that you need to read and become informed on what you're trying to investigate, because that body of knowledge and knowing who the players are in that story is important... when you go to social media, that body of knowledge gives you a base to be able to go 'that doesn't sound right, that does sound right, that fits in here', and it helps you put the pieces together (Z2).

This stance is best exemplified by Participant D5's comment in relation to the 24/7 news environment, and how it is imperative to beat competitors to the punch:

... I'm not interested in being a reporter that stands back and waits. You've got to get in there first and beat the competitors. So, I'm all for breaking news. After all, that's the name of the game these days (D5).

4.3   Witness as Citizen-Informant

The evolving media landscape includes professional journalists in a plethora of 'social roles' [19]. Bloggers and user-generated content are inextricably woven into the news production process, the result being an incorporation of varied content, diversification of source material and multiplicity of actors. Today, eyewitnesses providing reports on news events is *de rigueur*. Yet, many of these actors do not consider themselves to be part of the citizen media contingent. In legal parlance, the definition of a citizen-informant is an ordinary citizen who has either been the victim of or witness to a crime and reports the pertinent facts to law enforcement officials.[2] I therefore propose that this definition be reconceptualised in the news milieu. The ordinary citizen as an eyewitness who has reported on a news event but does not consider themselves to be an amateur journalist, nor a part of the citizen media contingent, is henceforth known as a citizen-informant.

With the challenge for journalism to reinvent itself in the digital media environment comes the challenge for scholars to review their methods and question the durability of findings. Given the need to redirect the focus of research from the system to the user, a cross-disciplinary approach is a valuable way to inspire and generate new ideas and reflection [20].

5   Conclusion

This paper examined our participatory digital media culture, discussing the nature of this interaction, the multiplicity of actors and how the role of the journalist has evolved. The findings reveal that digital journalism facilitates richer story-telling, with connectivity between experts, journalists and the public. The author suggests that the citizen-informant is reconceptualised in the news milieu. Two theoretical frameworks from the discipline of Information Science were introduced in order to re-orient research practices in participatory media. It is hoped that these theories will help redirect the focus of research in this field, from techno-centrism to the importance of considering social, situational and contextual factors.

References

1. Martin, N.: Information Verification in the Age of Digital Journalism. Paper presented at the Special Libraries Association Annual Conference, Vancouver, June 8-10, 2014. https://www.sla.org/wp-content/uploads/2014/07/Information-Verification.pdf
2. Bryman, A.: Social Research Methods. OUP, Oxford (2012)
3. Domingo, D., Le Cam, F.: Journalism in Dispersion. Digital Journalism 2(3), 310–321 (2014). doi:10.1080/21670811.2014.897832
4. Lewis, J., Williams, A., Franklin, B., Thomas, J., Mosdell, N.: The quality and Independence of British Journalism. Project Report, MediaWise (2008). http://www.mediawise.org.uk/wp-content/uploads/2011/03/Quality-Independence-of-British-Journalism.pdf
5. Godler, Y., Reich, Z.: How Journalists "Realize" Facts. Journalism Practice 7(6), 674–689 (2013). doi:10.1080/17512786.2013.791067
6. Shapiro, I., Brin, C., Bédard-Brûlé, I., Mychajlowycz, K.: Verification as a Strategic Ritual. Journalism Practice 7(6), 1–18 (2013). doi: 10.1080/17512786.2013.765638
7. Dervin, B., Dewdney, P.: Neutral Questioning: A New Approach to the Reference Interview. Reference Quarterly 25(4), 506–513 (1986)

---

[2] *Wallace v. State*, 964 So.2d 722 (District Court of Appeal of Florida, 2007). In *Wallace*, Justice Wallace wrote 'Generally speaking, a citizen-informant is an ordinary citizen who has either been the victim of or a witness to a crime and who reports the pertinent facts to law enforcement officials,' Duhaime's Criminal Law Dictionary http://www.duhaime.org/Legal-Dictionary/C/CitizenInformant.aspx

8. Glaser, B.G., Strauss, A.L.: Basics of Grounded Theory Analysis. Sociology Press, Mill Valley (1967)
9. Chatman, E.A.: The Impoverished Life World of Outsiders. J. Am. Soc. Inf. Sci **47**(3), 193–206 (1996)
10. Hersberger, J.A.: Are the Economically Poor Information Poor? Does the Digital Divide Affect the Homeless and Access to Information? Can. J. Inform. Lib. Sci. **27**(3), 44–63 (2003)
11. Jericho, G.: The Rise of the Fifth Estate: Social Media and Blogging in Australian Politics. Scribe, Brunswick (2012)
12. Baker, L.M.: Monitoring and blunting. In: Fisher, K.E, Erdelez, S., McKechnie, L. (eds.) Theories of Information Behavior. Information Today, Medford (2005)
13. Hedman, U., Djerf-Pierre, M.: The Social Journalist. Digital Journalism **1**(3), 368–385 (2013). doi:10.1080/21670811.2013.776804
14. Olsson, M.: Gently to Hear, Kindly to Judge: the Affective Information Practices of Theatre Professionals and Journalists. Information Research **18**(3) (2013). http://InformationR.net/ir/18-3/colis/paperC22.html
15. Nielsen Online Ratings.: IpsosMediaCT, people 14+ for the twelve months ending December 2013. emma™ (Enhanced Media Metrics Australia) (2013)
16. Jarvis, J.: For the Record | Comment. The Guardian, December 1, 2007. http://www.theguardian.com/commentisfree/2007/nov/30/fortherecord
17. Olsson, M.: Information Practices in Contemporary Cosmopolitan Civil Society. Cosmopolitan Civil Societies Journal **6**(2), 79–93 (2014). doi: 10.5130/ccs.v6i2.3948
18. Steele, B.: Journalism ethics then and now. In: McBride, K., Rosenstiel, T. (eds.) The New Ethics of Journalism, pp. vii–ix. CQ Press, Thousand Oaks (2014)
19. Kovach, B., Rosenstiel, T.: Blur: How to Know What's True in the Age of Information Overload. Bloomsbury, New York (2010)
20. Larsson, U. (ed.): Cultures of Creativity. Science History Publications (2006)

User Motivations for Tweeting Research Articles: A Content Analysis Approach

Jin-Cheon Na[✉]

Wee Kim Wee School of Communication and Information,
Nanyang Technological University, Singapore, Singapore
tjcna@ntu.edu.sg

Abstract. Nowadays Twitter is used to disseminate scientific findings to the general public, and how often research articles are tweeted is a major metric in altmetrics. So it is important to understand tweet authors' citation motivations and attitudes (or sentiments) towards the articles they cite. A content analysis approach was used to analyze 2,016 English tweets citing academic papers in the field of psychology. The results showed that most tweets (52.88%) cited articles to summarize the scientific findings of the studies. 11.81% of the tweets contained only the titles and URLs of the articles, and 19.05% of the tweets were retweets. Most tweeters held a neutral attitude towards the articles they tweeted, and only 5.15% showed negative feeling. In summary, most of the tweets do not convey in-depth critical discussion of academic papers, but they provide good access to some interesting research findings.

Keywords: Twitter · User motivations · Scholarly communication · Altmetrics · Psychology · Content analysis

1 Introduction

Measuring research impact is a critical task for universities, research organizations, and funding agencies in decision making and policy setting including recruitment, promotion and grant allocation. In digital libraries, it is also important to measure and present the research impact of articles to help users find impactful articles. As a measurement, citation count has been a strong indicator upon which to draw conclusions about research impact. It is also the machinery behind other major research measures such as journal impact factor, g-index, and h-index. However, citation count and other traditional metrics, which were originated in print processes and are based on literary output alone, are increasingly failing to keep pace with the new ways that researchers can generate impact in today's digital world [1]. A key limitation is timeliness, since it may take years for an article to get cited [2]. In addition, these metrics do not recognize non-scholarly and other online uses of an article in today's digital environment [3].

In the scientific community, scientometricians are now exploring the possibility of using social media activities as indicators of research impact. Among the attempts to develop non-citation-based metrics, altmetrics (short for alternative metrics) receive considerable attention due to the ease with which data can be collected and the

© Springer International Publishing Switzerland 2015
R.B. Allen et al. (Eds.): ICADL 2015, LNCS 9469, pp. 197–208, 2015.
DOI: 10.1007/978-3-319-27974-9_20

availability of a wide range of open data sources [4]. Altmetrics intend to assess Web-driven scholarly interactions, such as how often research is tweeted, blogged about, downloaded, or bookmarked [5]. Thus, to evaluate the significance of scholarly works better, we should pay more attention to informal discussions on social media. Therefore, the purpose of this study is to explore the motivations of users tweeting research. Twitter is a popular social network service which enables users to broadcast and read short 140-character messages called "tweets" [6]. Recently, it is not only an urban lifestyle tool to share locations and activities, but also a social application to spread academic research and viewpoints. Using a content analysis approach, this study aims to answer the following research question: "What are the motivations of users citing research articles on Twitter?" The field of psychology was selected for the study since the findings from psychology articles are commonly discussed on Twitter. The contribution of this study is to understand the various motivations of users tweeting research, and it will help to determine whether or not the simple counting of mentions of research articles on Twitter is a meaningful and strong indicator upon which to draw conclusions about research impact in altmetrics.

The layout of this paper is as follows. First, we provide related work, followed by the research method for studying the motivations of users tweeting research. This is followed by the discussion of the analysis results of the tweets, and finally conclusion.

2   Related Work

Twitter has been explored as an alternative measure for scholarly impact. Referencing articles via URLs is considered an act of citation, and mentions of articles in tweets positively affect traditional indicators of scholarly influence, e.g., download rates or citations in scholarly publications [7]. Weller, Droge, and Puschmann [8] analyzed the use of Twitter during scientific conferences and considered all the URLs (e.g., blog, conference, media, press, project, publication, slides, and twitter) in tweets as citations. But, generally, in the studies of altmetics including this paper, only URLs for peer-reviewed articles are counted as citations.

Veletsianos [9] analyzed 4,500 tweets of 45 scholars. The researcher found that the practice of sharing information, media, and resources was the dominant activity of the scholars' participation (39% of the data was coded as this category), and digital identity and impression management was another common theme for drawing attention to the scholars' work and professional endeavors. Ebner and Schiefner [10] also found that a typical scholarly usage of Twitter is recommending literature. Holmberg and Thelwall [11] reported that 27% of the tweets for the sampled researchers were retweets, in comparison to about 3% of the tweets for the average Twitter user.

Priem and Costello [12] conducted interviews and analyzed 2,322 tweets from 28 scholars. They found that these scholars used Twitter to cite articles, and 6% of the tweets were Twitter citations, half of them linking directly to the reference articles. The participants mentioned that Twitter citations represent and transmit scholarly impact. They also found that Twitter citations were much faster than traditional ones, with 40% appearing within one week of the cited resource's publication. However, this study didn't consider non-scholars who tweet research articles. In the proposed study, we are analyzing the motivations of any users (i.e. both scholars and non-scholars) tweeting research.

Thelwall et al. [13] conducted a content analysis of 270 tweets linking to academic articles, and found little evidence of active discussion about research, with most tweets simply repeating the article title (42%) or providing a brief summary of the article contents (41%). They also found that 4% of the tweets were positive about the articles and none were negative. In addition, 5% of the tweets mentioned that the articles were interesting, but 95% expressed no opinion about the article. Our study is similar to this work, but we are conducting a content analysis of 2,016 tweets linking to articles in a specific domain, i.e. psychology journal articles, with more detailed motivation categories. Mahrt et al. [6] stated that tweeting behavior is still too understudied to determine the validity of Twitter metrics. According to Haustein et al. [14], the presence of social media metrics across scientific publications is still quite low. Even if Twitter is the main platform, it only covered 22% of the publications in their study.

3   Research Method

3.1   Data Collection

We collected articles and their altmetric data (i.e. the number of mentions on Twitter) in the top 70 journals of the psychology discipline from altmetric.com. The top 70 journals were chosen based on their 2013 impact factors. There are 10 subcategories for the psychology discipline in the Thomson Reuter Social Science Citation Index, and we chose the top 10 journals of each subcategory. Considering the large dataset, it was unfeasible to take every tweet into account. Therefore, the articles in the top 70 journals were ranked by the number of mentions on Twitter. Then, the recent tweets of the top ranked articles (around 133 articles) were collected from `altmetric.com`. For each article, up to 20 English tweets were collected, and completely repeated tweets were removed while retweets were included. A total of 2,016 tweets were collected for content analysis.

3.2   Content Analysis of Citation Motivations

Shema et al. [15] studied the motivations of blog citations through a content analysis approach, and we adopted their motivation categories with slight modifications for Twitter. Table 1 shows the 10 motivation categories of users tweeting research, and most of the categories have several subcategories. Firstly, the motivations of 200 tweets from the 10 most tweeted articles were tagged by two coders. The agreement rate between the two coders was 80%, with occasional discussion of ambiguous cases. This initial coding helped to finalize motivation categories and their definitions. The rest of the 1,816 tweets were divided into two datasets, and each dataset was tagged by individual coder. The author also validated the tagged data with the help of another coder, and corrected wrongly tagged data. When the coding was carried out, each tweet was tagged with one or more motivations since a tweet can convey several motivations. Also, the abstract of each article was read before coding since it is not straightforward to infer the tweeter's motivations only with the tweet content.

Table 1. Motivation categories and their frequencies

Category	Motivation	Overall Frequency	% of Tweets
Discussion	1.1 Discussing factors which influence a psychology condition / lifestyle	250	12.40%
	1.2 Discussing social phenomena	86	4.27%
	1.3 Discussing a psychology problem	45	2.23%
	1.4 Discussing treatment for psychology conditions	63	3.13%
	1.5 Discussing possible practical / social outcomes of a research	8	0.40%
	1.6 Summarizing the scientific findings of the studies Explaining the importance of scientific findings	1,066	52.88%
	Overall Discussion	**1,518**	**75.30%**
Criticism	2.1 Raising methodological issues	26	1.29%
	2.2 Criticism of a practice	12	0.60%
	2.3 Disputing a belief	23	1.14%
	2.4 Criticizing an article's conclusions / recommendations	44	2.18%
	Overall Criticism	**105**	**5.21%**
Advice	3.1 Providing practical advices and recommendations	43	2.13%
	3.2 Advocacy against certain treatment / life style / intervention	34	1.69%
	Overall Advice	**77**	**3.82%**
Trigger	4.1 Reaction to a topic in the news / current event	5	0.25%
	4.2 Invitation for further discussion	49	2.43%
	4.3 Reaction to a question / comment by tweet readers	18	0.89%
	4.4 Reaction to another tweet post	62	3.08%
	4.5 Announcing the publication of a new article / Recommending this good / interesting article	350	17.36%
	4.6 Retweeting / Heard Through (HT)	384	19.05%
	4.7 Raising a question to think	81	4.02%
	4.8 Reaction to an article (commentary)	3	0.15%
	4.9 Sharing to specific friends, specific groups of people, or directing the article to their followers.	141	6.99%
	Overall Trigger	**1,093**	**54.22%**
Extensions	5.1 Recommending other materials (reading, podcast, video, etc.)	50	2.48%
	5.2 Suggesting future research directions	18	0.89%
	Overall Extensions	**68**	**3.37%**
Self	6.1 Sharing personal experience	43	2.13%
	6.2 Expressing self-preference	109	5.41%
	6.3 Publisher citation	106	5.26%
	6.4 Self-citation	40	1.98%
	6.5 Relating one's self or network in the context of the research	1	0.05%
	Overall Self	**299**	**14.83%**
Controversy	7.1 Discussing controversy	19	0.94%

Table 1. (*continued*)

Data	8.1 Asking for paper sources	15	0.74%
	8.2 Providing paper sources / facts with practical implications	105	5.21%
	Overall Data	**120**	**5.95%**
Ethics	9.1 Discussion of ethical questions	4	0.20%
Other	10.1 Purely tweeting	238	11.81%
	10.2 Others	39	1.93%
	Overall Other	**277**	**13.74%**

4 Experiment Results

4.1 Sentiments towards Articles

To investigate tweeters' attitudes or sentiments towards research articles, we analyzed the tweets and classified them into four categories: positive, neutral, partially negative, and negative. Most tweeters didn't express their opinions towards the articles.

As a result, most of the tweets (84.77%) were classified to neutral category, and the second most common category was positive (10.07%). The tweets only containing negative remarks were taken as a negative attitude, as in the following example:

"Study shows ladies love the face fuzz. My favourite #bad science ever I think. #beardgods http://t.co/Ap84Wda7i6 (Paper: The role of facial hair in women's perceptions of men's attractiveness, health, masculinity and parenting abilities)"

We categorized tweets as having a partially negative attitude when they confirmed a part of the research results but also raised some shortcomings, such as methodological issues, as follows:

"Quality of life in autism across the lifespan http://t.co/0yShXjVzGA Age, IQ & symptom severity did not predict QofL (but small N) (Paper: Quality of life in autism across the lifespan: A meta-analysis)"

The distributions of sentiments toward the articles are shown in Table 2.

Table 2. Sentiments toward articles

Sentiments	Number of Tweets	% of Tweets
Positive	203	10.07%
Neutral	1,709	84.77%
Partially Negative	66	3.27%
Negative	38	1.88%
Total	2,016	100.00%

4.2   Classification of Citation Motivations

The 2,016 tweets were classified into 10 motivation categories and their subcategories, and the overall motivation frequencies of the tweets are shown in Table 1. In this section, we discuss frequently occurring motivations and their examples. Some motivations, such as "Controversy" and "Ethics", didn't appear frequently, and are not discussed in detail.

Discussion. This is the most common main category coded, with 75.30% of the tweets. The most common subcategory under "Discussion" is "1.6 Summarizing the scientific findings of the studies", which covered 52.88% of the tweets. In most cases, these tweets summarize the significant finding of the studies, or explain the importance of research findings. Usually these tweets also have additional specific motivations, such as "1.1 Discussing factors which influence a psychology condition / lifestyle" (12.40%) and "1.3 Discussing a psychology problem" (2.23%). The following tweet not only summarizes the important findings of the article, but also discusses a factor which influences a psychology condition.

"Talking about suicide may in fact lead to improvements in mental health http://t.co/k4sHi7Wp9L (Paper: Does asking about suicide and related behaviours induce suicidal ideation? What is the evidence?)"

The motivation "1.2 Discussing social phenomena" (4.27%) includes tweets talking about common social preferences about thinking and doing things. "1.3 Discussing a psychology problem" mainly deals with the introduction, promotion, and prevention of certain psychology problems. "1.4 Discussing treatment for psychology conditions" (3.13%) is usually used when treatment is the focus of tweets. "1.5 Discussing possible practical / social outcomes of a research" (0.40%) discusses the practical implication of the research findings.

Criticism. 5.21% of the tweets were tagged with the "Criticism" motivation, which is not necessarily directed towards the articles. Opposing a certain behavior and belief was also included in this category. Thus, the percentage of this motivation is not equal to the one of negative attitude (i.e. both partially negative and negative) towards the articles. "2.1 Raising methodological issues" showed up in 1.29% of the tweets which discuss methodological problems or other issues of the studies, including topic selection. The following tweet is an example of this motivation.

"Mindfulness-based therapy: A comprehensive meta-analysis http://t.co/vKDBdWeolO Remiss of same authors not to give data on blinding again!"

Tweets criticizing common guidelines or practices are considered as "2.2 Criticism of a practice" (0.60%). The following tweet criticizes the peer-review practices of psychological journals.

"Revealing   experiment   on   the   arbitrariness   of   academic #peer #review:http://t.co/c2yKflEhoU (in psychology) (Paper: Peer-review practices of psychological journals: The fate of published articles, submitted again)"

"2.3 Disputing a belief" (1.14%) includes the tweets which correct misconceptions of traditional or widely-accepted beliefs. "2.4 Criticizing an article's conclusions / recommendations" covered 2.18% of the tweets. The following tweet is an example of "2.3 Disputing a belief".

"Contrary to popular belief "talking about suicide may reduce, rather than increase, suicidal ideation" http://t.co/xkbc22uxix from @WesselyS (Paper: Does asking about suicide and related behaviours induce suicidal ideation? What is the evidence?)"

Advice. This motivation consists of two subcategories and covered 3.82% of the tweets. The first one is "3.1 Providing practical advices and recommendations" (2.13%) which is meant for giving practical advice and recommendations about practices, treatments, or guidelines, and the second one is "3.2 Advocacy against certain treatment / life style / intervention" (1.69%) which includes tweets arguing against certain phenomena. An example tweet of "3.1 Providing practical advices and recommendations" is shown as follows.

"http://t.co/GipcictUKm Maybe we should ban #gayporn to protect #homophobes from themselves. (Paper: Is homophobia associated with homosexual arousal?)"

Trigger. This motivation was found in 54.22% of the tweets. "4.6 Retweeting and Heard Through" is the most common subcategory of Trigger motivation, occupying 19.05% shares. Tweets containing the following symbols (RT / MT / HT/ "@..." / via) were tagged with this subcategory. When tagging a retweet, if there is no additional remark on its original tweet, the motivation of the original tweet was also tagged. Otherwise, we tagged the motivations of the retweet based on the tweeter's additional statements. In the following case, additional motivation of the retweet is "1.6 Summarizing the scientific findings of the studies."

"RT @le_feufollet: Peer-review illusion: 8/9 papers resubmitted to the journals that published them were rejected. http://t.co/7rdb480iJa (Paper: Peer-review practices of psychological journals: The fate of published articles, submitted again)"

"4.5 Announcing the publication of a new article / Recommending this good or interesting article" is also a frequently occurred motivation, appeared in 17.36% of the tweets. One example tweet of this motivation is as follows.

"NEW! Scent of the Familiar: An fMRI Study of Canine Brain Responses to Familiar and Unfamiliar Human and Dog Odors. http://t.co/Y1Z40z5Zdq"

The next two popular subcategories are similar but suit slightly different situations. "4.7 Raising a question to think" (4.02%) refers to the tweets which put forward a question related to the article for readers to think over. If a question in a tweet could be addressed after reading the article, the tweet was tagged as this motivation. On the other hand, "4.2 Invitation for further discussion" (2.43%) often raises a question or asks readers to read an article for further discussion. The following first and second tweets are examples of "4.7 Raising a question to think" and "4.2 Invitation for further discussion" respectively.

"Bad in video games, but good in real life? http://t.co/HRTfolluFn #ethics (Paper: Being Bad in a Video Game Can Make Us Morally Sensitive)"

"This paper in our journal attracting lots of interest - identifying #autism risk at 9 months - what are your views? http://t.co/slreGtEEiV" (Paper: Identification of infants at risk for autism spectrum disorder and developmental language delay prior to 12 months)"

A tweet was tagged as "4.1 Reaction to a topic in the news / current event" (0.25%) when the news coverage of a topic or a current event triggered discussion of an article. The motivations "4.3 Reaction to a question / comment by tweet readers" (0.89%) and "4.4 Reaction to another tweet post" (3.08%) were not judged only by tweet contents. The former one was applied when a tweeter replied to the reader's question / comment in his/her own tweet while the latter one was applied to tweets where the tweeter made comments on others' tweets. While collecting tweets from altmetrics.com, we marked these two subcategories if we observed these patterns.

A tweet mentioning a commentary / critique / review on another article was tagged with "4.8 Reaction to an article (commentary)" (0.15%). The motivation "4.9 sharing to specific friends, specific groups of people, or directing the article to their followers" (6.99%) includes tweets in which tweeters use cc or @ symbol for targeting specific readers, which should be clearly separated from retweets and tweets containing "@author name" to show the copyright. An example tweet sharing to a specific friend is as follows.

"What a superb research article! (CC @SenatorHealy) http://t.co/V7UwK83nIq (Paper: The role of facial hair in women's perceptions of men's attractiveness, health, masculinity and parenting abilities)"

Extensions. This motivation consists of two subcategories with the coverage of 3.37% of the tweets. When tweets recommend related articles to read or other forms of the articles like slides and videos to watch, they were tagged with "5.1 Recommending other materials (reading, podcast, video, etc.)" (2.48%). In the following tweet, the podcast information of an article is recommended. The motivation "5.2 Suggesting future research directions" occupied 0.89% of the tweets.

"Excited to confirm that our next #podcast will be with Dr Liz Pellicano @CRAE_IOE discussing her #openaccess article http://t.co/IcUfg6M9TK (Paper: What should autism research focus upon? Community views and priorities from the United Kingdom)"

Self. This category (14.83%) covers tweeters' personal attitude and experience as well as the voices of article authors and journal publishers. When a journal publisher cites an article to announce or promote the publication, the tweet was tagged as "6.3 Publisher citation" (5.26%). "6.4 Self citation" (1.98%) was used when a paper author cites his/her article. These subcategories were marked when the tweets were collected, as we did not gather Twitter account information. "6.2 Expressing self-preference" (5.41%) includes tweets showing personal preference or opinion toward articles, lifestyle, etc. For instance, a tweeter expresses his interest in an article as follows.

"I look forward to reading this. http://t.co/YxnkMMJJll" (Paper: Scent of the Familiar: An fMRI Study of Canine Brain Responses to Familiar and Unfamiliar Human and Dog Odors)"

The motivation "6.1 Sharing personal experience" (2.13%) puts more emphasis on particular personal experience related to an article, such as the following tweet.

"We wish this study had come out when we were in high school! More/source: http://t.co/rli9zDjwEj http://t.co/O8teX5BF8G (Paper: What ever happened to the "cool" kids? long-term sequelae of early adolescent pseudomature behavior)"

Data. This motivation contains tweets asking for or providing paper sources, and was found in 5.95% of the tweets. Compared to "8.1 Asking for paper sources" (0.74%) which is asking where to get the full text of the article or other related resources, "8.2 Providing paper sources / facts with practical implications" (5.21%), which is offering access to a specific article or related resources, was more common. The following is a self-citation tweet which provides a paper source.

"Is Adolescence a Sensitive Period for Sociocultural Processing? Mail me or @le_feufollet for pdf if can't access it: http://t.co/0ZrStHq5c0"

Other. This motivation was found in 13.74% of the tweets. 11.81% of the tweets were "10.1 Purely tweeting". This subcategory contains tweets with no meaningful comments. It covers three cases. First, a tweet only contains the title or part of the title of an article with a hyperlink attached. Second, merely a hyperlink is provided. Third, a publishing journal name is referred to besides the title and hyperlink as the following example.

"Does asking about suicide and related behaviours... [Psychol Med. 2014] - PubMed - NCBI http://t.co/ZYudQ4lmD4"

"10.2 Others" (1.93%) accommodates tweets which could not be understood due to contexts or cultural differences. It also includes other motivations which are not predefined, such as explaining research settings.

4.3 Frequent Words in the Tweets

In order to understand the overall topics in each motivation category, 10 frequently occurring, meaningful words were extracted from top 30 words in each motivation category, and are shown in Table 3. In a corpus of 2,016 tweets, tweeters tended to express their viewpoints mainly in the fields of autism and depression when citing psychological papers (see frequent words in "Overall" in Table 3). For instance, "RT" is the most commonly used word in "Trigger" category to retweet or forward tweets to acquaintances. For "Self" and "Controversy" categories, "I" and "debate" are most frequently mentioned words respectively. As for "Data" category, "access", "available", and "open access" are frequently used to provide paper sources to followers. "Facebook" is also referred to frequently, since the psychological effects of Facebook are commonly investigated in the field of psychology.

Table 3. Frequent words in each motivation category

Motivation Category	Frequent Words
Discussion	study, rt, autism, research, people, Facebook, children, depression, women, and social
Criticism	research, study, suicide, autism, serotonin, depression, myth, think, violent, and data
Advice	Facebook, people, sleep, eating, life, decision, choices, control, help, and problems
Trigger	rt, study, research, article, paper, interesting, mt, read, review, and published
Extensions	research, article, autism, study, paper, podcast, see, lessons, video, and blog
Self	I, study, paper, article, rt, good, published, read, editorial, and interesting
Controversy	debate, influences, unconscious, behaviour, health, retire, theory, controversial, decision, and estimates
Data	paper, article, access, available, free, full, see, online, open access, and link
Ethics	ethics, bad, myth, busting, low, problem, standards, treatments, assumptions, and buster
Other	autism, Facebook, review, social, child, study, research, cognitive, effects, and impact
Overall	study, autism, rt, research, I, article, paper, Facebook, children, and depression

4.4   Discussion

We get some interesting findings from a content analysis of 2,016 tweets citing psychology research articles. First, over half of the tweets (52.88%) cited research articles to summarize the scientific findings of the studies. In this motivation, most tweets paraphrased either the titles of research articles or research findings from the abstract, and usually tweeters did not express their feelings or opinions directly.

11.81% of the tweets were purely tweeting, which means no comment was added to the tweets except the titles and URLs of the articles. Likewise, 17.36% of the tweets were used to announce or recommend new interesting articles by sharing paper sources. Also, 19.05% of the tweets were retweeted, in which most of the tweets include no meaningful comment. Even though these four foremost subcategories are valuable motivations, they do not convey in-depth critical discussion of academic papers.

For this phenomenon, we can think of three possible reasons. First, Twitter has a character limit (140) for each post, which does not allow users to adequately describe their opinions and sentiments. Not surprisingly, the majority of the tweets (84.77%) hold a neutral attitude towards the papers they cited. Second, 67.50% of Twitter users are between 16 and 22 years old [16], and they are interested in fascinating and fresh research findings, but the main intention of tweeting research is not to discuss scholarly issues deeply. As a result, they share the research findings they are interested in, but they are not keen to make more remarks. Another reason is the existence of non-active users who are only retweeting others' tweets. So Twitter seems not to be a good platform to discuss or debate research issues deeply, but provides good access to some interesting research findings.

5   Conclusion

In this study, we analyzed a corpus of 2,016 tweets to investigate user motivations for tweeting research articles in psychology. Our findings are in line with the ones by Thelwall et al. [13]. In summary, Twitter was mainly used to disseminate scientific findings to the general public without discussing academic issues deeply. Tweeters infrequently expressed their opinions towards the articles, and negative tweets (5.15%) were enough of a minority to be ignored for the purpose of altmetrics. Therefore, the simple count of mentions of a research article on Twitter appears a reasonable indicator for the importance of the article, and probably a good predictor for future citations. And so, in digital libraries, the provision of the counts of mentions of online articles in tweets will help users to find impactful or popular articles. Since the content analysis results of this study cannot reflect the complete aspects of research tweets in all disciplines, we plan to investigate user motivations for tweeting research articles in other disciplines.

References

1. Alternative Metrics Initiative: Phase 1 White Paper. National Information Standards Organization (NISO). http://www.niso.org/apps/group_public/download.php/13809/Altmetrics_project_phase1_white_paper.pdf
2. Sud, P., Thelwall, M.: Evaluating altmetrics. Scientometrics 98(2), 1131–1143 (2014). doi:10.1007/s11192-013-1117-2
3. Galligan, F., Dyas-Correia, S.: Altmetrics: Rethinking the Way We Measure. Serials Review 39(1), 56–61 (2013). doi:10.1016/j.serrev.2013.01.003
4. Thelwall, M., Haustein, S., Larivière, V., Sugimoto, C.R.: Do Altmetrics Work? Twitter and Ten Other Social Web Services. PLoS ONE 8(5), 1–7 (2013). doi:10.1371/journal.pone.0064841
5. Howard, J.: Scholars Seek Better Ways to Track Impact Online (2012). http://chronicle.com/article/As-Scholarship-Goes-Digital/130482/
6. Mahrt, M., Weller, K., Peters, I.: Twitter in scholarly communication. In: Weller, K., Bruns, A., Burgess, J., Mahrt, M., Puschmann, C. (eds.) Twitter and Society. Digital Formations, vol. 89, pp. 399–410. Peter Lang, New York (2014)
7. Eysenbach, G.: Can tweets predict citations? Metrics of social impact based on Twitter and correlation with traditional metrics of scientific impact. Journal of Medical Internet Research 13(4) (2011). doi:10.2196/jmir.2012
8. Weller, K., Droge, E., Puschmann, C.: Citation analysis in twitter: approaches for defining and measuring information flows within tweets during scientific conferences. In: Making Sense of Microposts Workshop, Crete, Greece (2011)
9. Veletsianos, G.: Higher education scholars' participation and practices on Twitter. Journal of Computer Assisted Learning 28(4), 336–349 (2012)
10. Ebner, M., Schiefner, M.: Microblogging—more than fun? In: Arnedillo-Sanchez, I., Isaias, P. (eds.) IADIS Mobile Learning Conference, pp. 155–159. Algarve, Portugal (2008)
11. Holmberg, K., Thelwall, M.: Disciplinary differences in Twitter scholarly communication. Scientometrics 101(2), 1027–1042 (2014)
12. Priem, J., Costello, K.L.: How and why scholars cite on twitter. In: Conference on ASIST, October 22–27, 2010, Pittsburgh, PA, USA (2010)

13. Thelwall, M., Tsou, A., Weingart, S., Holmberg, K., Haustein, S.: Tweeting Links to Academic Articles. International Journal of Scientometrics, Informetrics and Bibliometrics **17**(1) (2013)
14. Haustein, S., Costas, R., Larivière, V.: Characterizing Social Media Metrics of Scholarly Papers: The Effect of Document Properties and Collaboration Patterns. PLOS ONE **10**(3), 1–21 (2015). doi:10.1371/journal.pone.0120495
15. Shema, H., Bar-Ilan, J., Thelwall, M.: How Is Research Blogged? A Content Analysis Approach. Journal of the Association for Information Science and Technology **66**(6), 1136–1149 (2015)
16. Sloan, L., Morgan, J., Burnap, P., Williams, M.: Who Tweets? Deriving the Demographic Characteristics of Age, Occupation and Social Class from Twitter User Meta-Data. PLOS ONE **10**(3), 1–20 (2015). doi:10.1371/journal.pone.0115545

Xamobile: Usability Evaluation of Text Input Methods on Mobile Devices for Historical African Languages

Sunkanmi Olaleye(⊠) and Hussein Suleman

Department of Computer Science, University of Cape Town, Private Bag,
Rondebosch, Cape Town 7701, South Africa
{solaleye,hussein}@cs.uct.ac.za

Abstract. Customized text input editors on mobile devices for languages with no standard language models, such as some African languages, are vital to allow text input tasks to be crowdsourced and thus enable quick and precise participation. We investigated 4 different mobile input techniques for complex language scripts like |Xam and collected accuracy data from experiments with the Xwerty, T9, Pinyin script and hierarchical entry methods for mobile devices and also usability data from the participants. Our results on usability testing show that Xwerty methods offer substantial benefits to the majority of users in terms of speed for |Xam text entry and ease of use.

Keywords: Error correction · Human factors · Input devices · Text entry · Text entry metrics

1 Introduction

The Bleek and Lloyd collection of handwritten notebooks document the language and culture of some Khoi-San people in South Africa. All the pages of this collection have been scanned but are yet to be completely transcribed. It is made up of about 20000 pages of text in the |Xam and !Kun languages. A Web crowdsourcing platform designed for the transcription of the |Xam text requires desktop computer systems and Internet access, which has limited the potential of this tool [1]. However, volunteer workers of this Transcribe Bleek and Lloyd project indicated a preference for a mobile platform for the transcription tasks. This paper presents the outcome of our users' interaction and testing study on how best transcription can be done with low cost mobile devices using four different input methods (Xwerty, T9, Pinyin script and hierarchical) with |Xam text. Our research focuses on a mobile transcription input editor for |Xam called Xamobile. It currently has 4 text entry techniques. It is designed for Android OS mobile devices and tested on small touch screen phones.

2 Keyboard Design

We carried out a usability experiment that evaluates the text entry rate and ease of using the four input methods shown in Fig. 1 (a-d). We tested these input methods using text entry methods implemented on a Samsung GT-S5301.

© Springer International Publishing Switzerland 2015
R.B. Allen et al. (Eds.): ICADL 2015, LNCS 9469, pp. 209–214, 2015.
DOI: 10.1007/978-3-319-27974-9_21

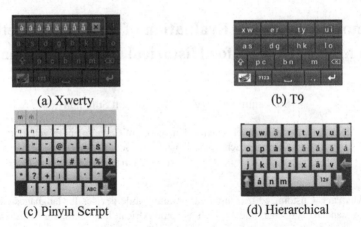

(a) Xwerty   (b) T9

(c) Pinyin Script   (d) Hierarchical

Fig. 1. (a) – (d) Xamobile Input methods

Fig. 2 shows the characteristics of |Xam text used in this experiment. The substring in a red rectangle is made up of a single base character 'a' with diacritic marks above and below, and combined base characters 'nn' with diacritic marks spanning across them.

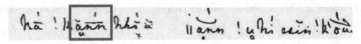

Fig. 2. |Xam text

Each of the input methods has some unique feature as an advantage over the other. Xwerty is based on the existing qwerty touchscreen keypad on mobile devices, with popup keypad templates for keys that are polymorphic. T9 uses the 2 key multi-tap feature, with the number of keys reduced compared to Xwerty. It has a word list choice suggestion based on the key pressed [2]. Pinyin script is a qwerty based technique based on Mandarin Chinese text entry techniques but differing in implementation. This does not make use of a keyboard popup for the representation of diacritical based characters, but has a Pinyin Renderer (PR) for the rendering of complex characters with diacritics using the proposed model in Fig 3a. It makes use of the |Xam character model, with 3 columns for base characters, 3 columns for diacritics above and 2 columns for diacritics below. It has 2 frames above the soft keyboard [3].

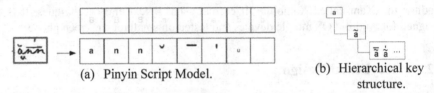

(a) Pinyin Script Model.   (b) Hierarchical key structure.

Fig. 3. Proposed |Xam text entry models

The topmost frame is for PR, where character and diacritics are entered in sequence and PR converts it to suitable |Xam text and displays suggested representations on the second frame below it (Fig 3a). The hierarchical technique reuses its keypad layout for the rendering of the children keys of its immediate parent. It renders the children key text as boldface to highlight them (see Fig 3b). It uses the first keypad layout repeatedly, unlike the Xwerty and T9 popup keypad template. We developed the four input methods for Xam and the text entry evaluation prototype using Java with Eclipse IDE, Android ADT and the Android SDK. The prototype is called Xamobile. Fig 4 shows the entry methods for our evaluation.

Fig. 4. Xamobile text entry methods

3   Evaluation

15 subjects (5 males, 10 females) were recruited to participate in a pilot study. All were recruited from the university campus, aged from 22 to 45, with an average of 1 year of Android QWERTY soft keyboard usage. The criteria for selecting subjects for the study was that they must know how to identity Latin and non-Latin characters from the presented text on the soft keyboard. All participants received their primary education in English.

Subjects were given pre- and post-experiment questionnaires to complete. Pre-questionnaires captured background information while the post-questionnaire captured their rating of the different input methods used in terms of how fast and complex it is for entry of the |Xam phrases on a 5-point Likert scale, where 1 was strongly disagree and 5 was strongly agree. A session consisted of a practice session where participants would familiarize themselves with the chosen text entry method for that session and, after correct entry of the practice presented |Xam phrase, a real session started with 20 different presented |Xam phrases. The experimental design was a within-subjects one-factor analysis of variance. The single factor was 'text entry interface' with four levels: X for Xwerty, T for T9, P for Pinyin script and H for Hierarchical. Table 1 shows the experiment order - T1, T2, T3 and T4, which was governed by a balanced Latin Square. We randomly assigned participants to an experiment order and each participant performed 30 minutes of text entry for each input technique. After each participant completed the experiments using the four input methods in the experiment order assigned, the post-questionnaires were filled and submitted.

Table 1. Balanced Design Model

T1	X	T	P	H
T2	T	P	H	X
T3	P	H	X	T
T4	H	X	T	P

Our experiment results for the highest and lowest typing speeds for the study were 14.88 and 2.92 words per minute (WPM), respectively. An ANOVA analysis established that there was a significant effect of entry techniques on the text input speed ($F_{3,56} = 5.32$, p < .005). This shows that Xwerty is the fastest text entry method with the highest word per minute (WPM) for |Xam text. The average WPM for the Xwerty, T9, Pinyin Script and Hierarchical techniques were 7.45 (SD = 1.76), 5.33 (SD = 1.31), 4.43 (SD = 1.18) and 4.85 (SD = 1.42), respectively. The post-survey asked users to comments on speed (Q1 [xwerty], Q3 [t9], Q5 [Pinyin], Q7 [hierarchical]) of text entry. Fig 5a shows the results of the survey regarding the speed of use and Xwerty is clearly the fastest method, followed by Pinyin and then the other methods. Likewise, the ANOVA analysis established that there was a significant difference in the error rates among the entry techniques ($F_{3,52} = 6.66$, p < .001). Our results show that hierarchical is the most accurate, with the least error rate for |Xam text. The average MSD for the Xwerty, T9, Pinyin Script and Hierarchical techniques were 17.38 (SD = 13.41), 15.72 (SD = 10.50), 27.68 (SD = 10.62) and 10.80 (SD = 4.52), respectively. There was no significant difference in error rates between Xwerty and T9, but these were significantly more accurate than the Pinyin Script entry technique. Also, our result from the post-survey asked on complexity of use (Q2 [Xwerty], Q4 [T9], Q6 [Pinyin], Q8 [hierarchical]) of text entry as displayed on Fig 5b. It shows that the Pinyin and hierarchical methods are noted as being marginally more complex than the other techniques, with Xwerty being the least complex. One of the comments from our users about Pinyin was that;

"Pinyin was very difficult. It was like old computing 'punch in card system'. What worked well was its ability to make many complex symbols/characters that one could not be easily found in the other systems. If Pinyin could be combined with Xwerty system, it will get better results because it is familiar and it should be able to create complex characters"

This comment further supports both our qualitative and quantitative findings from the experiment and survey in terms of speed of use. Contrarily, results from our usability survey on accuracy of text entry disagree with that of the computation from extracted data for accuracy but the majority of our users after the survey confirmed hierarchical is easy to use, which supports our quantitative findings that the hierarchical technique is the most accurate.

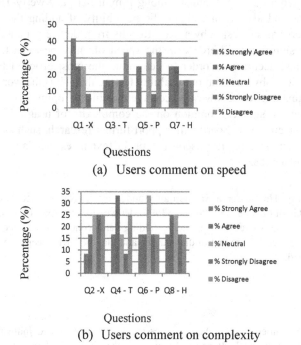

(a) Users comment on speed

(b) Users comment on complexity

Fig. 5. Questions and opinion of subjects based on Likert scale

4   Related Work

Digitization of local languages and text processing activities like text translation and transcription are typical applications of crowdsourcing. In recent times, low cost and small devices were used for crowdsourcing. Wismer et al. [4] evaluated input methods using text and image based CAPTCHAs on mobile devices by investigating five different touch and voice input techniques. The outcome of this survey shows that users prefer touch based CAPTCHAs or the voice based CAPTCHAs. Ilinkin and Kim [5] made use of 3 Korean text input methods, namely Chon-ji-in, EZ-Hangul, and SK on mobile for their evaluation. This study is similar in its implementation but differs due to the models of languages used. Korean is a standard language with known character sets but |Xam is a resource-scarce language.

5   Conclusions

Our research findings show that users prefer the Xwerty text entry technique. Our computed results from device generated data indicate Pinyin Script as the worst of the four tested techniques but contrarily, results from our usability testing indicates

Pinyin script was the next to Xwerty in terms of text entry rate and ease of use. Further research is required to distinguish among Pinyin Script, Xwerty-T9 and hierarchical techniques and also to investigate the possibility of adding the Pinyin script model with Xwerty as suggested by a user. Results from device generated data show that there is no significant difference in the speed of entry between these three in terms of speed and accuracy in order to determine the most efficient technique for |Xam text entry. It is obvious with our usability testing that T9 is the worst entry technique for |Xam text due to the lowest percentage in subjects' opinion on speed and the highest percentage in subjects' opinion on the complexity of usage. Ultimately, the fastest and most accurate keyboard will support further research, such as crowdsourcing of transcriptions that require users to type in text in extinct languages such as |Xam on a mobile device.

Acknowledgements. This research was partially funded by the National Research Foundation of South Africa (Grant numbers: 85470 and 83998), University of Cape Town and Telkom SA Ltd. The authors acknowledge that opinions, findings and conclusions or recommendations expressed in this publication are that of the authors, and that the NRF accepts no liability whatsoever in this regard.

References

1. Munyaradzi, N., Suleman, H.: Quality assessment in crowdsourced indigenous language transcription. In: Aalberg, T., Papatheodorou, C., Dobreva, M., Tsakonas, G., Farrugia, C.J. (eds.) TPDL 2013. LNCS, vol. 8092, pp. 13–22. Springer, Heidelberg (2013)
2. Soukoreff, R.W., MacKenzie, I.S.: Metrics for text entry research: an evaluation of MSD and KSPC, and a new unified error metric. In: ACM Proceedings of the SIGCHI Conference on Human Factors in Computing Systems, pp. 1–3 (2003)
3. Liu, Y.: Chinese Text Entry with Mobile Devices, Ph.D., University of Tampere (2010)
4. Wismer, A.J., Madathil, K.C., Koikkara, R., Juang, K.A., Greenstein, J.S.: Evaluating the usability of CAPTCHAs on a mobile device with voice and touch input. In: Proceedings of the Human Factors and Ergonomics Society 2012 Annual Meeting, pp. 1228–1232 (2012)
5. Ilinkin, I., Kim, S.: Evaluation of text entry methods for korean mobile phones, a user study. In: CHI(2010), pp. 2023–2026 (2010)

Investigating Image Processing Algorithms for Navigating Cultural Heritage Spaces Using Mobile Devices

Ayodeji Olojede[✉] and Hussein Suleman

Department of Computer Science, University of Cape Town, Rondebosch,
Cape Town 7700, South Africa
Oljayo001@myuct.ac.za, hussein@cs.uct.ac.za

Abstract. The use of mobile devices is increasing in the cultural heritage and museum context. The most common approach is to provide a customized mobile device to the museum visitor to navigate museum spaces. In this paper, a mobile cultural heritage guide is presented, which enables image based navigation of rock art sites using computer vision and image processing algorithms for rock art image feature detection and extraction. Traditionally such systems have used algorithms such as Scale-Invariant Feature Transform (SIFT), Speeded-Up Robust Features (SURF) and Oriented Fast and Rotational Brief (ORB). The three algorithms have been integrated in a prototype and their performance has been evaluated. It was observed that digital recognition of rock art images is possible under certain image preprocessing conditions. Also, the evaluation result shows that, generally, SIFT has good accuracy and, when used in conjunction with K Nearest Neighbor, has acceptable matching speed.

Keywords: Cultural heritage · Rock art images · Content based image retrieval system

1 Introduction

Cultural Heritage is a composition of physical artifacts, cultures and attributes from the past that a nation considers significant and decides to pass on to current and future generations. Examples include cultural artifacts such as rock art. Rock art is a term used to describe human-made engravings and paintings on stones [1]. Commonly associated with a nation's rich archaeological past, rock art represents an important asset for tourism and is also found at the centre of culture and education. A survey by Euro barometer in 2013 on cultural access and participation shows that cultural heritage objects are often isolated and difficult to appreciate, thereby resulting in low user engagement [2]. This has generated research interest all over the world, seeking ways to make cultural heritage more desirable and more accessible. A novel approach that is still currently being researched is the use of users' smart mobile phones, by providing a suitable mobile application that can be downloaded onto the users' device. Leveraging this approach and with an emphasis on rock art, this study is focused on investigating the feasibility of using images to navigate cultural heritage spaces like

© Springer International Publishing Switzerland 2015
R.B. Allen et al. (Eds.): ICADL 2015, LNCS 9469, pp. 215–224, 2015.
DOI: 10.1007/978-3-319-27974-9_22

the rock art sites using computer vision image processing and matching algorithms on mobile devices. To assist with this investigation, a Content Based Image Retrieval System was developed. Most heritage (rock art) sites are often left in their historical context found many miles away from civilization; the ambience of the site context is lost if the cultural heritage artifact is removed from its original location [3]. The proposed system will enable the camera of a mobile device to act as a cultural heritage guide. The user points the camera of his mobile device at the rock art of interest and takes a picture. Computer vision image processing technology recognizes the input picture and provides a ranked list of results to the user. Details such as the title and description of each returned result can be easily communicated back to the user. Such an application could help users appreciate rock art and also make it more accessible.

In the first part of this paper, we introduce cultural heritage and the issue of user engagement with cultural heritage. We then propose a mobile application that may help to tackle the problem. The other sections of this paper discuss the related work, the research approach, a discussion of the selected algorithms for feature extraction, descriptors and matching. Further, the paper presents an experiment to assess and compare the performance of the selected algorithms under realistic conditions.

1.1   Problem Definition

User engagement with culture has been a problem that has persisted for many years. Although attempts have been made to address this problem, especially with current advances in mobile technology that have given rise to a number of mobile applications for personalized cultural heritage content delivery, very little work has been done in addressing this problem from a rock art context. Literature has shown that digital recognition of rock art images is difficult due to their cluttered and rough nature, which makes it difficult for most computer vision algorithms to process them.

1.2   Related Works

Many years ago, personalized content delivery in the heritage and museum context was only achieved through audio-guides, where an audio system is used to guide users in experiencing an exhibit in a museum or a heritage site [4]. Current advances in mobile digital technology have given rise to many mobile applications to support personalized delivery of multimedia content to the user from a digital archive.

In CAPTCHA (Completely Automated Public Turing test to tell Computers and Humans Apart) rock [1], feature detection and extraction steps are outsourced to the user as the authors argued that current image feature detection and extraction algorithms performed poorly on rock art images. In captcha rock, the user takes a picture of a petroglyph and traces out the object of interest and submits to the application. The application extracts features and does similarity checks with a database of features to find corresponding matches. Mobile Vision [5] was designed for tourism in an urban setting. A user takes a picture of a place in his line of sight and the application intelligently returns all tourism objects around the picture taken. The application makes use of GPS to detect the user's location and Internet to return the tourism objects around the user's location. Map Snapper [6] was designed to allow users to query a remote information system based on photos of a paper map taken with the camera of a mobile device. The information system could then return useful information to the user via the device. For example, the returned information could include such things as events, facilities, opening times, and accommodation in the geographical region depicted by the query.

1.3   Description of System

Heritage Vision is a mobile application developed with simplicity and personalized rock art multimedia content delivery in mind. The application does not depend on Internet connectivity to function. All image processing is done on the mobile device. Keeping in mind the high computational requirements of image processing algorithms, this application was developed with consideration for the speed and memory constraints of mobile devices. As illustrated in Figure 1 below, the mobile application enables the user to take a picture of the rock art of interest with a mobile device.

Fig. 1. Usage of Heritage Vision

The picture is automatically processed by the image processing engine that runs on the mobile device. The image processing library intelligently pre-processes the image and detects distinct features and extracts descriptors. These descriptors are then matched with the descriptors in the database of training images preloaded in the application. When the application finds matches based on a Euclidean distance calculation, a ranked list of results is displayed back to the user. Information such as title and description are communicated to the user.

2   Research Approach

2.1   Collection of Data

During data collection, we did a physical tour of two rock art sites at the Cederberg Region in Western Cape, South Africa. The rock art sites are about 3 hours drive away from the University of Cape Town. Two students also accompanied us to the site. Each of the students had at least a camera phone. The goal was to make sure all data collection was done on the same day. Training images were taken from different view points and orientation with a 16Mega Pixel digital camera. The students took pictures from the same rock art sites using their mobile phone camera. They took pictures in a way that was comfortable for them to ensure that experimentation was done based on a real life scenario. Most pictures were taken in daylight. Some rock arts were hidden in caves, which creates a good opportunity for taking pictures under different light conditions. See figure 2 for sample data.

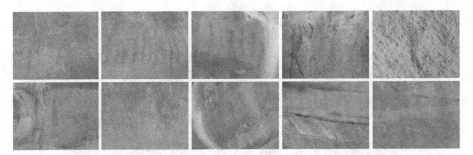

Fig. 2. Sample rock art images taken from the two sites at the Cederberg Region, Western Cape, South Africa

2.2   Mobile Application Prototype

A user centered design approach was adopted in the application prototype design. An operational prototype was implemented at this stage. Operational prototyping is a combination of a throwaway prototype and evolutionary prototype [7]. A throwaway prototype enables user engagement in the design process by producing diagrams of prototypes on paper for user evaluation. An evolutionary prototype is the actual system. In an evolutionary prototype, a clear set of requirements is developed while evaluation results from the throwaway prototype are used to complete the aspects of evolutionary prototype with an unclear set of requirements.

2.3   Image Preprocessing

The nature of rock art images makes it difficult for image processing algorithms to process them. Even the ones that eventually succeeded took a lot of time, hence the preprocessing step is necessary. Image processing involves importing, analyzing and manipulating an image. This process helped in simplifying the image thereby making it easy to process the image further. The output of this stage is usually an enhanced or compressed image.

2.4   Image Feature Extraction and Description

In order to match images, features or region have to be detected and extracted for each image. Such a feature or region can be defined as an interesting part of the image. A single image can contain hundreds to thousands of features. The following algorithms were chosen due to their general performance.

SIFT (Scale Invariant Feature Transform) algorithm is used for extracting distinctive invariant features from images that can be invariant to scale, rotation and illumination [8]. SIFT approximates the Laplacian of Gaussian (LoG) with difference-of-Gaussian (DoG) function to identify potential interest points, which are invariant to scale and orientation. SIFT has been tested and proven to be the most robust local invariant descriptor but it is mainly designed for gray scale images.

SURF (Speeded Up Robust Features) was proposed at the ECCV 2006 conference in Graz, Austria [9]. SURF is a local feature detector and descriptor that was partly inspired by SIFT. Its purpose was to ensure high speed in feature detection and description. SURF uses integral images to reduce computation time. For key point detection, SURF uses a Hessian blob detector which can be computed with 3 integer operations using a precomputed integral image. The authors argued that the Hessian matrix is used as a key point detector because of its good performance in computation speed and accuracy. For feature description, SURF uses the sum of the Haar wavelet responses around the point of interest in horizontal and vertical directions, which are also computed using integral images [9]. SURF descriptors can be used to find and track objects in an image or video. The authors claimed SURF is several times faster than SIFT and more robust against different transformations. Literature shows SURF is good at handling images with rotation and blurring, but not good at handling viewpoint change and illumination change. SURF is also mainly designed for gray scale images [10].

ORB (Oriented Fast and Rotational Brief) [11] was developed as a better alternative to SIFT and SURF in terms of computational cost, matching performance and mainly dealing with the patent issue. ORB uses FAST (Features from Accelerated Segment Test) to detect key points and then apply the Harris corner measure to find top N points among them. ORB uses enhanced BRIEF (Binary Robust Independent Elementary Features) descriptors which are invariant to rotation.

2.5   Feature Matching

The best candidate match for each feature was found by identifying its K nearest neighbors in the feature database of the training images. The nearest neighbors are defined as the key points with minimum Euclidean distance from the given descriptor vector [9]. This is a straight forward approach that linearly searches through the key points in no particular order.

3   Experiment

3.1   Experimental Apparatus

Image Dataset. As mentioned in the previous section, training images were gathered from the field. Images were taken with a 16mega pixel Samsung digital camera. Images were taken at different angles and orientation. All pictures were taken in daylight. As of the time of this experiment, we were able to gather over 500 images. Only 460 images were used as the set of training images. The remaining were rock art pictures taken with a mobile phone camera which would be used as Query images for testing.

Hardware. This experiment is focused on developing the application on the Android platform. A mobile device with processing speed of at least 1GHZ and RAM of at least 1 Gigabyte is considered the minimum hardware requirement. The minimum Android version is 3.0. For this experiment, we made use of an HTC Desire 816 with a Snap Dragon processor and a memory capacity of 1.5GB.

Software. Eclipse ADT (Android Developer Tools) bundle was used as the development IDE. The ADT bundle is specifically customized for developing Android applications. The Android SDK is also included in the ADT bundle. OpenCV (Open Source Computer Vision) is a library of programming functions mainly aimed at developing real time computer vision applications.[1] The library is free for use under the open source BSD license. The library is cross-platform. It has C++, C, Python and Java interfaces and supports Windows, Linux, Mac OS, iOS and Android. In this experiment, we made use of the OpenCV library in C++. The Android aspect is written in Java. Compilation was made possible using the Android NDK for Eclipse, which allow for compiling and executing native programs in Android.

3.2   Experimental Process

In the first stage of the experimental process, we needed to archive the image dataset mentioned above. In this stage, features of the images were extracted and their descriptors stored in the database. Prior to this, it was important to pre-process the images as the un-refined form was very difficult for the algorithms to process. The algorithms that eventually made it through took over a minute to extract features.

In the pre-processing stage,

1.   The Application normalizes the size of each image such that the final size is 288 x 216 pixels.
2.   The image was split into R, G, and B channels. The Green channel was preferred as rock art paintings were more visible under this channel. For a visual reference, see the image below. In the image below, the Green channel output is the circled section.
3.   The application performs a contrast enhancement (linear normalization) to [0, 255] as rock art images have low contrast.

---

[1]   http://opencv.org/

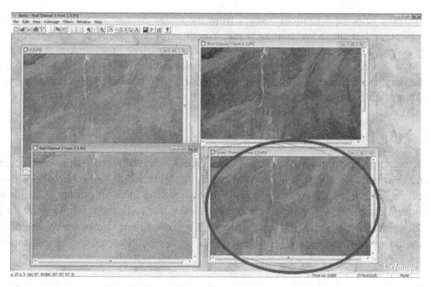

Fig. 3. A view of the Original Image, R Channel, G Channel and B channel. The Green channel is circled.

The image in Figure 4 below shows the final output of the image pre-processing.

Fig. 4. Result of linear normalization (contrast enhancement) of the green channel output

In the second stage, a separate apparatus for each algorithm was created. This process will enable us to visually quantify the difference between the numbers of features detected by each algorithm and also the quality of these features. It will also enable us to easily evaluate the performance of each algorithm. All apparatuses are similar in setup and image dataset. The feature detection method of each algorithm (SIFT, SURF & ORB) was executed first on the image dataset. Extracted feature descriptors were stored in the database.

We then selected 5 random images from the image dataset set aside as query images. Remember these were images taken with a camera phone by students. There were no particular guidelines as to how they took the picture. It was taken at their own discretion. We ran the experiment with this image dataset on the set of query images in the database. As mentioned earlier, we used the K Nearest Neighbor matching method for establishing and sorting match results.

3.3   Experiment Results

After the experiment process, we discovered SURF detected more features on rock art than the other two algorithms. We set a default value for the amount of key point detection for both SIFT and ORB. SURF does not offer such an option. We did this because most of the key points detected have very low radius and would slow down the descriptor storage and matching process. The table below shows the results of the feature extraction and descriptor process. ORB is fast but detected the fewest number of key points.

Table 1. Shows feature detection and descriptor comparison on a random query dataset. **Total Desc** is the total number of descriptors and **Time (ms)** is total time taken to extract descriptors

	SIFT		SURF		ORB	
Query	Total Desc	Time (ms)	Total Desc	Time(ms)	Total Desc	Time(ms)
Image 1	500	1552	421	691	387	103
Image 2	500	3709	1119	948	500	194
Image 3	500	2700	786	709	488	129
Image 4	500	3621	981	935	496	149
Image 5	500	5537	1535	1210	500	157
Average Speed (ms)		3423		898		146

We also found out that the majority of the key-points were detected outside of the actual paintings. The key point concentration was more in the background region. Very few were detected around the paintings, which is likely to have a negative impact on feature matching.

When the painting region was cropped out from the background and submitted to the algorithms for processing, features were detected around the painting region. It is unclear why key points were focused on the background region at this time.

K Nearest Neighbor was adopted to compare key points. This exhaustive search was used because of its simplicity and because, at the time of this experiment, there were 460 training images in the database. The method re-arranges the image results according to its confidence level. This method searches linearly and may be ideal for training images of single rock art sites but will not be ideal for a larger database of training images from different rock art sites.

3.4   Evaluations

We have evaluated the performance of the algorithms based on precision (how many returned documents are relevant) and recall (what fraction of the relevant documents was found). We also calculated the average precision.

From the table below, it is clear SIFT outperforms SURF and ORB. It has demonstrated competence in all queries when used with K Nearest Neighbor Matching.

Table 2. Shows the precision and recall for each algorithm, and average precision

	SIFT		SURF		ORB	
Query	Precision	Recall	Precision	Recall	Precision	Recall
Image 1	0.35	0.8	0.15	0.37	0.1	0.25
Image 2	0.35	0.7	0.2	0.4	0.05	0.1
Image 3	0.3	0.35	0.2	0.22	0.5	0.58
Image 4	0.55	1	0.4	0.7	0.2	0.36
Image 5	0.55	0.3	0.25	0.14	0.4	0.23
Average Precision	**0.42**		**0.24**		**0.25**	

We also evaluated the application performance in terms of speed. From the result table below, the K Nearest Neighbor match spent more time matching features from SURF and this is evident in the feature descriptor result where SURF detected more key points than SIFT and ORB. SIFT descriptors produced more results that are relevant to the user query even when there were scale and rotational changes. ORB was the fastest but the majority of the returned results were irrelevant to the query.

Table 3. Total time taken for application to perform search

	SIFT	SURF	ORB
Query	Time to Match (ms)	Time to Match (ms)	Time to Match (ms)
Image 1	15472	20542	680
Image 2	15802	15674	676
Image 3	15184	20072	583
Image 4	16968	15875	661
Image 5	15136	22016	637
Average Time (ms)	**15712**	**18836**	**647**

4   Conclusion

In this paper, we have been able to show the feasibility of digital recognition of rock art images under certain image pre-processing conditions. We also have been able to demonstrate the feasibility of object recognition on a mobile device with a particular configuration. However, further experiments will be required, most especially for the matching algorithm as K Nearest Neighbor match will not be ideal for a large image database. With feature vectors such as SIFT and SURF, it will be ideal to make use of Randomized KDTree technique. This will ensure indexing of feature vectors for fast retrieval. ORB makes use of binary features and an approximate nearest neighbor search using Local Sensitive Hashing (LSH) index may help to improve search speed in a large database of feature descriptors.

Acknowledgments. This research was partially funded by the National Research Foundation of South Africa (Grant numbers: 85470 and 83998), University of Cape Town and Telkom SA Ltd. The authors acknowledge that opinions, findings and conclusions or recommendations expressed in this publication are that of the authors, and that the NRF accepts no liability whatsoever in this regard.

References

1. Zhu, Q., Wang, X., Keogh, E., Lee, S.H.: An Efficient and Effective Similarity Measure to Enable Data Mining of Petroglyphs. Data Mining Knowl. Disc. **23**, 91–127 (2011)
2. Cultural Access and Participation. European Commission: Special Eurobarometer 399, April-May 2013. TNS OPINION & SOCIAL, Brussels [Producer]
3. Silver, C.S.: The Rock Art of Seminole Canyon State Historic Park: Deterioration and Prospects for Conservation (1985). Report #4000-430 may be obtained from Texas Parks and Wildlife, 4200 Smith School Road, Austin, TX 78744
4. Tellis, C., Proctor, N.: Workshop: Handhelds in Museums, Museums and the Web, Boston (2002)
5. Fritz, G., Seifert, C., Luley, P., Paletta, L., Almer, A.: Mobile vision for ambient learning in urban environments. In: The Third Annual International Mobile Learning Conference MLEARN 2004, Lake Bracciano, Rome (2004)
6. Hare, J., Lewis, P., Gordon, L., Hart, G.: MapSnapper: engineering an efficient algorithm for matching images of maps from mobile phones. In: Proc. SPIE 6820, Multimedia Content Access: Algorithms and Systems II, p. 68200L (2008)
7. Davis, A.M.: Operational Prototyping: A New Development Approach. IEEE Software, 71, September 1992
8. Lowe, D.: Distinctive Image Features from Scale-Invariant Keypoints. International Journal of Computer Visions **60**(2), 91–110 (2004)
9. Bay, H., Ess, A., Tuytelaars, T., Van Gool, L.: SURF: Speeded-Up Robust Features. Computer Vision and Image Understanding **110**(3), 346–359 (2008)
10. Zhang, T., Hirsch, B., Cao, Z., Yichang, H.L.: Automatic target recognition and image analysis. In: MIPPR (2009)
11. Rublee, E., Rabaud, V., Konolige, K., Bradski, G.: ORB: an efficient alternative to SIFT or SURF. In: IEEE 13th International Conference on Computer Vision (2011)

Crowdsourcing a Text Corpus is not a Game

Sean Packham[✉] and Hussein Suleman

Centre for ICT4D, Department of Computer Science, University of Cape Town,
Cape Town, South Africa
pcksea001@uct.ac.za, hussein@cs.uct.ac.za

Abstract. Building language corpora for low resource languages such as South Africa's isiXhosa is challenging because of limited digitized texts. Language corpora are needed for building information retrieval services such as search and translation and to support further online content creation. A novel solution was proposed to source original and relevant multilingual content by crowdsourcing translations via an online competitive game where participants would be paid for their contributions. Four experiments were conducted and the results support the idea that gamification by itself does not yield the widely expected benefits of increased motivation and engagement. We found that people do not volunteer without financial incentives, the form of payment does not matter, they would not continue contributing if the money is taken away and people preferred direct incentives and the possibility of incentives was not as strong a motivator.

Keywords: Crowdsourcing · Gamification · Translation · Language corpora · Information retrieval

1 Introduction

isiXhosa (Xhosa) is the second most spoken first language in South Africa, spoken by more than 8 million people - 16% of the country's population [1]. isiXhosa is categorised as a low resource language with a scarcity of digital content and well defined linguistic models and tools [2]. isiXhosa is a morphologically rich and a highly agglutinative language, forming words by gluing together part to a word's base form [3]. For example the base form of the isiXhosa word for month is "inyanga", gluing "i" in front produces the plural form "iinyanga". Developing automatic translation systems for agglutinative languages with few morphological models is particularly challenging because the base form of words are often incorrectly categorised [4]. Low resource languages are further challenged by the difficulty of assembling sufficient content to build language corpora, a problem worsened when trying to assemble multilingual language corpora. Attempts to assemble monolingual and multilingual isiXhosa corpora from South African governmental websites [2], [4] or by crawling isiXhosa specific websites [5] found that the quantity and quality of the content was not sufficient to produce a working machine translation system [4,5].

© Springer International Publishing Switzerland 2015
R.B. Allen et al. (Eds.): ICADL 2015, LNCS 9469, pp. 225–234, 2015.
DOI: 10.1007/978-3-319-27974-9_23

A gamified crowdsourcing system was proposed as a novel approach to affordably gather original multilingual content for building language corpora for low resource languages. A custom crowdsourcing system was created and evolved over four experiments. The aim of the experiments was to investigate if intrinsic motivation or gamified motivation could influence users to perform a clearly important social task, with monetary payments being only secondary. Thus, 2 of the experiments appealed to the users based on the intrinsic value of the task. The other 2 experiments offered payments, but these were gamified to test whether the game element appealed to users more than the financial reward. Additional motivation factors, such as physical rewards and user feedback, were not considered for this study. Furthermore, motivation factors for sustained participation weren't explored [6] because of the short duration of the experiments.

The rest of this paper describes these experiments and their results, preceded by a discussion of related literature.

2   Crowdsourcing

Crowdsourcing is the process of outsourcing tasks normally done by an employee or contractor to an anonymous crowd [7]. Crowdsourcing can be successful on projects that can be subdivided into small repeatable Human Intelligence Tasks (HITs), which are challenging for computers to perform but can be performed by a human in a reasonable amount of time [8]. Zaidan and Burch used crowdsourcing to produce Urdu to English translations where the quality was near professional levels by using redundant translations, translation edits and translator screening to automatically select the best translations [9]. Crowdsourcing has also been used for emergency response after the Haiti earthquake in 2010 to translate more than 40,000 emergency messages over six days from Haitan Kreyol to various languages [10]. A systematic classification of 46 crowdsourcing projects identified motivation via remuneration and quality control via a pre-qualification assessment to be prominent and important characteristics of successful crowdsourcing projects [11].

Table 1 shows the results of a literature survey that was conducted to sample the reward amounts for translation HITs on crowdsourcing platforms such as Mechanical Turk and CrowdFlower. The survey uncovered payment points for both translating and ranking tasks. A few studies specified payment points per task rather than per word and where possible a translation word cost was calculated. The survey shows that it was normal to find translation jobs between 2009 and 2014 that offered rewards between $0.01 and $0.25 to translate/edit a sentence.

Crowdsourcing marketplaces such as Mechanical Turk (MTurk) or CrowdFlower offer a crowdsourcing platform and access to a large number of users. A sampling of MTurk users revealed that 85% were from the United States and India and the remaining 15% were scattered across the rest of the world [8], therefore alternative means of specifically gathering bilingual English-isiXhosa speakers were investigated.

Table 1. Rewards offered by various crowdsourcing translation studies

Source	Task Detail	Reward	/Word
[9]	Translate Urdu to English	$0.10	$0.005
	Edit 10 sentence	$0.25	
	Rank 4 translation groups	$0.06	
[12]	Translate English to Spanish		$0.01
	Validate translation		$0.002
[13]	Rank 5 German to English machine translations	$0.01	
	Translate German to English	$0.10	
	Detect if a machine translation	$0.006	
[14]	Translate Spanish to English	$0.01	
	Translate Teluga to English	$0.02	
	Translate English to Creole	$0.06	
	Translate Urdu to English	$0.03	
	Translate Hindi to English	$0.03	
	Translate Chinese to English	$0.02	

2.1   Gamification

Gamification is the process of using gaming elements in a non-gaming context to improve user experience and motivation [15]. Rewarding a person with virtual points [16,17,18,19] and badges or achievements [19,20,21,22,23] for completing tasks are all examples of gamification. Like many games, gamification can be implemented as a competitive system where users compete against others for placement on a leaderboard [16], [18], [22], [24].

3   Methodology

The four experiments allowed users to translate English sentences from Wikipedia articles on South African topics on a custom created online crowdsourcing website. Each sentence needed to be translated by three separate users and the translations ranked in order of correctness by another three separate users. The ranks for each translation were totalled and the translation with the lowest score selected as the model translation. For example if all the users agreed and ranked the same translation first, that translation will be the model answer because it will have the lowest total ranking of $3 = 1 + 1 + 1$. Users were rewarded with points for each contribution and their total score was reflected on a leaderboard.

Experiment 1 was conducted during the early stages of the research as a pilot project to find out if participants could be gathered from Twitter, a social network for sharing short messages called tweets to followers, and also to prototype a custom crowdsourcing system with scoring, leaderboards and support for paying participants.

The design of experiment 2 was inspired by games that offer increasing rewards from increasing effort over time. For the purpose of comparison, accompanying schemes that offered consistent and decreasing rewards from increasing effort and constant effort were designed. Using the surveyed rewards from past studies and a sampling of professional translation rates, a payment model was developed to select translation and ranking rewards for all the payment groups. The model took into account task redundancy and the national minimum wage for workers with a secondary school education.

The scoring system was designed to have one to one mapping to money earned - each point was equivalent to ZAR0.01. Users were rewarded with points for translating and ranking and the number of points awarded depended on which group they were in. Each group had its own leaderboard. All the payment schemes for the 6 groups were designed with a cap of 100 translations and 100 rankings. Setting a cap allowed predictable payment values to be calculated for each group. Task payment points were first chosen for the groups in the constant set and adjusted appropriately for the increasing set and decreasing set. The groups in the increasing set were adjusted to start at a lower rate and end at a higher rate. The groups in the decreasing set were adjusted to start at a higher rate and end at a lower rate. All the groups had the same average payment per task if the cap was reached. This design created a predictable reward system where rewards could not spiral out of control or become meaningless if no cap existed. All the payment groups were balanced so that users in either could earn the same amount if they reached the cap, with an average reward per sentence translated of $0.06 and reward per sentence ranked of $0.03, putting it in the range of the surveyed rewards in Table 1. The reward amounts for the increasing and decreasing groups differed by 100% at the start and end of the task limit. The selected articles had an average sentence length of 22 words, which resulted in total cost of translating one sentence, including ranking and duplication to be 5-30 times cheaper than sampled local and international translation services.

In South Africa the smallest bank note available is a R10 note. Therefore a participant's money earned was rounded down to the nearest R10; for example a score of 9100 would round down to R90.00. Paying users with cash was not an option because of the large number of expected users. It was decided to use mobile wallet and cardless transaction services offered by many of South Africa's large banks. To send money, the sender deposits cash or selects an account to pay from, and provides the recipient's mobile number. On payment, the recipient gets an SMS detailing the transaction and instructions on how to withdraw the money. The money can be withdrawn from one of the sending bank's branches, cash machines or from a list of authorized partners.

The third experiment replaced the multiple payment groups with a single group, and tested whether the same students from the University of Cape Town would contribute without any financial reward. Users were awarded 1 point for translating or ranking and a single leaderboard was used. Translation and ranking caps were removed, as there was no budget that could be exhausted.

The final experiment tested whether paying users based on where they placed on the contributions leaderboard rather than per contribution would be better at motivating users to contribute more and produce more affordable rates than experiment 2.

An increasing reward for increased effort approach was adopted when choosing the payment points, which resulted in the rewards seen in Fig 1 for the users who contributed the most translations and rankings. Only the top 40 positions were allocated a reward. The experiment was designed to create a sense of heightened competition between users by having them focus on the marginal difference between their contributions and the next user's contributions. Experiment 4 allocated double the budget used in experiment 2 to rewards to further motivate participants.

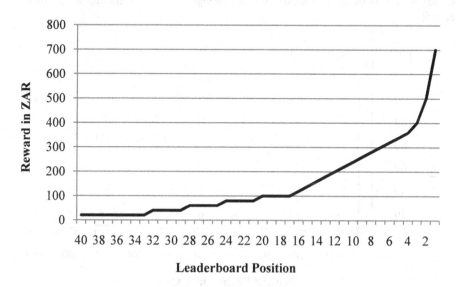

Fig. 1. Leaderboard payment scheme used in experiment 4

4   Results

Experiment 1 was run over three days from 5 August 2014. Five tweets were sent to the author's 132 followers who then shared the project four times; by the end the experiment website was visited 10 times but no one contributed any translations. There are a number of expected reasons for why people did not contribute: the author's network and extended network were not reaching isiXhosa speakers or they were not willing to contribute for free.

Experiment 2 was run for a week from 19 November 2014 (after final exams) with volunteering students from the University of Cape Town. Approximately 24,000 students were sent a "call for participants" email, 200 signed up to participate, 121 made at least one contribution and 61 users contributed enough to receive a reward. 3600 individual translations and 2589 individual rankings were contributed. 1088 sentences received 3 translations and 734 sentences received 3 rankings and could be reassembled into isiXhosa articles. The total cost of the experiment was ZAR3020.

An analysis of the translation times over the duration of the experiment showed no noticeable trends but this was due to the varying sentence length and low number of contributions in each group. Ranking times for all payment groups exhibited a similar downward trend over the duration of the experiment. This showed that the length of a sentence and its translations did not affect the time it took a user to rank it. Furthermore the different payment groups did not affect the users' motivation to rank faster.

Fig 2 shows that only 3 users reached both the translation and ranking limit and earned the maximum reward of ZAR100.00. A large percentage of users who did earn money contributed only enough to earn the first reward of ZAR10.00. 70% of the users did not contribute enough to qualify for any reward, showing that the incentive of payment was enough to motivate users to sign up but not enough to get them to contribute.

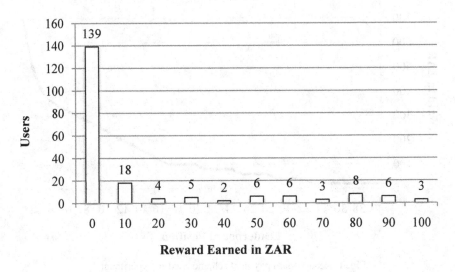

Fig. 2. Number of users per reward tier

Experiment 3 was run at the start of the 2015 academic year in February. 47 users registered and only 12 made at least one contribution. The activity of the users was considerably lower than that of Experiment 2: the most active user contributed 11 translations and 2 rankings. Only 11 sentences were translated 3 times and 2 sentences were ranked 3 times. Offering a monetary reward was considerably more successful at attracting and engaging participants.

Experiment 2 showed that only 61 out of the 200 users earned money therefore experiment 4 was designed to offer rewards to only the most active users. Experiment 4 received 147 users, 57 users contributed 1865 individual translations and 1767 rankings. 39% of users in experiment 2 and 61% of users in experiment 4 made at least one contribution, a considerable difference in activity. 617 sentences received 3 translations and 584 sentences received 3 rankings. Due to the lower activity and the pre-chosen budget, experiment 4 achieved a translation cost of ZAR0.22 per word, almost double the rate of experiment 2.

Table 2. Sample of the experiment 4 leaderboard

Rank	Contributions	Reward (ZAR)	Value vs. Experiment 2
1	444	700	0,32
2	401	500	0,40
3	372	400	0,47
4	284	360	0,39
5	259	340	0,38
6	245	320	0,38
7	192	300	0,32
8	156	280	0,28
9	143	260	0,28
10	133	240	0,28
36	8	20	0,20
37	8	20	0,20
38	7	20	0,18
39	7	20	0,18
40	5	20	0,13

Table 2 shows a sample of the activity of the top 10 and bottom 5 money earners in experiment 4. The second column shows how many contributions it took to reach the respective leaderboard position and reward and the fourth column shows how the translation cost the user achieved compared to that of experiment 2 in terms of value. No user achieved a translation cost equivalent to even half that of experiment 2. The value was worse at the bottom of the paid leaderboard but steadily improved, as users were more competitive higher up the leaderboard.

It would be interesting to know if users feel more comfortable to contribute in smaller groups, like those in experiment 2, which had on average 33 users, rather than a larger group like experiment 4. Users may feel they have a greater chance at reaching the top leaderboard position when there are fewer competitors.

5   Conclusion

Employing gamification in a crowdsourcing game to translate English to isiXhosa showed that people do not volunteer without payment, the form of payment does not matter, participants would not contribute if payment is taken away and finally people wanted a guaranteed rate and the possibility of incentives is not as strong a motivator.

The guaranteed rates offered by the various payment groups in experiment 2 were considerably more effective at getting participants to contribute than the leaderboard payment scheme of experiment 4. This was an interesting result as it was expected that linking payments to leaderboard positions would create a greater competitive environment but it may have had the reverse effect and scared off users who were late to join or slow to start.

The over-arching hypothesis of this project was that gamification of a crowdsourcing system with a task with strong intrinsic motivation would make it possible to gather important data with payment being a secondary factor rather than a primary one. The various experiments have illustrated that this is indeed not true. The student users were purposefully chosen to have a higher than average level of education and to not have a desperate need for the small amounts of money paid. Ultimately, the experiments have illustrated that monetary payment is still a stronger motivation factor than intrinsic motivation or motivation because of gamification. While these results were obtained with a specific task in a specific part of the world, the fundamental lessons learnt are likely to be applicable to corpus generation projects elsewhere.

6   Future Work

Additional motivation factors such as physical rewards can be assessed and compared to financial rewards and various gamification factors. Furthermore an analysis of similar experiments conducted in low resource environments can be performed.

A deeper analysis of user behaviour will be performed by examining translation and ranking durations across groups. Expert users will be used to assess the quality of the crowdsourced data. The developed system and techniques will be improved and used to gather further data for the development of isiXhosa language processing algorithms and tools.

Acknowledgements. This research was partially funded by the National Research Foundation of South Africa (Grant numbers: 85470 and 88209) and University of Cape Town. The authors acknowledge that opinions, findings and conclusions or recommendations expressed in this publication are that of the authors, and that the NRF accepts no liability whatsoever in this regard.

References

1. Statistics South Africa: Census 2011 Census in Brief. Statistics South Africa, Pretoria (2012)
2. Eiselen, E., Puttkammer, M.: Developing text resources for ten South African languages. In: Proceedings of the LREC (2014)
3. Webb, V.N.: African Voices: An Introduction to the Languages and Linguistics of Africa. Oxford University Press (2000)
4. Johnson, K.K.: Xhosa-English Machine Translation: Working with a Low-Resource Language (2011)
5. Drummer, A.: Phrase-Based Machine Translation of Under-Resourced Languages (2013)

6. Jackson, C.B., Osterlund, C., Mugar, G., Hassman, K.D., Crowston, K.: Motivations for sustained participation in crowdsourcing: case studies of citizen science on the role of talk. In: 2015 48th Hawaii International Conference on System Sciences (HICSS), pp. 1624–1634 (2015)
7. Howe, J. Crowdsourcing: How the Power of the Crowd is Driving the Future of Business. Random House (2008)
8. Ross, J., Irani, L., Silberman, M., Zaldivar, A., Tomlinson, B.: Who are the crowdworkers?: shifting demographics in mechanical turk. In: CHI 2010 Extended Abstracts on Human Factors in Computing Systems, pp. 2863–2872 (2010)
9. Zaidan, O.F., Callison-Burch, C.: Crowdsourcing translation: professional quality from non-professionals. In: Proceedings of the 49th Annual Meeting of the Association for Computational Linguistics: Human Language Technologies, vol. 1, pp. 1220–1229 (2011)
10. Munro, R.: Crowdsourced translation for emergency response in Haiti: the global collaboration of local knowledge. In: AMTA Workshop on Collaborative Crowdsourcing for Translation (2010)
11. Geiger, D., Seedorf, S., Schulze, T., Nickerson, R.C., Schader, M.: Managing the crowd: towards a taxonomy of crowdsourcing processes (2011)
12. Negri, M., Mehdad, Y.: Creating a bi-lingual entailment corpus through translations with mechanical turk: $100 for a 10-day rush. In: Proceedings of the NAACL HLT 2010 Workshop on Creating Speech and Language Data with Amazon's Mechanical Turk, pp. 212–216 (2010)
13. Callison-Burch, C.: Fast, cheap, and creative: evaluating translation quality using amazon's mechanical turk. In: Proceedings of the 2009 Conference on Empirical Methods in Natural Language Processing, vol. 1, pp. 286–295 (2009)
14. Ambati, V., Vogel, S.: Can crowds build parallel corpora for machine translation systems? In: Proceedings of the NAACL HLT 2010 Workshop on Creating Speech and Language Data with Amazon's Mechanical Turk, pp. 62–65 (2010)
15. Deterding, S., Sicart, M., Nacke, L., O'Hara, K., Dixon, D.: Gamification. Using game-design elements in non-gaming contexts. In: CHI 2011 Extended Abstracts on Human Factors in Computing Systems, pp. 2425–2428 (2011)
16. Eickhoff, C., Harris, C.G., de Vries, A.P., Srinivasan, P.: Quality through flow and immersion: gamifying crowdsourced relevance assessments. In: Proceedings of the 35th International ACM SIGIR Conference on Research and Development in Information Retrieval, pp. 871–880 (2012)
17. Farzan, R., DiMicco, J.M., Millen, D.R., Brownholtz, B., Geyer, W., Dugan, C.: When the experiment is over: deploying an incentive system to all the users. In: Proceedings of the Symposium on Persuasive Technology, in conjunction with the AISB (2008)
18. Farzan, R., DiMicco, J.M., Millen, D.R., Dugan, C., Geyer, W., Brownholtz, E.A.: Results from deploying a participation incentive mechanism within the enterprise. In: Proceedings of the SIGCHI Conference on Human Factors in Computing Systems, pp. 563–572 (2008)
19. Montola, M., Nummenmaa, T., Lucero, A., Boberg, M., Korhonen, H.: Applying game achievement systems to enhance user experience in a photo sharing service. In: Proceedings of the 13th International MindTrek Conference: Everyday Life in the Ubiquitous Era, pp. 94–97 (2009)
20. Anderson, A., Huttenlocher, D., Kleinberg, J., Leskovec, J.: Steering user behavior with badges. In: Proceedings of the 22nd International Conference on World Wide Web, pp. 95–106 (2013)

21. Denny, P.: The effect of virtual achievements on student engagement. In: Proceedings of the SIGCHI Conference on Human Factors in Computing Systems, pp. 763–772 (2013)
22. Dominguez, A., Saenz-de-Navarrete, J., De-Marcos, L., Fernández-Sanz, L., Pagés, C., Martínez-Herráiz, J.-J.: Gamifying Learning Experiences: Practical Implications and Outcomes. Comput. Educ. **63**, 380–392 (2013)
23. Fitz-Walter, Z., Tjondronegoro, D., Wyeth, P.: Orientation passport: using gamification to engage university students. In: Proceedings of the 23rd Australian Computer-Human Interaction Conference, pp. 122–125 (2011)
24. Halan, S., Rossen, B., Cendan, J., Lok, B.: High score! - motivation strategies for user participation in virtual human development. In: Safonova, A. (ed.) IVA 2010. LNCS, vol. 6356, pp. 482–488. Springer, Heidelberg (2010)

Semi-automatic Metadata Generation Workflow for Developing a Continuing Education Resource Repository

Jung-ran Park$^{(\boxtimes)}$ and Andrew Brenza

Drexel University, Philadelphia, USA
{jp365,apb84}@drexel.edu

Abstract. This paper presents a high-level conceptualized workflow for the development of a repository related to continuing educational resources for the metadata professions. One of the major challenges facing cataloging and metadata communities concerns current developments and emerging trends in standards and technologies for managing digital information. Through utilization and integration of available open-source (semi)automatic metadata generation tools, we attempted to design a repository that maximizes the self-sufficiency of the system components while also generating high quality metadata records for metadata resources. We also attempted to design a workflow that will permit the repository to serve its primary function as a continually updated warehouse of material that will constitute a centralized resource of continuing education needs of metadata.

Keywords: Metadata · Repository · Extensible Markup Language (XML) · Semantic Web · Web Ontology Language (OWL) · Library and information science · Continuing education · Open-source · (Semi) automatic metadata · Metadata generator · Linked Data

1 Introduction

One of the major challenges facing cataloging and metadata communities concerns current developments and emerging trends in standards and technologies for managing digital information. The ongoing shift from traditional print-based to digital Web-based services has created a critical need for highly trained cataloging and metadata professionals equipped with 21st century skills to facilitate resource description, use, management, and preservation in the digital environment. Park, Tosaka, Maszaros, and Lu [1] have identified critical issues regarding the institutional capacity of the LIS community to support efforts to improve the knowledge and skills of practitioners in the cataloging and metadata field. One of the major findings is a gap between continuing education needs and the accessibility of professional development resources and opportunities. Professionals indicate an active interest in seeking continuing education opportunities to stay abreast of current developments and trends. However, the current state of continuing education is not able to completely satisfy needs in the delivery of training programs and learning objects.

© Springer International Publishing Switzerland 2015
R.B. Allen et al. (Eds.): ICADL 2015, LNCS 9469, pp. 235–245, 2015.
DOI: 10.1007/978-3-319-27974-9_24

Tosaka & Park [2] highlight several major gaps between the continuing education needs expressed and the type of professional training received. While continuing education topics have tended to focus on descriptive metadata creation and controlled vocabularies for subject access, practitioners show a strong interest in receiving future training in topics relating to metadata quality control mechanisms and documentation practices, markup languages (e.g. Extensible Markup Language (XML)) and Semantic Web technologies including Resource Description Framework (RDF) and Web Ontology Language (OWL).

While we have seen efforts to develop an online clearinghouse where LIS faculty could share metadata education materials [3] there has been no comparable attempt to develop a comprehensive framework upon which to create an effective system dedicated to professional development programs and resources available for practitioners in the field [4]. As any single continuing education provider cannot be expected to provide all relevant training programs that meet the diverse needs of professionals, it is essential to develop a portal that brings scattered professional development resources together in a meaningful manner and provides a platform for virtual communication and collaboration.

The purpose of this paper is to present a high-level concept workflow for the functioning repository. Through utilization and integration of available open-source (semi)automatic metadata generation tools, we have attempted to design a repository that maximizes the self-sufficiency of the system components while also generating high quality metadata records for metadata resources related to the library profession. Thus, our aim is to present a workflow that leverages the power of (semi)automatic metadata generation tools in order to optimize the discoverability and use of continuing education resources.

2   Literature Review

Despite the development of (semi)automatic metadata generation tools of sufficient quality, most of these tools still exist as independent applications [5]. Most tools have been designed to solve one or a few issues, such as title or keyword extraction, within an experimental context [6,7,8]. This means that there is a lack of integration of (semi)automatic metadata generation tools that constitute comprehensive metadata generation applications for the creation of a broad range of metadata elements. As a result, researchers wishing to create comprehensive applications must customize disparate tools so that they work in concert, typically through scripts that integrate the independent tools into a single, coherent system [9]. The workflow outlined in this paper will similarly use scripts to integrate the functionality of the various tools used to generate complete Dublin Core metadata records for the DSpace application. Since the focus of this paper is on the high-level concept of the workflow, details regarding the integration of the tools have been omitted.

Kurtz [10] analyzes consistency of Dublin Core metadata records for three repositories using DSpace. Kurtz [10] further points out that DSpace offers the capability to automatically extract a number of Dublin Core technical metadata element values. DSpace can automatically extract values for the Dublin Core elements of Date, Format, Identifier, and Provenance, as well as for various qualifications for each [10]. Although there are a number of applications that are capable of extracting these types of technical metadata, the proposed repository is currently designed as a DSpace repository. Thus, we intend to take advantage of such capabilities in the design of our workflow.

In addition to leveraging the efficiencies of DSpace, we aim to streamline the repository workflow using tools that offer the broadest range of extraction capabilities. Specifically, we will explore tools like Data Fountains, a suite of applications developed at the University of California for the development of digital libraries, which includes applications that permit the automatic extraction of many metadata values, including but not limited to values held in HTML meta-tags as well as the automatic generation of values for descriptions, titles, creators, and languages [8]; or Kea,[1] a key phrase extraction algorithm developed at the University of Waikato in New Zealand, capable of mapping extracted terms to controlled vocabularies. We hope that through the use of the most complete and sophisticated tools currently available we will ease the task of tool integration while exploiting the most advanced techniques of (semi)automatic metadata generation.

Similarly, in order to ensure the ease with which the workflow of our repository can be established, maintained, and improved, the modularity of the different applications in the system is emphasized. As Deng and Reese [9] show in their development of a number of digital projects which incorporated the automated batch loading of metadata, modularity allowed for the systematic troubleshooting of components so that difficulties could be isolated and addressed. Furthermore, Deng and Reese's modularity also permitted the potential for enhancing the system as capabilities improved [9]. In a similar fashion, we have designed our workflow in a modular fashion in order to take advantage of these capabilities.

Despite the capabilities of current tools to enhance the metadata generation process through (semi)automatic means, there is little literature on the development of metadata workflows which incorporate (semi)automatic tools. Furthermore, we are not aware of any (semi)automatic tools incorporated into a self-sustaining digital repository. Generally, the literature reflects the utilization of (semi)automatic tools for batch processing of existing metadata records, either to convert records into a standard format in the creation of a specific digital project [9],[11], or for the automated interaction of repositories of metadata objects.

Another example of the incorporation of (semi)automatic tools in metadata generation workflows is that offered by Green [12]. Green and his colleagues show how the (semi)automatic metadata generation tool RepoMMan can assist contributors to digital repositories with the management of their scholarly documents [12]. This usage is primarily to assist users who are unfamiliar with metadata practices. In a similar vein, Devaul, Diekema and Otswald [13] employ natural language processing techniques in order to automatically populate as many metadata fields as possible for review by metadata librarians. It is our intention to contribute to these efforts through the workflow design presented for the remainder of this paper.

3   Workflow for Metadata Generation

The goal of the workflow proposed in this paper is to develop a self-sustaining digital repository that allows the metadata community to find and access professional devel-

---

[1] http://www.nzdl.org/Kea/index_old.html

238   J.-r. Park and A. Brenza

opment resources for self-directed lifelong learning on emerging/new data standards and technologies. The key objective of this project is to create a searchable digital repository that will serve as a clearinghouse providing information about learning materials and contents for practitioners. In particular, the content will focus on new and emerging standards and technologies encompassing Semantic Web and Linked Data topics including Simple Knowledge Organization System (SKOS), RDF and Semantic Web applications in library catalogs. The resources themselves will be focused on those that are freely available on the Web.

The project repository, built on DSpace software and hosted on a server at Drexel University, is designed with self-sustaining and governing mechanisms. As topics are identified, the automated workflow monitors the Web, continually populating the repository with continuing education resources. The development of these automated mechanisms is a key project objective that will create a functioning repository with scalability, currency, minimal operating costs, and sustainability.

In this portion of the paper, we present a high-level workflow conceptualization for the (semi)automatic generation of metadata records related to resources relevant to the metadata community. This model focuses on the manual and automatic discovery of Web resources, their ingest into DSpace, and the subsequent extraction and/or manual assignment of Dublin Core metadata values in order to create full metadata records within the repository. Figure 1 below provides a diagram of this workflow. Each step in the process has been numbered and each number corresponds to each of the subsections below. Table 1 provides a list of the 15 Dublin Core metadata elements that will be populated as a result of this workflow. These elements are matched to the mechanism that will be used to assign values to each of the Dublin Core elements.

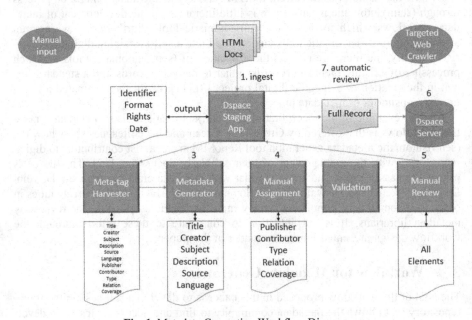

Fig. 1. Metadata Generation Workflow Diagram

 The goal of this workflow is to provide a system for the development of a repository that leverages the potential of (semi)automatic metadata generation tools to create, maintain, and update metadata records for the metadata Web resources relevant to the educational needs of the library community. In order to ensure that each metadata record contains a minimum set of core bibliographic data, profiles/guidelines will be developed that define these requirements. These profiles will also define the format for element values, including the application of any controlled vocabularies or metadata content standards, in order to maximize interoperability of the records and help with the development of a validation mechanism which will be incorporated into the workflow.

Harvested resources developed through an automatic crawler will be stored in the staging area before ingesting them into DSpace, so the first step (ingestion) needs to be modified. In the staging area, the harvested resources will be evaluated in terms of their relevance to the scope of our project repository. Project application profile/best practices/guidelines are being developed; in this profile, we specify core elements such as title, subject, and date. Administrative metadata (provenance metadata) and preservation metadata need to be included as core elements. This profile will work as a validation mechanism of the metadata records. If core elements are missing, metadata will be manually created. If a meta-tag harvester creates all the core elements, this will be stored in the staging area or directly in DSpace.

Table 1. Dublin Core Elements with Corresponding Methods of Metadata Generation

Dublin Core Element	Metadata Generation Method
Title	Meta-tag harvester/Metadata generator
Creator	Meta-tag harvester/Metadata generator
Date	DSpace/ Meta-tag harvester
Subject	Meta-tag harvester/Metadata generator
Description	Meta-tag harvester/Metadata generator
Source	Meta-tag harvester/Metadata generator
Rights	DSpace/Meta-tag harvester
Coverage	Meta-tag harvester/Manual
Relation	Meta-tag harvester/Manual
Language	Meta-tag harvester/Metadata generator
Type	Meta-tag harvester/Manual
Identifier	DSpace
Format	DSpace
Publisher	Meta-tag harvester/Manual
Contributor	Meta-tag harvester/Manual

3.1   Ingestion

Ingestion represents the first step in the process of developing the proposed repository. We have identified three means by which relevant resources may be identified and referred to the system. First, we plan on implementing a developed Web crawler that can be trained to identify relevant resources. Based on the evaluation of hyperlinks, anchor text and Website content, the Web crawler will identify resources and initiate the process of generating metadata records. Data Fountains, a suite of metadata generation tools developed at the University of California, Davis, includes a targeted Web crawler that can search for resources within any user-defined subject domain. Because of Data Fountains' flexibility and its relevance to the library community (it was developed to support the creation of digital libraries), it is a likely candidate for the implementation of this step.

Once relevant resources are identified, they will be converted to XML files and submitted to the staging version of the DSpace application for the first phase of metadata value extraction. The conversion to XML will facilitate the processing of records by the various applications used throughout the workflow. Since DSpace is capable of automatically extracting some types of technical metadata, these will be the first to be generated. Values for the Dublin Core elements of Identifier, Format, Rights and Date will be populated at this point. Once these elements have been populated, the XML files will be sent to the meta-tag harvester to be processed in the second step of the workflow.

In addition to the automatic identification of metadata resources through the implementation of a developed Web crawler, resources can also be referred to the system manually. This will likely take the form of a URL referral to the Web crawler, which will then use this URL to process the resource as usual. Finally, users will also be presented with a mechanism to manually upload relevant materials to the repository. These too will be processed as any other resource.

3.2   Meta-tag Harvester

Meta-tag harvesting is the second step in the workflow. Meta-tag extraction is a computing process whereby values for metadata fields are identified and populated through an examination of metadata tags within documents. In other words, it is a form of metadata harvesting and/or conversion of that metadata into other formats. Thus, meta-tag harvesting relies on the identification of pre-existing metadata values which are then used to populate the values within a given schema. In the case of this repository, metadata located within HTML meta-tags will be identified and mapped to relevant Dublin Core elements. Various tools have already been developed to accomplish this task, such as Web services like Editor-Converter Dublin Core Metadata and Firefox Dublin Core Viewer Extension as well as the downloadable meta-tag harvester developed as part of the Data Fountains suite of tools.

The project team is still evaluating these tools and a final selection has not yet been reached. Nevertheless, it is worth noting that the usefulness of these tools is entirely dependent on the quality of metadata embedded in HTML documents at the time of processing. It may be that, for some HTML documents, embedded values for all or most of the Dublin Core elements are already present, leading to a completed record at this stage of the workflow that can move directly to the Manual Review stage in step 5. Or, as is more likely the case, none or only a few meta-tags will be identified, in which case the record will then proceed to step 3 (Manual Generation) for processing by more sophisticated (semi)automatic metadata generation tools.

3.3   Metadata Generation

Metadata Generation is the third step in the workflow. At this stage, the metadata record for any given resource may be more or less incomplete, depending on the number and quality of the meta-tags embedded in the document. The collection of (semi)automatic metadata generation programs will be engaged to complete as much of the record as possible. For instance, the suite of tools that comprise Data Fountains include applications that can extract the Dublin Core elements of Title, Creator, Language, Subject, Description and Source from the free text of HTML documents. Thus, if these elements are not represented in meta-tags, the metadata generation tools will populate them with values.

A significant aspect of this step is the assignment of terms to the Dublin Core Subject element. In order to accomplish this step, we plan to use clustering or classifying algorithms, such as those developed by Kea or Data Fountains, which extract keywords from free text documents and map those keywords to some kind of vocabulary. For this project, we developed a list of subject terms that will be used to organize resources within the repository. These terms are relevant to the subject of metadata in the library professions. They will allow users to search and browse through the resources in the repository. So that this step can be accomplished with maximum accuracy and utility to the user, the developed algorithms will be trained using machine learning techniques, which involve the processing of known resources.

3.4   Manual Assignment of Metadata

Manual Assignment of Metadata is the fourth step in the workflow. At the beginning of this stage, each record will be validated against a mechanism which reflects the requirements of the repository profiles. Validation will include a check for values in mandatory elements and an evaluation of element value formats. Following validation, any metadata fields that could not be populated by the automatic means described above will be presented to repository managers for manual input. Depending on the success of the previous steps in the workflow, the completeness of a metadata record for any given resource may be variable.

If, for instance, a given resource contained a comprehensive list of meta-tags, and the metadata generator was able to map extracted keywords to subject terms successfully, the record may be virtually complete. In the case of a complete and validated record, the record would in fact bypass this step and move immediately to the Manual Review step described next in the workflow. However, as is more likely the case, the record will be incomplete in some fashion. The repository managers will then fill in any remaining Dublin Core fields with relevant values and re-submit the record to be processed in the next step of the workflow. The absence of values for mandatory elements and improperly formatted element values will be highlighted for special consideration. Repository application profiles will guide repository managers with the manual creation of any Dublin Core element value to be added to the record.

It is worth noting here that a number of Dublin Core elements have defied efforts by programmers to develop tools for their automatic generation. These elements are Publisher, Contributor, Type, Relation, and Coverage. Since we are currently unaware of any tools except meta-tag harvesters that can automatically generate values for these elements, the repository managers will have to be responsible for their input. However, as the repository is in an early stage of development, we are also in the process of examining the utility and necessity of each Dublin Core element for continuing education resources. It may be determined that values for these Dublin Core elements are unnecessary for the optimal functioning of the repository, in which case some of these more difficult elements may not be included in the final workflow.

3.5   Manual Review

Once all of the Dublin Core elements have been populated for a given resource, the metadata record is sent through the validation mechanism again prior to its incorporation into the functional repository. Following the second validation, the metadata record will be presented to repository managers for final review and evaluation. The repository managers will have the option to edit all Dublin Core elements at this point in the workflow and will be prompted to correct any validation errors. Like the manual-creation-metadata stage, repository guidelines and profiles will assist managers with the correction of any element values. Following any changes made by the managers, the record will once again be processed by the validation mechanism with any errors presented for correction. Once a record passes validation, it can then be approved for final ingestion into the repository, where it will become available for use.

3.6   Record Storage

Although Record Storage is the penultimate step in the workflow process, it represents the final step in incorporating a record within the repository. At this point in the workflow, the metadata record should be complete. The record is then saved to the live version of DSpace hosted on the Drexel Server. Thus, the record is incorporated into the repository and is available for use.

3.7   Automatic Review

Automatic Review represents the final step in the workflow. At this stage of the process, completed records have been stored on the server for use by the repository's users. However, in order to ensure the currency of established resources, we plan on including a mechanism by which the developed Web monitoring will periodically review incorporated resources and update them as needed. Thus, resources will be fed back into the Web crawler and re-evaluated. If changes are detected, then a process of generating a replacement record will be initiated. This review process will mimic the workflow for the creation of a new record, but will replace the older record instead of creating a brand new one. In this way, we hope to create a mechanism whereby the repository updates its contents as well as continually searching for new resources.

4   Discussion

We will use a rapid prototyping approach to develop the repository, its components and the integration of those components. Rapid prototyping replaces the requirement analysis and design processes of the traditional system development life cycle with an iterative process of prototype refinement. Thus, the evolutionary prototype is used as a tool for clarifying repository requirements and evaluating design as the repository is being developed. This approach will allow us to develop a functioning repository as quickly possible while permitting the refinement of the repository as complications arise and difficulties are overcome. This will be enhanced by the proposed workflow design, which emphasizes the modularity of each of the components used. Modularity affords the opportunity to make refinements within portions of the workflow without complete system redesign. Additionally, should other relevant tools become available, these can also be integrated into the workflow without serious threat to the integrity of system functionality.

One aspect of the current workflow that will need to be addressed as the prototype develops is the possibility of data conflicts that emerge as result of the (semi)automatic metadata generation process. In other words, there is the possibility that different stages of the workflow will generate different values for a given element. In order to resolve such conflicts, scripts will need to be developed so that the system will be able to decide which value for a specific element is preferred. For instance, the meta-tag harvester and the metadata generator may produce different values for the Title element. A script would be needed to inform the system that the meta-tag is the preferred value, should that be determined to be more reliable data. If such conflicts cannot be resolved by the workflow, a mechanism would also need to be incorporated that would present the issue to repository managers at the manual input stage of the process.

As suggested above, another issue is related to the fact that there are currently no (semi)automatic means to generate values for certain Dublin Core elements beyond the use of meta-tag harvesters. Again, these elements are Publisher, Contributor, Type, Relation, and Coverage. Because it is more than likely that these elements will need to be populated manually, they pose a significant potential strain on repository resources. Thus, we are in the process of determining exactly which values will be necessary for the optimal functioning of the repository from the user perspective. This evaluation may result in the designation of some of these more difficult elements as optional.

One of the more important considerations related to the determination of the mandatory/optional nature of certain Dublin Core elements will simply be related to time. Since the repository is designed to function at the highest level of autonomy as possible, with a minimum of manual intervention, time constraints on the ability of repository managers to manually input data will be a significant factor. Thus,

244 J.-r. Park and A. Brenza

depending on the number and complexity of identified resources, a balance between the ability of managers to generate manual metadata and the optimization of discovery capabilities will need to be addressed.

Thirdly, there is the issue of optimizing the usability of the repository within the networked environment. Because the repository is intended to be a warehouse of metadata resources which can be located and consumed on the Web, the metadata records for these resources need to be optimized for their discovery online. This may mean that the Dublin Core records stored within the Drexel Server instance of DSpace may ultimately need to be converted to some form of RDF prior to Web exposure. Additionally, these records may also need to be mapped to BIBFRAME, the Library of Congress's model for the representation of bibliographic records in the networked environment. This mapping would further the discoverability of resources on the Web while ensuring a higher degree of interoperability with other library systems and repositories.

Perhaps the greatest benefit to encoding and exposing the repository records in RDF would be that the major search engines would crawl and index the resources in the repository. This would certainly enhance the discovery of records on the Web. Encoding the repository records in some form of RDF or BIBFRAME also offers the advantage of permitting users, and the repository itself, to find and use resources related to those resources in the repository. RDF encodings are structured in such a way as to allow certain types of applications to find related resources. Regarding the repository itself, such a mechanism could be used to inform the targeted Web crawler of new resources to ingest.

5   Conclusion

This paper has presented a high-level conceptualized workflow for the development of a repository related to continuing educational resources for the metadata professions. We have attempted to design a workflow which maximizes the self-sufficiency of the repository through the utilization of state-of-the-art (semi)automatic metadata generation tools and minimal human supervision. We have also attempted to design a workflow that will permit the repository to serve its primary function as a continually updated warehouse of educational material that will constitute a centralized resource of continuing education needs of metadata. Although the repository is in an early stage of development, its successful implementation will become a vital resource for the metadata community.

Acknowledgements. This study is supported through an award from IMLS 21st Century Laura Bush program for the project entitled *Building a Workforce of Information Professionals for 21st Century Global Information Access* for a three year period (2014-2017). Special appreciation goes to Miralee Schulte for her help in formatting and proofreading the paper.

References

1. Park, J.R., Tosaka, Y., Maszaros, S., Lu, C.: From Metadata Creation to Metadata Quality Control: Continuing Education Needs Among Cataloging and Metadata Professionals. Journal of Education for Library & Information Science **51**(3), 158–176 (2010)
2. Tosaka, Y., Park, J.R.: RDA Training and Continuing Education Needs: Perspectives of Cataloging and Metadata Professionals. Journal of the American Society for Information Science & Technology **64**(4), 651–662 (2014)
3. Vellucci, S.L., Hsieh-Yee, I., Moen, W.E.: The Metadata Education and Research Information Commons (MERIC): A Collaborative Teaching and Research Initiative. Education for Information **25**(3/4), 169–179 (2007)
4. Pinkston, J.: Wanted: A revolution in library continuing education. Public Library Quarterly **28**(4), 295–311 (2009)
5. Park, J.R., Brenza, A.: Evaluation of (Semi)Automatic Metadata Generation Tools: A Survey of the Current State of the Art. Information Technology and Libraries **34**(3) (2015). doi:10.6017/ital.v34i3.5889
6. Dobreva, M., Kim, Y., Ross, S.: Designing an automated prototype tool for preservation quality metadata extraction for ingest into digital repository. In: Cunningham, P., Cunningham, M. (eds.) Collaboration and the Knowledge Economy: Issues, Applications, Case Studies 2008. Information and Communication Technologies and the Knowledge Economy Series, vol. 5. IOS Press, Amsterdam (2008)
7. Greenberg, J., Spurgin, K., Crystal, A.: Final Report for the AMeGA (Automatic Metadata Generation Applications) Project. Technical report, Library of Congress (2005)
8. Polfreman, M., Broughton, V., Wilson, A.:Metadata Generation for Resource Discovery. Joint Information Systems Committee (2008)
9. Deng, S., Reese, T.: Customized Mapping and Metadata Transfer from DSpace to OCLC to Improve ETD Work Flow. New Library World **110**(5/6), 249–264 (2009)
10. Kurtz, M.: Dublin Core, DSpace, and a Brief Analysis of Three University Repositories. Information Technology and Libraries **29**(1), 40–46 (2010)
11. Walsh, M.P.: Batch Loading Collections into DSpace: Using Perl Scripts for Automation and Quality Control. Information Technology and Libraries **29**(3), 117–127 (2010)
12. Green, R., Dolphin, I., Awre, C., Sherratt, R.: The RepoMMan Project: Automating Workflow and Metadata for an Institutional Repository. OCLC Systems & Services: International Digital Library Perspectives **23**(2), 210–215 (2007)
13. Devaul, H., Diekema, A.R., Ostwald, J.: Computer-Assisted Assignment of Educational Standards Using Natural Language Processing. Journal of the American Society for Information Science and Technology **62**(2), 395–405 (2011)

The Effects of Collaboration and Competition on Players' Perceptions in Human Computation Games

Ei Pa Pa Pe-Than[✉], Dion Hoe-Lian Goh, and Chei Sian Lee

Wee Kim Wee School of Communication and Information,
Nanyang Technological University, Singapore, Singapore
{ei1,ashlgoh,leecs}@ntu.edu.sg

Abstract. Human Computation Games (HCGs) harness human intelligence through games to address computational problems. Collaboration and competition have emerged as the most commonly used HCG genres. Yet, little research has examined the effects of such genres on players' perceptions. Through an experimental study with 95 participants, this study investigates the effects of collaboration and competition on perceived enjoyment and output quality in mobile content sharing HCGs. The findings suggest that competition yielded better perception of output accuracy than collaboration. However, players derived more behavioral enjoyment from collaboration than competition in HCGs. The implications of these findings are discussed.

Keywords: Human Computation Games · Location-based content · Mobile multiplayer games · Information sharing · Enjoyment · Output quality

1 Introduction

Human Computation Games (HCGs) harness human intelligence through enjoyable gameplay to address computational problems that are beyond the power of computer programs but trivial for humans [1,2]. One well-known example is the *ESP Game* [3] in which two randomly-paired players are tasked with creating tags for images, and awarded points for every matching tag. HCGs also yield benefits for the creation of digital libraries. For instance, photo digital libraries, such as PhotoGeo [4], that enable users to annotate photos with metadata attributes to facilitate future retrieval could utilize games to motivate participation.

Recent studies suggest that players either collaborate or compete during HCG play [2]. In collaborative HCGs, players work together as a team, and the outcomes are shared among team members. In contrast, players develop strategies to play against others in competitive HCGs, and only one player at a time can achieve the winning condition [5]. It has been argued that collaboration can promote positive behaviors, which in turn influences enjoyment and performance in the task performed, whereas competition can promote negative behaviors and outcomes [6]. Accordingly, competitive HCGs may be more enjoyable than collaborative ones, but they may not yield high-quality outputs. Therefore, it is imperative to investigate the potential effects of these genres on players' perceptions.

© Springer International Publishing Switzerland 2015
R.B. Allen et al. (Eds.): ICADL 2015, LNCS 9469, pp. 246–251, 2015.
DOI: 10.1007/978-3-319-27974-9_25

Enjoyment is known to be a success factor of hedonic systems, while output quality is regarded as a significant factor of task-oriented systems [7]. As HCGs intertwine gaming with output generation [1], both enjoyment and output quality could be critical aspects. In addition, prior studies advocate the multidimensionality of enjoyment and output quality [8,9], and hence, treating such constructs as unidimensional may overlook the importance of specific influential dimensions. Put differently, researchers have yet to examine whether the multiple dimensions of perceived output quality and enjoyment differ across HCG genres.

Thus, this study aims to examine the effects of HCG genres (collaborative vs. competitive) on perceived output quality and enjoyment, using three custom-developed mobile HCGs for location-based content sharing. Findings from our work will provide a better understanding of the influence of collaboration and competition in HCG play, and with such information, better design decisions can be made.

2   Perceived Output Quality and Perceived Enjoyment

Perceived output quality is defined as an individual's perception of the quality of output provided by an information system [7]. It has been suggested that accuracy, completeness, relevancy, and timeliness are significant dimensions of online social content [10]. As a HCG is a type of online system and the most visible feature is the quality of its shared content [11], such quality dimensions may also be relevant to HCGs. Prior studies found that individuals in collaborative gameplay situations exhibited more trust in their partners, leading to higher levels of performance [5]. In contrast, [2] argues that players may take advantage of collaboration by colluding with other players on unusable information, possibly resulting in lower levels of perceived output quality. Hence, we propose the following research questions:

RQ1: What are the differences in perceived a) accuracy, b) completeness, c) relevancy, and d) timeliness between collaborative and competitive HCG genres?

Perceived enjoyment refers to the degree to which an individual perceives fun or pleasure when performing an activity [7]. [9] argues that enjoyment consists of three dimensions: affective, cognitive and behavioral, which may mutually exert influence on each other. Scholars believe that competition undermines enjoyment, as individuals are more likely to focus on winning rather than on the activity itself [6]. Other scholars have argued that competition poses exciting challenges, making individuals more involved and promoting enjoyment [5]. With regard to collaboration, research has shown that working as a team could engender a sense of relatedness with other team members, which is a crucial source of enjoyment [5]. However, collaboration may hinder enjoyment when individuals perceive the group goal as controlling, resulting in a loss of autonomy [6]. These inconsistent findings warrant further examination. Hence, the following research questions are asked:

RQ2: What are the differences in perceived a) affective, b) cognitive, and c) behavioral enjoyment between collaborative and competitive HCG genres?

3   Methodology

3.1   Applications Developed for the Study

Three location-based content sharing applications were developed. The reasons for developing our own applications were that we would have better control over the look-and-feel of the interfaces and the accessibility of the generated data. All three applications offer a map-based interface that indicates locations with content, which are overlaid with mushroom houses (see Fig. 1). Each house has a number of units, and each of these holds comments created inside. A comment comprises the title, tags, descriptions, media elements (e.g. photos) and ratings.

First, *Collabo* (collaborative HCG) enables players to form a team with other players to rescue the starving pets in their vicinity. The starving pets appear sad and have a darker tone (see Fig. 2). To rescue the pets, players need to feed them with comments or rate those created by others. All activities of players are shown on the "Activities tab" (see Fig. 3). Players earn an equal amount of points once a pet is rescued.

Fig. 1. A map-based interface   **Fig. 2.** A list of pets residing in a location   **Fig. 3.** Players' activities on the pet.   **Fig. 4.** A pet owned by "gigo".

Second, *Clash* (competitive HCG) allows players to compete with others for pet ownership. The name of the current pet owner is displayed on the nametag (see Fig. 4). The player can challenge the current owner to a duel, and he/she will win if the total of his/her strength and daily luck (a random number generated upon the first login of each day) is greater than that of the challenged player. The strength of the player is based on the quantity and recency of comments, and the number of ratings.

Finally, *Share* is a non-game application that serves as a control. It does not have any game elements, and offers the basic features for contributing and accessing content. Players are not awarded with any game points or rewards for their activities. Instead, they can view statistics such as the number of comments and ratings created.

3.2   Participants and Experimental Procedure

Ninety-five participants (49 males and 46 females) with an average age of 23 were recruited from two local universities. The majority of the participants (81.3%) indicated that they were game players. Participants were from diverse educational backgrounds such as computer science (47.8%) and Engineering (38.8%).

A within-subjects experimental design was adopted. The experiment was conducted across separate sessions with each session having three to nine participants. Before the experiment began, participants were given instructions on how to use the applications together with a short 15–minute practice session. Participants used all three applications on Android-based mobile phones on three different days, each spaced one day apart. On each day, participants followed a given usage scenario which includes joining a team to rescue a pet (for *Collabo*), winning a pet (for *Clash*), and viewing the usage statistics (for *Share*) in addition to creating, viewing, and rating comments, and they completed a questionnaire for respective application. Participants were paid an incentive of $20.

3.3   Measures Used

A questionnaire was developed to elicit participants' perceptions of the study's constructs. All question items were adapted from prior research [12], [8], [11], and measured on a 5-point Likert scale ranging from 1 (strongly disagree) to 5 (strongly agree). A principal component factor analysis with varimax rotation and reliability analyses were conducted. As suggested by prior research [13], items that were most highly loaded on their respective factors (0.5 and above) were retained in the analysis.

Perceived information quality was assessed with 12 items. Four factors were extracted from the factor analyses, namely, accuracy, completeness, relevancy, and timeliness. Similarly, perceived enjoyment was evaluated using 12 items. The three factors emerged were affective, cognitive, and behavioral enjoyment. All constructs exhibited acceptable internal reliabilities with a Cronbach's alphas of at least 0.93.

4   Results

Table 1 shows the means and standard deviations of participants' perceptions for all applications. The results of the ANOVAs indicated that there were significant differences with respect to accuracy $[F(2,282)=15.08, p<.01]$, completeness $[F(2,282)=19.95, p<.01]$, relevancy $[F(2,282)=10.86, p<.01]$, affective $[F(2,282)=8.54, p<.01]$, cognitive $[F(2,282)=11.09, p<.01]$, and behavioral $[F(2,282)=10.81, p<.01]$.

The results of Tukey's test revealed that participants felt that the output from *Share* was more accurate, complete, and relevant than from both HCGs. They recognized a higher level of accuracy in *Clash* than in *Collabo*. However, the differences in completeness and relevancy between both HCGs were not significant. Next, participants perceived that *Collabo* and *Clash* provided higher levels of affective and cognitive enjoyment than *Share*, but no differences in ratings between both HCGs were found. In terms of behavioral enjoyment, *Collabo* performed better than both *Clash* and *Share*, though differences in perceptions between the latter two applications were non-significant.

Table 1. Means and standard deviations for perceived output quality and enjoyment (N=95).

Variable	Type of application / Mean (SD)		
	Collabo	*Clash*	*Share*
Accuracy*	2.89 (0.91)	3.13 (0.98)	3.43 (0.75)
Completeness*	2.88 (0.83)	2.80 (0.83)	3.36 (0.97)
Relevancy*	3.02 (0.85)	2.86 (1.00)	3.36 (1.08)
Timeliness	3.01 (0.82)	2.98 (0.93)	3.09 (0.93)
Affective*	3.21 (0.99)	3.01 (1.08)	2.62 (0.94)
Cognitive*	3.64 (0.95)	3.34 (1.06)	2.99 (0.89)
Behavioral*	2.99 (1.09)	2.62 (1.08)	2.30 (0.90)

*Statistically significant differences between the three applications at $p<0.01$.

5   Discussion and Conclusion

This experiment yielded the following findings. First, *Share* was perceived to offer more accurate, complete, and relevant outputs than both *Collabo* and *Clash*. Both HCGs required players to perform gaming activities, and such extra work could have been perceived to be deviating from output generation, leading to a lack of confidence in quality. Next, the output of *Clash* was perceived to be higher in accuracy than that of *Collabo*. Perhaps, competition that drives players to strive for victory [6] conveyed an impression that more accurate output would be generated than via collaboration. This offers an explanation for the finding of prior work [11] where the relationship between accuracy and HCG enjoyment was non-significant, suggesting that game genres could have moderated such a relationship. Interestingly, timeliness was perceived similarly across all three applications. Perhaps, due to the assumption that online environments provide current information [10], HCGs appeared to instill confidence that their outputs were as timely as that of the non-game variant.

Second, participants derived greater enjoyment from HCGs as opposed to the non-game application. This underlines the potential of the game-based approach for human computation. Both game genres were found to be equally effective in evoking positive emotions and thoughts, giving rise to affective and cognitive enjoyment. Our results show that participants using *Collabo* derived more behavioral enjoyment than *Clash*. Perhaps, participants experienced the benefit of being part of a team, which may have spurred them to be more committed to the gameplay [5], thereby inducing behavioral enjoyment. Compared to prior work in which enjoyment is treated unidimensionally [11], this study provides a detailed understanding that HCG enjoyment comes from multiple sources that may vary due to the game mechanics employed. Hence, multiple dimensions (e.g., affective, cognitive, and behavioral) should be use when assessing HCG enjoyment and its impact.

This study yields the following implications. One, we discovered that collaboration has a similar effect on perceived affective and cognitive enjoyment, and even presents a greater impact on behavioral enjoyment, compared to competition. This provides evidence for the need to create different strategies to evoke enjoyment of HCGs. Two, this study indicates a gulf between gaming and output quality and hence, better design strategies to bridge these two aspects needs to be sought. Three, our results suggests that a co-op mode where people form long- or short-term groups is needed to make them more deeply involved in HCGs. Further, competitive elements are needed to influence perceptions of output accuracy. Taken together, the study bodes well for digital libraries that may wish to consider using games to enhance user engagement.

Although this study yields valuable findings, some limitations should be addressed. For instance, this study relied on basic, but commonly used, gameplay mechanics in HCGs. Future research may investigate the differential effects of a larger set of gameplay mechanics, such as those used in adventure and simulation games.

Acknowledgements. This work was supported by MOE/Tier 1 grant RG64/14.

References

1. Goh, D.H., Ang, R.P., Lee, C.S., Chua, A.Y.K.: Fight or unite: Investigating game genres for image tagging. J. Am. Soc. Inf. Sci. Tec. **62**, 1311–1324 (2011)
2. von Ahn, L., Dabbish, L.: Designing games with a purpose. Commun. Acm. **51**, 58–67 (2008)
3. von Ahn, L., Dabbish, L.: Labeling images with a computer game. In: SIGCHI Conference on Human Factors in Computing Systems, pp. 319–326. ACM Press, New York (2004)
4. de Figueiredo, H.F., Lacerda, Y.A., de Paiva, A.C., Casanova, M.A., de Souze Baptista, C.: PhotoGeo: A photo digital library with spatial-temporal support and self-annotation. Multimed. Tools. Appl. **59**, 279–305 (2012)
5. Waddell, J.C., Peng, W.: Does it matter with whom you slay? The effects of competition, cooperation and relationship type among video game players. Comput. Hum. Behav. **38**, 331–338 (2014)
6. Tauer, J.M., Harackiewicz, J.M.: The effects of cooperation and competition on intrinsic motivation and performance. J. Pers. Soc. Psychol. **86**, 849–861 (2004)
7. Davis, D., Bagozzi, P., Warshaw, R.: Extrinsic and intrinsic motivation to use computers in the workplace. J. Appl. Psychol. **22**, 1111–1132 (1992)
8. Lee, Y.W., Strong, D.M., Kahn, B.K., Wang, R.Y.: AIMQ: A methodology for information quality assessment. Inform. Manage. **40**, 133–146 (2002)
9. Nabi, R.L., Krcmar, M.: Conceptualizing media enjoyment as attitude: implications for mass media effects research. Commun. Theor. **14**, 288–310 (2004)
10. Schaal, M., Smyth, B., Mueller, R. M., MacLean, R.: Information quality dimensions for the social web. In: International Conference on Management of Emergent Digital EcoSystems, pp. 53–58. ACM Press, New York (2012)
11. Pe-Than, E.P.P., Goh, D.H.L., Lee, C.S.: Making work fun: Investigating antecedents of perceived enjoyment in human computation games for information sharing. Comput. Hum. Behav. **39**, 88–99 (2014)
12. Fang, X., Zhao, F.: Personality and enjoyment of computer game play. Comput. Ind. **6**, 342–349 (2010)
13. Costello, A.B., Osborne, J.W.: Best practices in exploratory factor analysis: four recommendations for getting the most from your analysis. Pract. Assess. Res. Eval. **10**, 1–9 (2005)

More Than Just Black and White: A Case for Grey Literature References in Scientific Paper Information Retrieval Systems

Aravind Sesagiri Raamkumar[(✉)], Schubert Foo, and Natalie Pang

Wee Kim Wee School of Communication and Information,
Nanyang Technological University, Singapore, Singapore
{aravind002,sfoo,nlspang}@ntu.edu.sg

Abstract. In this paper, we start by analyzing the presence of grey literature (GL) references in the bibliographies of different article-types using an extract of 122,406 articles from the ACM Digital Library. GL articles accounted for about 16% of the overall references with highest presence in proceedings (17.61%). Boosting techniques for promoting GL references are proposed for information retrieval systems for two specific scenarios. A simple IR experiment was conducted with 103,739 articles to validate the proposed boosting techniques with 10 research topics. Results show that GL references were consistently pushed to the top of the search results along with an increased visibility in top 20 results.

Keywords: Grey Literature · Citation analysis · Boosting techniques · Scientific paper information retrieval · Digital libraries

1   Introduction

Scientific papers are the key information resources for literature review and information seeking purposes of researchers. The scientific nature of these papers is asserted through the rigorous review process enforced by commercial publication houses. The findings of studies in such papers are accepted as part of the body of knowledge for corresponding research topics. Grey Literature (GL) materials are alternate resources produced by researchers, practitioners and the common public. These resources are not part of the traditional publishing lifecycles. Grey Literature is defined as *"information produced on all levels of government, academia, business and industry in electronic and print formats not controlled by commercial publishing"* [1]. Websites, technical reports and dissertations are considered GL across all disciplines. Conference proceedings are considered GL in medical, social sciences and humanities disciplines, while computer science and engineering disciplines consider them as scientific materials. In this paper, we regard proceedings as scientific papers while the article-types websites, technical reports, dissertations, patent and unpublished are considered GL materials.

© Springer International Publishing Switzerland 2015
R.B. Allen et al. (Eds.): ICADL 2015, LNCS 9469, pp. 252–257, 2015.
DOI: 10.1007/978-3-319-27974-9_26

Even though there has been debate on whether GL materials should be included in systematic literature reviews and meta-analyses [2], inclusion of GL in scientific papers has been largely left to authors' discretion. There have been efforts in the past to accumulate and index GL materials at both institutional and national levels for facilitating easier access [3]. There have also been arguments made for using open access repositories in the indexing of both GL and non-GL articles [4]. Academic databases and search systems that provide integrated access to scientific and GL papers are few, since the scope of collecting and indexing papers is immense. In the systems where both types of papers are available, lesser preference is given to GL materials while ranking the search results, thereby reducing their visibility to searchers. Nevertheless, past studies have shown sustained referencing of GL materials in scientific papers over the years [5].

Research interest in GL has ranged from recognition of the availability of GL to development of GL initiatives such as conferences, journals and repositories [2]. The usability of GL materials has been acknowledged in the context of conducting literature reviews [6]. However, the inclusion of GL articles in meta-analysis has been subject to debate due to the difficulty of assessing the methodological quality of the studies [7]. Yasin et al. [8] reported the presence of GL references in about 9.22% of 183 Systematic Literature Reviews (SLR) articles, with conference proceedings and technical report as the most cited GL types (68%). In a citation analysis study [5] conducted on a sample set of articles in Google Scholar, data indicated that around 34.3% of the retrieved articles were GL, with technical reports (26%) being the most used type. These studies indicate the notable presence of GL materials in scientific papers.

There are two main objectives in the work proposed in the paper. The first objective is to analyze the referencing extent of GL materials in an extract of papers from ACM Digital Library (ACM DL). The analysis aims to examine the extent of GL cited by authors, and hence its importance if so, to warrant the motivation to push GL materials higher in the results list in specific scenarios. The second objective is to propose boosting techniques for pushing GL materials in Information Retrieval (IR) system settings due to their applicability in digital libraries. Digital libraries can benefit from having such functionality, especially if such GL resources are found to be particularly relevant for specific domains and contexts. Our scope was restricted to the GL materials that are cited as bibliographic references in the articles of ACM DL extract used in the current study. We conducted a simple experiment to validate the IR boosting technique with 10 research topics selected from the ACM DL. Our experiment showed that the boosting technique helped push GL references into the top 20 search results.

2   Analysis of Bibliographic References in ACM DL Extract

As a part of ongoing studies towards building a task-based scientific paper recommender system, we have been using an extract of the ACM Digital Library (ACM DL). The extract contains full text and metadata of articles from the ACM DL published between the years 1951 and 2010. A sample set was built from the extract, containing the articles that have keywords, abstract and references entirely present in the extract. The total count of valid articles in the sample set is 122,406, with 103,739 proceedings articles and 18,667 periodicals articles. The bibliography parsing service AnyStyle was used for parsing the bibliographies. AnyStyle assigns the references type based on the BibTeX entry types. A total of 2,320,345 references were parsed and the required fields were extracted and stored in a MySQL database.

Based on this information, the percentages of GL and non-GL references by different article types are shown in Figure 1. The GL Percentage (GLP) on the whole for proceedings and periodicals was 17.61% and 14.48, In ACM DL, journals, magazines and transactions constitute periodicals. Within periodicals, articles are mainly classified as research articles while some journals also allow review/survey articles. Survey articles have the lowest GLP (12.86%). Contrastingly, referencing behavior in conferences, symposiums and workshops is observed to be comparatively less stringent. There are different article-types under proceedings. The types demos (18.71%) and tutorials (17.98%) have the highest GLP, as the references in articles of such types are of miscellaneous nature.

The current examination is limited to quantifying the referencing of GL articles in the extract. In-depth qualitative studies need to be conducted to identify the citation motivations of authors based on the citation contexts of GL references in articles. As stated earlier, the argument being made in this paper is to better utilize the available data within digital libraries in order to help researchers in finding sufficient and useful articles as a part of their literature review. Since digital libraries parse the full text of articles to extract structured data, the bibliographic references could be utilized for enhancing user search.

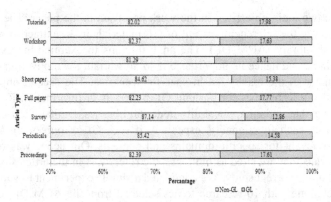

Fig. 1. GL vs Non-GL References Percentage in ACM DL Articles

3   Experimentation with GL Boosting Technique

In academic search systems and digital libraries, the article metadata along with full text is indexed. Papers are retrieved based on the matching of search keywords and the indexed text. The final results are sorted using citation count, search keyword relevance, recency, and other factors. Bibliographic references from articles are also indexed in some of these systems, although these items are rarely displayed in the search results. For promoting GL references in IR systems, the technique of document boosting can be adopted. A separate field known as 'boosting weight' can be added to each document when the indexing process is performed. The boosting weights can be used during the retrieval process to compute a new similarity score on top of the basic similarity score. Using this technique, GL materials that get additional weightage due the boosting rules will have a higher probability of getting a better rank in the search results, thereby increasing their visibility to users.

We briefly discuss the results of an experiment carried out to validate the GL references boosting technique applicable for scientific paper IR systems. For this experiment, the proceedings articles of the ACM DL extract were used. A total of 103,739 articles and corresponding 2,320,345 references were indexed in a Lucene index file. The fields indexed were *article id, article title, article abstract, article-type* and the *boosting weight* (gl_w). For all the proper full-text articles, article-type was set as 'in-proceedings' and for the references, the type was set based on the reference-type identified using the AnyStyle reference parsing service. Okapi BM25[9] (k=2, f=0.75) was used for the initial similarity score calculation. The boosting weight rules used are provided as follows: *-Rule 1: If the article or the reference is of non-GL type, the boosting weight is 1.0, Rule 2: If the reference is of GL type and its reference count is more than 2, the boosting weight is 1.5, Rule 3: If the reference type is a thesis, the boosting weight is 1.25.* Rules 2 and 3 are the two scenarios used for boosting GL materials in this study. The boosting weights for these rules are samples for this study since the aim is elevate certain GL articles. A separate experiment is required to arrive at ideal weights for boosting rules.

Ten research topics were used as the search keywords for the experiment. These topics are part of the top 50 author specified keywords in the ACM DL. For each research topic, a search was performed and the top 100 results were retrieved based on the BM25 similarity score. For the BM25 similarity score calculation, the title and abstract fields of the articles were used. From the retrieved 100 results, the top 20 results were ranked using four techniques. The proposed GL Boosting Technique (GBT) was benchmarked against two traditional ranking techniques and one combined ranking technique. The three benchmarking ranking techniques were Citation Count Technique (CCT) in which the results were ranked based on article's citation count, BM25 Similarity Score Technique (BST) in which the ranking was based on the computed BM25 similarity score and thirdly, the Combined Score Technique (CST) where the values of citation count and BM25 similarity score were added to form a combined score. In the proposed GBT, the ranking was based on the values which were computed by multiplying the BM25 similarity score with the boosting weight (gl_w).

In order to perform a proper evaluation, a novel evaluation metric Grey Literature Availability Measure (GLAM) had to be conceptualized that accounted for both the retrieved GL articles count as well as the corresponding ranks. GLAM is based on two base metrics: GL Count (GLC) which is the count of GL materials that are retrieved in the query, and in-query MRR (iMRR), a modified version of Mean Reciprocal Rank [10]. Unlike MRR, which is calculated across a set of queries, iMRR is calculated within a single query. First, the reciprocal ranks of GL articles in the query are identified. Second, the sum of the reciprocal ranks is divided by the GL articles count (GLC) to form the iMRR value. The main evaluation metric Grey Literature Availability Measure (GLAM) is calculated by adding up GLC and iMRR for each query. Higher GLAM values indicate higher presence of GL articles in the query results, along with better ranks.

The evaluation was done with two ranked lists (N@10 and N@20) for each research topic. Figures 2 and 3 provide the GLAM values computed using the four techniques for the 10 research topics at N@10 and N@20 respectively. For N@10, GL boosted technique (GBT) has higher GLAM than the benchmarking techniques as the GL count (GLC) is higher for all research topics. For N@20, except for two research topics 'interaction design' and 'wireless networks' where CCT technique has a higher GLAM, the GBT technique produces the best results for all other research topics. Thus, the experiment shows the GL boosting technique produces the expected results for the majority of the input research topics.

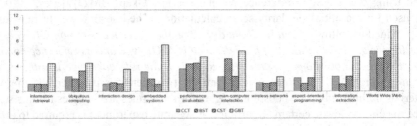

Fig. 2. Comparison of GLAM Values for the Four Techniques (N@10)

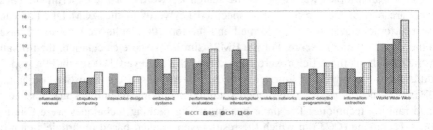

Fig. 3. Comparison of GLAM Values for the Four Techniques (N@20)

4   Conclusion and Future Work

In this paper, we have analyzed the bibliographic references of articles from an extract of the ACM Digital Library for ascertaining the level of GL referencing. We found that GL materials were found in nearly 16% of the references overall. GL referencing was higher in proceedings article-types, particularly tutorial, demo and workshop papers. The referencing was comparatively lower in periodicals, particularly in the literature survey article-type. Two scenarios were identified for boosting GL materials in the context of digital libraries where bibliographic references are parsed and indexed along with article metadata and full text. Boosting techniques for pushing GL references have been proposed for IR settings. An IR experiment was conducted to validate the effectiveness of the boosting technique using a novel evaluation metric. Future user evaluation techniques can also be carried out to evaluate the relevance of the GL found in the result lists. These proposals have practical implications for implementation in academic digital libraries, since current systems don't properly make use of all types of bibliographic references of articles indexed in the corpus. GL articles which satisfy certain pre-set rules are candidates for a higher presence in the search results. As a part of our current work, the proposed IR boosting techniques will be implemented in a task-based scientific paper recommender system for reading list generation and also for shortlisting papers for inclusion in research manuscripts.

Acknowledgements. This research is supported by the National Research Foundation, Prime Minister's Office, Singapore under its International Research Centres in Singapore Funding Initiative and administered by the Interactive Digital Media Programme Office.

References

1. Schöpfel, J., Stock, C., Farace, D.J., Frantzen, J.: Citation analysis and grey literature: stakeholders in the grey circuit. In: GL6: Sixth International Conference on Grey Literature (2005)
2. Farace, D., Schöpfel, J. (eds.): Grey literature in library and information studies. Walter de Gruyter (2010)
3. Stock, C., Henrot, N.: From OpenSIGLE to OpenGrey: Changes and Continuity. Grey J. **7**, 93–97 (2011)
4. Banks, M.A.: Towards a continuum of scholarship: The eventual collapse of the distinction between grey and non-grey literature. Publ. Res. Q. **22**, 4–11 (2006)
5. Di Cesare, R., Luzi, D., National, I.: The impact of Grey Literature in the web environment: A citation analysis using Google Scholar. Grey J. **4**, 83–96 (2008)
6. Booth, A., Papaioannou, D., Sutton, A.: Systematic approaches to a successful literature review. Sage (2011)
7. Cook, D.J., Guyatt, G.H., Ryan, G., Clifton, J., Buckingham, L., Willan, A., McIlroy, W., Oxman, A.D.: Should unpublished data be included in meta-analyses?: Current convictions and controversies. Jama **269**, 2749–2753 (1993)
8. Yasin, A., Hasnain, M.I.: On the quality of grey literature and its use in information synthesis during systematic literature reviews (2012)
9. Jones, K.S., Walker, S., Robertson, S.E.: A probabilistic model of information retrieval: development and comparative experiments: Part 2. Inf. Process. Manag. **36**, 809–840 (2000)
10. Voorhees, E.M.: The TREC-8 Question Answering Track Report. TREC **99**, 77–82 (1999)

A Comparison of User Engagement with the CDC Facebook Page During Health Crisis and Ordinary Periods

Sue Yeon Syn[✉]

The Catholic University of America, Washington, DC, USA
syn@cua.edu

Abstract. This study investigated the Centers for Disease Control and Prevention (CDC) Facebook Page to understand how users engage differently in ordinary and health crisis situations. The posts and user activities, such as shares, likes, and comments, at different times and situations were collected and compared. The findings showed that users engage more actively during health crises. The types of engagement differed depending on the seriousness of the event. The results showed that users engage based on the content of the posts during both ordinary and health crisis situations. The findings of the study contribute in further understanding of users' behavior on social media in different situational contexts.

Keywords: Social media · Crisis informatics · Health communication · User engagement · Facebook

1   Introduction

Social media is used popularly as a health communication tool [1,2]. When seeking health-related information, social media users seek professional and personalized information [3]. Social media is also considered a channel for online word-of-mouth communication during crisis situations [4]. A survey found that web users consider social media an alternate channel to request help in emergency situations, and social media serves as one of the most popular sources of emergency information during a disaster [5].

Major advantages of using social media during health crisis situations include the services being free, supporting direct communication among users and between an organization and users, having already established a large audience body which allows effective dissemination of information [6], and allowing sharing of contextualized information and emotional support among users who are impacted by such situations [7]. However, there are also concerns in using social media in health crisis situations, in many cases related to ethical issues such as verification of the sources [6], and dissemination of false or misleading information.

© Springer International Publishing Switzerland 2015
R.B. Allen et al. (Eds.): ICADL 2015, LNCS 9469, pp. 258–263, 2015.
DOI: 10.1007/978-3-319-27974-9_27

Previous studies have investigated the use of social media during crisis situations such as Japan's tsunami disaster [8], the UT Austin shooting [9], and the Virginia Tech shooting [10]. However, little has been examined about the use of social media in a national or organizational health crisis situation. Health crisis situations, especially for epidemic cases, are unique because the boundary of time and people who are impacted is not easy to identify, and people who are not currently impacted may be influenced some time later. This leads to different types of information needs and behaviors from other crises.

This study investigates how Facebook users engaged with information during the Ebola outbreak event in the United States and during ordinary situations. Research questions of this study include: how does users' engagement differ in a health crisis situation from ordinary engagement? and do the types of information influence users' engagement during health crisis and ordinary situations?

2   Methods

The data was collected using the Facebook Graph API from the Centers for Disease Control and Prevention (CDC) Facebook Page (www.facebook.com/CDC). Facebook is selected as it provides various kinds of user engagement such as likes, shares, and comments. Moreover, Facebook is the most popularly used social media by American adults [11]. The CDC functions as the national public health institute of the United States and aims to protect public health and prevent disease. It was the government organization to respond to the Ebola outbreak and was one of the major authoritative sources for the updates of status in the U.S. The CDC Facebook Page is a public environment that enables observation of user engagement. Since Page posts are mainly created by the CDC, users' participation can be observed from their reactions to the wall posts such as comments and likes.

This study collected the contents and types of posts, the numbers of posts, shares, likes, and comments per posts, and the dates of creation for the posts to analyze the patterns of user engagement during crisis and general health communication. The data was collected for July 1, 2014 to January 31, 2015 based on the timing of the Ebola outbreak events in the U.S. (October 2014), covering the previous and following 3 months. The data in the previous year was collected for the same time period, from July 1, 2013 to January 31, 2014, for comparison.

3   Findings and Discussion

The collected data includes a total of 1,295 Facebook posts with means of 225.32 shares, 232.37 likes, and 41.98 comments per post. Table 1 shows the counts of posts and averages of user engagement per post by month.

Table 1. Counts of posts and averages of user engagement on CDC Facebook Page

Months		Posts (count)	Shares (avg.)	Likes (avg.)	Comments (avg.)
2013	7	114	62.00	85.80	11.32
	8	115	74.48	103.11	20.86
	9	117	57.79	68.37	5.41
	10	40	66.65	92.08	14.88
	11	90	78.00	89.90	6.04
	12	93	47.84	74.53	6.13
	1	94	46.12	62.19	4.68
TOTAL		663	61.56	81.73	9.76
2014	7	90	103.33	164.12	20.93
	8	103	567.91	545.89	84.04
	9	90	273.24	289.32	35.27
	10	113	1044.81	821.68	258.46
	11	74	200.36	291.43	31.05
	12	68	192.46	252.22	22.96
	1	94	101.8	192.83	11.88
TOTAL		632	397.36	390.4	75.78

To make sure the comparison between health crisis and ordinary situation is made appropriately and ensure that the selected period of ordinary situation (July 1, 2013 to January 31, 2014) did not include other public health events, the Facebook posts were examined with word appearance counts to identify issues mentioned. The most frequently appeared words during the ordinary period include CDC, health, new, learn, help, healthy, Dr, prevent, public, know, etc. The words list represents that the discussion focus on general public health issues. The posts from Ebola outbreak period have different word selection such as Ebola, Africa, outbreak, spread, risk, and virus. Figure 1 shows visualized word frequencies with word clouds.

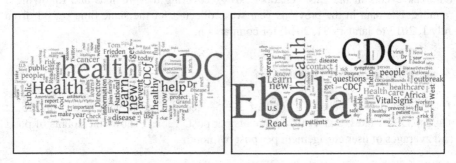

Fig. 1. Word clouds comparison based on word frequency in CDC Facebook Page posts (left from posts in 2013 period; right in 2014 period) (produced with Wordle)

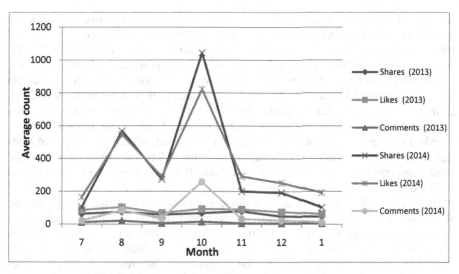

Fig. 2. Averages of shares, likes, and comments by month

Table 2. The significance of differences in user engagement among months

		2013							2014						
		7	8	9	10	11	12	1	7	8	9	10	11	12	1
2014	7	NS/NS/NS	NS/NS/NS	NS/NS/NS	NS/NS/NS	NS/NS/NS	NS/NS/NS	NS/NS/NS							
	8	NS/***/**	NS/***/*	*/***/***	NS/***/NS	NS/***/**	NS/***/**	NS/***/**	NS/***/*						
	9	NS/**/NS	NS/*/NS	NS/**/NS	NS/NS/NS	NS/*/NS	NS/**/NS	NS/**/NS	NS/NS/NS	NS/***/NS					
	10	***/***/***	***/***/***	***/***/***	***/***/***	***/***/***	***/***/***	***/***/***	***/***/***	NS/***/***	***/***/***				
	11	NS/*/NS	NS/*/NS	NS/**/NS	NS/NS/NS	NS/*/NS	NS/**/NS	NS/**/NS	NS/NS/NS	NS/***/NS	NS/NS/NS	***/***/***			
	12	NS/NS/NS	NS/NS/NS	NS/NS/NS	NS/NS/NS	NS/NS/NS	NS/NS/NS	NS/*/NS	NS/NS/NS	NS/***/NS	NS/NS/NS	***/***/***	NS/NS/NS		
	1	NS/NS/NS	NS/NS/NS	NS/NS/NS	NS/NS/NS	NS/NS/NS	NS/NS/NS	NS/NS/NS	NS/NS/NS	NS/***/**	NS/NS/NS	***/***/***	NS/NS/NS	NS/NS/NS	

1. Presented in the order of shares/likes/comments
2. *** p < .001, ** p < .01, * p < .05, NS = not significant

Although the numbers of posts by the CDC were generally consistent during the two periods (on average, 94.71 posts per month in 2013 and 90.29 in 2014), the averages of shares, likes, and comments became extremely high during the health crisis situation (Table 1 and Figure 2). One-way ANOVA tests further showed that there are significant differences in all user engagements by month ($F(13, 1258) = 6.735$, $p < 0.001$ for shares, $F(13, 1294) = 41.332$, $p < 0.001$ for likes, and $F(13, 1294) = 29.891$, $p < 0.001$ for comments). The post hoc tests with Tukey HSD showed that most of the significant differences are from active participation in October 2014, when the Ebola outbreak happened in the U.S. However, it is notable that these mean differences demonstrate that users start engaging with likes, and as the crisis situation becomes severe, they engage further with shares and comments (Figure 2 and Table 2).

When the types of information posted were examined, among the 6 types of posts defined by Facebook Graph (i.e., status, photo, link, video, and event), photo was the most dominant type of post on CDC Facebook Page (on average 53.25% of posts each month). The tendency of user engagement was compared for different types of posts based on the existence of a health crisis situation. In ordinary engagement, shares and likes were the types of user engagement that showed significant differences among post types ($F(4, 644) = 9.600$, $p < 0.001$ for shares, and $F(4, 662) = 13.678$, $p < 0.001$ for likes). On the other hand, when there is a health crisis, likes was the only user engagement type that showed a significant difference among post types ($F(4, 631) = 3.386$, $p < 0.009$). These findings can be understood to indicate that users share or comment on posts when they are willing to participate in the communication, regardless of its type.

A similar tendency was observed from the contents of the posts, when the posts with the highest levels of engagement (top 5) were examined. During general situations, the most shared, liked, commented posts include photos, statuses, and links, with content that included calling for participation or actions, medicine information for awareness, and the organization's situational information. During the health crisis situation, the most shared, liked and commented posts were all related to the crisis, in this case the Ebola outbreak. The types of posts varied including statuses, links, and photos. The content of posts with the most user engagement was disease (Ebola)-related information including infection channels and diagnosis facts and situational information, mainly about how the government was handling the situation. The findings seem to be consistent with the discussion from previous studies that social media users expect to acquire useful information [12] and find professional and personalized information on health-related issues. In a similar sense, the results show that the contents of the posts matter most to users and motivate their engagement during health crisis or ordinary situations.

4   Conclusion

This study investigated the CDC Facebook Page to understand how users engage differently in general and health crisis situations. The posts and user engagement activities, such as shares, likes, and comments, were examined. The findings showed that users engage more actively during health crises; however, the types of engagement changed depending on the seriousness of the crisis. The results showed that users engage based on the content of the posts shared, not necessarily the types of posts, and this tendency was consistent during ordinary and health crisis periods.

This study investigated only one community related to one health crisis situation on Facebook. Users' engagement may differ in other types of communities, situations, or social media; and such cases can be explored for a future study to better understand users' engagement in health crisis communication on social media.

References

1. Chou, W.S., Hunt, Y.M., Beckjord, E.B., Moser, R.P., Hesse, B.W.: Social media use in the United States: Implications for health communication. J. Med. Internet Res. **11**(4), e48 (2009)
2. Thackeray, R., Neiger, B.L., Smith, A.K., Wagenen, S.B.V.: Adoption and use of social media among public health departments. BMC Public Health **12**, 242 (2012)
3. Oh, H.J., Lauckner, C., Boehmer, J., Fewins-Bliss, R., Li, K.: Facebooking for health: An examination into the solicitation and effects of health-related social support on social networking sites. Comput. Hum. Behav. **29**(5), 2071–2080 (2013)
4. Austin, L., Liu, B.F., Jin, Y.: How audiences seek out crisis information: Exploring the social-mediated crisis communication model. J. Appl. Commun. Res. **40**(2), 188–207 (2012)
5. American Red Cross. More Americans using mobile apps in emergencies. http://www.redcross.org/news/press-release/More-Americans-Using-Mobile-Apps-inEmergencies
6. Crowe, A.: The social media manifesto: A comprehensive review of the impact of social media on emergency management. Journal of Business Continuity & Emergency Planning **5**(1), 409–420 (2011)
7. Yates, D., Paquette, S.: Emergency knowledge management and social media technologies: A case study of the 2010 Haitian earthquake. Int. J. Inform. Manage. **31**(1), 6–13 (2011)
8. Acar, A., Muraki, Y.: Twitter for crisis communication: Lessons learned from Japan's tsunami disaster. International Journal of Web Based Communities **7**(3), 392–402 (2011)
9. Li, L.T., Yang, S., Kavanaugh, A., Fox, E. A., Sheetz, S., Shoemaker, D., Whalen, T., Srinivasan, V.: Twitter use during an emergency event: the case of UT austin shooting. In: Proceedings of the 12th Annual International Digital Government Research Conference, pp. 335–336 (2011)
10. Palen, L., Vieweg, S., Liu, S.B., Hughes, A.L.: Crisis in a networked world: Features of computer-mediated communication in the April 16, 2007 Virginia Tech event. Soc. Sci. Comput. Rev. **27**(4), 467–480 (2009)
11. Duggan, M., Ellison, N.B., Lampe, C., Lenhart, A., Madden, M.: Social media update 2014. Pew Research Center (2015)
12. André, P., Bernstein, M.S., Luther, K.: Who gives a tweet? Evaluating microblog content value. In: Proceedings of the Conference on Computer Supported Cooperative Work (CSCW 2012), pp. 471–474 (2012)

Aesthetic Experience and Acceptance of Human Computation Games

Xiaohui Wang[1(✉)], Dion Hoe-Lian Goh[1], Ee-Peng Lim[2], and Adrian Wei Liang Vu[2]

[1] Wee Kim Wee School of Communication and Information,
Nanyang Technological University, Singapore, Singapore
{Wang0870,ashlgoh}@ntu.edu.sg
[2] School of Information Systems, Singapore Management University, Singapore, Singapore
{eplim,adrianvu}@smu.edu.sg

Abstract. Human computation games (HCGs) are applications that leverage games to solve computational problems that are out reach of the capacity of computers. Game aesthetics are critical for HCG acceptance, and the game elements should motivate users to contribute time and effort. In this paper, we examine the effect of aesthetic experience on intention to use HCGs. A between-subjects experiment was conducted to compare a HCG and a human computation system (HCS). Results demonstrated that HCGs provided a greater sense of aesthetic experience and attracted more intentional usage than HCSs. Implications of this study are discussed.

Keywords: Human Computation Games · Aesthetic experience · Acceptance

1 Introduction

The paradigm of "human computation" seeks to harness human intelligence to solve large-scale problems that are out of reach of the capacity of computers [1]. Humans act as processers in a distributed system and each performs a small part of a massive computation. Such systems are known as human computation systems (HCSs) [2].

In a parallel development, video games have experienced a rapid worldwide growth in recent years. As a consequence, a significant amount of research has been done on the use of games to motivate individuals to perform computational tasks [3]. These are called Human Computation Games (HCGs) [4] where individuals perform computational tasks as by-products of gameplay [5]. Compared to HCSs which mainly rely on contributions from online volunteers or paying for human resources, HCGs have the potential to effectively access a large amount of voluntary participants by providing entertainment [1]. They have thus been widely employed to build online collections in digital libraries and other information systems, such as multimedia tagging, location annotation, and ontology construction [6].

One of the first attempts to use video games as a medium for computation was the ESP Game [7], designed to collect labels for images. Randomly paired players are showed the same images and tasked to guess the keywords their partner would provide. Points are awarded for matches. The matched keywords then become labels for

© Springer International Publishing Switzerland 2015
R.B. Allen et al. (Eds.): ICADL 2015, LNCS 9469, pp. 264–273, 2015.
DOI: 10.1007/978-3-319-27974-9_28

the corresponding images. The ESP game collected over 50 million labels contributed by 200,000 players within a two-year period. These labels can be used to improve Web-based image search. This demonstrates the potential of human computation games in establishing and improving digital libraries. Other attempts include *Moodswing*, a game to record labels of the time-varying mood in a music clip [8], and *Eyespy*, a content sharing game which allows players to tag geographic locations with photos or text [9].

Like any other information system, encouraging user participation in HCGs is critical for success and is a challenging task [10]. This calls for an understanding of the driving factors of HCG acceptance. In related literature, studies suggested that enjoyable game experience in HCGs was the primary determinant of behavioral intention [11]. However, past research generally focused on explaining the hardcore game experience which emphasized the role of challenge and social interaction [12,13], while the casual game experience is seldom recognized. On the other hand, HCGs focus on solving computation problems that can be easily divided into bite-size subtasks. Thus, the casual game genre is an efficient approach to embed such computational tasks [4].

In this research, we employ the aesthetic experience to articulate the casual game experience in HCGs and examine its effect on HCG acceptance. Doing so will deepen understanding of the HCG experience and provide guidelines for HCG evaluation. Furthermore, experimental studies that examine the causal effect of game aesthetics on user acceptance are lacking in the literature. This study thus fills this gap and investigates whether aesthetic experience in HCGs motivates intentional use by comparing the performance of a HCG with a HCS.

Our objectives are thus twofold. We develop a music video tagging game incorporating various aesthetic elements. Next, we conduct an experiment to uncover the role of aesthetic experience in determining the acceptance of HCGs. The remaining sections of this article are organized as follows. First we highlight the research related to user experience of HCGs. We then present the methodology used in this study, followed by the results and discussions. Finally, we conclude with implications of the findings and future work.

2   Theoretical Background

2.1   Acceptance Research

Acceptance research seeks to investigate the contributing factors of individuals' willingness to employ an information technology [6]. User acceptance is the primary measure of the success of any information system, including HCGs. Prior studies in HCGs examined some predictors of individual acceptance, such as usability factors, output quality, and enjoyable game experience [14]. In particular, game enjoyment has been suggested as a pertinent factor in influencing user acceptance. For instance, [8] conducted a survey to investigate the influence of aesthetic experience as well as perception of output quality on intention to use a HCG. They found that aesthetic experience was the primary predictor.

The literature is unequivocal in stating that HCGs perceived positively by players are more likely to attract intentional use [14]. Nevertheless, there has been lacking effort examining the causation effect of aesthetic experience on HCG acceptance with experimentation, which is a limitation of [8]. An experimental study can examine the causal effect with all the other confounding factors controlled, which provides more rigorous evidence for the role of game enjoyment on HCG adoption. Moreover, comparing individuals' perceptions and acceptance of the HCG with those of a HCS could help clarify the question of how game elements motivate human computation.

2.2   Aesthetic Experience - The Casual Game Experience

Game enjoyment is a vital determinant of acceptance in the hedonic context. However, most of the current game experience models, such as flow [15] and gratifications [16], emphasize a sense of challenge and fellowship and focus on explaining the experience of hardcore gameplay. The experience of casual gameplay, that is, the desire to seek relaxation or kill time, is essential to game experience but rarely emphasized. Here, [17] proposed a categorization of game enjoyment in which four types of fun are accounted: hard fun, easy fun, serious fun, and social fun. This categorization explains how each game category provides the necessary motivations for different gamers in each type of game. Hard fun refers to the expectation to be challenged, to compete with others, with a program, or even with one's own previous achievements (i.e. score). Social fun refers to the expectation to build social connections with other players. Easy fun refers to the inspired curiosity, feeling of relaxation, and killing time with less involvement. Serious fun refers to the improvement of a player's internal state or achievement of real-world benefit. Hard fun and social fun are probably the most important motives for hardcore gameplay [18]. However, for casual gameplay, the primary motives may be achieving a sense of easy fun. Previous work demonstrated that an easy form of fun, such as relaxing, passing time, and narrative were vital driving forces of players playing casual games [19,20].

In light of this, the aesthetic experience is proposed to construct the casual game experience. Aesthetics in games is defined as the emotional responses that players feel as a result of interacting with a game [19]. Instead of emphasizing a flow experience, aesthetic experience covers the emotional elements among players during their interactions with the game. [20] proposed a taxonomy of game aesthetics which includes eight categories: sensation, narrative, fantasy, challenge, fellowship, discovery, expression, and submission. This taxonomy provides a concrete way of talking about game enjoyment. Besides, it emphasizes the role of visuals, narrative, relaxation, and passing time in the game experience. Compared with previous game enjoyment models, the aesthetic experience articulates the components of game experience explicitly with an emphasis on easy fun. Thus, the taxonomy of aesthetic experience could be a more appropriate framework to describe the casual game experience. Accordingly, this study adopts the taxonomy of aesthetic experiences to describe HCG game enjoyment. By doing so, researchers and designers could improve their knowledge about components of the casual game experience. The study could also provide guidance for developers of HCGs to design systems with high levels of enjoyment and improve acceptance.

3   Application Development

To accomplish this study, two versions of an application were developed: a HCG named Kpoprally, and a HCS version. Kpoprally is a HCG based on a guessing game genre for collecting tags of K-pop music videos (Figure 1a). We choose the K-pop music genre because of its large following in Asian countries. Players annotate music videos through contributing answers to questions. As incentives, they obtain points as well as ranking in the game. Questions in Kpoprally come in two categories. Objective questions, such as *"What is the name of the artist performing in the video"* and *"What is the title of the song"*, are included to differentiate experienced players from novices. Next, subjective questions, such as *"What is the mood of the video"* and *"What is the color of the video"* (Figure 2b), are designed to collect subjective tags. Objective tags can be provided by music publishers and automatic annotation systems. However, annotating for music videos is particularly challenging when it comes to capturing highly subjective human perceptions [21]. Here, human computation can be applied to collect subjective tags for music videos. Such tags would enhance the description of music videos and allow for more accurate video search and recommendation.

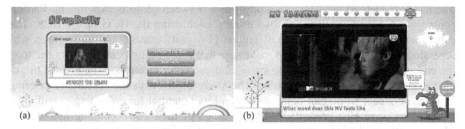

Fig. 1. Screenshots of Kpoprally. (a) Main Menu; (b) Gameplay Session

Kpoprally integrates a series of aesthetic elements to foster a positive game experience: sensation, narrative, challenge, fellowship, and submission. Specifically, sensation represents a sensory arousal among players. This is provided by an appealing visual design. Narrative refers to the sense of drama in the game, operationalized as an avatar presenting the backstory. Players are told that their mission is to help the virtual avatar achieve a good ranking in a K-pop music competition. Challenge means an appropriate level of difficulty matching players' skills. This is operationalized as questions of varying difficulty. Fellowship means fostering social connections in the game. In Kpoprally, players can invite their friends and share their in-game achievements on Facebook, creating a sense of community. Submission represents the game as a tool for passing time. Here, Kpoprally keeps players engaged with attractive tasks and multiple goals, such as such as earning more points for the avatar and fighting for higher rankings in the leaderboard.

Correspondingly, a HCS was developed to serve as a control group to compare against the performance of Kpoprally (Figure 2a). The HCS duplicated all the computational mechanisms of Kpoprally, but removed some game-based aesthetic elements. These included the storyline, avatar, ranking system, and achievement mechanism. The interface design of the HCS was changed to a non-game version (Figure 2b). Nevertheless, users of the HCS would still have an aesthetic experience through functions such as *Mes-*

sage Board and *Invite Friends*. *Message Board* in the HCS acted as a communication channel for users to discuss K-pop topics and leave comments. *Invite Friends* allowed users to invite Facebook friends to use this system. These elements might arouse a sense of social interaction and thus an aesthetic experience.

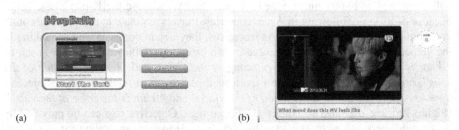

(a)   (b)

Fig. 2. Screenshots of the HCS (a) Main Menu; (b) Task session

4   Methodology

The research method used for this study was a between-subjects experiment. Participants were randomly assigned to two groups, each using the HCG or the HCS. The experiment was conducted in small groups (3-6 participants), and each group was separated from others. This was to make sure that every participant clearly understood the concepts and procedures in the study, and each participant had the chance to ask the researcher if he or she had doubts. The study began with the researcher briefing about the concept of human computation and its potential for collecting useful data. Participants were also presented with the usage of their corresponding application. They were then asked to test the assigned application for about 15 minutes.

Once concluded, participants completed an online questionnaire that captured their aesthetic perception and acceptance of the assigned application. In particular, perceived aesthetic experience was measured to ascertain perceptions towards the HCG and the HCS. This was assessed with five constructs (sensation, narrative, challenge, fellowship, and submission) adopted from the taxonomy of aesthetic experiences. Player acceptance, our dependent variable, was operationalized as attitude, intention to use, and intention to recommend the Kpoprally. Questions were adopted from previous work [5], [17] and were all rated on a 7-point scale ranging from 1 (strongly disagree) to 7 (strongly agree). The reliability of the constructs was assessed with Cronbach's alpha. Most of the scores were above the good level (that is, above 0.80), while challenge was in the acceptable level ($0.60 < \alpha < 0.80$) [22]. Participants were also asked to provide qualitative comments of what they like and dislike about the application.

A total of 95 participants were recruited from local universities. There were 60 males and 35 females, with ages ranging from 18 to 40, and an average age of 23.5 years. Participants were typical casual game players who played casual games once a month or more (82.1%). 57.9% of the participants also had experience playing hardcore games. Further, 39 participants (41.1%) listened to K-pop music once a month or more. Forty-eight participants were assigned to the HCS group and 47 to the HCG group.

5   Results

Table 1 shows the means and standard deviations of participants' perceptions of the aesthetic elements. Unsurprisingly, participants rated all constructs higher for the HCG than the HCS. To investigate which aesthetic elements were significantly different between the HCG and the HCS, t-tests were performed with groups as the independent variable and aesthetic elements as dependent variables. Results showed significant differences between the HCG and the HCS in terms of fantasy [t(1, 93) = 8.31, $p < .01$], narrative [t(1, 93) = 10.34, $p < .01$], and submission [t(1, 93) = 4.66, $p < .05$]. However, tests for sensation [t(1, 93) = .78, $p = .38$], challenge [t(1, 93) = 3.55, $p = .06$], and fellowship [t(1, 93) = .65, $p = .42$] were not significant.

Table 1. T-test Results for Perceptions of Aesthetic Elements.

Variables	HCG Group (n = 47)		HCS Group (n = 48)	
	Mean	SD	Mean	SD
Sensation	4.98	1.15	4.77	1.18
Fantasy**	4.90	0.98	4.23	1.23
Narrative**	4.74	1.16	3.89	1.38
Challenge	4.58	1.10	4.16	1.08
Fellowship	4.75	1.05	4.57	1.11
Submission*	4.63	1.19	4.09	1.29

Table 2 shows the means and standard deviations of participants' perceptions and acceptance of the applications. On the whole, participants rated all the constructs higher for the HCG than the HCS. A MANOVA was performed to examine the difference in the perception and acceptance variables. The independent variable was the group and the dependent variables were Perceived Aesthetic Experience (PAE), Attitude (ATT), Intention to Use (USE), and Intention to Recommend (REC).

Results showed that there was a statistically significant difference between the HCG and the HCS groups [F(1, 93) = 2.62, $p < .05$; Wilk's Λ = .82, partial η^2 = .17]. The univariate F tests showed that PAE of the HCG was statistically higher than the HCS [F(1, 93) = 5.41, p < .05]. With regards to acceptance, results showed that the HCG group was statistically higher than the HCS group in terms of USE [F(1, 93) = 9.01, $p < .05$], and REC [F(1, 93) = 10.12, $p < .05$]. The difference in ATT among the two applications was statistically non-significant [F(1, 93) = 2.12, $p = 0.22$].

Table 2. MANOVA Results for Acceptance.

Variables	HCG Group (n = 47)		HCS Group (n = 48)	
	Mean	SD	Mean	SD
Perceived Aesthetic Experience *	4.76	0.14	4.29	0.14
Attitude	4.89	0.18	4.58	0.17
Intention to Use *	4.73	0.20	4.12	0.19
Intention to Recommend *	4.83	0.18	4.18	0.19

6   Discussion

The present study adopted the aesthetic experience to measure players' casual game experience in HCGs and examined its effect on player acceptance. A between-subjects experiment was conducted with participants randomly allocated into two groups evaluating a HCG and a HCS. Analysis of the experimental data yielded the following findings. With regards to perceptions of the applications, participants found that the HCG provided a better aesthetic experience compared to the HCS. Put differently, participants appreciated the aesthetic features of the HCG and found it more enjoyable. Consequently, participants showed higher intention to use and intention to recommend the HCG than the HCS. However, no difference was found in attitude towards those two applications. These findings are discussed next.

As expected, the t-test results showed that participants perceived the HCS and the HCG as significantly different in terms of narrative, fantasy, and submission. Stated differently, the HCG provided a greater sense of aesthetic experience compared to the HCS. This demonstrates that the aesthetic elements in HCGs are able to influence perceptions of game enjoyment. Participants liked the narrative, fantasy, and submission elements in the HCG and found it leading to positive emotions. This finding is reflected in the qualitative feedback. Here, participants commented with *"imaginative"*, *"relax and make me feel at ease"*, and *"nice interface, color, and graphics"* when asked about their favorite game features.

Consequently, participants showed higher intention to use the HCG and intention to recommend it to others when compared with the HCS. This implies that aesthetic elements in terms of fantasy, narrative, and submission significantly affect individuals' adoption behavior. This study thus demonstrates that HCGs which provide a greater level of aesthetic experience can attract more intentional usage and recommendation from users.

Moreover, this study provides empirical evidence for the effect of easy fun on HCG acceptance. Kpoprally employed aesthetic elements such as a storyline, an avatar, and multiple tasks. These elements likely aroused a sense of curiosity, role play, and killing time, hence supporting easy fun [17]. Here, participants' feedback on the HCG focused on the visual design and storyline, such as *"catchy UI"*, *"(interface) very pleasing to eyes"* and *"interactive story"*, which are all easy fun elements. Unsurprisingly, participants found that these aesthetic elements affected their adoption behavior hence demonstrating the effect of easy fun on HCG acceptance.

While the effect of aesthetic experience on behavioral intention was demonstrated, no significant difference was found in individuals' attitude towards the HCG and the HCS. One possible explanation could be that attitudes of these two systems were established by different antecedents. For attitude towards HCGs, the most dominant predictor may be aesthetic experience. However, for HCSs, the most dominant predictor could be utility factors instead of enjoyment [23]. Qualitative feedback from participants suggested that individuals' preference of the HCS may largely depend on the usability and functionality of the system. When asked about the favorite aspect of the HCS, most of the comments provided by participants focused on two aspects: interface usability and computation. Comments such as *"clear and straightforward interface"*, *"simple instructions and easy to use"*, *"overall, it is easy to learn to use and effective"*, *"creative and interesting idea (human computation)"*, and *"the system can help me when I want to find some videos*" were mentioned as the preferred aspects of the HCS. It seems that, for utility-oriented systems, interface quality and functions of the system were the focus areas of participants' attention, and whether the system was enjoyable or not was not their primary concern.

7   Conclusion

HCGs that harness human power to perform computational tasks through an entertainment-oriented approach have experienced an increase in popularity in the past decade, and their usefulness has been documented in previous studies. This study examines the effect of aesthetic experience on acceptance of HCGs by comparing a HCG with a HCS. Results demonstrate that our HCG provided a higher level of aesthetic experience and attracted more intentional usage than our HCS.

The following implications can be derived from our findings. First, our work contributes to the understanding of factors that influence the usage of entertainment-oriented information systems. Previous studies used sophisticated models to examine the association between game enjoyment and acceptance. Nevertheless, there has been a lack of work investigating the extent to which aesthetic experiences affect user acceptance with experimentation. This experimental study thus provides more rigorous evidence for the effect of aesthetic experience on adoption.

In addition, results of this study suggested that game elements such as fantasy, narrative, and submission could improve individuals' behavioral intention of HCGs. This study examines the effect of easy fun on HCG acceptance and details the understanding of components of HCG enjoyment. Future research in HCG enjoyment should thus include those elements.

Findings of this study also suggest a number of design implications for HCGs.

- First, fantasy is a vital aesthetic element that can be incorporated into HCGs. A major appeal of the HCG is an environment that evokes mental images which do not exist in real life. This could be achieved through an avatar representing the system or the user. For HCGs, avatars can be an interface element which players use to control the game, or an image that represents the player's identity.

- Next, appealing narrative should be considered. Developing HCGs with storylines can provide players with a sense of curiosity and thus attract them to linger. Besides, a storyline is also an appropriate approach to embed computational tasks. HCG developers can transform computational goals into turn points in narratives. Driven by curiosity about the uncharted plots, players may be highly motivated to finish the computational tasks.

- Finally, submission is a vital component of aesthetic experience and should be pursued in HCG development. People play casual games to kill time. HCGs can thus be designed as a tool to facilitate this and achieve easy fun. Developers can enhance the accessibility of HCGs to make it possible for people to play with time and attention limitations, such as enabling quick start and quit. On the other hand, HCGs should have complex features to keep players occupied with game activities. For instance, HCGs with the quiz genre should shorten the duration of each round of play but set interrelated and also progressive goals, so that players can play in short fragments of time but stay attracted by larger, overarching goals.

Although this study has yielded valuable findings, they are subject to several limitations. First, this research conducted a cross-sectional study that only captured a single snapshot of users' perception and acceptance. It remains an open question o what extent the effect of perceptions on acceptance differs across time. Thus, future research can be done to further the understanding of HCG acceptance by focusing on how aesthetic experience and its effect on acceptance change over time. Second, results were generated based on the evaluation of one type of game and one type of platform. It would be worthwhile to evaluate different HCG genres because game elements of different game genres are previously found to satisfy different aesthetic experiences, which may affect users' performance and preference of these games.

Acknowledgements. This work was supported by MOE/Tier 1 grant RG64/14.

References

1. Law, E., Von Ahn, L.: Human computation. Synthesis Lectures on Artificial Intelligence and Machine Learning **5**, 1–121 (2011)
2. Yuen, M.C., Chen, L.J., King, I.: A survey of human computation systems. In: Proceedings of the CSE 2009, pp. 723–728. IEEE Press, New York (2009)
3. Šimko, J., Tvarožek, M., Bieliková, M.: Human Computation: Image Metadata Acquisition based on a Single-Player Annotation Game. International Journal of Human-Computer Studies **71**, 933–945 (2013)
4. Von Ahn, L., Dabbish, L.: Designing Games with a Purpose. Communications of the ACM **51**, 58–67 (2008)
5. Goh, D.H.-L., Lee, C.S.: Perceptions, Quality and Motivational Needs in Image Tagging Human Computation Games. Journal of Information Science **37**, 515–531 (2011)
6. Pe-Than, E.P.P., Goh, D.H.-L., Lee, C.S.: A Typology of Human Computation Games: An Analysis and a Review of Current Games. Behaviour & Information Technology **34**, 1–16 (2013)
7. Von Ahn, L., Dabbish, L.: Labeling images with a computer game. In: Proceedings of the SIGCHI, pp. 319–326. ACM Press, New York (2004)
8. Kim, Y.E., Schmidt, E.M., Emelle, L.: Moodswings: A collaborative game for music mood label collection. In: Proceedings of the 9th International Conference of Music Information Retrieval, pp. 231–236 (2008)
9. Bell, M., Reeves, S., Brown, B., Sherwood, S., McMillan, D., Ferguson, J., Chalmers, M.: Eyespy: supporting navigation through play. In: Proceedings of SIGCHI Conference on Human Factors in Computing Systems, pp. 123–132. ACM Press, New York (2009)
10. Dillon, A., Morris, M.G.: User Acceptance of New Information Technology: Theories and Models. Annual Review of Information Science and Technology **14**, 3–32 (1996)
11. Wang, X., Goh, D.H.-L., Lim, E.-P., Vu, A.W.L.: Player acceptance of human computation games: an aesthetic perspective. In: Tuamsuk, K., Jatowt, A., Rasmussen, E. (eds.) ICADL 2014. LNCS, vol. 8839, pp. 233–242. Springer, Heidelberg (2014)
12. Qin, H., Rau, P.L.P., Salvendy, G.: Effects of Different Scenarios of Game Difficulty on Player Immersion. Interacting with Computers **22**, 230–239 (2010)
13. Hamari, J., Koivisto, J.: Social Motivations to Use Gamification: An Empirical Study of Gamifying Exercise. http://aisel.aisnet.org/ecis2013_cr/105

14. Pe-Than, E.P.P., Goh, D.H.-L., Lee, C.S.: Enjoyment of a mobile information sharing game: perspectives from needs satisfaction and information quality. In: Chen, H.-H., Chowdhury, G. (eds.) ICADL 2012. LNCS, vol. 7634, pp. 126–135. Springer, Heidelberg (2012)
15. Sweetser, P., Wyeth, P.: GameFlow: A Model for Evaluating Player Enjoyment in Games. Computers in Entertainment **3** (2005)
16. Sherry, J.L., Lucas, K., Greenberg, B.S., Lachlan, K.: Video game uses and gratifications as predictors of use and game preference. In: Vorderer, P., Bryant, J. (eds.) Playing Video Games. Motives, Responses, and Consequences, pp. 213–224. Lawrence Erlbaum Associates, Mahwah (2006)
17. Lazzaro, N.: The Four Fun Keys. In: Isbister, K., Schaffer, N. (eds.) Game Usability: Advancing the Player Experience, pp. 315–344. Elsevier, Burlington (2008)
18. Neys, J.L., Jansz, J., Tan, E.S.: Exploring Persistence in Gaming: The Role of Self-Determination and Social Identity. Computers in Human Behavior **37**, 196–209 (2014)
19. Fencott, C., Clay, J., Lockyer, M., Massey, P.: Game Invaders: The Theory and Understanding of Computer Games. Wiley-IEEE Computer Society Press, Los Alamitos (2012)
20. Hunicke, R., Leblanc, M., Zubek, R.: MDA: a formal approach to game design and game research. In: AAAI Workshop on Challenges in Game AI, vol. 4 (2004)
21. Morton, B.G., Speck, J.A., Schmidt, E.M., Kim, Y.E.: Improving music emotion labeling using human computation. In: Proceedings of the ACM SIGKDD Workshop on Human Computation, pp. 45–48. ACM Press, New York (2010)
22. Kline, P.: Handbook of Psychological Testing. Routledge, London (2013)
23. Ahn, T., Ryu, S., Han, I.: The Impact of Web Quality and Playfulness on User Acceptance of Online Retailing. Information & Management **44**, 263–275 (2007)

On-Demand Big Data Analysis in Digital Repositories: A Lightweight Approach

Zhiwu Xie[1(✉)], Yinlin Chen[1], Tingting Jiang[1], Julie Speer[1],
Tyler Walters[1], Pablo A. Tarazaga[2], and Mary Kasarda[2]

[1] University Libraries, Virginia Polytechnic Institute and State University,
Blacksburg, USA
{zhiwuxie,ylchen,virjtt03,jspeer,tylerw63}@vt.edu
[2] Department of Mechanical Engineering,
Virginia Polytechnic Institute and State University, Blacksburg, USA
{ptarazag,maryk}@vt.edu

Abstract. We describe a use and reuse driven digital repository integrated with lightweight data analysis capabilities provided by the Docker framework. Using building sensor data collected from the Virginia Tech Goodwin Hall Living Laboratory, we perform evaluations using Amazon EC2 and Container Service with a Fedora 4 repository backed with storage in Amazon S3. The results confirm the viability and benefits of this approach.

Keywords: Big data · Data management · Docker · Scholarly digital divide · Use and reuse driven approach

1 Introduction

The open data and open science movements have gained significant momentum in recent years. Many funding agencies have now instituted new mandates and policies to pressure even the most reluctant researcher towards sharing data for validation and reuse. Eagerly embracing this trend, academic and research libraries are aspiring to lead the management of these research outputs, especially their dissemination, preservation, and curation [1]. To achieve the ultimate goal of openness, it is critical to position the library's role in the larger context of the research data lifecycle [2] to facilitate, not impede the free flow of information, and avoid self-servingly turning library services into extra barriers to entry or even data graveyards.

It has long been argued that shallow openness does not necessarily lead to effective use of information. This is particularly critical for sharing data sets of high volume and high velocity. The "digital divide" not only exists to marginalize the rural population with insufficient IT infrastructure but is also prevalent among academic researchers and domain experts. Lacking appropriate access to big data infrastructure, knowledge, or tools, a large number of these researchers are more and more distanced from participating in data-intensive science [3]. This paper addresses the scholarly digital divide by developing a library service that goes beyond open access and preservation. In addition to traditional repository functions, we also provide a flexible and low barrier data analysis infrastructure to allow researchers to submit their own

R.B. Allen et al. (Eds.): ICADL 2015, LNCS 9469, pp. 274–277, 2015.
DOI: 10.1007/978-3-319-27974-9_29

algorithms for execution against the preserved big data sets in an on-demand fashion. As a result, researchers can focus more on their own research instead of struggling with computing complexities.

2   Use and Reuse Driven Big Data Management

A use and reuse driven approach to manage big data [4] differs from the traditional library repository in that the emphasis is geared more towards serving the researcher's needs to answer domain-specific research questions, instead of building "preservation-ready" systems to satisfy the librarian's urge to document and arrange materials in certain ways to facilitate unspecified future access. The argument is that unless we make fresh data immediately usable and reusable to researchers in their research process, the data will quickly turn cold, become less valuable for long-term preservation, and crowd out limited IT resources for big data management.

Due to this shift of mission and philosophical stance, the OAIS Reference Model [5] is considered inadequate. We need to add an important component missing from the traditional library repository, namely a co-located data analysis infrastructure, to accomplish the goals laid out. Our prior research [4] compared a number of IT infrastructure options with which the use and reuse driven approach may be implemented. Given the IT environment and conditions currently prevalent in most academic libraries, we proposed the public cloud as a viable candidate. Indeed, cloud computing has been attributed to democratizing science [6] and is well positioned to bridge the scholarly digital divide. This paper furthers our prior exploration by adopting a light- weight approach.

3   A Lightweight Approach for On-Demand Analysis

Our prior approach [4] used the computing cloud in its most conventional sense by provisioning virtual machines in lieu of physical machines. We then installed user-supplied analysis code on each of them, and crunched data as if we had a traditional computing cluster on hand. While effective, this approach accrues higher computational overhead since the strong isolation between virtual machines, not essential to data analysis, is enforced nonetheless.

Docker [7], on the other hand, is more lightweight and cheaper since multiple Docker Containers can share the same kernel and application libraries. It requires one extra step from the researchers to "dockerize" their analysis algorithms, but this can usually be automated and does not involve a steep learning curve. We describe the details of our implementation in the next section.

4   Evaluation

The lightweight approach was evaluated using sensor data collected from the Virginia Tech Goodwin Hall Living Laboratory. As the world's most instrumented building for vibration, the Goodwin Hall facility can accumulate more than 60TB of vibration data per year, forming a fertile ground for researchers to explore how humans interact with the built environment [8]. Since this research field is inherently multidisciplinary and explorative, we must not dictate how researchers build the algorithm and use the data. This makes prebuilt analysis inappropriate, but it does make virtualization and on-demand analysis necessary.

Following our prior system architecture, implementation, and evaluation, we added Amazon EC2 Container Service (ECS), Amazon cloud's support for Docker, to our technology stack. We then dockerized the three simple algorithms used to test 1) ingestion of the data into a Fedora 4 based repository and extraction of technical metadata, 2) calculation of the maximum, minimum, mean, and median value for each of the sensor data file, and 3) visualization of the data file by plotting the HDF5 source files into a diagram, then ingesting the diagram back to the repository. The source code developed for this paper is openly available from Github at `https://github.com/VTUL/ICADL`. The dockerized code can run on any system supporting Docker, but due to the data co-location requirement, it is much cheaper to deploy in a cloud environment.

We evaluated the performance of the analysis algorithms against 160GB sensor vibration data, collected from one single channel over 24 hours. The data are stored in Amazon S3 and linked from a Fedora 4 based metadata repository running on an EC2 instance in the same availability zone. Instead of provisioning 1, 2, 4, 8, and 16 EC2 instances to perform the heavyweight analysis, we ran up to 4 EC2 instances; each runs up to 4 ECS tasks to perform the same analysis. Table 1 shows the total time required for each test to analyze all the data.

Table 1. Time in seconds spent to complete the computation of the test cases

Test	Number of ECS Tasks				
	1	2	4	8	16
1	240.33	180.52	65.86	33.75	16.68
2	676.07	612.52	314.93	159.18	74.03
3	83263.11	53572.53	35035.10	10780.09	5447.75

As in the prior study [4], the results clearly show a linear scalability with the increase in the number of ECS tasks. The only significant exception is when the number of ECS tasks equals 2, where the test case is completed within more than half the duration of using a single ECS task. When we double the number of ECS tasks to 4 and further, the linear scalability reverts to what is expected. We initially thought this might be a mistake, but repeated tests show the same phenomenon. This exception may be due to certain Amazon ECS oddities.

Running the same test using ECS also results in about 1/3, 100%, or 10% longer running time respectively than what the heavyweight approach results in using the same number of EC2 instances as ECS tasks. However, the total cost is much lower, since here we mostly use only 1/4 of EC2 instances as was used in the heavyweight approach. The extra time is expected, since the lightweight approach shares the same EC2 instance within multiple ECS tasks. Although data processing may be more efficient by fully utilizing the shared CPU and memory, the network bandwidth and disk I/O becomes a bottleneck. This is clearly illustrated in both Test 1 and Test 2, where copying data from the storage to the processing node then reading into the CPU clearly dominates the workload. When the number crunching outweighs the network and disk I/O, as is the case in Test 3, the efficiency gain of the lightweight approach is much more evident.

The lightweight approach described here is similar to the yt project [9], although the latter is only targeting data size in the range of tens of gigabytes, in which case moving data around is not as expensive as in most big data management scenarios.

5   Summary and Future Work

As the Docker technology gains popularity in IT operations, digital libraries should consider leveraging its strengths to facilitate use and reuse driven data management. The lightweight approach described in this paper allows cheaper and more efficient execution of user submitted algorithms against the big data sets archived in a digital library. We will conduct more experiments using algorithms from the domain scientists to evaluate the actual performance of this approach and gain deeper understanding of its benefits and limitations.

References

1. Akers, K.G., et al.: Building Support for Research Data Management: Biographies of Eight Research Universities. International Journal of Digital Curation 9(2), 171–191 (2014)
2. Higgins, S.: The DCC curation lifecycle model. International Journal of Digital Curation. 3(1), 134–140 (2008)
3. Farcas, C., et al.: Biomedical cyberinfrastructure challenges. In: Proceedings of the Conference on Extreme Science and Engineering Discovery Environment: Gateway to Discovery, pp. 6:1–6:4. ACM, New York (2013)
4. Xie, Z., et al.: Towards use and reuse driven big data management. In: Proceedings of the 15th ACM/IEEE-CS Joint Conference on Digital Libraries, pp. 65–74. ACM, New York (2015)
5. ISO 14721:2003: Open Archival Information System - Reference Model (2003)
6. Barga, R., et al.: The Client and the Cloud: Democratizing Research Computing. IEEE Internet Computing 15(1), 72–75 (2011)
7. Turnbull, J.: The Docker Book: Containerization is the new virtualization. James Turnbull (2014)
8. Hamilton, J.M., et al.: Characterization of human motion through floor vibration. In: Catbas, F.N. (ed.) Dynamics of Civil Structures, vol. 4, pp. 163–170. Springer International Publishing (2014)
9. Turk, M.J., et al.: yt: A Multi-code Analysis Toolkit for Astrophysical Simulation Data. ApJS. 192(1), 9 (2011)

Identification of Tweets that Mention Books: An Experimental Comparison of Machine Learning Methods

Shuntaro Yada[✉] and Kyo Kageura

Graduate School of Education, The University of Tokyo, 7-3-1 Hongo,
Bunkyo-ku, Tokyo 113-0033, Japan
{shuntaroy,kyo}@p.u-tokyo.ac.jp

Abstract. In this paper, we address the task of the identification of tweets on Twitter that mention books (TMB) among tweets that contain the same strings as full book titles. Although this task can be treated as a kind of Named Entity Recognition, the fact that book titles consist of ordinary expressions (such as "The Girl on the Train") makes the task harder. Furthermore, if tweets are gathered through a dictionary-based search, the tweets that contain the same strings as full book titles are often spam. However, assuming a complete list of book titles (i.e. from a union catalogue from a library or commercial bibliographic data from a book store), this task can be solved by text classification. Thus, we proposed a two-step pipeline consisting of spam filtering and TMB classification based on supervised learning with a small amount of labelled data. We constructed optimal classifiers by comparing combinations of four proven supervised learning methods with different features. Given the difficulty of the task, our pipeline performed highly (about 0.7 in terms of F-score).

Keywords: Machine Learning · Japanese text classification · Named entity recognition on twitter · Book title identification

1 Introduction

In this paper, we comparatively examine four machine learning (ML) methods with different combinations of features in the task of identifying tweets on Twitter that mention books (henceforth TMB).

We are currently developing a book recommendation system that aims to simulate the situation where a person discovers books by chance through daily informal conversation with her/his friends [1]. We are observing drastic changes in the environment of reading (or discovering books). Information seeking is becoming more and more personalized in general. With the advent and spread of e-books, we have fewer opportunities to be exposed to books by chance and/or unconsciously[1]. Although we

---

[1] Online information is in general optimised for those who intentionally look for specific information, and mechanisms to promote accidental encountering with further information (e.g. PR banners and links) are arranged from the point of view of information providers [2].

© Springer International Publishing Switzerland 2015
R.B. Allen et al. (Eds.): ICADL 2015, LNCS 9469, pp. 278–288, 2015.
DOI: 10.1007/978-3-319-27974-9_30

do not yet exactly know to what extent passive and unconscious exposure to books may contribute to a person's reading habits, this contribution could be substantial. It is therefore important to design and construct mechanisms and environments which emulate or simulate the experience of physical exposure to books in the digital world. We proposed the above system based on the idea that it is likely that one's social capital will unconsciously inspire one's behaviour. The identification of TMBs, which we report on in this paper, constitutes a core technical module of this system. Our focus is Japanese book titles and Japanese Twitter.

An informal observation of Japanese tweets revealed that the majority of TMBs contain book titles in full, while a small portion uses informal abbreviations of titles (e.g. "Gatsby" for "The Great Gatsby") and/or combinations of circumstantial information (e.g. "Gatsby published by Kadokawa" or "the latest novel by Haruki Murakami")[2]. We focus here on the task of identifying TMBs that contain full book titles; in addition to the fact that they are the majority, this task will allow us to gain insight into identifying tweets that do not contain full book titles.

The identification of tweets containing full book titles is naturally defined as the task of identifying the book titles in tweets, i.e. a kind of named entity (NE) recognition task [3]. In the case of our current task, the existence of an up-to-date, comprehensive list of book titles can be assumed (by collecting book titles from the union catalogues of libraries and commercial bibliographic data including the site `amazon.co.jp`). Therefore, it is easy to gather tweets containing book titles in full from Twitter. The major problem comes from the fact that a substantial portion of book titles consists of ordinary expressions such as "Kidnapping" or "A Night in Paris". Furthermore, while TMBs seldom appear within a given user's tweet timeline, tweets that literally contain full book titles are often spam. Thus, the major issue that we have to address here is classifying tweets that contain strings which are the same as book titles into TMBs and non-TMBs (tweets that contain strings that happen to be identical to full book titles but do not mention books) with high precision and high recall.

Taking these factors into consideration, we introduced a two-step pipeline consisting of spam filtering and TMB/non-TMB classification based on supervised learning with a small amount of labelled data, and examined the combination of features and learning algorithms. We have shown that the optimal combination of the learning algorithm and features in our two-step pipeline framework achieves a reasonably high — in fact very high, if we take into account the difficulty of the task — performance, both in terms of both recall and precision. We have also suggested that the methods proposed here can be applied to similar tasks dealing with different NE types, such as TV programs, films, and song titles.

The rest of the paper is organised as follows. In Section 2, we briefly review related work. Section 3 describes the setup of our experiment, including the choice of ML methods and features. Section 4 describes and examines the results of our experiments. Section 5 concludes the paper.

---

[2] Manga and young-adult novels are the exception as they tend to be referred to by abbreviated titles.

2   Related Work

Application-oriented text classification work has been carried out in relation to a variety of tasks, including the classification of news reports into topic categories, opinion mining, sentiment analysis and spam filtering [4,5]. Such ML methods as naive Bayes [6], maximum entropy modelling (MaxEnt) [7], Support Vector Machine (SVM) [8] and Random Forest [9] have been widely used. These methods have also been applied to the classification of tweets in Twitter, for identifying spam tweets [10,11], or for sentiment and opinion analysis [12,13], showing different results in terms of ML methods, depending on their applications and parameter settings.

There are also studies that use tweet classification for the identification of specific information most typically represented by NEs, including the identification of useful information related to software products [14], for influenza patients [15], and related to health conditions of Twitter users [16]. While these studies are related to our task, there has been no work addressing the identification of TMBs.

Liu et al. (2011) and Ritter et al. (2011) reported NER from Twitter [5], [17]. They pointed out three characteristics of tweets data which make NER difficult, i.e. informal expression, small number of characters, and infrequent occurrence of NEs (with the exception of personal and location names). The situation for identifying TMBs is the same.

There are many studies that target particular types of NEs, e.g. the identification of biochemical-substance names [18,19] and film titles with some other relevant NEs [20]. While there are studies on the identification of bibliographic information, most are concerned with academic papers [21,22]. There are some works devoted to the identification of book titles [23,24], but none deal with tweets.

3   Methodology

3.1   Data Set

We first collected 74,330 Japanese tweets containing the same strings as book titles from the Twitter Streaming API (from 30th April to 5th May, 2015), using the Japanese morphological analyser MeCab[3] with a comprehensive book title dictionary generated from the bibliographic database of the Japanese union catalogue[4] [25].

For manual annotation, we selected tweets containing only one book title string (70,844 tweets). Then, we chose the tweets containing book titles that were mentioned less than three times in total (10,791 tweets). As the distribution of books has a 'long tail', we can cover a wide variety of cases by selecting low frequency titles.

Finally, the authors annotated 8,528 tweets manually so that each tweet was labelled of 'TMB' or 'Spam,' or was unlabelled. The label 'Spam' is applied when (i) the main contents of the tweet are affiliate marketing links or (ii) the tweet is posted by an automated program. We obtained 350 TMBs, 4,040 Spam tweets and 4,138 unlabelled tweets. Annotated tweets can be described using the matrix below (Table 1) with two points of view: tweet author, and whether the tweet mentions books.

---

[3] http://taku910.github.io/mecab/
[4] This dictionary is not strictly kept up to date, but we assume it to be within the margin of error due to the small proportion of the newest books.

From the standpoint of the system we are developing, in Table 1, only 'TMB' tweets are targeted while 'Spam TMB,' 'Spam' and 'TnMB' are excluded. This is because we aim to extract tweets that mention books in the context of daily conversation in which many topics are referred to [1]. While Spam TMBs do refer to books, they do not satisfy this criterion.

Table 1. Descriptive matrix of tweets in our data set.

	Mentioning Books	**Not Mentioning Books**
Spam	Spam Tweets Mentioning Books (Spam TMB)	Spam Tweets Not Mentioning Books (Spam)
Not Spam	Tweets Mentioning Books (TMB)	Tweets Not Mentioning Books (TnMB)

3.2   Pipeline

According to our preliminary research [25] and the manual annotation, spam tweets appear much more frequently than TMBs, but can be easily detected thanks to their format. On the other hand, there is great variety in the textual expression of TMBs. Hence, we propose the following two-step pipeline: (1) Spam filtering (Spam + Spam TnMB vs. TMB + TnMB); (2) TMB/non-TMB classification (TMB vs. TnMB). In Section 4, we examine the effectiveness of this approach through comparative experiments focusing on both precision and recall from the point of view of the overall aim of our application.

3.3   Machine Learning Methods

For our task, we chose four ML methods that have been frequently applied and have performed well in text classification (as we saw in Section 2): Naive Bayes, MaxEnt, SVM, and Random Forest. These classifiers can be applied to TMB/non-TMB classification as well as to spam detection. Although there is great diversity in the textual expressions of TMBs, word-level features related to mentioning book references are still considered to be still relevant in distinguishing TMBs from TnMBs. As for the implementation of ML algorithms, we utilised scikit-learn[5] Python library.

We tuned the following parameters (notation provided in parentheses) for each ML method in the first phase of experiments. We will call it Phase 1, and its detailed procedure will be shown in Section 4.1.

- **Naive Bayes:** Additive smoothing (α).
- **MaxEnt:** The norm used in the penalisation (henceforth 'NP'; L1 or L2 term was used) and the inverse of regularisation strength (C).
- **SVM:** The penalty parameter of the error term (C) and the RBF kernel coefficient (γ)[6].

---

[5] http://scikit-learn.org/

[6] We use a radial basis function (RBF) kernel for SVM because it showed better result in our preliminary experiment than other kernels such as linear, polynomial, and sigmoid.

- **Random Forest:** The number of trees in the forest (N_t) and the function deciding the maximum number of features to consider when looking for the best split (henceforth 'MF'; we used 'sqrt': $f(x) = \sqrt{x}$ or 'log2': $f(x) = \log_2 x$).

Two points should be noted here. First, the multinomial model is used for naive Bayes, which generally performs better than the Bernoulli model in text classification [4]. Second, we conducted feature reduction using Latent Semantic Analysis (LSA) when applying Random Forest.

3.4   Feature Selection

We selected a different feature set for each classifier. As for spam filtering, we mainly used URL-based and user-based features because of their popularity in spam detection on Twitter [26]. In TMB/non-TMB classification, tokens in tweets were used as main features.

Features Used for Spam Filtering

- **URL domain:** Almost all spam tweets contain URLs, and lead users to some promotional sites or fraudulent websites. These URLs are diverse but can be summarised by their domain.
- **URL query keys:** Many spam tweets have affiliate links. These links consist of query keys that identify affiliate program user-IDs. This can be utilised to distinguish links that are simply introducing books and inducing readers to make a purchase.
- **SSL:** Since fraudulent and spam websites seem to be less likely to use SSL certification, we added some weight to links using SSL. We computed the ratio of the numbers of SSL-certified URLs contained in each tweets.
- **Hashtag count:** We exploit this frequently-utilised feature because spam tweets tend to contain a relatively high number of hashtags [10].
- **Following and follower count:** Twitter rules[7] says that if an account shows "randomly or aggressively following" behaviour, it may be a spam account. This behaviour can be indicated by unbalanced following and follower counts.
- **Application name:** Our preliminary investigation showed that most spam tweets are posted via automatic bot applications [25].

Features Used for TMB/non-TMB Classification

- **URL domain:** We found that many TMBs also have URLs linking the tweets to book-related websites such as book stores and book review sites, while URLs in TnMBs refer to other media such as news articles and videos [25].
- **Application name:** TMBs are posted not only via official or third-party client applications, but also via social reading services. The latter case is not observed with TnMBs.

---

[7] https://support.twitter.com/articles/253501-twitter

- **Tokens within tweets:** To utilise tokens as a feature, we conducted three kinds of preprocessing due to their importance in informal text such as tweets [27]. We first normalised the differences in character width, as this is just typographical variations. Second, we replaced all blank characters (space, return) with %S% so as to consider them as a feature, since these characters are explicitly used for formatting in a Japanese context. Thirdly, after the work [10], the URLs and mentioned user names with the @ symbol were replaced with %URL% and %REPLY% respectively. We then applied morphological analysis and obtained tokens from each Japanese tweet, from which we extracted the following additional features as options (henceforth *token options*). We tried all combinations of these options with each ML method, in order to find the best combinations (Section 4).
  - **POS tag:** Distinguishing the same strings using Part-Of-Speech (POS) tags can be effective. This option adds POS tags to each token string.
  - **NE abstraction:** If common NE types are detected through morphological analysis, then these NEs are replaced with their class name, for example, "person's name" or "organisation name".
  - **Identifying tokens surrounding the title:** Each tweet in our data set contains full book title string, and the tokens around the strings tend to be different for TMBs and non-TMBs. In this option, the title string is converted into %TITLE%, and postfixes of '-/+' are added to every token if it appears before/after the title respectively.

We computed the TFIDF values of above features except *Following and follower count* and *SSL*, the computation of which has two options. The first is whether or not all the non-zero term counts (TF) are set to 1, which is denoted by *BinaryTF* (True or False).

The second is *MaxDF*, which means that the terms are ignored if they have a higher DF value than this threshold (1.0 or 0.8). Note that we did not use tokens in tweets from spam filtering because they did not contribute to classification performance in our preliminary experiment.

4   Experiments

4.1   Experimental Setup

We conducted experiments in two phases. In the first phase (Phase 1), we carried out two experiments in order to find the best combination of parameters and feature set for the ML methods for (a) spam filtering and (b) TMB/non-TMB classification. In the second phase (Phase 2), based on the results obtained in the experiments in Phase 1, we evaluated the performance of our proposed method, i.e. (c) the two-step pipeline consisting of spam filtering and TMB/non-TMB classification. For comparison, we conducted a controlled experiment in which (d) spam-included tweet data were directly classified into TMBs and non-TMBs.

In other words, the Phase 1 experiments were carried out to find the best choice of methods, while the Phase 2 experiments were carried out to confirm the actual usability of our proposed method in the TMB recognition task we defined within the framework of our application.

Phase 1

- **Experiment (a):** To find the best ML algorithm and combination of parameters and feature set for spam filtering, exhaustive grid searches were conducted using all of the tweet data. We defined the best combinations by their F-score, or the harmonic mean of precision and recall.[8]
- **Experiment (b):** Using spam-excluded data, we conducted grid searches for the TMB classifier as well as Experiment (a). The F-score was also used in defining the best combination.

Phase 2

- **Experiment (c):** A two-step pipeline was built for each of the best classifiers obtained in Phase 1, and this pipeline was applied to spam-included data. In the training stage, the spam filter used spam-included training data, while the TMB/non-TMB classifier used a spam-excluded subset of the same training data set as with that of the spam filter. In the first step of the pipeline, the spam filter predicted spam tweets, and removed them from the test data. In the second step, the TMB/non-TMB classifier predicted the TMBs. Evaluation was conducted by average precision, recall, and F-score, in addition to TMB loss rate. The Precision-Recall curve was also shown for further diagnosis.
- **Experiment (d):** This was intended to be a controlled experiment to Experiment (c); all TMB/non-TMB classifiers with the best settings (obtained in Phase 1) were trained on spam-excluded tweets and tested on spam-included tweets. We computed the average precision, recall, and F-score.

In all experiments, classifiers were trained and tested within our data set, through 10-fold cross validation manner with random and stratified sampling.

4.2   Evaluation

The result of spam filtering in Experiment (a) (Table 2) shows that MaxEnt performed best in spam filtering. The score (0.978 F-score) reached a level equivalent to other spam filtering research (over 0.9 F-score) [10,11]. As for the TMB/non-TMB classification in Experiment (b) (Table 3), SVM performed the highest (0.699 F-score). The tokens surrounding the title turned out to be an important feature for identifying TMBs. We can also observe that BinaryTF contributes to every ML method. This seems to correspond to the fact that each expression related to books (such as "read" and "book") tends to appear at most once within each TMB.

The result of Experiment (c) (Table 4) shows that our pipeline performed very highly in comparison with Experiment (d) (Table 5). In addition, for practical application to our book recommendation system, this performance can be called as desirable based on the following three points:

(a) Spam filtering also performed very highly in terms of TMB loss (only 5.7%; Step 1 in Table 4) as well as spam removing scores;

---

[8]   Precision is defined as "true positive / (true positive + false positive)," while recall is defined as "true positive / (true positive + false negative)." F-score is "(2 • precision • recall) / (precision + recall)," which can summarise the values of both precision and recall.

(b) Although the TMB/non-TMB classifier still required improvement in the high recall area (Fig. 1, 2), its performance (about 0.7 F-score; Step 2 in Table 4) is very promising considering the small amount of training data;

(c) Therefore, the Precision-Recall curve drawing 'shoulder' in the upper right of Fig. 1, 2 suggests that further improvement can be achieved while maintaining both precision and recall.

Table 2. The best parameters, feature sets and F-scores for the four ML methods in spam filtering. Notations in parameters and TFIDF options are the same as in Section 3.4.

ML methods	Parameters	TFIDF options		F-score
		BinaryTF	MaxDF	
Naive Bayes	$\alpha = 0$	True	1.0	0.772
MaxEnt	$C = 10.0$, NP: L1	False	0.8	**0.978**
SVM	$C = 10.0$, $\gamma = 0.001$	True	1.0	0.542
Random Forest	MF: sqrt, $N_t = 100$	False	0.8	0.937

Table 3. The best parameters, feature set and F-scores for the four ML method in TMB/non-TMB classifier trained and tested on spam-excluded tweets. 'Title' in token options denotes *identifying tokens surround title*. 'NEabst' denotes *NE abstraction*.

ML methods	Parameters	TFIDF options		Token options			F-score
		BinaryTF	MaxDF	Title	NEabst	POS	
Naive Bayes	$\alpha = 0.05$	True	0.8	True	True	True	0.577
MaxEnt	$C = 10.0$, NP: L1	True	0.8	True	False	False	0.656
SVM	$C = 10.0$, $\gamma = 0.1$	True	1.0	True	False	False	**0.699**
Ran. Forest	MF: sqrt, $N_t = 100$	True	1.0	True	True	True	0.503

Table 4. Performance of the two-step pipeline consisting of MaxEnt and SVM. TMB loss in Step 2 are shown by $1 - Recall$

Steps	Precision	Recall	F-score	TMB loss
1. Spam filtering	0.978	0.978	0.978	**0.057**
2. TMB/non-TMB classification	0.698	0.681	**0.686**	(0.319)

Table 5. The performance of direct TMB/non-TMB classification (trained on spam-excluded tweets) for the four ML methods with the best parameters and feature sets.

ML methods	Precision	Recall	F-score
Naive Bayes	0.287	0.426	0.342
MaxEnt	0.291	0.161	0.389
SVM	0.331	0.666	0.439
Random Forest	0.892	0.343	0.490

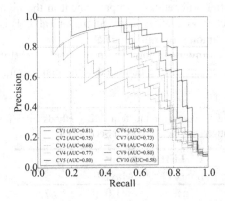
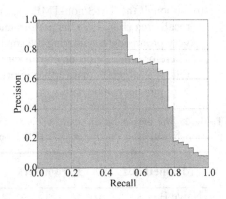

Fig. 1. Precision-Recall curve with Area Under the Curve (AUC) of all iterations of cross validation (CV) in Experiment (c).

Fig. 2. Precision-Recall curve of the iteration resulting median AUC (0.73; CV7 in Fig. 1) in Experiment (c).

5   Conclusions

In this paper, we tackled the task of identifying Japanese tweets that mention books from spam-included tweets, which can be defined as one type of NE (book title) recognition. We proposed a two-step pipeline consisting of spam filtering and TMB/non-TMB classification, and observed that the best combination is MaxEnt and SVM, which performed desirably for our book recommendation system in terms of F-score (0.686).

While this paper focused on the identification of book titles, our methods can be readily extended into the recognition of a wider range of document titles, such as research paper titles. Our results should also be useful for other, similar kinds of NE, such as TV programs, films, and song titles, which tend to take the form of ordinary phrases. The combination of spam filtering and TMB/non-TMB classification will also be applicable in recognising these kinds of NE in tweets.

In this research, we excluded TMBs containing abbreviated book titles. Although they are not the majority, in order to cover them, we plan to build a dictionary of abbreviated titles automatically by exploiting redirects of online knowledge bases such as Wikipedia [28]. Furthermore, applying the pipeline to our remaining unlabelled tweets, we also plan to augmentation of training TMB data, which will improve classification performance.

References

1. Yada, S.: Development of a book recommendation system to inspire "infrequent readers". In: Tuamsuk, K., Jatowt, A., Rasmussen, E. (eds.) ICADL 2014. LNCS, vol. 8839, pp. 399–404. Springer, Heidelberg (2014)
2. Adobe: Click Here: The State of Online Advertising. Tech. rep., Adobe Systems Incorporated (2013)

3. Nadeau, D., Sekine, S.: A Survey of Named Entity Eecognition and Classification. Ling-visticae Investigationes **30**(1991), 3–26 (2007)
4. Aggarwal, C.C., Zhai, C.: A survey of text classification algorithms. In: Aggarwal, C.C., Zhai, C. (eds.) Mining Text Data SE - 6, pp. 163–222. Springer US, Boston (2012)
5. Liu, X., Zhang, S., Wei, F., Zhou, M.: Recognizing named entities in tweets. In: 49th Annual Meeting of the Association for Computational Linguistics, pp. 359–367. ACL, June 2011
6. McCallum, A., Nigam, K.: A comparison of event models for naive bayes text classification. In: AAAI Workshop on Learning for Text Categorization, pp. 41–48 (1998)
7. Nigam, K.: Using maximum entropy for text classification. In: Workshop on Machine Learning for Information Filtering, pp. 61–67 (1999)
8. Cortes, C., Vapnik, V.: Support-Vector Networks. Machine Learning **20**(3), 273–297 (1995)
9. Breiman, L.: Random Forests. Machine Learning **45**(1), 5–32 (2001)
10. McCord, M., Chuah, M.: Spam detection on twitter using traditional classifiers. In: Calero, J.M., Yang, L.T., Mármol, F.G., García Villalba, L.J., Li, A.X., Wang, Y. (eds.) ATC 2011. LNCS, vol. 6906, pp. 175–186. Springer, Heidelberg (2011)
11. Lea, D.: Detecting spam bots in online social networking sites: a machine learning approach. In: Foresti, S., Jajodia, S. (eds.) Data and Applications Security and Privacy XXIV. LNCS, vol. 6166, pp. 335–342. Springer, Heidelberg (2010)
12. Go, A., Bhayani, R., Huang, L.: Twitter Sentiment Classification Using Distant Supervision. Tech. rep., Stanford (2009)
13. Pak, A., Paroubek, P.: Twitter as a corpus for sentiment analysis and opinion mining. In: Calzolari, N., Choukri, K., Maegaard, B., Mariani, J., Odijk, J., Piperidis, S., Rosner, M., Tapias, D. (eds.) The 17th International Conference on Language Resources and Evaluation, pp. 1320–1326. ELRA, Valletta (2010)
14. Prasetyo, P.K., Lo, D., Achananuparp, P., Tian, Y., Lim, E.P.: Automatic classification of software related microblogs. In: 28th International Conference on Software Maintenance, pp. 596–599. IEEE, September 2012
15. Aramaki, E., Maskawa, S., Morita, M.: Twitter catches the flu: detecting influenza epidemics using twitter. In: The Conference on Empirical Methods in Natural Language Processing, pp. 1568–1576. ACL, Stroudsburg (2011)
16. Tuarob, S., Tucker, C.S., Salathe, M., Ram, N.: An Ensemble Heterogeneous Classification Methodology for Discovering Health-related Knowledge in Social Media Messages. Journal of Biomedical Informatics **49**, 255–268 (2014)
17. Ritter, A., Clark, S., Mausam, Etzioni, O.: Named entity recognition in tweets: an experimental study. In: Conference on Empirical Methods in Natural Language Processing, pp. 1524–1534. ACL, July 2011
18. Kou, Z., Cohen, W.W., Murphy, R.F.: High-recall Protein Entity Recognition Using a Dictionary. Bioinformatics **21**(Suppl 1), i266–i273 (2005)
19. Yoshida, K., Tsujii, J.: Reranking for biomedical named-entity recognition. In: Workshop on Biological, Translational, and Clinical Language Processing, pp. 209–216. ACL, June 2007
20. Murai, H., Kawashima, T., Kudou, A.: Quantitative Analysis Concerning the Relationships and Roles of Pronouns in Movie and Theater Critiques (in Japanese). Journal of Japan Society of Information and Knowledge **22**(1), 23–43 (2012)
21. Abekawa, T., Nanba, H., Takamura, H., Okumura, M.: Automatic Extraction of Bibliography with Machine Learning (in Japanese). IPSJ SIG Notes **2003**(98), 83–90 (2003)

22. Kousha, K., Thelwall, M.: An Automatic Method for Extracting Citations from Google Books. Journal of the Association for Information Science and Technology 66(2), 309–320 (2015)
23. Brin, S.: Extracting patterns and relations from the world wide web. In: Atzeni, P., Mendelzon, A.O., Mecca, G. (eds.) WebDB 1998. LNCS, vol. 1590, pp. 172–183. Springer, Heidelberg (1999)
24. Downey, D., Broadhead, M., Etzioni, O.: Locating complex named entities in web text. In: International Joint Conference on Artificial Intelligence, pp. 2733−2739 (2007)
25. Yada, S., Kageura, K.: Categorization of tweets mentioning books based on text clustering (in japanese). In: IEICE Technical Committee of Natural Language Understanding and Models of Communication, pp. 61−66 (2015)
26. Chinnasamy, D.G., Mohanraj, V.: A Survey on Spam Detection in Twitter. International Journal of Computer Science and Business Informatics 14(1), 92–102 (2014)
27. Ostrowski, D.A.: Feature selection for twitter classification. In: Eighth International Conference on Semantic Computing, pp. 267–272. IEEE, June 2014
28. Kashioka, H.: Analysis of synonym obtained from redirection of wikipedia (in japanese). In: The 13th Annual Meeting of the Association for Natural Language Processing, pp. 1094−1096 (2007)

Mining Variations in Hangul Orthography

Juyoung An and Robert B. Allen

Department of Library and Information Science, Yonsei University, Seoul, South Korea
anjy@yonsei.ac.kr, rba@boballen.info

Abstract. There are many nuances in Korean Hangul orthography. While there has been an attempt at standardization by the National Language Deliberation Council, usage has continued to evolve. We collected data from Twitter to show that usage sometimes differs greatly from the standard and that while the Council has proposed revisions of the standard on the basis of usage, there are other cases with an even greater imbalance usage which the Council did not change. Thus, we recommend that the Council consider the results of text mining studies as a part of their deliberations.

Keywords: Hangul · Korean orthography · Text-Mining

Contemporary written Korean (Hangul) follows a phonetic script which was developed in 1443. It was used to a limited extent until the 1940s and since then has become widespread. Overall, Hangul has been very successful and has helped to reduce illiteracy in Korea, but in some cases the most appropriate orthography is difficult to determine [1]. There are several reasons for this. (a) There are many homonyms and people introduce variations in the written form for clarity. For example, the words '자장면' and '짜장면' are both used to refer to a specific type of noodle. (b) People tend to write the words as they pronounce them. Because it is hard to pronounce all of final consonants those final consonants may be lost or written inconsistently. (c) People tend to write words in a way from which they can easily infer the meaning. '차지다' (sticky) is an example of this last point: because the word for sticky rice cakes is 찰떡, the word sticky is sometimes written as '찰지다'.

Because of the difficulties in orthography, the National Language Deliberation Council was established to recommend standard usage. According to the first provision of the *Korean orthography rule*, there are two principles: idealism and opportunism. In other words, idealism is the principle that all notations have to be the same and unified regardless of the settings of the notation. Opportunism asserts that the notation has to follow the common pronunciation of the people. [2,3] As a result, the National Language Deliberation Council held a large meeting to modify some rules on Korean orthography as the language has evolved. However, the Council typically does not systematically consider detailed data about usage in its deliberations.

In order to examine the nature and frequency of these orthographic inconsistencies, a large sample of Korean Tweets was collected from Twitter. Specifically, we examined Tweets from 2010 to 2014. To find terms where there was likely confusion, several seed

© Springer International Publishing Switzerland 2015
R.B. Allen et al. (Eds.): ICADL 2015, LNCS 9469, pp. 289–290, 2015.
DOI: 10.1007/978-3-319-27974-9

texts such as news articles and news groups about these issues were examined and some filtering was applied. For instance, words imported from Chinese were excluded. After that, the larger corpus of Korea Tweets was searched for these terms.

In 2011, the Council recommended making '짜장면' the standard form over '자장면' because of the discrepancy in usage frequency. In the Twitter corpus, we found that the frequency of '짜장면' is about 3.3 times the frequency of '자장면'. However, as shown in the first row of Table 1, we found that there were quite a few other words where there was as much or greater confusion in usage. Based on our observations, we believe that text mining could help the members of Council make recommendations.

Table 1. Many non-standard words occur more often than the corresponding standard word.

Recommendations	Non-Standard words	Semantic Confusions
Words to be modified from Non-standard word to Standard word (3.3<value)	겨땀, 궁시렁거리다, 넝쿨, **되려***, **모듬***, 씨부리다, **어리버리***, 우겨넣다, **찌질하다***, 체신머리, 흐리멍텅하다	곱등이, 귓불, 주구장창, **찰지다***
Words which might be modified from Non-standard to Standard word (1<value<3.3)	건네다, 닥달하다, 또아리, 뽀개다, 설레임, 아둥바둥, 오뚜기, 으시대다, 짜집기	되갚음, 한 끝 차이, 줄임말
Words which do not have to be modified (value<1)	넙다랗다, 돌맹이, 뒤치닥꺼리, 뒤치다거리, 뒷치닥걸이, 맛뵈기, 맛배기, 맛빼기, 배끼다, 새침대기, 어짜피, 얼버무리다, 여지껏, 우뢰, 임마, 졸립다, 짧다랗다, 웅큼	

References

1. Lee, J.H.: The Lesson and Process of the Revision of German Orthography (2013) http://www.korean.go.kr/nkview/nklife/2013_1/23_0111.html
2. Kim, J.N.: The Principle of the Korean Orthography: Centered on the Interpretation of the First Provision of General Rules. The Society of Korean Semantics **27**, 21–44 (2008)
3. Kim, J.S.: A History of the Hangeul Orthography and A Proposition for Its Amendments. The Society of Korean Language and Culture **37**, 111–128 (2008)

Development of an Imaginary Beings Knowledge Structure

Wirapong Chansanam[1] and Kulthida Tuamsuk[2(✉)]

[1] Information Technology Department, Chaiyaphum Rajabhat University,
Chaiyaphum, Thailand
wirapongc@cpru.ac.th
[2] Information and Communication Department, Digital Humanities Research Group,
Khon Kaen University, Khon Kaen, Thailand
kultua@kku.ac.th

Abstract. This paper presents an Imaginary Beings knowledge structure, expanded from the knowledge domain of "Belief Culture" in the authors' previous study. The knowledge was derived from several resources, content analysis was used, and then the knowledge structure was implemented in the KOS using the Idealized Cognitive model. This preliminary study found that the structure of knowledge on imaginary beings contains 5 sub-categories and 120 instances.

Keywords: Imaginary beings · Knowledge organization · Idealized cognitive model

1 Introduction

Several works have attempted to define the scope and meaning of belief culture and superheroes, but they varied based on the understanding of the people in each society and the context that surrounds them, such as religion, ethnic background, age, and geographic settings [1]. Imaginary beings, one of the aspects of belief culture, are creatures of the human imagination: a person or thing that exists only in legends, myths, fiction, movies, or comic books. The definition of modern imaginary beings is a made-up character having super powers and abilities, found in fantasy, science fiction, or children's literature. These kinds of literature and media are having psychological and social impacts on both children and adults [2]. Therefore, understanding the definition and scope of knowledge on imaginary beings in the old world and the modern world is a critical issue in humanity studies.

Borges' book, published in 1969, contained descriptions of 120 mythical beasts from folklore and literature [3]. Other than this, there were very few studies, especially those that included the contemporary imaginary beings. This study attempts to work on content analysis, and then organize the knowledge on contemporary imaginary beings using the knowledge organization concept. The findings will be used for ontology development in the next step of this research.

© Springer International Publishing Switzerland 2015
R.B. Allen et al. (Eds.): ICADL 2015, LNCS 9469, pp. 291–293, 2015.
DOI: 10.1007/978-3-319-27974-9

2   Methodology

The content analysis of knowledge on imaginary beings was done based on several resources, including the *Book of Imaginary Beings* [3], and electronic resources containing information relating to the appearances and characteristics of imaginary beings in the old world and modern world. The knowledge structure of imaginary beings was constructed in expansion of the "Belief Culture" knowledge structure in the previous study [1], and then implemented in the KOS using the Idealized Cognitive model [4].

3   Preliminary Findings

In the previous study, the knowledge domain of "Belief Culture" comprised of 3 classes: Object entities, Beings entities, and Process entities [1]. The knowledge on "Imaginary Beings" in this study is classified in the "Being entity" by its appearances' association. The knowledge of "Imaginary beings" is divided into 5 sub-categories including: Human, Animal, Plant, Object, and Multiple mixed. One-hundred and twenty instances and their values are also listed. An example is shown in Figure 1.

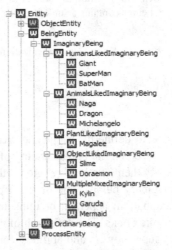

Fig. 1. An Imaginary beings knowledge structure

4   Future Work

This paper presents a preliminary study on the knowledge structure of imaginary beings contained in Borges' book and other resources. The details of knowledge structure and description will be done in the next step of the research. In addition, the ontology of knowledge on imaginary beings will also be developed for future semantic knowledge retrieval.

Acknowledgements. This research is funded by the Digital Humanities Research group of Khon Kaen University, Thailand.

References

1. Chansanam, W., Tuamsuk, K., Kwiecien, K., Ruangrajitpakorn, T., Supnithi, T.: Development of the belief culture ontology and its application: case study of the greater mekong subregion. In: Supnithi, T., Yamaguchi, T., Pan, J.Z., Wuwongse, V., Buranarach, M. (eds.) JIST 2014. LNCS, vol. 8943, pp. 297–310. Springer, Heidelberg (2015)
2. Fleck, A.: Effects of Superheroes on Children. http://everydaylife.globalpost.com/effects-superheroes-children-27905.html
3. Borges, J.L., Guerrero, M.: The Book of Imaginary Beings. Dutton, New York (1969)
4. Lakoff, G.: Women, Fire, and Dangerous Things: What Categories Reveal about the Mind. University of Chicago Press, Chicago (1987)

Semantic Knowledge Retrieval for Belief Culture

Wirapong Chansanam[1], Kulthida Tuamsuk[2(✉)], Kanyarat Kwiecien[2],
Taneth Ruangrajitpakorn[3], and Thepchai Supnithi[3]

[1] Chaiyaphum Rajabhat University, Chaiyaphum, Thailand
wirapongc@cpru.ac.th
[2] Khon Kaen University, Khon Kaen, Thailand
{kultua,kandad}@kku.ac.th
[3] National Electronics and Computer Technology Center, Pathum Thani, Thailand
{taneth.rua,thepchai.supnithi}@nectec.or.th

Abstract. This paper proposes a semantic knowledge retrieval methodology that comprises of the evaluation of resources and relationships between association resources, the identification of applicable information based on belief culture ontology, a semantic system of resources, attributes, and properties. The proposed method is based on a newly developed ontology focused on tacit knowledge of belief culture. From this study, domain experts can search semantically associated resources for their terminology query.

Keywords: Semantic knowledge retrieval · Belief culture · Knowledge-based systems

1   Introduction

Ontology is a widely used tool for describing knowledge representation. The benefits of ontology consists its interoperability to share common understanding among people or software agents, it enables the re-use of domain knowledge and explicit assumptions [1]. Some ontologies of cultural knowledge have been developed but they focused on tangible cultural heritage and are intended to be used as information resources rather than as tools for information retrieval.

A semantic search framework was adopted in several studies to handle information retrieval issue [2,3]. This research adopted a semantic knowledge retrieval framework for semantic preprocessing of documents and queries. A newly developed ontology focused on representing tacit knowledge on the "Belief culture" is used. The system was completely tested and evaluated using existent data acquired from the documents and domain experts as well as the corpus of actual NL queries in Thai language.

2   Methodology

In this research we present a realistic approach to designing and developing a complete knowledge-based system (KBS). The system was constructed on the semantic web and used the belief culture ontology to capture and explain the meaning of

© Springer International Publishing Switzerland 2015
R.B. Allen et al. (Eds.): ICADL 2015, LNCS 9469, pp. 294–295, 2015.
DOI: 10.1007/978-3-319-27974-9

domain expert queries that were expressed in natural language (NL). The system could be seen as a search engine which accepts NL queries and performs the search in the back-end KBS. In order to measure the accuracy of methods, we observed the top-5 and top-10 results for each query.

3   Findings

The effectiveness of the retrieval results of the semantic knowledge retrieval using ontology and the search results using search engines was compared. The improvement of accuracy is mainly due to the consideration of the semantic relationships between the target information and the query keywords in searching and indexing. The semantic knowledge retrieval method can retrieve resources that contain the query keywords in their textual descriptions as well as resources, attributes, and properties that are indirectly associated with the query keywords through semantic pathway. In contrast, the baseline search engines do not consider the indirect associations between the query keywords and the resources. In case of the Belief database, most of the key information of a publication is represented in a single text. Thus, the basic keyword-based search is sufficient to retrieve the relevant results for many queries; thereby the performance of the search engine is not worse compared to that of semantic knowledge retrieval method. On the other hand, in the Belief KBS, the indirect semantic relationships among resources, attributes, and properties play an important role in finding relevant results. As a result, the execution of the Belief KBS search knowledge retrieval is much worse than that of the existent search engine methods.

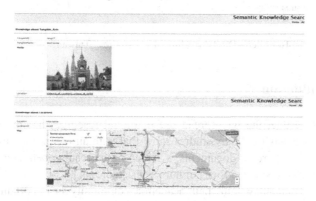

Fig. 1. A snapshot of the belief culture knowledge-based systems

References

1. Milton, S., Keen, C., Kurnia, S.: Understanding the benefits of ontology use for australian industry: a conceptual study. In: 21st Australasian Conference on Information Systems, 1–3 December 2010, Brisbane, Australia (2010)
2. Khan, L., McLeod, D., Hovy, E.: Retrieval Effectiveness of an Ontology-Based Model for Information Selection. The VLDB Journal **13**, 71–85 (2004)
3. Li, Z., Raskin, V., Ramani, K.: Developing Engineering Ontology for Information Retrieval. J. Comput. Inf. Sci. Eng. **8**, 1–13 (2008)

Digital Reading Behavior of LIS Graduate Students: A Case Study at National Taiwan Normal University

Chia-Hsiang Chen and Hao-Ren Ke

Graduate Institute of Library and Information Studies,
National Taiwan Normal University, Taipei, Taiwan
{80015003e,clavenke}@ntnu.edu.tw

Abstract. This study explores the digital reading behavior of graduate students from a Library and Information Science (LIS) Program. By making a connection between their habits and various forms of capital that may shape their reading behavior, this study adopts a qualitative approach, examining the four key concepts of Bourdieu's practice theory: habitus, economic capital, cultural capital, and social capital. Semi-structured interviews were conducted with fifteen students at National Taiwan Normal University. The result of this study indicates that the four key concepts of Bourdieu theory do influence the LIS graduate students' digital reading behavior, and may provide librarians, faculty, and students' thesis supervisors with suggestions for improving adaptive learning in the information society.

Keywords: Bourdieu · Digital reading · User studies · Taiwan

1 Introduction

Over the last decade, the widespread use of digital resources has dramatically impacted reading behavior. Many studies show that with an increasing amount of time spent on reading electronic documents, a screen-based reading behavior is emerging. Digital reading has become a focus of numerous studies [1].

Becoming grounded within their academic community is important to graduate students, because the professional training at school affects their career path. This behavior shapes the digital reading of graduate students, which is often very different from those of undergraduates [2].

In Taiwan, the first effort in library and information (LIS) studies began in 1955. National Taiwan Normal University initiated the Master's Program in Library and Information Studies in 2002, and its Ph.D. program was launched in 2009.[1] In the digital era, the LIS professional institute educates professionals qualified to face the challenges of the information society.

---

[1] http://www.glis.ntnu.edu.tw

© Springer International Publishing Switzerland 2015
R.B. Allen et al. (Eds.): ICADL 2015, LNCS 9469, pp. 296–297, 2015.
DOI: 10.1007/978-3-319-27974-9

This research begins by presenting Pierre Bourdieu's theory of practice [3]. Drawing upon his work to analyze the use of various reading sources, this study uses a qualitative approach to investigate how habitus, economic capital, cultural capital, and social capital shape students' digital reading behavior [4].

The paper presents material and findings that answer the following:

- Which factors influence graduate students' reading habitus?
- How do graduate students spend money on electronic devices that access digital content?
- What academic sources do graduate students use for academic activities?
- Which social networks do graduate students use to share and connect to others?

2   Method

A qualitative study using semi-structured interviews was conducted on graduate students in the Graduate Institute of Library and Information Studies at National Taiwan Normal University. Data was collected from 15 respondents: 9 female and 6 male, 12 masters and 3 doctoral students. The average interview lasted 50 minutes, and took place during 4 weeks in January and February 2015.

3   Concluding Remarks

This paper makes a timely contribution by applying Bourdieu's theory to explore the digital reading behavior of LIS graduate students in Taiwan. It connects learners' habits to the different forms of capital that shape their reading behavior.

This study has revealed students' reading behavior and their use of digital resources. Since the sample is small, future research should expand to an inter-school or inter-disciplinary scale in order to understand the digital reading behavior of different groups.

Acknowledgements. This research is sponsored by the Ministry of Science and Technology, Taiwan under NSC Grants No. NSC 104-2917-I-003-003.

References

1. Liu, Z.: Digital reading: An Overview. National Science Library, Chinese Academy of Sciences 5(1), 85–94 (2012)
2. Rempel. H.G.: A Longitudinal Assessment of Graduate Student Research Behavior and the Impact of Attending a Library Literature Review Workshop. https://ir.library.oregonstate.edu/xmlui/bitstream/handle/1957/19492/Rempel_LongitudinalAssessGradStudents.pdf
3. Bourdieu, P.: Reproduction in Education: Society and Culture. Sage, Thousand Oaks (1990)
4. Kvasny, L., Keil, M.: The challenges of redressing the digital divide: a tale of two US cities. Information Systems Journal **16**, 23–53 (2006). doi:10.1111/j.1365-2575.2006.00207.x

Performance of a Cloud-Based Digital Library

Yinlin Chen, Edward A. Fox, and Tingting Jiang

Department of Computer Science, Virginia Tech., Blacksburg, VA24061 , USA
{ylchen,fox,virjtt03}@vt.edu

Abstract. Cloud computing provides agility, elasticity, scalability, and many other features which a dedicated local hosting can not offer. In this study, we transfer a local hosting digital library, Ensemble, to become a cloud-based digital library. We measure the performance of three kinds of cloud computing architectures and present our results.

Keywords: Cloud computing · Digital library · Infrastructure · Performance

1 Introduction

Cloud computing provides agility, elasticity, scalability, and many features which a dedicated local hosting can not offer. Recent research used cloud computing limited in cloud instance and cloud storage [2]. Yet there are many cost-efficient cloud computing services we can use to build a digital library [1]. To determine how to do this with good performance, we transfer our local hosting digital library, Ensemble, into the cloud environment and measure performance among different cloud computing architectures.

2 Cloud Computing Architecture for Ensemble

To find a cloud computing architecture suitable for Ensemble, we designed three kinds of cloud computing architectures in this study. These are the Instance-based architecture, Service-based architecture, and Container-based architecture. The Instance-based architecture deploys the entire digital library inside an instance (virtual machine) provided by the cloud platform. The Container-based architecture packages each system component into a Docker image and has all the services running in the Docker engine inside an instance. The Service-based architecture replaces a system component with cloud services if there are matches. For example, MySQL in Amazon RDS can replace a local MySQL database.

To simplify the process to conduct experiments, we chose three of the most important Ensemble components to build a minimal digital library in each architecture. These components are: Ensemble interface and repository (Application component), Solr server (Index component), and MySQL database (Storage component). In the Instance-based architecture all of the components are connected internally. On the other hand, in the Container-based case, each component is running in the container and communicates with the others.

© Springer International Publishing Switzerland 2015
R.B. Allen et al. (Eds.): ICADL 2015, LNCS 9469, pp. 298–299, 2015.
DOI: 10.1007/978-3-319-27974-9

3   Experiments

We conducted multiple experiments on these three cloud computing architectures and measured their performance. We measured response time on the page view and search, and the concurrent user limit for each architecture. Our load testing dataset is the Ensemble log data from May 11, 2015 to July 26, 2015. We used the Apache JMeter loading test tool. During the experiments, we assigned the same computing resources and network bandwidth to each architecture and also the server that runs the Apache JMeter tool. For page view and search experiments, we added 10 concurrent users per second every minute, so varied from 10 to 100. For the concurrent user limit experiment, we started load testing from 500 concurrent users per second, and added 100 concurrent users per 1 minute until the digital library's error TPS (Throughput Per Second) was over 50. Table 1 shows the results.

Table 1. Cloud computing architectures performance

	Container(1VM)	Instance(1VM)	Service(3VMs)	Container(3VMs)
View	800ms	800ms	750ms	740ms
Search	800ms	450ms	340ms	440ms
Users	800	900	1200	1400

4   Conclusion

Our results show that the Container-based approach where each container has its own VM performs best though there is a 100ms slower search response time compared to the Service-based case. The cost of this architecture can be further reduced and the performance can be improved as long as we can adjust the size of instance resources according to the loading on the digital library components. Taking Ensemble for example, we can increase the MySQL component container VM size and reduce the Application component container VM size to reduce costs and achieve better performance. Utilizing the flexibility provided by cloud computing, you can find the optimal cloud-based architecture for your digital library. Authors of this paper were supported by the US NSF under Grant Number DUE-0840719.

Acknowledgments. Authors of this paper were supported by the US NSF under Grant Number DUE-0840719. The statements made herein are solely the responsibility of the authors.

References

1. Fox, E.A., Robert, M.A., Furuta, R.K., Leggett, J.J.: Digital Libraries. Commun. ACM **38**(4), 22–28 (1995)
2. Teregowda, P., Urgaonkar, B., Lee Giles, C.: Cloud computing: a digital libraries perspective. In: 2010 IEEE 3rd International Conference on Cloud Computing (CLOUD), pp. 115–122. IEEE (2010)

Assisting Retrieval of Academic Papers for User's Information Needs

Kosuke Furusawa[1], Hongjun Fan[1], Yoichi Tomiura[1], and Emi Ishita[2]

[1] Kyushu University, 744 Motoka, Nishi, Fukuoka 819-0395, Japan
{2IE14035Y,2IE14033P}@s.kyushu-u.ac.jp, tom@inf.kyushu-u.ac.jp
[2] Department of Library Science, Kyushu University,
Hakozaki, Higashi, Fukuoka 812-8581, Japan
ishita.emi.982@m.kyushu-u.ac.jp

Abstract. Search by terms is often used when researchers search academic papers. However, it is difficult to collect almost all papers that satisfy information needs using search terms alone. In this paper, we propose a support method to find papers that satisfy user's information needs with search by terms. This is achieved by searching abstracts that have been obtained with general search terms, and further analyzing them using a researcher's own provided abstract to identify the user's information needs.

Keywords: Support methods for academic papers · Types of sentences

1 Introduction

In the search for academic papers, it is generally necessary to search almost all papers that satisfy user's information needs. However, it is difficult to do with only search by terms. If a search is performed using specific search terms, this tends to limit the search results, which leads to important papers being omitted. This is because authors may use different terms both in describing papers and in searching for them, even though such terms may express a similar or near-identical meaning. Conversely, if a researcher conducts searches using general search terms, too many search results are returned for the researcher to inspect them all. The purpose of our study is to develop a support system for finding academic papers that satisfy user's information needs using general search terms while preventing search omissions.

For example, consider the case where a researcher is writing an academic paper. The researchers have written an abstract and want to collect papers to confirm the originality of their study. In this situation, we can consider the following support to the user. The system searches papers using the general search terms provided by the researcher, and then conducts clustering of abstracts from the search result and the researcher's own abstract. The abstracts in the cluster that includes their abstracts are similar to their abstracts. However, there may be are lots of abstracts returned in the search results that do not satisfy the researcher's needs. For example, a paper with an abstract that is similar in background to the researcher's abstract may not satisfy the researcher's specific needs.

Therefore, we have developed a method for a user to find academic papers more efficiently that satisfy the user's needs. This is achieved by searching abstracts that have been obtained with general search terms, and further analyzing them using types of sentences in abstracts and the user's abstract that express researcher's information needs.

© Springer International Publishing Switzerland 2015
R.B. Allen et al. (Eds.): ICADL 2015, LNCS 9469, pp. 300–301, 2015.
DOI: 10.1007/978-3-319-27974-9

2   Proposed Method

We present the following method for supporting a user in finding papers that satisfy the user's information needs. First, the user will input general search terms related to the user's information needs. Second, the system will search for papers using those search terms and obtain abstracts for each. Third, the user will input their own abstract that expresses the user's needs. Finally, the system conducts its search algorithm. This first step involves conducting topic analysis [1] for the resulting abstracts and the user's abstract. Then the system conducts clustering of them using topic information assigned to words, and extracts papers that satisfy the user's information needs using both the topic information and estimated types of sentences in abstracts. We consider three types of sentences to be identified within abstracts:

1. **Problem Sentence:** the sentence describing the problem that the paper deals with.
2. **Idea/Method Sentence:** the sentence describing an idea or a method to resolve the problem.
3. **Result Sentence:** the sentence describing the result of the paper.

When a user wants to confirm the originality of the user's own idea or method to resolve a certain problem P, the user's information needs can be met by the papers whose abstract describes the problem similar to P. We therefore expect that many information needs can be extracted precisely by defining the types of sentences in the abstract. Furthermore, we suppose that we would estimate type for each sentence in abstract by the method proposed by Hirohata et al. [2].

3   Experiment

We have interviewed researchers to obtain practical examples of information needs. We have then searched and obtained abstracts of papers for each of these examples with the search terms that were decided by consulting with the interviewed researchers. Then, we have classified abstracts into two groups; the abstracts that satisfy the information needs and those that do not. Furthermore, we manually classified the types of sentences within the abstracts. We then applied the proposed method to these datasets and calculate the precision and recall of extracting the papers that satisfy the information need. In our poster presentation, we report these findings.

Acknowledgements. This work was supported by JSPS KAKENHI Grant Number 15H01721.

References

1. Griffiths, T.L., Steyvers, M.: Finding scientific topics. Proceedings of the National Academy of Sciences of the United States of America **101**(Suppl. 1), 5228–5235 (2004)
2. Hirohata, K., et al.: Identifying sections in scientific abstracts using conditional random fields. In: Proc. of IJCNLP 2008, pp. 381–387 (2008)

Evaluating Library Escape: A Prototype Information Literacy Game

Yan Ru Guo and Dion Hoe-Lian Goh

Wee Kim Wee School of Communication and Information,
Nanyang Technological University, Singapore Singapore
{W120030,ashlgoh}@ntu.edu.sg

Abstract. The use of digital game-based learning has grown rapidly in recent years, including in information literacy (IL) education. However, many efforts have failed because users are not involved in the design process. The present study adopts a user-centered design approach to evaluate an educational IL game prototype, with data analyzed based on Pedagogical Playability Heuristics.

Keywords: Digital game-based learning · Information literacy · Pedagogical playability heuristics · User evaluation

1   Background

With the explosion of digital information, information literacy (IL) has become very important. University students routinely need to search for and synthesize information from multiple sources, such as digital libraries and databases, making IL skills critical to academic performance [1]. However, students find traditional instruction not engaging, and expect to be entertained [2]. Digital game-based learning (DGBL) can have a positive impact [2]. The University of Michigan reported success of its online game *BiblioBouts* to promote IL among students [1].

However, efforts to integrate current design heuristics with theoretically sound frameworks have been scarce, and largely make anecdotal claims [3]. Further, most IL game design does not involve end users. One exception is [1], which conducted the evaluation only after the game was developed. This study aims to fill this research gap by demonstrating how users may be involved in the initial conceptualization. Interviews were conducted to elicit potential users' comments and ideas. The data were analyzed using the Pedagogical Playability Heuristics (PPH), a theoretical framework to evaluate educational games [3] (see Table 1).

Table 1. Pedagogical Playability Heuristics

Captivation of Interest	The game should capture players' interest and stimulate their curiosity. The storyline should relate to players' life experiences, and there are variations in gameplay.
Meeting learning needs	The learning objectives and goals should be clear to players and teach new concepts and skills.
Building confidence	Challenges should match players' skills level. Players can easily get help, find it useful to achieve the learning objectives, and feel a sense of control.
Self-assessment	Players should receive immediate feedback and be able to track their progress.

© Springer International Publishing Switzerland 2015
R.B. Allen et al. (Eds.): ICADL 2015, LNCS 9469, pp. 302–303, 2015.
DOI: 10.1007/978-3-319-27974-9

2   Discussion and Analysis

Library Escape is an IL role-playing game for university students. The student protagonist failed an IL exam and was led to a haunted library which he must escape by finding IL knowledge hidden in objects. The six missions in the game are based on the Information Search Process Model [4]. Educational content covers basic concepts of IL and how to search, access, and evaluate information for academic purposes. Each mission features one section of the library, and players complete the tasks and quizzes in each step with the help of constructive feedback before progressing.

Ten students from a local university were recruited, presented with the low-fidelity game prototype, and interviewed for about an hour. Audio recordings were transcribed, combined with the notes taken during interviews, assigned anonymized names of "P1" to "P10", and coded based on the PPH.

Captivation of Interest. To make the game relevant, the protagonist is a student. Each mission takes place in a different area of the library to maintain players' attention. The backstory of failing one subject can also relate to their personal experience.

Meeting Learning Needs. Selection of appropriate content is important in DGBL. P5 said "*I think the content is too abstract and theoretical. I want to learn more about the hands-on stuff. Things I can use immediately.*" As a result, more practical tips on information search and catalog use will be included in the revised game.

Building Confidence. The level of challenge increases as the player progresses, starting simple to establish players' confidence. Players receive immediate scripted feedback after submitting their answers. P4 remarked that "*You should also tell them why they are right or why they are wrong [...] Or they just guess*".

Self-assessment. Quiz questions test how much players have learnt and give immediate feedback. The low-fidelity design did not have a progress indicator. P2, an experienced gamer, suggested adding a progress bar so players will know how many objects they have found and how many they still need.

In conclusion, our study sheds light on how users can be actively involved in DGBL design. For DGBL, both learning and gameplay enjoyment needs should be fulfilled. The PPH provide a theoretical understanding of the factors contributing to success. This study was limited because it used a low-fidelity, non-functioning prototype in the evaluation. To overcome this problem, the interviewer described each mission for participants. Other methods will also be valuable to triangulate the findings and provide a more comprehensive picture of DGBL evaluation as part of future work.

References

1. Markey, K., Leeder, C., Rieh, S.Y.: Designing Online Information Literacy Games Students Want to Play. Rowman and Littlefield, Lanham (2014)
2. Prensky, M.: Digital game-based learning. Computers in Entertainment 1(1), 21 (2003)
3. Tan, J.L., Goh, D.H.-L., Ang, R.P., Huan, V.S.: Child-centered interaction in the design of a game for social skills intervention. Computers in Entertainment 9(1), 2–17 (2011)
4. Kuhlthau, C.C.: Seeking meaning: A process approach to library and information services. Libraries Unltd Incorporated (2004)

Ontology-Based Digital Humanities System for the Development of Librarianship in Taiwan

Hao-Ren Ke, Xing-Zhi Fu, and Shun-Hong Sie

Graduate Institute of Library and Information Studies, National Taiwan Normal University,
Taipei City, Taiwan
{clavenke,60215005e,mayh}@ntnu.edu.tw

Abstract. This poster paper presents the establishment of an ontology-based system for supporting the description and illustration of the development of librarianship in Taiwan. The ontology leverages the professional path of a great librarianship personage in Taiwan, Professor Chen-Ku Wang, as the kernel. This system can assist digital humanities scholars in library and information science (LIS) to explore the historical development of librarianship in Taiwan.

Keywords: Digital humanities · Ontology · Resource description framework · Linked data · Librarianship

1 Introduction

Digital technology changes how humanities scholars conduct research and even the whole research environment. In the era of big data, it is essential to analyze and discover important but hidden information from big data for assisting humanities scholars to perform research, and this is the aim of digital humanities.

Ontologies originate from philosophy. According to Gruber [1], *an ontology is an explicit specification of a conceptualization, and is a systematic account of existence.* In information science, ontologies describe the important concepts in a domain and their relationships so as to empower computers to understand human knowledge.

This study attempts to create an ontology-based digital humanities system to describe and explore librarianship's development in Taiwan. Professor Chen-Ku Wang's professional path is employed to define the ontology for the development of a specific field, librarianship in this case. Professor Wang has been dedicated to librarianship for more than sixty years and plays a leading role in library development in Taiwan. Professor Wang helped set up an ideal paradigm for Taiwan's library education, library administration, organizational leadership, and academic research, and earned himself high respect and various honors.

2 System Development

The development of the proposed system comprises four steps. The first step collects information on Professor Wang. In 2014, the library of National Taiwan Normal

© Springer International Publishing Switzerland 2015
R.B. Allen et al. (Eds.): ICADL 2015, LNCS 9469, pp. 304–305, 2015.
DOI: 10.1007/978-3-319-27974-9

University organized an exhibition for celebrating Professor Wang's 90th birthday, and a great quantity of information was collected at that time. Additionally, there are two important books for this study, My Life with Books – 50 Years Librarianship and The Librarianship in Taiwan, both of which are written by Professor Wang.

Step two is ontology design. *Ontology Development 101* [2] guides the design of the ontology. The researchers comb the collected information to discover essential entities and properties. Some common ontologies from DBpedia are also used so that the proposed ontology can maintain its specificity, as well as being interoperable with famous ontologies. The design tool is Protégé, a free open ontology editor and knowledge acquisition system. The ontology created in this study classifies the entities into 42 classes, and links them by 45 object properties.

The third step transforms the ontology into Resource Description Framework (RDF) for complying with Linked Data standards. The D2RQ Platform provides the functionality of accessing relational databases in RDF.

The final step builds the Web Site and provides the user interface. The user interface integrates LodLive, which uses Linked Data standards to browse RDF resources. Furthermore, because every resource is described in RDF format, the system could access external resources (e.g. DBpedia) from the proposed system, and increase the value of resources.

3   Conclusion

The professional path of an influential personage in a specific field is beneficial for constructing the ontology for the development of the field. This poster paper outlines the steps for achieving the above purpose. A prototype system has been built. Future work includes polishing the system and user evaluation.

Acknowledgements. This work was a partial result of the project funded by the Ministry of Science and Technology (MOST 102-2410-H-003-121-MY3).

References

1. Gruber, T.R.: A Translation Approach to Portable Ontology Specifications. Knowledge Acquisition 5(2), 199–220 (1993)
2. Noy, N.F., McGuinness, D.L.: Ontology development 101: a guide to creating your first ontology. Stanford Knowledge Systems Laboratory Technical Report KSL-01-05 and Stanford Medical Informatics Technical Report SMI-2001-0880, March 2001

Designing Interface for Elderly Adults: Access from the Smartphone to the World

Ling-Ling Lai and Chia-Rou Lai

Tamkang University, Taipei, Taiwan

Abstract. The purpose of this research is to understand how elderly people use their smartphones to access and connect to the world of information. The focus is especially on their needs and preferences of the interface. With the ease of technology and touch-screen mobile phones, more elderly people have the intention to use smartphone to keep in close contact with their families and friends. With the rapidly growing numbers of the elderly population worldwide, including in Taiwan, it is important to know how our senior citizens could better access the world through the smartphone, which is increasingly popular with no doubt. The results of the study showed that elderly people encounter some problems while using smartphones, which could be valuable input for smartphone industries to take into account for future designs.

Keywords: Elderly users · Human computer interaction · Mobile information · Smartphone · Usability

1 Introduction

The purpose of this research is to understand how elderly people use their smartphones to access and connect to the world of information. The focus is especially on their needs and preferences of the interface. With the ease of technology and touch-screen mobile phones, more elderly people have the intention to use smartphone to keep in close contact with their families and friends. With the rapidly growing numbers of the elderly population worldwide, including in Taiwan, it is important to know how our senior citizens could better access the world through the smartphone, which is increasingly popular with no doubt. The results of the study showed that elderly people encounter some problems while using smartphones, which could be valuable input for smartphone industries to take into account for future designs.

2 Literature Review

According to the Annual Report of Mobile Advertisement [1], Apple smartphones occupied 37% of the market of mobile phone, Samsung accounted for 35%, followed by HTC (21%) and SONY (4%) in Taiwan. With Apple and its iOS system being the first place of the market share, it is however the Android system that accounts for the biggest share of mobile phone system at present. Based on Nielson's usability testing definition [2], including efficiency, errors, memorability, learnability, and

© Springer International Publishing Switzerland 2015
R.B. Allen et al. (Eds.): ICADL 2015, LNCS 9469, pp. 306–307, 2015.
DOI: 10.1007/978-3-319-27974-9

satisfaction, the interface design and usability of smartphones for the elderly users are put to test to identify the preference and problems of this group of users. The method of usability testing requires a small number of participants with repeated testing to examine an interface [3].

3   Research Method

With the assumption that not all smartphone functions are suitable for elderly users, four research questions are identified to examine their user behavior of smartphones, which are (1) the needs of smartphones for the elderly; (2) the preferences of smartphone functions for the elderly; (3) the usability of smartphones for the elderly, and (4) the difficulties of smartphones for the elderly. The study recruited 12 participants through the method of snowballing, starting from the seniors of the researchers' circle. From there, more participants are recruited. All participants are residents of Taipei city, have used smartphones, and are over 60 years old. Among the participants, four (33%) of them are in higher education system, others held a variety of job positions before their retirement, including government officials, childe care, and service related industries.

4   Findings and Conclusion

Specific tasks are designed for elderly users to perform and post-task interviews are carried out to obtain their comments and feedback. The researchers found that senior users have basic needs while using their smartphones, including making and receiving calls, enjoying audio-visual entertainment, accessing the Internet, taking notes, taking pictures, learning something new from the Internet, making emergency calls, setting alarms, etc. Reading online news and writing e-mails are less needed functions for this group of users in the study; besides, there is no obvious need for calendars and planners. Essentially, elderly people like to use smartphones for two reasons: the first is convenience; the second is the Internet access. As for the selection of the phone, there are two groups of users: one faithfully prefers traditional mobile phones over smartphones because they do not think smartphones are necessary at present; the other group prefers smartphones, but they would be happier to see smartphones more closely match their needs. Seniors have difficulties and problems when using smartphones in the areas such as: accidental dialing, small screen, complex emergency-calling system, much complicated steps of changing phone settings, sensitivity of the touch-screen, type errors, confusion about the meanings of the interface icons, and overall problem due to the lack of exposure to new technologies in the past.

References

1. Vpon Data Driven and Context-Based Advertisement: Annual Report of Mobile Advertisement in Taiwan (2013). (retrieved from) http://www.vpon.com/images/datafile/Vpon_2013tw.pdf
2. Nielson, J.: Usability Engineering. AP Professional, New York (1993)
3. Nielson, J.: Why you only need to test with 5 users. Alertbox (2000). (retrieved February 14, 2014, from) www.useit.com/alertbox/2000319.html

Investigating the Use of YouTube as a Self-Directed Learning Platform

Chei Sian Lee[1], Hamzah Osop[2], Gani Kelni[1], and Dion Hoe-Lian Goh[1]

[1] Wee Kim Wee School of Communication and Information,
Nanyang Technological University, Singapore, Singapore
{leecs,W110006,ashlgoh}@ntu.edu.sg
[2] Electrical Engineering and Computer Science School,
Queensland University of Technology, Brisbane, Australia
hamzahbin.osop@hdr.qut.edu.au

Abstract. Web 2.0 technologies have paved the way for self-directed online learning. YouTube, in particular, is a viable Web 2.0 platform that can be used to disseminate educational content and in the process empower users to take charge of their own learning. Through the lens of self-directed learning theory, we perform qualitative content analyses on comments contributed by learners after watching educational videos on YouTube. Results indicate that YouTube can play important roles in facilitating a self-directed learning platform.

Keywords: YouTube, Online learning, Self-Directed Learning

1 Introduction

Web 2.0 technologies have paved the way for new online avenues where users can initiate and conduct learning on their own which is also known as self-directed learning. Self-directed learning (SDL) is an initiative in which an individual takes, with or without the help of others, in finding out his own learning needs and goals, identifies the human and material resources for learning, decides and works out appropriate learning strategies, and evaluates the result of his/her learning [1].

We propose that YouTube, a Web 2.0 video-sharing site, can be an effective self-directed learning environment. It was envisaged that shared online videos will increasingly find a role in teaching and learning [2]. Further, YouTube can be used for delivery of learning content as it affords collaborative content creation and peer assessment which helps to enhance the social learning experience. Thus, YouTube has the potential to help learners to learn at their own pace and to take charge of their own learning. Through the lens of self-directed learning theory [1], we perform qualitative content analysis on comments generated by YouTube users, focusing on those who watched educational YouTube videos.

2 Literature Review

The basic principle underlying self-directed learning (SDL) is that individuals empower themselves and take responsibility for decisions related to their learning. This

© Springer International Publishing Switzerland 2015
R.B. Allen et al. (Eds.): ICADL 2015, LNCS 9469, pp. 308–310, 2015.
DOI: 10.1007/978-3-319-27974-9

means that learners have to take control to direct resources to achieve a learning goal [3]. Four dimensions were identified in the literature [4,5]. First, the *control* dimension is concerned with how a learner is able to direct his or her learning [4]. Second, the *initiative* dimension examines how a learner is able to proactively take steps toward decisions and actions [1]. Third, the *motivation* dimension explores the desire of the learner in taking actions and steps towards his or her learning goals [6]. Lastly, the *self-efficacy* dimension is concerned with the learner's belief in his or her capabilities to produce an outcome. Here, this study examines how the four dimensions (i.e. control, initiative, motivation and self-efficacy) are facilitated in YouTube.

Our aim in this study is to investigate on whether YouTube provides an effective platform for self-directed learners by drawing from the dimensions of SDL. From the perspective of learners who consume educational videos, we propose to examine the research question: *how effective is YouTube as a SDL platform from the perspective of self-directed learning theory?*

3   Methodology

A customized software application was developed using Google YouTube API to extract videos in the domain of computing, programming and computer science. A sample of 150 educational videos was selected. Qualitative content analysis was conducted to examine the comments generated by learners who watched the selected videos. Here, our primary coding instrument focused on characterizing the four dimensions - Control, Initiative, Motivation, and Self-Efficacy [4]. We sampled 300 comments (i.e. 30 comments from each video) from the 10 videos for content analysis. The sentiments (i.e. positive, negative and neutral) were also coded for each comment.

4   Results and Discussion

Our results (shown in Table 1) demonstrate that YouTube affords online learners a positive self-directed learning environment. Specifically, our results indicate that learners were generally positive with regards to taking *control* of their learning in YouTube as features on YouTube (e.g. recommendations, searching) empower learners to take control. With regards to *initiative* and *motivation*, our results suggest that learners who searched for educational videos on YouTube appeared to be motivated individuals who took initiative and proactive steps towards acquiring knowledge on a particular topic. In particular, we found that many learners were using the educational YouTube videos to supplement their formal learning. With regards to *self-efficacy*, we found that learners felt that they had gained knowledge by watching the videos. On a broader scale, we see that educational videos on YouTube have the potential to create impact on making education more affordable and accessible. Thus, educational videos on YouTube are in the direction towards creating digital libraries of educational content accessible by global users and hence closing the gap in the digital divide.

Table 1. Sampled results of qualitative content analysis

Dimension	Sentiments	Findings
Control	Positive	Learners would take control by highlighting their learning difficulties and they might ask questions and/or give suggestions or even direct what the video contributors could do to help in their learning. *"hey men this is a great tutorial I never done programming I will like you if u can explain the lines of code ...' and what that means thank you and god bless you"* .
Initiative and Motivation	Positive	Initiative and motivation dimensions were not mutually exclusive as the two concepts are interrelated. Learners who watched YouTube educational videos typically were intrinsically motivated to initiate and proactively take steps to advance their learning. *"...after searching for ages tutorials on different languages I gave up and just searched `How to start programming`. I'm glad I found your site :)".* *"I'm going to be following your tutorials for a menu I have to do for the Uni."*
	Negative	Learners lacking the motivation to learn. *"really hate this program but [I] am forced to learn it at college".*
Self-efficacy	Positive	Learners felt that learning on YouTube enhances their knowledge on the topic. *"....with the help of this course I am now moving on to advanced programming..."* *"these videos gave me the basic ways of thinking when working with programming.."*
	Negative	Learners complained about the content posted. *"Videos covering programming problems are incredibly useless."* *"I can t imagine this would be very useful.I absolutely hate python."*

References

1. Knowles, M.S.: Self-Directed Learning. Association Press, New York (1975)
2. Holt, L., Brockett, R.G.: Self Direction and Factors Influencing Technology Use: Examining the Relationships for the 21st Century Workplace. Computers in Human behavior **28**(6), 2075–2082 (2012)
3. Robertson, J.: The Educational Affordances of Blogs for Self-Directed Learning. Computers & Education **57**(2), 1628–1644 (2011)
4. Stockdale, S.L., Brockett, R.G.: Development of the PRO-SDLS: A Measure of Self-Direction in Learning Based on the Personal Responsibility Orientation Model. Adult Education Quarterly **61**(2), 161–180 (2011)
5. Delahaye, B.L., Smith, H.E.: The Validity of the Learning Preference Assessment. Adult Education Quarterly **45**(3), 159–173 (1995)
6. Bonk, C.J.: YouTube anchors and enders: the use of shared online video content as a macrocontext for learning. In: American Educational Research Association (AERA) 2008 Annual Meeting, New York, NY (2008)

Linked Data for Professional Education (LD4PE) Project

Sam Oh[1], Marcia L. Zeng[2], Michael Crandall[3], Stuart A. Sutton[3],
and Thomas Baker[1]

[1] Sungkyunkwan University, Seoul, South Korea
samoh21@gmail.com, tom@tombaker.org
[2] Kent State University, Kent, Ohio, USA mzeng@kent.edu
[3] University of Washington, Seattle, WA, USA
{mikecran,sasutton}@uw.edu

Abstract. This poster reports on the Linked Data for Professional Education (LD4PE) project, which leads to the development of a professional education resource *Exploratorium* for teaching and learning Linked Data practices in design, implementation, and management.

Keywords: Competency-based teaching and learning · Learning resources · Linked data

The Linked Data for Professional Education (LD4PE) project responds to the need for Linked Data Competencies in the professional workforce while aligning competencies and learning outcomes with learning resources available in the open Web. The poster reports on the progress of the project and introduces the major building blocks in developing a professional education resource *Exploratorium* for teaching and learning Linked Data practices in design, implementation, and management. These major building blocks are:

- *Learning Resources* have been collected, including curricular structures and syllabi, packages of "how-to" videos and step-by-step instructions targeted to specific learning outcomes, and tools and codes prepared for exercises, all available on the Web through both open and commercial providers. The learning resources are described with metadata based on the Learning Resource Metadata Initiative (LRMI) standard.[1] In addition to general descriptions and rights, pedagogy, accessibility, and competencies are also described in great detail for each learning resources. The web-based authoring editor can be configured in multiple languages (at the moment they are English, Spanish, and Korean) and support automatic generation of RDF/JSON data.
- A Web-based, Linked Data *Exploratorium* website is designed to enable the management and innovative use of these learning resources. The backbone of this *Exploratorium* will be a competency framework for Linked Data practice

---

http://www.lrmi.net/

© Springer International Publishing Switzerland 2015
R.B. Allen et al. (Eds.): ICADL 2015, LNCS 9469, pp. 311–313, 2015.
DOI: 10.1007/978-3-319-27974-9

that supports indexing of learning resources according to the specific competencies they address. The Exploratorium website will also support social recommendation mechanisms to highlight the best learning resources and their alignment to the *Competency Index*. The environment will provide built-in broadcast and responsive communication channels for community engagement and continuous feedback. The *Exploratorium* itself is modeled in RDF and implements Linked Data principles.[2] International Unified Identifiers (IRIs) are assigned to statements of competence. The IRIs are used to map learning resource metadata to nodes in the *Competency Index*.

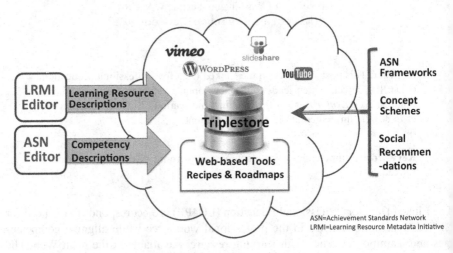

Fig. 1. Exploratorium architecture

- A *Competency Index* has been developed and continually modified. The RDF- modeled "Competency Index for Linked Data" employs the Achievement Standards Network (ASN)[3] Description Language for describing formally promulgated competencies and benchmarks. The *Index* will be a cohesive, stakeholder-developed set of RDF-modeled assertions defining competencies, knowledge, and skills needed for using Linked Data in the library, archive, and museum (LAM) environment.
- A set of openly available, web-based *tools* aims to support the creation of learner trajectory maps expressing curricular structures or personal learning journeys superimposed over the competency framework. In other words, the tools are developed to enable teachers, trainers, and learners to map their own pathways through the *Competency Index* graphs. These diverse and creative pathways for learning can also be saved as named graphs. They provide different roadmaps for discovering and traversing lesson plans, "how to" recipes, webinars, and tutorials that have been described and aligned to the competency nodes of the *Index* graphs.

---

[2] http://www.w3.org/DesignIssues/LinkedData.html
[3] http://www.achievementstandards.org/

The LD4PE project considers a wide range of target audiences to be served: teachers and trainers in LAMs as users (and contributors) of learning resources indexed in the *Exploratorium*; learners engaged in formal education and in continuing professional development; employers of professionals engaged in Linked Data activities; and content providers of Linked Data educational resources (such as curricula, tutorials, webinars and best practice recipes).

The research team is composed of iSchool educators from University of Washington and Kent State University in the United States and Sungkyunkwan University in South Korea, with partners from OCLC, Elsevier, Synaptica, and Access Innovations. The *Exploratorium* will be maintained by the Dublin Core Metadata Initiative (DCMI) as a basic framework for development of its education and training agenda. The project will continue to engage domain experts, teachers and trainers, learners, and resource providers in both development and user experience testing stages.

Recommender Knowledge-Based System for Research on the Development of Northeastern Thailand

Jirapong Panawong and Kulthida Tuamsuk[✉]

Information and Communication Department, Faculty of Humanities and Social Sciences,
Khon Kaen University, Khon Kaen, Thailand
jirapong.p@gmail.com, kultua@kku.ac.th

Abstract. This research aimed to develop a recommender knowledge-based system for research on the development of northeastern (NE) Thailand. The data from research on the development of NE Thailand were retrieved from NRCT and ThaiLIS databases. More than 1000 records from 2002 to 2012 were used in this study. The knowledge was organized and constructed based on the framework of research strategies (B.E. 2012-2016) for the NE region. The ontology was developed using the Hozo editor. The recommender knowledge-based system was developed and evaluated by experts and researchers in the field.

Keywords: Northeastern Thailand · Research information system · Recommender knowledge-based system

1   Introduction

This research aims to develop a recommender knowledge-based system for scholars using three research and development techniques: 1) knowledge organization and construction, based on the policy and frameworks for research strategy for northeastern Thailand's development of the National Research Council of Thailand (NRCT) [1], 2) ontology development, and 3) semantic technology for recommender knowledge-based searching. It is expected that the contents of research on the development of northeastern Thailand will be accessed via semantic search. The system can provide the search results in a manner of recommendation according to the queries, such as who are the experts in the specific research areas, what are the research methodologies used for that topic, what are the similar studies that have been done on that topic, etc.

2   Methodology

This research used research and development methodology. The research was divided into three phases: 1) Knowledge organization and construction using content analysis and classification [2]. 2) Ontology development using Ozaka University's Hozo-ontology editor [3]. 3) Development of the recommender knowledge-based system

© Springer International Publishing Switzerland 2015
R.B. Allen et al. (Eds.): ICADL 2015, LNCS 9469, pp. 314–315, 2015.
DOI: 10.1007/978-3-319-27974-9

using the National Electronics and Computer Technology Center (NECTEC), Thailand's Ontology-based Application Management (OAM), which comprised functions for knowledge management and semantic search processing.

3   Findings

The knowledge has been categorized into two domains. First, the contents domain, comprised of 5 main classes including social development, economic development, natural and environmental resources development, research innovation and human resources development, and research system development. Second, the research documents domain, divided into two main classes: publications and methodology. Each main class was divided into sub-classes and the relationships of the topics were identified. The knowledge structure from phase 1 was analyzed and used for ontology development using University of Ozaka University's Hozo-ontology editor [3,4] and then validated by ontology experts. The ontology comprised of 19 concepts, and 349 classes and sub-classes.

The recommender knowledge-based system was developed using semantic web technology for its main function [4]. NECTEC's OAM software was used for semantic search tool. The data of 1058 research records from the NRCT and ThaiLIS databases between 2002 and 2012 have been input and then the relationships between the ontology and input data were mapped. The techniques included data mapping, property column mapping, vocabulary mapping, and development of resource description framework (RDF) [4]. The recommender knowledge-based system can support semantic search, therefore the contents of research on the development of northeastern Thailand can be accessed and provide results in a more innovative manner according to the researchers' needs.

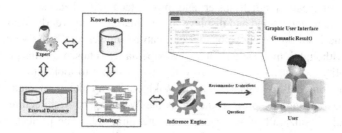

Fig. 1. Architecture of the recommender knowledge-based system

References

1. National Research Council Thailand (NRCT): The Framework of Research Strategies of Thailand (2012–2016). National Research Council Thailand, Bangkok (2011)
2. De Wever, B., et al.: Content Analysis Schemes to Analyze Transcripts of Online Asynchronous Discussion Groups: A Review. Computers & Education **46**(1), 6–28 (2006)
3. National Electronics and Computer Technology Center (NECTEC): Hozo-ontology Editor: A Handbook. NECTEC, Bangkok (2012)
4. Sicilia, M.A.: Metadata, Semantics, and Ontology: Providing Meaning to Information Resources. International Journal of Metadata, Semantics and Ontologies **1**(1), 83–86 (2006)

Schema.org for Wikipedia's Articles on Architecture

Jay Park

Yonsei University, Seoul, South Korea
j.kelly.park@gmail.com

Abstract. This paper focuses on how Wikipedia's architectural data can be improved using Schema.org. First, there will be a selection of which information should be represented from the WikiProject Architecture's infobox templates. Then the selected information will be categorized according to Schema.org. Finally, this will be represented in the most suitable language.

1   Introduction

Architecture presents an ambiguity problem because it is both an art and a science of structures. It has to be identified with an independent schema.

Schema.org was launched in 2011 by Bing, Google and Yahoo!. The goal was to create a shared collection of schemas for the web. This allows the information to be machine-readable. Search engines depend on this type of markup to display search inquiries. By constructing Wikipedia with Schema.org, Wikipedia will be able to contribute information much faster and more accurately because search engines would be able to understand and display the information in an orderly fashion.

Wikipedia is an online encyclopedia that can be viewed as a massive open-source database. Although it may lack accuracy, Wikipedia was chosen for this project due to its availability and vastness. The goal of this paper is not to look into the validity of the information, but to organize all of Wikipedia's architectural data. Wikipedia currently has an ongoing project known as the WikiProject Architecture. It aims to connect and organize all of Wikipedia's architectural data. The project sets infobox (information box) templates to guide authors and help the viewers see certain information at a glance. The templates have parameters that need to be filled out. The goal of this paper is to select and correlate the parameters according to Schema.org.

2   Information Selection and Organization

The WikiProject Architecture provided one infobox template for architects and four for buildings according to the building type. The four building templates were viewed as one, since several parameters overlapped. The parameters were superfluous and, since Schema.org focuses on consistency and generalizations, had to be narrowed down. 18 out of the 19 architect parameters and 37 out of the 72 building parameters were selected with exception to the optional parameters.

© Springer International Publishing Switzerland 2015
R.B. Allen et al. (Eds.): ICADL 2015, LNCS 9469, pp. 316–317, 2015.
DOI: 10.1007/978-3-319-27974-9

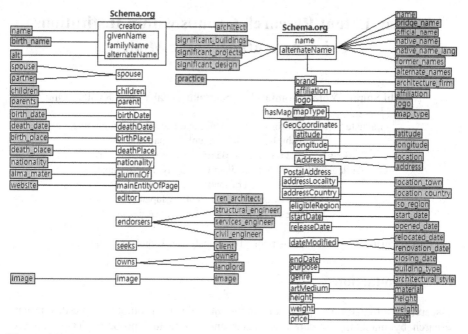

Fig. 1. This shows a correlation between the parameters of WikiProject Architecture's infobox templates to Schema.org. Some parameters correlate to two or more properties and vice versa. Wikipedia's infobox parameters are shown in gray boxes and schema.org in white boxes.

3   Markup Language

Wikipedia has its own language known as the Wiki markup, also known as wikitext or wikicode. Wiki markup marks up sections, line breaks, indenting text, aligning text, and text formats. Wikipedia additionally uses HTML elements for presentation formatting. However, it does not define the type of the information. This will be the role of Schema.org. Schema.org can be marked up using microdata, RDFa, and JSON-LD. JSON-LD is the most suitable for this project because of its simplicity and the ability to link data. JSON-LD is an extension of JSON, which is used to transmit data between websites and browsers. Linked data is a way of publishing data on the web so that one website can refer to another website. This is crucial because the infobox templates are highly interconnected. It will also eliminate duplicity, save storage space and the time needed to encrypt Schema.org to the existing data.

4   Conclusion

Architecture communities can build their websites based on this model for organizational purposes. Firms can also contribute and advertise their architects and buildings. Although the scope is narrow and hypothetical, this hypothetical model can be resourceful to architectural organizations and search engine companies.

Mining Latent Research Groups within Institutions Using an Author-Topic Model

Takeshi Shirai[1], Yoichi Tomiura[1(✉)], Shosaku Tanaka[2], and Ryutaro Ono[3]

[1] Graduate School of Information Science and Electrical Engineering,
Kyushu University, Fukuoka, Japan
{takeshi.shirai,tom}@inf.kyushu-u.ac.jp
[2] College of Letters, Ritsumeikan University, Kyoto, Japan
sho@lt.ritsumei.ac.jp
[3] RICOH Company, Ltd., Tokyo, Japan
ryuutaroh.ono@nts.ricoh.co.jp

Keywords: Research administrator · Topic analysis · Author-topic model

1 Introduction

Research Administrators play an important role in promoting interdisciplinary research by managing research strategies and intellectual property. They can also contribute meaningfully to the planning and management of interdisciplinary studies. The aim of this study is to develop a support system that Research Administrators can use to identify latent research groups within an institution.

2 Method

A latent research group is a pair of researchers who share collaborative potential. It can be considered to exist when the following two conditions are satisfied:

1. The researchers are each conducting different studies.
2. There are mutually related elements in each study of the researchers.

We use topic analysis with an author-topic model [1] that estimates the occurrence probability distribution of topics for each author and the occurrence probability distribution of words for each topic in order to analyze the studies or interests of researchers. A pair of researchers A and B satisfies condition 1 when the distributions of topics for researchers A and B are considerably different. The pair satisfies condition 2 when some topic a occurs from researcher A with significantly high probability, some topic b occurs from researcher B with significantly high probability, and topics a and b are related in some manner. Topics a and b are related when they appear simultaneously in a thesis written by a third-party. However, it seems impractical to collect extensive theses written by third-parties, add them to the theses written by target researchers and conduct topic analysis on all of them. We therefore use a thesis search engine. Of course we cannot search theses directly with topics obtained in the topic analysis. So we make a list of words that generate from topic t with significantly high probability and tend not to appear in the other topics, and we conduct an AND-search with a

R.B. Allen et al. (Eds.): ICADL 2015, LNCS 9469, pp. 318–319, 2015.
DOI: 10.1007/978-3-319-27974-9

query containing more than one word in the list contain the topic t. In this manner, we get theses containing topic a and theses containing topic b. If there is a common thesis in two theses groups, the thesis contains both topics a and b, and the two topics are regarded as related. Furthermore, the thesis can be used as evidence of the relation between the two topics.

The speed of the topic analysis method is upgraded using the same approach as in Approximate Distributed Latent Dirichlet Allocation (AD-LDA) [2].

3   Experiments

In order to confirm that the method described in section 2 is effective, we conduct an experiment on extracting the latent research groups from 435 pairs of researchers, all possible combinations of 30 researchers belonging to Kyushu University. We collected theses written in Japanese from Kyushu University Institutional Repository (QIR). We left only entries of Japanese Wikipedia, removed other words for each thesis, and made a set of documents. We treated Wikipedia entries as one word and conducted topic analysis on the set of documents.

When conducting topic analysis with a small number of topics, we can expect that the proposed method has high recall and low precision. The method needs to have high recall and some dozens percent (for example, at least 20%) precision to work well as a support system for Research Administrators. We therefore executed an extraction of latent research groups using topic analysis with 600 topics, and with 2000 topics, and compared the results on recall and precision. We used CiNii[1] as the thesis search engine to check if two topics are related. In the case with 600 topics, 179 pairs were extracted as latent research groups. And we judged that 31 of these pairs could be regarded as having collaborative potential. The precision is 0.173, and the recall is 0.449. In the case with 2000 topics, 143 pairs were extracted as latent research groups. And we judged 32 of these pairs could be regarded as having collaborative potential. The precision is 0.224, and the recall is 0.463.

Acknowledgements. This work was supported by JSPS KAKENHI Grant Number 25540151.

References

1. Rosen-Zvi, M., Griffiths, T., Steyvers, M., Smyth, P.: Learning Author Topic Models from Text Corpora. ACM Transactions on Information Systems (TOIS) **28**(1), January 2010
2. Newman, D., Asuncion, A., Smyth, P., Welling, M.: Distributed inference for latent dirichlet allocation. In: 21st Annual Conference on Advances in Neural Information Processing Systems 20, December 2007

---

[1] http://ci.nii.ac.jp/

E-Government in Kazakhstan as a Segment of a Semantic Digital Library

Gulmira S. Sultanbaeva, Nurgul P. Saparkhojayeva, and Elmira S. Sultanbayeva

Al-Farabi Kazakh National University, Almaty, Kazakhstan
sultanbaeva_g@mail.ru, nurgul.saparkhojayeva@gmail.com

Abstract. E-government has become a relevant possibility due to the development of digital technologies in the Republic of Kazakhstan. In addition to optimizing mechanisms of governance management due to the gradual introduction of services connecting the state with other branches of government, businesses and citizens, electronic government provides for the socially important formation of digital (electronic) democracy. Prerequisites for its formation makes it the introduction of the latter, as the company is promoting the use of IT capabilities at the state level to the society. The duties of e-government are the creation of internal and external government computer-information networks and a central database of information, offering activities focused on the needs of citizens and society through the Internet, and the development of new control methods that meet the requirements of society.

1 Introduction

According to scientists, a digital library can be characterized by the range of purposes it serves or the area in which it operates, such as training, education, e-government, e-commerce, entertainment, customer support, or supporting communication between users [1]. We propose to consider a digital library as an information system. In this case, the e-government as a kind of an information system is a digital library. Any information system has to deal with digital content. The main objective of the project "Electronic Government" is the creation of an information space for Kazakhstan and its development. The strategic goal of e-government is for the interests of citizens to have an impact on how the state reacts to important issues, and to ensure citizens' active participation in the processes of state management.

This study monitored the information activity of Kazakhstani society, analyzed provided online services, and conducted a content analysis of the portal egov.kz.

2 Background

Electronic government consists of the following relations: G2C, or Government-to-Citizen; G2B, or Government-to-Business; G2G, or Government-to-Government, between the various branches of the state bodies; and G2E, or Government-to-Employees, between the government and civil servants [2].

© Springer International Publishing Switzerland 2015
R.B. Allen et al. (Eds.): ICADL 2015, LNCS 9469, pp. 320–321, 2015.
DOI: 10.1007/978-3-319-27974-9

The following are major issues of the information society in Kazakhstan:

- The integration of information (electronic resources, user profiles, taxonomies) based on various metadata, containing expressive semantic descriptions
- Support for e-government interaction with other information systems with the help of metadata, either at the level of communication
- Providing a reliable, convenient and adaptable search and interfaces of view of electronic documents [2].

3   Results

Results show that the closing citizens and the government on the platform of e-government ensures the stability of the state and acts to maintain social and political equality. In assessing the near future project of e-government in Kazakhstan, 35% of experts consider that it will reduce of bureaucracy and corruption in the government, and 24% optimistically conclude that it will help authorities promptly respond to requests from the public and increase the openness of state activities (Figure 1).

How do you estimate the nearest future of a project of e-government in Kazakhstan?

- Achieved openness of activity of state structures
- Decreased bureaucracy and corruption of authorities
- Authorities respond promptly to requests from citizens
- Citizens will be able to make political decisions

Fig. 1. Expert opinions about the future of e-government, by % of respondents

By implementing e-government in Kazakhstan, the government opens up the following possibilities: the public receives objective and timely political information; forming a positive public opinion about the institutions of government; rapid and effective implementation of government programs; effective and efficient operation of the state and local government offices (akimats); the implementation of local government and planning; and strengthened public faith in the government.

References

1. Soergel, D.: Digital libraries and knowledge organization. In: Kruk, S.R., McDaniel, B. (eds.) Semantic Digital Libraries, pp. 9–39. Springer, Heidelberg (2009)
2. Sultanbayeva, G.S.: Political Communication in Mass Media: Foreign Experience and Kazakhstan, Almaty (2012)

Study of Color Universal Design in Digital Games

Kazuya Takemata[1(✉)], Tsubasa Takeda[2], Misa Tanaka[2], and Akiyuki Minamide[1]

[1] Kanazawa Technical College, Kanazawa, Japan
{takemata,minamide}@neptune.kanazawa-it.ac.jp
[2] Kanazawa Institute of Technology, Nonoichi, Japan

Abstract. Color perception tests that were mandatory in grade schools in Japan are no longer conducted due to the amendment to the School Health Law in 2003. Therefore, there are cases where one is not aware that he or she has color vision deficiencies (color anomaly) until he or she either gets employment or progresses to the next stage in their education, and are forced to change their course for this reason. Accordingly, the goal of this research is to develop game software which can equally be enjoyed by those with color vision deficiencies in order to help under these circumstances.

Keywords: Color universal design · Color vision · Game software

1   Introduction

Color perception tests that were mandatory in grade schools in Japan were excluded from periodical health examinations due to the revision to the School Health Law in 2003. Therefore, there are cases where one is not aware that he or she has color vision deficiencies (color blind) until he or she either gets employment or progresses to the next stage in their education, and are forced to change their course due to this [1]. Accordingly, the goal of this research is to develop game software which can equally be enjoyed by those with color vision deficiencies in order to improve these circumstances. We also will investigate if it is possible to promote color perception tests to those who may possibly be color blind by playing this game.

2   Color Vision Deficiency

A human possesses three types of cones with differing spectral characteristics. These are L cones (red cones), M cones (green cones), and S cones (blue cones). People with these three types of cones, and with color vision of these three colors are called people with normal color vision. A person without either the L cone (red cone) or the M cone (green cone) is called a Protanope or Deuteranope, respectively. Moreover, a person whose L cone spectral characteristics are off, and resemble those of M cones is called Protanomaly, and a person whose M cone spectral characteristics are off, and resemble L cones is called Deuteranomaly. Most color deficiencies can be classified as Protanope, Protanomaly, Deuteranope, or Deuteranomaly, and the ratio in Japanese males is

© Springer International Publishing Switzerland 2015
R.B. Allen et al. (Eds.): ICADL 2015, LNCS 9469, pp. 322–323, 2015.
DOI: 10.1007/978-3-319-27974-9

about 5%. In case of Japanese females, it is about 0.2%. Therefore, in this study, we simulated the color vision of color blind people, and investigated the difference in the amount of information that they receive compared to people with normal color vision in order to develop games that they can also enjoy.

3   Production of Shooting Games

This is a conventional 2-dimensional shooting game. One can move in all directions and shoot by operating the system. We prepared two types of ammunition for enemy attacks. One type of ammunition is red (numerical color RGB values of 255.0.0), and the other is yellow (numerical color RGB values 255.255.0). Background color is set to brown (numerical RGB values 93.85.36). Due to this, color blind individuals will have a hard time discriminating the red ammunition because they will assimilate with the background. The attacks from the enemy are set so that both red and yellow ammunition will be shot simultaneously. A person with defective color vision will tend to deal with only the yellow ammunition during play, and this action by the game player will show the possibility of the player being color vision defective. Fig. 1 is a screen shot of the shooting game. The red ammunition is pointed by the arrow in the figure. Due to this, players with color vision deficiencies will have a hard time discriminating the red ammunition because they will assimilate with the background.

Fig. 1. Original Game Scene (Left) and Simulated Game Scene of Color Anomaly (Right)

4   Conclusion

We submitted the prototype shooting game to the festival of a Junior High School within our local area. The game received high marks from Junior High Schoolers, and many played multiple times. Most gave positive opinions, such as they "enjoyed" the game. However, we did not find people that showed discomfort about discriminating the two colors. We observed them when they played games, and we feel that it would be difficult to find players with color vision deficiencies during game play. We would like to improve the game software we developed, and finish it to a level deployable in the field.

References

1. Shimbun, Y.: Delay in "detecting" color anomaly, an investigation by the Ophthalmologists Association (article in the Yomiuri Shimbun, September 20, 2013)

Staff Development of Academic Librarians to Improve Information Literacy Education in the Digital Age

Yukiko Watanabe and Kenshi Hyodo(✉)

Kyushu University Library, 6-10-1 Hakozaki, Higashi-ku, Fukuoka 812-8581, Japan
{watanabe.yukiko.935,hyodo.kenshi.896}@m.kyushu-u.ac.jp

Abstract. For enhancing skills related to information literacy instruction in the digital age, we developed an education program for academic librarians, based on knowledge of learning science and educational technology. We evaluated the program in practice and discovered that: 1) Academic librarians want to acquire basic knowledge of learning science and instructional design, 2) Lectures about theory alone are insufficient, but the combination of theory with practical workshops is effective for promoting the integration of participants' knowledge, and 3) Some practical examples support understanding of the theory.

Keywords: Academic library · Instruction librarian · Education program

1 Introduction

In the digital age, information literacy is increasingly indispensable to digital library users, and information professionals have great responsibilities for information literacy education. In North America, the Association of College and Research Libraries (ACRL) showed the standards of competency and framework for information literacy for higher education [1], and the position of "instruction librarian," which involves proficiencies in instructional design and teaching skills, has become established in academic libraries [2]. However, academic librarians in Japan have few opportunities to gain such skills and educational programs for them are not organized systematically, even though the government has promoted educational reform and expects librarians to enhance information literacy education in the university. In this paper, we developed an education program for academic librarians based on the knowledge of learning science and educational technology with specialists, and evaluated it in practice to improve skills related to information literacy instruction in the digital age.

2 Education Program Outline and Evaluation

The education program covers two categories of ACRL's proficiencies: teaching skills and instructional design skills. The learning objective is that librarians should be able to recognize the positive effect of learner-centered approaches and that librarians should be able to point out which theory or model of instructional design is applicable

© Springer International Publishing Switzerland 2015
R.B. Allen et al. (Eds.): ICADL 2015, LNCS 9469, pp. 324–325, 2015.
DOI: 10.1007/978-3-319-27974-9

to improve information literacy education. The program consists of two parts. Part I offers two sessions in a one-day seminar. The first session contains an introductory lecture on learning science and an activity on a collaborative learning strategy known as the "jigsaw technique." The second session contains an introductory lecture on instructional design, and provides references for learning about each theory and model more deeply. In addition to acquiring knowledge and skills, the program focuses on applying them to a real task. Thus, Part II is held as a one-day workshop one or two months after the seminar. Participants make a practical proposal to improve their own situation, and utilize what they have learned. Specialists, who were the lecturers in Part I, also give feedback to participants at the workshop and by online communication during the preparation period for Part II.

We implemented the education program and hosted Part I in November 2014 and Part II in January 2015 at the Kyushu University library. Forty-one librarians, both from the university and from outside, joined Part I. Nine librarians from the university joined Part II. Participants answered questionnaires for assessing the program after joining each part. The results of the survey were as follows: response rates were 75.6% for Part I and 100% for Part II. Among Part I responders, 97% answered that what they had learned from the first session was useful for improving educational activities at their own institution while 58% responded that the second session was useful. In particular, 16% made a positive comment on experiencing the practical activity of collaborative learning in the first session. For the second session, there were comments indicating the difficulty of connecting theory with practice. Among Part II responders, 56% strongly agreed and 44% agreed that they would review their proposal further and would implement it in their actual situation.

3   Future Development

Through developing and putting in practice a new education program, we discovered that: 1) Academic librarians want to acquire basic knowledge of learning science and instructional design, 2) Lectures about theory alone are insufficient, but the combination of theory with practical workshops is effective for promoting the integration with the participants' knowledge, and 3) Practical examples support understanding of the theory. By opening the workshops to librarians from other universities, we will continue to improve this program and develop an e-learning program of lecture videos combined with workshops while improving the evaluation strategy of the program.

Acknowledgements. This work was supported by JSPS KAKENHI Grant Number 26280120.

References

1. ACRL: Framework for Information Literacy for Higher Education (2015). http://www.ala.org/acrl/standards/ilframework
2. ACRL: Standards for Proficiencies for Instruction Librarians and Coordinators (2007). http://www.ala.org/acrl/standards/profstandards

A Window of Opportunity to Create a Portal to Digital Libraries and Digital Archives in Hawai'i

Andrew B. Wertheimer

Library & Information Science Program, University of Hawaii, Honolulu, USA
wertheim@hawaii.edu

Abstract. In the nearly two decades since the establishment of the California Digital Library, most American states have established similar statewide digital libraries and digital archive portals. Hawai'i remains one of the only holdouts. This paper briefly takes a managerial and policy approach to suggest the present is a window of opportunity to develop a consortium and proposes steps towards considering creation of a statewide digital collection.

Keywords: Digital libraries · Digital archives · State digital library portals · Portals · Digital librarianship · Digital library consortia · Consortial management · Hawaii · Pacific

1 Introduction

The Library of Congress's American Memory Project has a page with links to digital libraries and archive projects in each of the 50 states.[1] Although the list contains at least one digital library or archive in each state, fewer than five have no statewide digital consortium. These sites are portals to digital collections of published materials (digital libraries) or unpublished materials (digital archives), sometimes combined with an online encyclopedia about the state and other features such as Open Access Publishing and P-20 educational materials. The creation of state digital archives and libraries was gently encouraged by the Library of Congress and the Institute of Museum and Library Services (IMLS) through their Grants to States Program and the Library Services and Technology Act.

Since these sites are so ubiquitous, the fact that Hawai'i is one of the few without a statewide portal merits analysis. This paper takes a managerial-policy approach by suggesting that the present time offers a unique window of opportunity to create a portal, and proposes a process to establish a digital space that is useful to cultural heritage institutions and their users.

2 The Hawaiian Context

At a first glance, one might assume that Hawai'i would be an ideal place for the development of a statewide portal. Although Honolulu is a large metropolis with many

---

[1] https://www.loc.gov/rr/program/bib/statememory/

© Springer International Publishing Switzerland 2015
R.B. Allen et al. (Eds.): ICADL 2015, LNCS 9469, pp. 326–328, 2015.
DOI: 10.1007/978-3-319-27974-9

archives, libraries, museums, and universities, the state is spread out over six islands, some of which are quite sparsely populated.

Although the Hawaiian State Public Library System (HSPLS) quietly resigned from taking a role on creating a digital portal, the Hawai'i State Archives and University of Hawai'i (UH) at Mānoa both took the lead in establishing their own digital collections. At the same time, another independent set of self-defined digital libraries emerged, created by the Native Hawaiian Community. Sometimes these followed standard library and archival practices, but often not.

3   Window of Opportunity

Although it has been a decade since the last major steps were taken to develop a statewide digital portal, there may be a new window of opportunity. A key factor is the appointment of a new state librarian. The Board of Education selected Stacey Aldrich, who has been involved in a number of developing library technology projects, including playing a key role in Maryland's state network [1].

State Archivist Susan Shaner and UH Mānoa Librarian Irene Herold continue to support digital efforts in their institutions. Another part of the window of opportunity could come from the relatively new President of the UH System, who was the former head of technology services and helped secure a major grant to extend broadband connections to the state. In his former role, President Lassner was highly supportive of open source platforms, and ITS, UH Libraries, and Outreach College are supporting Open Education Resources, which could be a real part of any digital portal. Another potential supporter is the new State Governor, who was previously an engineer and made promoting technology jobs part of his campaign platform.

3.1   Other Partners

All of the aforementioned groups are potential collaborators. The Hawai'i State Museums Association has already made progress on a parallel venture, the Connecting to Collections statewide planning IMLS grant, so we have a good set of partners available [2]. Most of the libraries are partners already on several ventures, such as the Database Consortium. The UH LIS Program is another possible partner, especially since several faculty members have experience with digital libraries.

Our statewide professional associations can help move this agenda forward. In the past the associations seemed to almost be competing against each other for survival, but a spirit of cooperation seems to be rising, as can be seen by the strong participation in recent joint events and an upcoming joint conference. The recent success of Na Hawai'i Imi Loa, as an association of Native Hawaiian LIS students and alumni, suggests ways that these professionals can use their skills and cultural competence. A key example is the recent thesis of Shavonn Matsuda, which calls for a Native Hawaiian Knowledge Organization System [3]. Other possible partners, explored in my larger paper, include Brigham Young University-Hawaii and the Bishop Museum. There are a number of smaller libraries and archives in the state that might want to join in the effort, including the Hawaiian Historical Society, historical societies on neighbor islands, and ethnic community collections.

Outside of the traditional circle of libraries, archives, and museums, other key partners would include the University of Hawai'i Press, which is already partnering with university libraries on a number of scholarly publishing ventures. There are also a number of small and medium size publishers in the state, and many are creating eBooks. Hawai'i is also home to the online newspaper *Civil Beat*, which has published a few issues supporting libraries, as has the *Honolulu Star-Bulletin.*

The state portal does not need to be a static collection of published books or electronic records, but could become an integral access point to local information as well as a creative space to share creative works as well as a political discourse. Interesting examples include the works of Kanu Hawaii, an online site dedicated to sustainability, as well as Kapiolani Community College, which has created digital exhibits about Nisei veterans, a Native Plants Hawaii site, and a creative effort that allowed chefs to learn about the current availability of local farm produce.

4   Next Steps

In order to take advantage of this current window of opportunity, I would suggest that the Hawai'i Library Association or Association of Hawai'i Archivists hold a set of meetings involving the major libraries and archives. Each repository interested in participating should be invited to send one or two people, ideally a director and someone with technical experience with digital projects. Major stakeholders should be encouraged to respond to the key questions. At a second meeting, it would be good to review notes and attempt to formulate some way of moving forward. This needs to become an organization so that it can be democratic, transparent, and develop reporting methods to bring in stakeholders who can assist with the process. Doing this in 2015, rather than 2005, many parties in Hawai'i have a better understanding of digital libraries, digital archives, and the importance of cooperative work on establishing quality relevant controlled vocabularies, as well as standards for intellectual property, scanning quality, and preservation methods.

Working to create one digital archive or portal might will not bring an end to Hawai'i's digital divide or create major immediate change, and it is a very real possible that all of the participants might agree that the best step would be to simply create one simple homepage with links to the various digital projects in the state or to partner with the Digital Public Library of America (DPLA) Hub; however, it would be a worthwhile exercise for all stakeholders to visualize what a digital archive and digital library platform could offer.

References

1. Library Journal.: Stacey Aldrich: Movers & Shakers 2003, March 15, 2003. http://lj.libraryjournal.com/2003/03/people/movers-shakers-2003/stacey-aldrich-movers-shakers-2003/
2. Hawai'i Museum Association: Nūhou: HMA's quarterly newsletter **45**(4) (2014). http://www.hawaiimuseums.org/wp-content/uploads/2014/03/nuhou-winter-2014.pdf
3. Matsuda, S.-H.: Toward A Hawaiian Knowledge Organization System. (MLISc), Univ. of Hawai'i at Mānoa (2015)

Extracting Structure from Scientific Abstracts Using Neural Networks

Paul Willot[1,2]([⊠]), Kazuhiro Hattori[1], and Akiko Aizawa[1]

[1] National Institute of Informatics, Tokyo, Japan
[2] Université Pierre et Marie Curie, Paris, France

Abstract. *Objective:* Knowing the structure of a scientific paper abstract is useful in a variety of NLP tasks such as information extraction or paper writing assistance. Existing methods classify abstract sentences into predefined structural roles, achieving good results but only on specific fields. In this poster we investigate a method that works well across domains. *Method:* We propose a classifier based on neural networks, and compare it with conventional classifiers, using labeled abstracts from the bio-medical domain as a training corpus, and manually annotated computer science abstracts as test data. *Result:* Early experiments demonstrate that our neural-network–based method significantly outperforms conventional methods in the cross-domain classification task.

1 Background

Abstract segmenting tools are useful for text retrieval, allowing users to search in a specific section, and for any task benefiting from structured information.

Most of the previous researches have been conducted on the Medline database, a bio-medical bibliographic database, exploiting the significant numbers[1] of structured abstracts in which sections are explicitly marked by headings. In their experiment K. Hirohata et al.[1] evaluate support vector machines and conditional random field classifiers to categorize sentences, reporting accuracies of 93% and 95% respectively. We use these two classifiers as a baseline for our experiments.

2 Proposed Method

We work on 500,000 structured abstracts extracted from the Medline database, and use 20% of it as test set along with a manually annotated collection of ACL and ACM abstracts.

First, we pre-process each sentence by lemmatizing the words, replacing the numbers with a '#' symbol, and adding the relative sentence location in the abstract as a complementary feature to the sentence content. We chose to consider the four structuring labels Background, Method, Results and Conclusion as recommended by G.Y. Chung[2].

---

[1] Approximately 3 million, as of 2015.

© Springer International Publishing Switzerland 2015
R.B. Allen et al. (Eds.): ICADL 2015, LNCS 9469, pp. 329–330, 2015.
DOI: 10.1007/978-3-319-27974-9

We introduce a new classifier based on a long short-term memory neural network (LSTM), which is a neural network fitted for sequence labeling. This network is able to take the full context into account[3], which is advantageous because it improves the abstraction of the classifier from domain specific language by taking the context into account for each word, whereas a CRF only considers the context outside of the sentence, as it process a sequence of sentences and not a sequence of words[1].

3 Evaluation

We first evaluate our neural network on the Medline corpus, then we evaluate the baseline and our network on a manually annotated corpus of ACL and ACM abstracts. This annotated corpus is constructed by averaging annotations independently made by three experts in the field on 100 abstracts from ACL and ACM. We obtain a Fleiss' kappa value of 0.64, indicating a fair annotation agreement. Because we allowed the annotator to choose the best labels regardless of the previous one (e.g. we can have the sequence Background, Method, Background, Conclusion), we observed that the CRF performed poorly on the task as it predicted strictly ordered labels. We therefore compared our neural network with SVM for the second corpus. Our neural network achieved a 90.1% precision on the Medline corpus (93.3% CRF, 92.9% SVM) and a 61.9% precision on the ACL/ACM corpus, compared to 46.3% for SVM, with respective recall of 65% and 48%. The results showed that because of the specificity of bio-medical vocabulary, higher accuracy on the Medline corpus doesn't imply higher accuracy on our evaluation set.

4 Conclusion

Our experiments showed that the proposed system generalizes better to new domains than previously proposed methods, and can therefore be used to extract structure from scientific paper abstracts across multiple domains.

In addition to adding complementary features and improving the neural network performance, transfer training may provide improved results in future work.

Acknowledgments. This work was supported by JSPS KAKENHI Grant Numbers 15H01721, 15H02754.

References

1. Hirohata, K., Okazaki, N., Ananiadou, S., Ishizuka, M.: Identifying sections in scientific abstracts using conditional random fields. In: Proceedings of the 3rd International Joint Conference on Natural Language Processing 2008, pp. 381–388 (2008)
2. Chung, G.Y., Coiera, E.: A study of structured clinical abstracts and the semantic classification of sentences. In: Proceedings of the Workshop on BioNLP: Biological, Translational, and Clinical Language Processing 2007, pp. 121–128 (2007). doi:10.3115/1572392.1572415
3. Sundermeyer, M., Schluter, R., Ney, H.: LSTM neural networks for language modeling. In: INTERSPEECH 2012, pp. 194–197 (2012)

A Survey and a Comparative Study of Natural Disaster Taxonomies of Current Practice

Li Yang[1](✉) and Yejun Wu[2]

[1] School of Computer Science, Southwest Petroleum University, Chengdu, Sichuan, China
yangli0027@163.com
[2] School of Library and Information Science, Louisiana State University, Baton Rouge, USA
wuyj@lsu.edu

Abstract. This paper presents a survey and a comparative study of natural disaster taxonomies of current practice. Four taxonomies are studied and compared, including AIRS/211 LA County Taxonomy of Human Services, Disaster Category Classification and Peril Terminology for Operational Purposes, Peril Classification and Hazard Glossary, and Human Security Taxonomy. Taxonomic structure, subject coverage, and applied databases are compared and key findings are presented. The structure of a common, comprehensive taxonomy of natural disaster is proposed.

Keywords: Classification · Comparative study · Natural disaster · Taxonomy

1   Introduction

Natural disaster information, such as a systematic record and evaluation of disaster events can be important to disaster preparedness, response and recovery [1]. Databases at all levels are used by experts and organizations to manage natural disaster information. Different databases may use different taxonomies to organize information, resulting in the same information items being categorized into different classification structures. For instance, Avalanche may be categorized into Earthquake (upper level), and can also be a category itself at the same level as Earthquake. Differences in natural disaster taxonomies may affect information use and sharing, and may even cause misunderstanding. The goal of this study is to survey major natural disaster taxonomies and conduct a comparative analysis to examine their commonalities and differences. Our ultimate goal is to develop a common, comprehensive taxonomy of natural disasters for information management.

2   Background and Method

Natural disaster taxonomy is a subject of natural disaster based classification that organizes terms in a controlled vocabulary into a hierarchy [2]. Many research outcomes, such as AIRS/211 LA County Taxonomy of Human Services (1983), Taxonomy of Disasters and Their Victims [3], Global Environmental Risk Taxonomy [4],

© Springer International Publishing Switzerland 2015
J.B. Allen et al. (Eds.): ICADL 2015, LNCS 9469, pp. 331–333, 2015.
DOI: 10.1007/978-3-319-27974-9

Taxonomy of GEM Building [5], Taxonomy of Threats for Macro-Catastrophe Risk Management [1], and Hazard Taxonomy [6], have been published. These taxonomies indicate the lack of a common classification and definition of terms.

The comparative study of natural disaster taxonomies is expected to identify the commonalities and differences between the taxonomies, and to set a foundation for a comprehensive taxonomy of natural disasters, which can be useful for organizing information in digital libraries for natural disaster information management.

Taxonomies were collected from the Web using Google. Queries include (Natural) Disaster Taxonomy, (Natural) Disaster Classification, Disaster Category, Earthquake Taxonomy, (Natural) Disaster Database, (Natural) Disaster Digital Library.

3   Case Studies of Taxonomies

More than 10 taxonomies were collected. Four of them were selected for the study.

- AIRS/211 LA County Taxonomy of Human Services (THS). THS is both extensive and specific [7]. It does not aim for natural disaster information management specifically, but has a complete section of Disaster Services about human services before and after disasters, during which precaution/warning and emergency rescue/relief are key to reducing losses and suffering.
- Disaster Category Classification and Peril Terminology for Operational Purpose (DCC+PTOP). DCC+PTOP is based on a "triggering hazard/event" logic, and classifies hazards only [8]. Human activities are not included.
- Peril Classification and Hazard Glossary (PCHG). PCHG is an improved and revised framework of DCC+PTOP. Each category, main event and peril has a corresponding definition, which is called a Hazard Glossary, to facilitate selection and appropriate use [9]. Human activities are not included.
- Human Security Taxonomy (HST) (v2.2). HST is based on existing humanitarian and GIS data of both natural and technical disasters, with 13 base layers, 28 GIS layers and more than 890 data elements [10]. It includes natural and technical disasters, and has relatively complete subject coverage from precaution before disaster, to relief after disaster, with a simple classification of natural hazards.

4   Comparison and Findings

Table 1 shows a comparison of the four taxonomies. The Human Security Taxonomy (HST) has the broadest coverage, but its human services section is not as comprehensive or specific as the Taxonomy of Human Services (THS). It covers disaster types but they are not as specific as DCC+PTOP. When developing a comprehensive natural disaster taxonomy, HST can be used as the foundation, DCC+PTOP can be used to enrich disaster types, and THS can be used to enrich human services. The definition of terms in THS serve as good references when developing the taxonomy. In order to facilitate the use of taxonomies, detailed definitions and extensions including Used For, See Also, External Terms, Related concepts and Bibliography Reference can be applied.

Table 1. A comparison of four taxonomies

	THS	DCC+PTOP	PCHG	HST
Pub. Year	1983	2009	2014	2013
Levels	6	4	3	3
Subject coverage	human services, disaster services	disaster types	disaster types (revised version of DCC+PTOP)	infrastructure, disaster source data, disaster types, human services
Term definition	detailed	detailed	detailed	simple
Databases	Multiple types of human services	NatCatSERVICE, EM-DAT	Multiple types of loss databases	Databases of pre-event hazard mitigation, emergency response, materiel pre-positioning

Each of the four taxonomies that are used in databases to organize information has its own structure and subject coverage. The findings of this study can be used to create a comprehensive taxonomy for organizing natural disaster information. The Human Security Taxonomy can be used as a foundation, and the other three taxonomies can be used to enrich the parts of disaster types and human services.

References

1. Coburn, A., Bowman, G., Ruffle, S., Ralph, D., Tuveson, M.: A Taxonomy of Threats for Macro-catastrophe Risk Management. Cambridge Centre for Risk Studies (2013)
2. Garshol, L.M.: Metadata? Thesauri? Taxonomies? Topic maps! Making sense of it all. Journal of Information Science 30(4), 378–391 (2004)
3. Taylor, A.J.: A Taxonomy of Disasters and Their Victims. Journal of Psychosomatic Research 31(5), 535–544 (1987)
4. Babut, G., Moraru, R.: Considerations Regarding Global Environmental Risk Taxonomy And Assessment. Wiertnictwo, Nafta, Gaz **26**(3), 471–476 (2009)
5. GEM Building Taxonomy v2.0: Evaluation and Testing Report. http://www.nexus.globalquakemodel.org/gem-building-taxonomy/posts/report-on-evaluation-and-testing-of-the-gem-building-taxonomy-released
6. Safety Management International Collaboration Group Standardization. http://www.skybrary.aero/index.php/Category:SM_ICG_Standardization
7. Los Angeles County: Structure and Contents - AIRS/211 LA County Taxonomy of Human Services (2015). https://211taxonomy.org/publicfiles/view/Intro-Structure_and_Contents.pdf
8. Below, R., Wirtz, A., Guha-Sapir, D.: Disaster Category Classification and Peril Terminology for Operational Purposes. Published: CRED: Brussels, MunichRe: Munich (2009)
9. Integrated Research on Disaster Risk: Peril Classification and Hazard Glossary (2014). http://www.irdrinternational.org/2014/03/28/irdr-peril-classification-and-hazard-glossary/
10. Worldwide Human Geography Data Working Group: Human Security Taxonomy (2013). http://www.geoplatform.gov/wwhgd-home

eScience and Living Analytics

Palakorn Achananuparp

Singapore Management University, Singapore Singapore
palakorna@smu.edu.sg

Abstract. Massive amount of digital traces left behind by life in the modern world have brought about the emergence of a *computational social science*. This presentation introduces research at Living Analytics Research Centre (LARC) where problems in consumer and social analytics are solved through the use of large-scale data, computational techniques, and closed-loop experimentation.

Keywords: Computational social science · eScience · Living analytics

1   Introduction

Recent advances in Internet and telecommunication technology have dramatically transformed modern life. Everything we do leaves digital traces that reveal detailed information about ourselves and the relationships with others. We broadcast our feelings, thoughts, interests, and friendships through the use of online social networks like Facebook and Twitter. Our professional networks are virtually visible to anyone through our LinkedIn profile. Our physical locations and movements can be tracked through ubiquitous sensors embedded in arrays of mobile devices. The massive amount of data about people and society have transformed the ways scientific research is conducted. In social science, a few Internet companies, e.g., Google and Yahoo, and academic researchers have pioneered the studies and applications of large-scale data, leading to a paradigm shift in computational social science [1].

In this presentation, I will give a brief overview of Living Analytics Research Centre (LARC), a joint research collaboration between Singapore Management University (SMU) and Carnegie Mellon University (CMU). Established with a five-year (2011-2015) grant from the government of Singapore, LARC's mission is to bring together multidisciplinary teams of researchers in data mining and machine learning, statistics, social and behavior science, management science, and network science, to expand computational social science.

LARC focuses on five key research areas, including 1) intelligent systems for mining and analytics; 2) social and management science; 3) network experimentation; 4) security, data fusion, and privacy preservation; and 5) systems and infrastructure. Unique to LARC's approach to research is the iterative aspects of analytics.

© Springer International Publishing Switzerland 2015
R.B. Allen et al. (Eds.): ICADL 2015, LNCS 9469, pp. 334–335, 2015.
DOI: 10.1007/978-3-319-27974-9

Essentially, the analytic loop starts with the *Observation* stage that involves observing user interactions and relationships within a network to collect their digital traces. Next, the *Analyze and Predict* stage will analyze the digital traces to find interesting patterns and generate hypotheses about the observations. Then, in the *Experiment* stage, experiments are designed to investigate how individuals and groups in the network will respond to changes introduced by the experimenters. Finally, in the *Human Actions* stage, individuals' and groups' responses in the experiments are analyzed. The experimental findings will determine the optimal way to implement the changes in real setting and the next iteration begins.

In the second part of the presentation, I will introduce some of the research projects conducted by LARC researchers and collaborators, covering a wide range of topics. For example, how digital traces of theme park visitors were used to improve their personal experience, how social media messages were used to gain more insights about real-world events, such as elections [2]. Lastly, I will conclude by reflecting on the challenges in realizing living analytics.

2   Presenter

Palakorn Achananuparp is a research scientist at Living Analytics Research Centre (LARC). He received his Ph.D. from Drexel University where his research focused on extractive text summarization for complex question answering. At LARC, he led the research and development of several social media analytics [3] and experimentation [4] systems. His research interests include social media mining, web and text mining, and personal informatics. His publications appeared in broad venues, such as ACL-HLT, HICSS, and Social Networks. He served as a program committee of various conferences (DSAA, ICADL, SocInfo, etc.) and reviewed for many journals (JASIST, TIST, TKDE, etc.) and conferences.

References

1. Lazer, D., Pentland, A., Adamic, L., Aral, S., Barabasi, A.-L., Brewer, D., Christakis, N., Contractor, N., Fowler, J., Gutmann, M., Jebara, T., King, G., Macy, M., Roy, D., Van Alstyne, M.: Life in the Network: The Coming Age of Computational Social Science. Science 323(5915), 721–723 (2009)
2. Skoric, M., Poor, N., Achananuparp, P., Lim, E.-P., Jiang, J.: Tweets and votes: study of the 2011 singapore general election. In: Proceedings of 45th Hawaii International International Conference on Systems Science (HICSS-45 2012), pp. 2583–2591. IEEE (2012)
3. Achananuparp, P., Lubis, I.N., Tian, Y., Lo, D., Lim, E.-P.: Observatory of trends in software related microblogs. In: Proceedings of the 27th IEEE/ACM International Conference on Automated Software Engineering - ASE 2012, p. 334. ACM Press, New York (2012)
4. Lim, K.H., Lim, E.-P., Achananuparp, P., Vu, A., Kwee, A.T., Zhu, F.: LASER: A Living Analytics Experimentation System for Large-Scale Online Controlled Experiments (2014)

Linking Digital Art History Content to the Web of Data: From Online Exhibitions to Linked Taiwan Artists

Shu-Jiun Chen

Institute of Taiwan History, Academia Sinica, Taipei, Taiwan
sophy@sinica.edu.tw

Abstract. Following humanities' digital turn, Art History, a traditional humanities research field, has shifted to "Digital Art History". This report presents the Linked Taiwan Artist project which aims to construct a linked open data based digital research environment for art history researchers.

Keywords: Digital art history · Digital humanities · Linked open data

This report presents Academia Sinica's first digital art history project, which demonstrates the evolution of semantic approaches to constructing a digital research environment for art history learners and researchers. The "Starting out from 23.5°N: Chen Cheng-po" bilingual website [1] has been lunched at the first stage attempting to explore the life and time of the important Taiwanese artist Chen Cheng-po (1895– 1947) through objects and visualization. Many items in Chen's archive and his painting style reveal a strong influence of both Japanese and Post-Impressionist art with cross-cultural encounters, and intensive social networks among him and his fellows [2,3,4]. The website, featuring more than 500 pieces of artwork, correspondence and other documents, is organized into 10 themes based on Chen's personal history, travelling paths, and social networks. A number of tools such as timelines, Google maps, network graphs, and the Art & Architecture Thesaurus (AAT) of the Getty Research Institute, among others, are cleverly woven into the graceful interface of the website, making it an intriguing and educational experience for viewers. The project involves the creation of different types of Chinese-English bilingual metadata records and authority files for the objects, people, places, events, and multiple timelines. We also have used controlled vocabularies, for instance, in the "subject" element of the artwork metadata records. In addition, GIS-applications with historical maps have been integrated into the projects. The website serves an online exhibition showing how the different types of digital art history content can be linked together to help users read the artist in the backdrop of Taiwan under Japanese Rule.

However, all the expressions of relationships in the online presence, such as social networks among artists have been already pre-defined in the databases. The project at its second stage has adopted Linked Open Data (LOD) principles [5] to model and publish the existing different types of datasets with a purpose to enhance semantic retrieval and exploration and allow for the expression of complex relations between information objects. A number of selected use cases have been created based on the

© Springer International Publishing Switzerland 2015
R.B. Allen et al. (Eds.): ICADL 2015, LNCS 9469, pp. 336–337, 2015.
DOI: 10.1007/978-3-319-27974-9

interview with art historians. For instance, scholars would like to query which artworks are created in different stages of an artist that depict a specific place, and among these works, which ones have been selected for a specific event. We have reused seven sets of terms from well-known linked open vocabularies, including the schema.org, CIDOC-CRM, Getty Vocabularies, DBpedia, RDF Schema, SKOS, and DCMI Metadata Terms. The art history ontology following an RDF Data model has been created with 30 classes and 57 properties. The application of Linked Taiwan Artists [6] has been developed with four features as follows: (1) open data: publishing the collection semantically, 5-star open data scheme with a SPARQL endpoint which allows others to reuse the data; (2) faceted navigation and inferring of semantic relationships: supporting exploration and discovery objectives, for instance, the search result can dynamically show the different types of relationship between two artists by the system's inductive reasoning, and users can take a look at what happened in a specific place, for example, who was born, died and resided in Taipei, or which works, by whom depicted scenes of Taipei; (3) contextualizing research materials: giving data sets essential context and increases their discoverability; and (4) allowing data from different sources to be interconnected & queried.

In summary, the report demonstrates a preliminary result constructing Linked Open Data for the digital collection of a painter and his related archives, social network and events in the age of Taiwan Modern Art History (1895-1947). We set up use cases & reuse LOD vocabularies to help design an art history ontology for the study. The Linked Open Data application, Linked Taiwan Artists, has been published on the Web with four essential features. More complete functions will be explored and implemented for the application, for instances, an integrated space-time tracking system in support of representation, analysis, and visualization of artists' activities and interactions in physical and virtual spaces.

References

1. Academia Sinica Digital Center: Starting out from 23.5°N: Chen Cheng-po (2014). http://chenchengpo.asdc.sinica.edu.tw/
2. Lin, Y.C.: The real scenes and images Utopia in Chen Cheng-po's journey of life. In: Lin, Y.C., Lee, W.F. (eds.) Journey Through Jiangnan: A Pivotal Moment in Chen Chen-po's Artistic Quest, pp. 6–15. Taipei Fine Arts Museum, Taipei (2012)
3. Hsiao, C.R.: Surging waves: the historical significance of Chen Cheng-po's 120th birthday anniversary touring exhibition [Introduction]. In: Yeah, T.S. (ed.) Surging Waves: Chen Cheng-po's 120th Birthday Anniversary Touring Exhibition, Tainan, pp. 10–25. Tainan City Government, Tainan (2014)
4. Mathison, C.B.: Identity, hybridity, and modernity: the colonial paintings of Chen Cheng-po. In: Lin, Y.C., Lee, W.F. (eds.) Journey Through Jiangnan: A Pivotal Moment in Chen Chen-po's Artistic Quest, pp. 50–63. Taipei Fine Arts Museum, Taipei (2012)
5. Bizer, C., Heath, T., Berners-Lee, T.: Linked data-the story so far. Semantic Services, Interoperability and Web Applications: Emerging Concepts, 205–227 (2009)
6. Academia Sinica Digital Center: Linked Taiwan Artists (2015). http://data.asdc.tw/LTA/

Modeling Digital Literary Texts "Literally"

Wayne de Fremery

Sogang University, Seoul, South Korea
wdefremery@gmail.com

Abstract. This panel presentation reports on recent collaborative experiments in textual modeling that illuminate mechanisms ordinarily concealed when digital reproductions of textual artifacts are enacted. Approaching digital texts the way analytical bibliographers approach printed books can produce fecund forms of literary, textual, technological, and historical critique. The talk concludes with a description of how textual models described in the presentation were printed using 3D printers. These new physical models of digital texts illuminate some of the artistic opportunities and documentary challenges presented by the panoply of modeling techniques described by Kirschenbaum as our ".txtual condition."

Keywords: 3D printing · Analytical bibliography · Comparative textual media · Korean literature · Modeling

This presentation reports on recent collaborative experiments in textual modeling that I have conducted as part of a larger project investigating how digital texts might be studied "literally," the way an analytical bibliographer would study a printed document. Models, in their wide variety of conceptual and material forms, are central to iterating texts. They articulate, for example, various digital standards such as Unicode and the logic of software controlling the conceptual objects we read as text on screen. They also shape physical documents designed using digital technologies. If we aim to study the mechanisms of textual production as they relate to interpretive textual practice in our digital age, models are a good place to begin. And modeling has been a topic of great interest in the digital humanities, although what is connoted by modeling among digital humanists is distinct from what I intend here. Indeed, some contend that specific kinds of modeling, such as topic modeling, which attempts to discern thematic structures in the content of digital texts, might stand for the field as a whole.[1]

This presentation will not address topic modeling directly, but will ask more general questions about modeling textual documents. How might a new generation of textual scholars (re)model digital texts to illuminate mechanisms that manifest texts in digital environments and our physical world? Can we develop models that reveal what bibliographer D.F. McKenzie has called the sociology of texts in a fashion that will advance practices in new fields such as comparative textual media? If we were to lend physical form to the various models that constitute digital objects, modeling them "literally,"

---

[1] In a 2012 issue of the *Journal of Digital Humanities* devoted to topic modeling, Elijah Meeks and Scott B. Weingart suggest that topic modeling can be considered a synecdoche for the digital humanities. They make this claim partly in jest, to highlight recent interest in the topic among digital humanists and critique stereotypes about digital humanities' practices [1].

© Springer International Publishing Switzerland 2015
R.B. Allen et al. (Eds.): ICADL 2015, LNCS 9469, pp. 338–339, 2015.
DOI: 10.1007/978-3-319-27974-9

what shapes might they take? What might these physical models of digital documents say about the idea of being "literal," meaning taking texts and words in their usual and most basic sense? This talk presents preliminary answers to these questions and suggests that the practice of modeling, if conceived more broadly by digital humanists, can enable insight, foster wonder, and promise cultural preservation.

The first half of the presentation recounts experiments designed to reveal mechanisms ordinarily concealed when digital reproductions of textual artifacts are enacted. Inspired by approaches pioneered by McKenzie, Jerome McGann, Johanna Drucker, Katherine Hayles and recent work by Matthew Kirschenbaum and Alan Galey, this section describes remodeling a digital copy of one issue of the important Korean colonial-era periodical *Kaebyŏk* (Creation), hosted on a website administrated by the National Institute of Korean History (NIKH). This was done by generating an alternate visual scheme for the Unicode values used as part of the computational procedures that present the July 1922 issue *Kaebyŏk* on the NIKH website. This engagement with the materials and computational elements of digital texts revealed itself as a fecund form of literary, textual, technological, and historical critique. Our experiment generated a number of domain-specific hypotheses about genre, translation, and compositional practice in colonial Korea while raising important questions about studies of culture that bracket either the material or discursive systems of cultural objects from view and the ways historical documents are "conserved" digitally. A narrow focus on the material-discursive details of a single issue of one periodical brought expansive, largely unexplored, fields of investigation into view.

The second half suggests that the practice of modeling can afford new expressive opportunities in addition to historical and literary insights. McKenzie famously argued that books are expressive forms. I suggest that new philological techniques can productively blur the material, conceptual, and, eventually, institutional boundaries that demarcate artistic and scholarly practice. To illustrate these creative horizons and the expressive opportunities presented by model-making in specific material, historical, sociocultural, and technological conditions, the talk concludes by describing how I projected the 2-dimensional models introduced in section one in three dimensions and printed the results in plastic and steel using 3D printers. I argue that these new physical models help us see some of the artistic opportunities and documentary challenges, scholarly prospects and creative conundrums presented by the more ubiquitous modeling techniques that constitute what Kirschenbaum calls our ".txtual condition." "Access is thus duplication, duplication is preservation, and preservation is creation and re-creation," writes Kirschenbaum; "this is the catechism of the .txtual condition" [2]. If this is the catechism, then creatively iterating and reiterating the models that constitute digital texts—in digital and physical form—promises a means of cultural preservation and access to the sociomaterial, technological, historical, and literary elements that constitute this condition.

References

1. Meeks, E., Weingart, S.B.: The Digital Humanities Contribution to Topic Modeling. Journal of Digital Humanities 2(1) (2012). http://journalofdigitalhumanities.org/2-1/dh-contribution-to-topic-modeling/
2. Kirschenbaum, M.: The.txtual condition. In: Hayles, K.N., Pressman, J. (eds.) Comparative Textual Media: Transforming the Humanities in the Postprint Era. University of Minnesota Press, Minneapolis (2013)

Digital Archives and Digital Methods:
A Indonesian Case Study

Miguel Escobar Varela

National University of Singapore, Singapore Singapore
m.escobar@nus.edu.sg

Abstract. Digital humanities methods, both quantitative (such as Stylometry and Network Analysis) and interpretive (interactive scholarship and tangible interfaces) can be used to analyze and present the data in digital archives of cultural heritage (such as performance documentation).

Keywords: Digital humanities · Network analysis · Performance archives · Stylometry · Tangible interfaces

The Contemporary Wayang Archive (CWA) is an online collection of full video recordings of new versions of *wayang kulit,* a form of puppet theatre that constitutes Java's most important theatrical tradition. Conventional shows last eight hours and are rarely watched by younger spectators. In contrast *kontemporer* (contemporary) shows are shorter and integrate new languages and media (such as hip hop music, digital image projections and narratives inspired by television). The CWA aims to systematically document innovations in *wayang* by presenting a video database of the key innovations in the form, with translations into English and explanatory notes.

An archive of this kind is a valuable resource for students, artists and researchers who want to watch the videos and learn more about the specific performances that have been archived. However, it is also a rich source of data, which can be processed and presented in a number of ways, using digital humanities methodologies. This paper considers a few examples of the kinds of research made possible by these approaches:

1) **Stylometric analysis of the performance texts.** Specifically, we have used Principal Component Analysis (PCA) to identify differences in authorial style, by considering the words shared by all authors in the sample. In the past, PCA has been extensively used for author identification of written texts. However, we have found that it can reveal different authorial styles of oral, improvised texts in languages such as Indonesian and Javanese.

2) **Network analysis.** *Wayang* performances mostly use characters from the Sanskrit epic narratives: the Mahabharata and the Ramayana. However, *kontemporer* shows only focus on a subset of the characters. Using network analysis we can compare the networks of the characters in traditional shows to those of *kontemporer* ones.

© Springer International Publishing Switzerland 2015
R.B. Allen et al. (Eds.): ICADL 2015, LNCS 9469, pp. 340–341, 2015.
DOI: 10.1007/978-3-319-27974-9

3) **Interactive scholarship.** A web platform that integrates, text, video and semi-quantitative visualizations derived from the archive is available at www.wayankontemporer.com.

4) **Tangible interfaces.** Using Arduino microprocessors and digital sensors we are in the process of building an exhibition booth that will enable visitors to to interact with the recordings of the archive by manipulating puppets and musical instruments equipped with sensors.

Digital archives are often considered within the context of Digital Humanities as an example of new scholarly outputs. However, digital archives can do more than just facilitate access to the cultural record. Digital archives can become the starting point for quantitative approaches to the study of culture (such as stylometric analysis and network analysis) and for creative and interactive tools used to display research findings (such as interactive scholarship and tangible interfaces).

Sharing Scientific Literature, Ontologies, Databases and Annotations for Open Science

Jin-Dong Kim

Database Center for Life Science,
Research Organization of Information and Systems, Tokyo, Japan
jdkim@dbcls.rois.ac.jp

Scientific knowledge has been accumulated for hundreds or even thousands of years. With 'accumulation', it means scientific discoveries have been recorded and published, mostly through scientific literature. By accessing the accumulated knowledge, development of new knowledge could be efficient. Particularly in life sciences, the existence of public online libraries, e.g. PubMed, has played an important role in enabling scientists to instantly access scientific articles of interest. As technology progresses, however, the velocity of knowledge extension is rapidly increasing, and it is becoming almost impossible for human researchers to comprehend even their own expert areas.

Meanwhile, important entities have been databased in structured databases to enable an instant access to information about them. Important concepts also have been organized in the form of taxonomy, controlled vocabulary and ontology. Recently, Linked Data (LD) is emerging as a new way of data publication. LD enables relevant data pieces across multiple databases to be linked to each other through a standard protocol. It may be said that while the amount of databased data pieces increased during the development of structured databases (mostly relational databases), the linkage between the data pieces is being significantly improved thanks to the technology of LD and Semantic Web. Particularly, life sciences form an area of rich public databases, e.g. gene databases (Entrez Gene), Protein databases (UniProt), or interaction databases (IntAct). Also, there is a central repository of life science ontologies, BioPortal.

While scientific literature may be regarded as a comprehensive chronological records of scientific discoveries, structural databases may be regarded as aiming at comprehensively enumerating entities of interest with their important properties, and ontologies as organization of the entities or abstractions of them. Compared to knowledge represented in scientific literature, however, the pieces of knowledge in structured databases or linked data often miss their contexts, e.g., experimental environments. As contexts of individual data pieces are often represented in scientific literature where they are referenced, finding references to the entities in literature and linking them to the corresponding entities is an important process which restores the contexts of the entities, from the perspective of databases, and indexes the contexts of literature by the entries of databases, from the perspective of the literature.

With this background, there are many projects on-going to produce semantic indexing of scientific literature using entities from structural databases, a.k.a. literature annotation. Literature annotation projects are particularly active in the area of life sciences,

© Springer International Publishing Switzerland 2015
R.B. Allen et al. (Eds.): ICADL 2015, LNCS 9469, pp. 342–343, 2015.
DOI: 10.1007/978-3-319-27974-9

partly due to the existence of public literature databases, e.g. PubMed. Although many of those annotation projects are conducted individually, fundamentally, they share the same target, i.e. PubMed articles. Since it is impossible for a single group to annotate the whole PubMed collection for every important aspect, individual projects annotate different parts of PubMed for different aspects of life science. It is like many blind men annotating a giant elephant. The annotations produced by an individual may be limited, but if all the annotations are collected and aligned, the chances of figuring out the whole picture are maximized.

As a solution to the situation, the PubAnnotation project is launched with the aim at providing an infrastructure for integration and public sharing of literature annotations.

Digital Humanities Research at Khon Kaen University, Thailand

Kulthida Tuamsuk

Information and Communication Department, Faculty of Humanities and Social Sciences,
Khon Kaen University, Khon Kaen, Thailand
kultua@kku.ac.th

Digital Humanities (DH) is a research issue emerging from integration of knowledge in computer science and humanities, which is an increasingly interesting field among academics in information studies. The issue has been listed as an important research agenda in many countries. Governments as well as academics themselves see the necessity for compilation, retention, and exploitation of humanity-related knowledge and cultural inheritances. By means of high-competent information technology and communication, it becomes possible to transform the information and store it in a digital format that is easily accessible and simple to learn when retrieved. Semantic and comparative dimensions, etc. can also be created which lead to development of critical as well as creative skills. Hence, a surprisingly great amount of monetary support has been allocated for establishment of research centers, research laboratories, or research societies worldwide in the field of DH in the world's leading universities.

Thailand has not as yet established a DH research community. However, it can be said that the doctoral degree program in information studies at KKU has enabled faculty members and students to develop their research competence in DH. Many studies have been published in international conference proceedings and journals. The faculty members also are of high competency in the DH research development and in creating internationally renowned works. Establishment of the research group in DH thus received the university's support as it will be the first of its kind in Thailand and in Southeast Asia.

The DH research work of the KKU-Digital Humanities Research Group (DHRG) is based on integration of knowledge in information science, computer science, and computer engineering for management of knowledge in the field of humanities and related fields. The objectives are as follows: 1) To collect, analyze, synthesize, store, and organize knowledge in humanities existing in various forms. This knowledge is usually rare, but reflects history, cultures and human's ways of living. Storage risks destruction and loss both from human naivety and natural disasters. 2) To use high technology to manage content in digital forms in order to open up opportunities for unlimited access to knowledge without any obstacles in distance, time, and place so as to avail learning in new and multiple dimensions. 3) To enable research with academics in humanities, a discipline with few innovation and integration of knowledge for application in humanity research so as to increase research studies and hence more research work outcomes in the field based on modern technology. Therefore, the framework of research of the KKU-DHRG can be classified in 3 subsets: (1) Organization (2) Retrieval & Access, and 3) Services, as illustrated in Figure 1.:

© Springer International Publishing Switzerland 2015
R.B. Allen et al. (Eds.): ICADL 2015, LNCS 9469, pp. 344–345, 2015.
DOI: 10.1007/978-3-319-27974-9

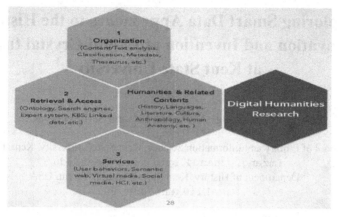

Fig. 1. Framework of research at KKU-DHRG

The research issues of the KKU-DGRG focus on: 1) Systems – Development of the systems for knowledge, metadata, ontology, semantic web, knowledge base, and an expert system for important humanities knowledge in Thailand or other countries in the Mekong Sub-region and ASEAN members, for example, folk tales, local histories, local wisdoms, ethnic groups, beliefs, ways of living, traditions, cultures, etc.; 2) Resources – Development of 3D Virtual Museum or digital learning resources for objects or major Thai art works. Examples are 3D virtual museums of antiques, silk, ancient buildings, human anatomy, musical instruments, Thai boxing, Thai dancing art, etc.; and 3) Processes and Behaviors – Knowledge management and study of information behaviors in humanities, for instance, knowledge exchanging process, knowledge transfer process, knowledge systematization process, etc.

Examples of the research works of doctoral students and the KKU-DHRG (both completed and on-going research):

- Knowledge organization and ontology: GMS' intangible cultural heritages, GMS' belief culture, GMS' folklore, imaginary beings, alternative medicine, Thai culture, Thai ethnic groups, historical sites, and Thai northeastern customs of the twelve months.
- Metadata: Metadata for Thai inscriptions, Thai palm leafs, and museum artifacts-ancient pottery.
- Semantic digital libraries or archives: Semantic digital libraries of Thai ethnic groups, Semantic web of Thai historical sites.
- Knowledge-based system: Knowledge-based system for the belief culture of Greater Mekong sub-region.
- Semantic 3D virtual museum: 3D virtual museum of masterpieces of Ban Chiang's potteries.

Future research will include the development of a semantic virtual museum of human skeleton which will collaborate with the Department of Anatomy, Faculty of Medicine, Khon Kaen University; and the development of semantic digital archives for knowledge management of the teaching works of Her Royal Highness Maha Chakri Sirindhorn at Chulachomklao Royal Military Academy which will collaborate with Chulachomklao Royal Military Academy, Thailand.

Exploring Smart Data Approaches to the History of Innovation and Invention at Liquid Crystal Institute at Kent State University

Marcia L. Zeng[1(✉)], Yin Zhang[1], Hongshan Li[2], and Serhiy Polyakov[1]

[1] School of Library and Information Science, Kent State University, Kent, USA
{mzeng,yzhang4,spolyako}@kent.edu
[2] Department of History, Kent State University, Kent, USA
hli@kent.edu

Abstract. This presentation reports on the preliminary findings of a research project that applies smart big data approaches to studying the history of innovation and invention in the case of the Liquid Crystal Institute that was established 50 years ago at Kent State University.

Keywords: Digital humanities · Innovation history · Smart data

Digital Humanities has commanded increasing attention worldwide over the past several years, and the field is still expanding. Although the definitions are being debated and the multifaceted landscape is yet to be fully understood, most agree that initiatives and activities in digital humanities are at the intersection between the humanities and digital information technology [1]. The field applies big data mathematical research techniques to the description and analysis of cultural objects—including art, literature, and technological artifacts themselves [2].

Advanced technologies—especially under the umbrella of big data and the Semantic Web—now allow researchers to access and reuse large volumes of diverse data, to discover patterns and connections formerly hidden from view, to reconstruct the past, to discover impacts in real and virtual environments, and to bring the complex intricacies of innovations to light, all as never before [3]. Nevertheless, in its raw form, data is just like crude oil; it needs to be refined and processed in order to generate real value. Data has to be cleaned, transformed, and analyzed to unlock its hidden potential [4]. Once tamed through organizing and integrating processes (including semantic analysis and coding through collaboration with subject-area experts), large volumes of unstructured, semi-structured, and structured data are turned into "smart data" that reflect the research priorities of a particular discipline or field. Smart data inquiries can then be used to provide comprehensive analyses and generate new products and services. Given its unprecedented power and effectiveness, the effort to tame big data has been made not only by natural scientists, engineers, and financial analysts, but also by researchers in the social sciences and humanities, ushering in a new era in digital humanities. New approaches to researching the history of innovation have found their relevance in the digital age. Historical narratives of invention and innovation based on networks and historical data modeling, graphics, statistics, and mathematics are intended to complement the classical study of the history of technology and science.

© Springer International Publishing Switzerland 2015
R.B. Allen et al. (Eds.): ICADL 2015, LNCS 9469, pp. 346–347, 2015.
DOI: 10.1007/978-3-319-27974-9

An interdisciplinary research team at Kent State University has been conducting a research project "Digital Humanities Research with Smart Big Data — A Network Framework of Innovation History" since the beginning of 2015. The research team consists of more than 10 faculty members and research assistants from library and information science, history, geography, physics, visual communication design, and journalism and mass communication. The first case is about the scientific innovations and inventions of the Liquid Crystal Institute (LCI) at Kent State University, the birthplace of liquid crystal displays and one of the most prominent innovation centers in the United States over the past five decades. Through the work of its alumni, LCI has had a significant impact on the way the world sees things – that is, the way we see things on our phones, tablets, and computer screens [5]. Like other historical studies, our project heavily relies on heritage materials that are not machine-processable, such as archival files, annual reports, and oral history materials, digitized or not. After gathering the facts about the people and organizations involved in the research, we have used existing databases and textual materials for patents, grants, academic publications, archives, social networks, named entities, geographical locations, etc. Some of these are available as whole datasets, while others need to be crawled. A significant amount of digitized contents still needs to be datafied by our team. On the methodology side, the application of methodologies defined by historiometrics, scientometrics, network theory, semantic analysis models, graph theory, and temporal-spatial data analytics, among others, demands knowledge in a variety of disciplines while also calling for collaboration in selecting relevant methods and connecting the findings. It is extremely valuable to have validation through engaging the scientists who are also the subjects of the study. Drawing across so many types of data simultaneously and interactively in such an unprecedented manner, this project aims at applying the methodology and technology to study the history of other innovations or inventions.

This presentation will share with digital humanities researchers about the challenges we encountered and the experiences we have accumulated in the first stage of the project around the efforts to collect, clean, mine, analyze, and synthesize the existing data, to apply various analytics techniques with available methodologies, and to produce the most accurate data and findings. The presentation will also discuss our efforts to narrow and close the gaps between available data and its under-utilization in historical research and to build a bridge to help researchers and educators overcome the challenges in researching the innovation history in the data-intensive environment.

References

1. Svensson, P.: The Landscape of Digital Humanities. Digital Humanities Quarterly 4(1), 1938–4122 (2010)
2. Svensson, P.: Humanities Computing as Digital Humanities. Digital Humanities Quarterly 3(3), 1938–4122 (2009)
3. Gardner, D.: An ocean of data [Introduction]. In: Smolan, R., Erwitt, J. (eds.) The Human Face of Big Data, pp. 14–17. Against All Odds Productions, Sausalito (2012)
4. TiECON East.: Data is new oil (2014). http://www.tieconeast.org/2014/big-data-analytics
5. Bos, P.: Impact of our graduates on the industry. In: Morgan, S., et al. (eds.) 50 Years of Innovation, pp. 34–35. Kent State University, Kent (2015)

Development of a Semantic Digital Library of Knowledge on Ethnic Groups in Thailand

Juthatip Chaikhambung[✉] and Kulthida Tuamsuk

Information and Communication Department, Faculty of Humanities and Social Sciences,
Khon Kaen University, Khon Kaen, Thailand
{cjutha,kultua}@kku.ac.th

Abstract. This concept paper focuses on the development of a semantic digital library for ethnic group's knowledge in Thailand. The research objectives include: 1) to analyze the scope and organize knowledge on ethnic groups in Thailand, 2) to develop ontology and metadata for the knowledge of ethnic groups in the country, and 3) to develop and assess the semantic digital library of the knowledge on ethnic groups in the country. The research and development method which comprises of a documentation analysis, a qualitative research, and a system development method will be used in the study.

Keywords: Ethnic groups · Semantic digital library · Thailand

1   Introduction

The development of every country in the world has mentioned the ethnic diversity that is associated with the development of the country. If countries ignore the importance of a country made up of ethnic diversity, development problems in terms of political, economic, social and cultural development will occur [1]. Therefore, knowledge of ethnicity is vital to national security and peaceful coexistence of the nation. Thailand has established the Office of Ethnic Affairs belonging to the Department of Social Development and Welfare. This office is responsible for overseeing policies on ethnic groups. There is recognition of the importance of the ethnic groups living in the country for achieve understanding and reconciliation that can coexist peacefully appeared in a master plan (2015-2017) prepared by Ministry of Social Development and Human Security [2].

In order to store, disseminate and access knowledge about ethnic groups in Thailand, a semantic digital library of knowledge about ethnic groups in Thailand should be developed. This is useful for the study of learning and research. The prototype model for the storage and utilization of knowledge about ethnic groups in Thailand will be developed as well.

2   Research Objectives

This research comprises of three objectives: 1) to analyze the scope and organize knowledge on ethnic groups in Thailand; 2) to develop ontology and metadata for managing the knowledge of ethnic groups in Thailand; and 3) to develop and assess the semantic digital library of knowledge on ethnic groups in Thailand.

© Springer International Publishing Switzerland 2015
R.B. Allen et al. (Eds.): ICADL 2015, LNCS 9469, pp. 348–349, 2015.
DOI: 10.1007/978-3-319-27974-9

3   Research Conceptual Framework

This research is based on knowledge organization, semantic digital library and metadata for digital library concepts. The research conceptual framework is shown in fig. 1.

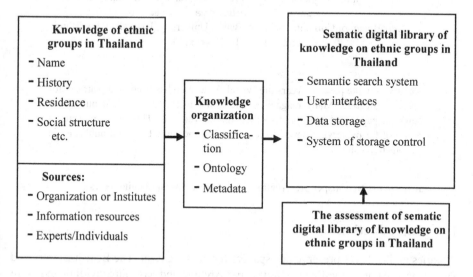

Fig. 1. Research conceptual framework

4   Research Methodology

This research is in line with digital humanities research aiming for using innovative technology for organizing and making use of the knowledge on ethnic groups in Thailand. The research and development method is used by combining the followings techniques and approaches: 1) content analysis, knowledge classification, ontology, and metadata development for knowledge organization; and 2) semantic technology and digital library management for the system development.

Acknowledgements. This research is supported by the Digital Humanities Research Group, Faculty of Humanities and Social Sciences, Khon Kaen University, Thailand.

References

1. Srisontisuk, S.: Cultural dynamics of ethnic diversity. In: Srisontisuk, S. (ed.) Discussion of I-San Culture in Researches, pp. 29–93. Department of Sociology and Anthropology, Faculty of Social Sciences, Chiang Mai University, Chiang Mai, Thailand (2015). (in Thai)
2. Ministry of Social Development and Human Security: Master plan to develop ethnic groups in Thailand (2015-2017) (2015). http://www.chatipan.dsdw.go.th/pdf/F001.pdf. (in Thai) (retrieved March 5, 2015)

Digital News Story Preservation Framework

Muzammil Khan[1(✉)] and Arif Ur Rahman[2]

[1] Department of Computer Science, Preston University, Islamabad, Pakistan
muzammilkhan86@gmail.com
[2] Department of Computer Science, Bahria University, Islamabad, Pakistan
badwanpk@bui.edu.pk

Abstract. In the past few years the World Wide Web has become a platform for news publication. Many magazines and newspapers have stopped publishing news on paper and only publish their digital versions. This paper presents a proposal for preserving news stories related to the same topic but published in various newspapers.

Keywords: Newspaper preservation · Story preservation · Digital news

1   Introduction

Libraries and archives preserve newspapers for the long term. The British Library and Findmypast maintain the British Newspaper Archive and have already digitized more than forty million scanned historical newspapers. The Irish newspaper archives cover 300 years of Irish history by scanned newspaper articles published in forty newspapers. A number of initiatives including the Internet Archive, Australian Web Archive i.e. PANDAS, Portuguese Web Archive, Reed Tech Archives, Preservica and Web-Preserver have been taken in last two decades [1]. These initiatives focused on various aspects of archiving like collection strategies, archival formats and information retrieval techniques in archives etc.

Newspapers cover stories about various types of events like acts of parliaments, events of political importance for countries, proceedings of courts related to important cases, births, deaths, marriages and sports. The lifespan of online newspapers vary from one newspaper to another i.e. from one day to a month. Though a newspaper may be backed up and archived, in the future it will be difficult to access particular information published in various newspapers about the same story. The issues become even more complicated if a story is to be tracked through an archive of many newspapers which require different technologies to access them. The issue may be addressed by linking stories to the same topic published in various newspapers and then preserving them in a standard format.

2   Research Objectives and Approach

The focus of the current proposal is on the preservation of news stores collected from various newspapers related to the same news. The following goals are to be achieved.

R.B. Allen et al. (Eds.): ICADL 2015, LNCS 9469, pp. 350–351, 2015.
DOI: 10.1007/978-3-319-27974-9

- **Story Selection Criteria:** The criteria for selecting stories related to a news from various newspapers is to be defined. People from different institutions like archivists from the National Library of Pakistan, journalists, analysts, researchers and academics will be contacted to define these criteria. Initially the selection may be done manually but later on a tool may be developed which helps in automating the process.
- **Identify Metadata:** Some metadata is explicitly stored with the content and is available at the source like the author of the story, the publication date, and the name of the newspaper. However, some metadata is not explicitly available at the source like the name of an act discussed in parliament and Parliamentarians who initially presented the bill. Such metadata will need to be identified and explicitly stored in the archive. The metadata is supposed to be helpful in ingesting stories to the archive and browsing the archive.
- **Archival Format and Archive Structure:** The stories will come from various news websites developed using various technologies. The stories related to the same news will need to be normalized to a standard format which should be able to integrate the metadata explicitly available at the source along with the content. Furthermore, it should include metadata identified in the previous objective. The structure of the archive needs to be optimal for search and retrieval. The metadata and different types of content i.e. text, images and videos should be linked in a manner which supports easy identification of relevant search results.
- **Search and Retrieval of Stories:** The archived news stories will be searched and retrieved through a web interface. This will allow search using keyword-based search as well as an interface to search the archive using the metadata e.g. dates, author names and newspaper names (advanced search). The search interface should be easy to use and platform-independent.

3   Conclusions

The proposal requires expertise in various domains including archives, metadata, newspapers, and information retrieval techniques. The outcomes will help institutions for preserving news about their activities as well as individuals interested in preserving news for any purpose.

References

1. Gomes, D., Miranda, J., Costa, M.: A survey on web archiving initiatives. In: Gradmann, S., Borri, F., Meghini, C., Schuldt, H. (eds.) TPDL 2011. LNCS, vol. 6966, pp. 408–420. Springer, Heidelberg (2011)

Information Exchanged in Mentoring Between Faculty Advisors and Their Doctoral Students

Jongwook Lee

School of Information, Florida State University, Tallahassee, FL, USA
nadoopro@gmail.com

Abstract. This dissertation explores the characteristics and activities of mentoring relationships and examines information behaviors with emphasis on identifying types of information exchanged in mentoring between faculty advisors and doctoral students in library and information science (LIS). The study draws upon a socialization content framework developed in organizational settings, as few frameworks are available in academic settings. The study relies on a mixed methods design that combines qualitative interview and quantitative survey methods.

1   Introduction

In doctoral education, mentoring by faculty advisors plays a significant role for students both in the learning and in the adjustment process (i.e., socialization) of doctoral students to their work, department, university, and discipline [1,2]. While a plethora of research has examined the socialization and mentoring of graduate students, little work has focused on the content/information dimension that can be used as an accurate measure of learning outcomes [3]. This dissertation research addresses that lack, exploring the characteristics and activities of mentoring relationships and examining information behaviors with emphasis on identifying types of information exchanged in mentoring between faculty advisors and doctoral students in library and information science (LIS). For investigation of the information dimension in mentoring, the study draws upon Klein and Heuser's socialization content framework developed in organizational settings, given that few frameworks specific to academic settings are available [3].

2   Research Questions

The overarching research questions for the dissertation are as follows:

1. Do LIS doctoral students think of their faculty advisors as mentors?
   (a) How do they characterize the role of faculty mentors?
   (b) Do they perceive differences between mentoring and non-mentoring relationships between LIS doctoral students and advisors? What are those differences?

© Springer International Publishing Switzerland 2015
R.B. Allen et al. (Eds.): ICADL 2015, LNCS 9469, pp. 352–353, 2015.
DOI: 10.1007/978-3-319-27974-9

(c) Are there differences in perceptions of relationships across stages of doctoral socialization? How are they different?

2. What types of information are exchanged between LIS doctoral students and their advisors?

(a) Do LIS doctoral students exchange information related to their doctoral work and their future profession with their advisors? What types of information are exchanged at the level of their job task, department/school, university, and discipline?

(b) Do LIS doctoral students exchange information related to balancing their professional obligations and their personal lives? What types of information are exchanged?

(c) Are there differences in types of information exchanged between mentoring and non-mentoring relationships?

(d) Are there differences in types of information exchanged across stages of doctoral socialization?

3. What modifications, if any, have to be made for Klein and Heuser's framework in order to make a fit to the context of LIS doctoral education?

3 Methods

The author found that Klein and Heuser's framework is applicable to doctoral mentoring after some modifications. For purposes of this dissertation, the author uses a mixed methods design that combines qualitative interview and quantitative survey methods. In the first stage, the author will conduct interviews with ten LIS doctoral students in the United States, testing the content framework and identifying possible modifications for the context of doctoral education. Thereafter, the author will test and generalize the findings of the qualitative study by surveying library and information science doctoral students in the United States. The results of the study will increase our understanding of the socialization and mentoring of doctoral students, will lay a foundation for information behavior research in mentoring, and will broaden the role of interpersonal information sources. In addition, the study results will have practical implications for the development of a socialization outcome measure as well as a computer-mediated mentoring system.

References

1. Austin, A.E.: Preparing the next generation of faculty: Graduate school as socialization to the academic career. Journal of Higher Education 73(1), 94–122 (2002)
2. Gardner, S.K.: Fitting the mold of graduate school: A qualitative study of socialization in doctoral education. Innovative Higher Education 33, 125–138 (2008)
3. Klein, H.J., Heuser, A.E.: The learning of socialization content: A framework for researching orientating practices. Research in Personnel and Human Resources Management 27, 279–336 (2008)

Business Ontology Model for Community Enterprise of Thai Local Wisdom

Chitlada Prommakorn[✉], Kulthida Tuamsuk, and Kanyarat Kwiecien

Information and Communication Department, Faculty of Humanities and Social Sciences,
Khon Kaen University, Khon Kaen, Thailand
prommagon_noey@hotmail.com, {kultua,kandad}@kku.ac.th

Abstract. This paper presents the research concept on the development of business ontology model for community enterprise of Thai local wisdom. A concept of "Business ontology" which provides the knowledge domains and structures of business processes and management will be used as a framework for this study. The business model of 230 community enterprises in Thailand which received best practices awards in 2013 will be studied. The results will provide the substances, methods, and knowledge management of community enterprises which will then be used for business ontology development.

Keywords: Business ontology model · Community enterprise · Thai local wisdom

1   Introduction

Community Enterprise is defined as the community's business of goods and services production which is operated by the community based on the people's participation. It aims for increasing and distributing the incomes and self-reliance of the people in the community [1]. Local wisdom is considered a foundation of life for the Thai community. It is a knowledge source of the community that has been shared and transferred from generation to generation [2]. Recently, local wisdom has been a significant asset of successful community enterprises. In the year 2013, there were announced 230 best-practiced community enterprises which earned significant incomes and were self-reliant [1]. A previous study [3] found that community enterprises have had unique business management, and most of them integrated knowledge management in their business processes.

A business model refers to the substances or methods or logics of the business processes that explains how the organization creates its value and revenue [4]. With the advance of information technology, the knowledge in a business model is collected and constructed by using an ontology concept, which is then called a "business ontology". Because the business model of Thai local wisdom's community enterprises is unique and valuable, the researchers aim to develop an ontology of the business. The ontology will help to understand the business processes and can be used as a tool for semantic web development.

© Springer International Publishing Switzerland 2015
R.B. Allen et al. (Eds.): ICADL 2015, LNCS 9469, pp. 354–355, 2015.
DOI: 10.1007/978-3-319-27974-9

This research aims for studying the business model of the community enterprises of Thai local wisdom and then develop the business ontology model for community enterprises management.

2   Research Conceptual Framework

The research conceptual framework is constructed based on the literature reviews. The following concepts and theories will be used in this study: community enterprises management, business model, knowledge management of Thai local wisdom, knowledge classification, and ontology development. (Figure 1)

Fig. 1. The research conceptual framework

3   Research Methodology

The research and development method is used for this study. Research approaches include 1) the content analysis, qualitative and quantitative studies for collecting data on the business model of 230 best-practice community enterprises in Thailand, and 2) the content classification and ontology modeling and construction.

References

1. SCEB: Community enterprises. Office of the Secretary of Community Enterprises Board (2015). http://www.sceb.doae.go.th/Ssceb2.htm
2. Na Talang, A.: Concept for knowledge management of local wisdom. In: Local wisdom and knowledge management, pp. 6–8. Ammarind Printing, Bangkok (2003)
3. Tuamsuk, K., Phabu, T., Vongprasert, C.: Knowledge management model of community business: Thai OTOP Champions. Journal of Knowledge Management **17**(3), 363–378 (2013)
4. Magretta, J.: Why business models. Harvard Business Review **80**(5), 86–92 (2002)

Development of 3D Virtual Museum for Ban Chiang Masterpiece of Potteries

Teerapol Suebchompu$^{(\boxtimes)}$, Kulthida Tuamsuk, and Kanyarat Kwiecien

Information and Communication Management Program, Faculty of Humanities and Social Sciences, Khon Kaen University, Khon Kaen, Thailand
autoa18@hotmail.com, {kultua,kandad}@kku.ac.th

Abstract. The study is on the development of 3D virtual museum for Ban Chiang masterpiece of potteries. The objectives of this research are to:(1) collect data and capture the artifacts to exhibition in 3D virtual museum, (2) organize data for Ban Chiang Masterpiece of potteries for museums database and (3) design and develop 3D virtual museum for Ban Chiang masterpiece of potteries. The research conceptual framework used in this study consists of: museum object, creation of 3D object, data organization, and design and development. Expected outcomes of the research are: (1) guidelines in the development of 3D virtual museum based on the research and development approach (2) metadata of knowledge description for Ban Chiang Masterpiece of Potteries, and (3) the 3D virtual museum for Ban Chiang Masterpiece of Potteries.

Keywords: 3D · Virtual museum · Ban Chiang pottery

1 Introduction

Ban Chiang National Museum is an important cultural heritage of Thailand and the world. The museum's exhibition displays various objects about the ancient times society's development to educate visitors, especially Ban Chiang potteries. The potteries have unique features, shapes and patterns that make them invaluable cultural objects. Beside this, they are academic evidence of knowledge creation in the Early Historic works of art by confirming the ancient Ban Chiang culture that had begun approximately 5,600 years ago. However, the artifacts are difficult for visitors to visit at the museum because of the lack of time and the distance away from town. The location problem may make visitors fail to appreciate the value of the ancient potteries [1]. Nowadays, with the advantage of information technology, we can create the museum's objects exhibition on web, which quickly gain more attention. In particular, by creating the application of 3D virtual reality technology to create an object by 3D model [2,3]. This research study developed by using a 3D virtual reality technology. Metadata is used for data organization, then the artifacts are digitized and storage in the database before presenting by using 3D virtual reality technology.

R.B. Allen et al. (Eds.): ICADL 2015, LNCS 9469, pp. 356–357, 2015.
DOI: 10.1007/978-3-319-27974-9

2   Research Objectives

1. To collect data and create 3D images for Ban Chiang masterpiece of potteries.
2. To develop metadata and digital collection for Ban Chiang Masterpiece of potteries.
3. To design and develop 3D virtual museum for Ban Chiang masterpiece of potteries.

3   Research Conceptual Framework

The Research conceptual framework comprises of the following concept and theories: (1) museum artifacts: select 30 of Ban Chiang masterpiece of potteries, (2) creation of 3D artifacts: by photographing and photogrammetry, (3) data organization: using VRA Core 4.0 to metadata for cultural objects and visual resources, and (4) design and development of the 3D Virtual Museum for Ban Chiang Masterpiece of Potteries.

4   Research Methodology

The research methodology is research and development. The research approaches are divided into three phases: (1) collect data and create 3D images for Ban Chiang masterpiece of potteries, (2) develop metadata and digital collect for Ban Chiang Masterpiece of potteries and (3) design and develop 3D virtual museum for Ban Chiang Masterpiece of potteries.

Acknowledgements. This research is supported by the Digital Humanities Research Group, Faculty of Humanities and Social Sciences, Khon Kaen University, Thailand.

References

1. Ban Chiang National Museum: Ban Chiang Heritage. Bangkok: The Fine Arts Department (2007). (in Thai)
2. Mclellan, H.: Cognitive Issue in Virtual Reality. Journal of Visual Literacy **18**, 175–199 (1998)
3. Stephen, B.D.: The Design of Virtual Environments With particular reference to VRML (1996). http://www.man.ac.uk

Knowledge Representation of Social Science Research Data for Data Curation and Reuse

Guangyuan Sun[✉] and Christopher S.G. Khoo

Wee Kim Wee School of Communication and Information,
Nanyang Technological University, Singapore637718, Singapore
gsun003@e.ntu.edu.sg, chriskhoo@pmail.ntu.edu.sg

Abstract. The proposed study is in the area of data curation and knowledge representation. It focuses on the issues and methods of curating quantitative social science data, to advance the methodology of data curation, and data reuse and integration in the social sciences. Socio-economic data will be the object of the study. They are defined as data that is related to people, organization and society which can be stored in a tabular format.

Keywords: Data curation · Data reuse · Data integration · Knowledge representation · Quantitative data · Social science

1 Introduction

Data curation is attracting substantial interest in the e-Science and e-Social Science communities. *Data curation* refers to the management of datasets (usually research data) to make them available for use by other researchers beyond the lifespan and purpose of the project for which the data was collected. The main purpose of data curation is to support reuse by other users and integration with other datasets. The U.K. Digital Curation Centre pointed out that research datasets can be reused later in other research projects: "Curation enhances the long-term value of existing data by making it available for further high quality research."[1]

Part of managing data for integration and reuse is to design the data representation format that supports data reuse by other researchers, and the integration of the curated data with other datasets for further analysis. Knowledge representation techniques, especially metadata schema and ontology, can be used to represent the structure of curated data and specify the meaning of data elements, as well as represent context information needed for interpretation and reuse by other researchers. The proposed study focuses on the knowledge representation issues of data curation.

In the past, data curation initiatives have focused on scientific communities, especially in the bioscience area. Data curation in social science is in a nascent stage. It is still not clear what kinds of data need to be curated, how they should be represented and stored, and how the curated data can be integrated and reused. The proposed study focuses on the issues and methods of curating social science data, to advance the methodology of data curation and data reuse in the social sciences.

---

[1] http://www.dcc.ac.uk/digital-curation/what-digital-curation

© Springer International Publishing Switzerland 2015
R.B. Allen et al. (Eds.): ICADL 2015, LNCS 9469, pp. 358–359, 2015.
DOI: 10.1007/978-3-319-27974-9

2   Research Objectives

This study will focus on the curation of quantitative social science data, which are numerical data related to people, organizations and society that can be stored in a tabular format (e.g., Microsoft Excel file, CSV file, SPSS file, etc.). The study is further limited to questionnaire survey data. However, as social scientists also make use of statistical data collected and published by government and international agencies, the scope of the study is extended to such official statistical data.

The objectives of the study are: 1) to develop a knowledge representation system for the data curation of quantitative social science research data; 2) to identify issues and solutions in the reuse and integration of curated data by social science researchers.

3   Research Method

Social science is a broad area that includes several disciplines. The study will focus on the discipline of sociology, which is arguably a core discipline in social science. However, the study will also investigate the extensibility of the knowledge representation system to two other social science disciplines—communication studies and information studies.

The knowledge representation system developed for representing sociology quantitative data has to satisfy certain requirements. It has to represent the following types of information accurately:

1. The meaning (semantics) of the data and dataset;
2. The research concepts that are operationalized in the questionnaire survey;
3. Various types of context information about the dataset;
4. Provenance of the dataset and relations with other datasets;
5. Other types of information needed to support researchers to find and evaluate the dataset for possible reuse, to integrate two or more datasets.

The first four types of information will be identified through content analysis of a sample of sociology questionnaires and the associated research reports. The last type will be identified through user (i.e. researchers in this case) studies. The requirements identified through content analysis will later be confirmed in the user study, to find out how useful these kinds of information are in supporting data reuse and integration, as well as to identify additional information needed.

Questionnaires will be collected from appendices of Master's theses and Doctoral dissertations in the ProQuest Dissertations and Theses database. Official statistical data will be collected from the online statistical services from government of public bodies. A group of 25 social science researchers in Singapore will be recruited as participants in the user study.

Author Index

Printed in the United States
By Bookmasters